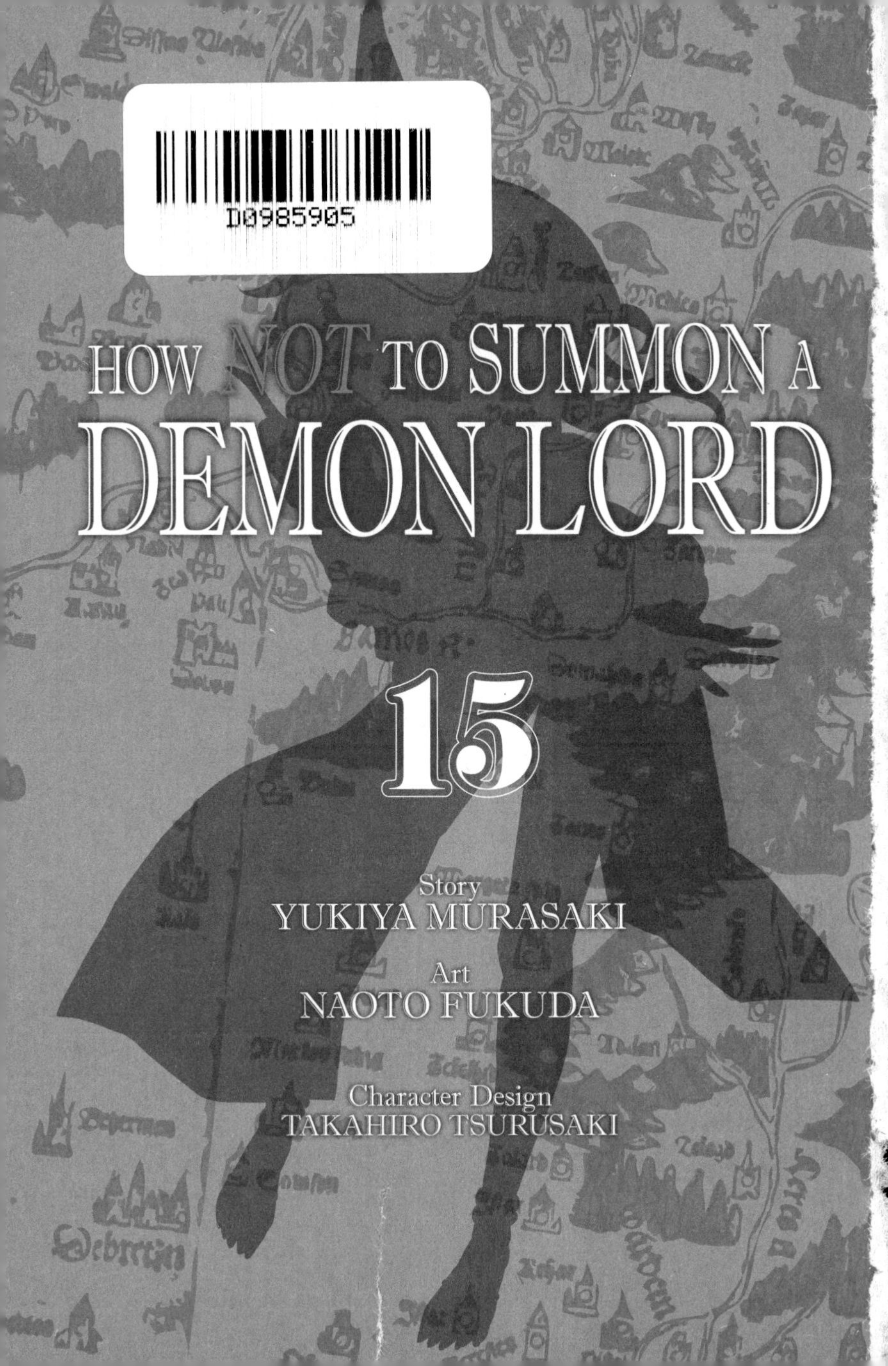

HOW NOT TO SUMMON A DEMON LORD

15

Story
YUKIYA MURASAKI

Art
NAOTO FUKUDA

Character Design
TAKAHIRO TSURUSAKI

HOW NOT TO SUMMON A DEMON LORD CHARACTERS

Race: Demon
Level: 150

Self-proclaimed Demon Lord from another world.

Thanks to the "Magic Deflection" effect of the Demon Lord's Ring, which Diablo received in-game, Rem and Shera's Enslavement Ritual backfired. Now *they're* the ones with Enslavement Collars. In the real world, Diablo was unpopular, didn't have a way with words, and couldn't interact with other people to save his life. But in this world, he's tall, handsome, and practically invincible! He still doesn't have a way with words, but he manages to make it through tough situations by acting like a Demon Lord.

Diablo (Sakamoto Takuma)

STORY

Takuma Sakamoto is an elite gamer in the fantasy MMORPG *Cross Reverie*. He is so overwhelmingly strong that he is known as the "Demon Lord." One day, he's summoned to a world nearly identical to the game by two girls: Shera, an Elf, and Rem, a Pantherian. Thanks to a pair of Enslavement Collars, Takuma Sakamoto--now Diablo--has control over the girls...but he really sucks at talking to other people!! To hide this, Diablo begins behaving like his Demon Lord persona from the game. While demonstrating his power, built up through skills he acquired by playing *Cross Reverie*, Diablo sets out on an adventure with Shera and Rem.

Last time, Diablo and the others wound up held prisoner in a confessional room, and in order to rescue them, Horn leapt to Level 80 via the guidance of Level-Up Goddess Babalon and a "Subjugation Contract Collar." Thanks to the "Charm" skill she acquired, she successfully infiltrated the Inner Sanctum, but got badly hurt in combat against the Paladin, Grun.

Until this point, Diablo had been letting Lumachina take the lead, but upon hearing Grun's scornful words about Horn, who'd been gravely wounded for the sake of her friends, his eyes were opened to the fact that a Demon Lord just needs to act like a Demon Lord would!! And now that the Demon Lord Diablo has awakened, he begins his counterattack!

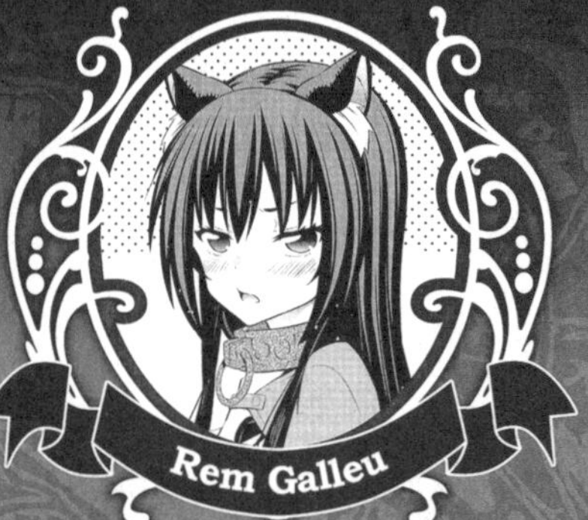
Rem Galleu

Race: Pantherian Level: 40
A Summoner and an Adventurer. She has catlike fluffy ears, a long tail, a small body, and is adorable. She's also flat as a board. Rem is always calm, though she's a bit of a prude.

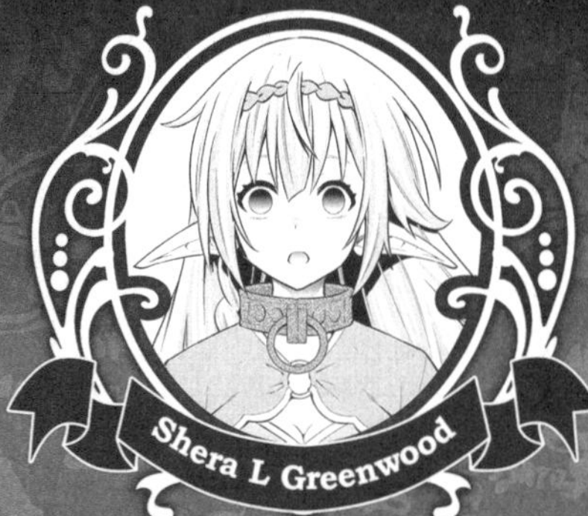
Shera L Greenwood

Race: Elf Level: 30
A Summoner and an Elf. She is slender and elegant, but also has an impressively large bosom that is at odds with the rest of her body. Her innocent and naive personality calms everyone around her.

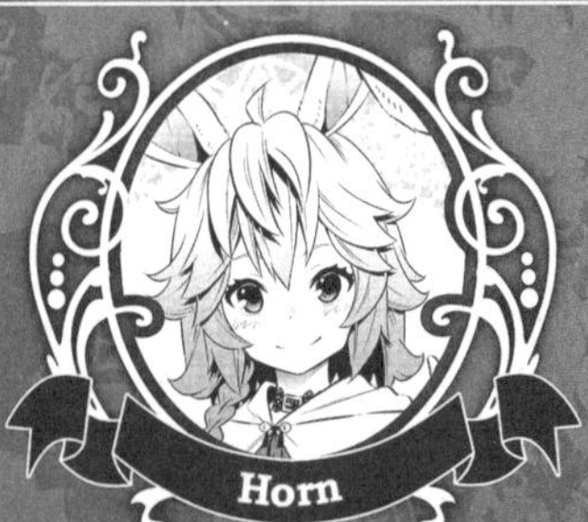
Horn

Race: Grasswalker
A girl who joined the party to guide them on adventures in Zircon Tower. Thanks to a "Subjugation Contract Collar," she has become a Level 80 "Seeker."

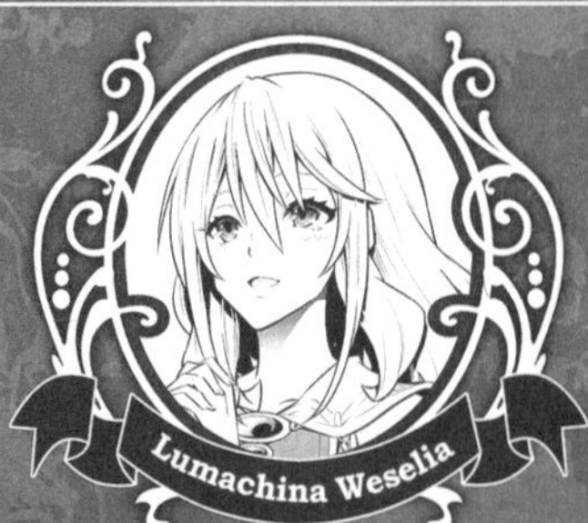
Lumachina Weselia

The High Priestess of the Church. Corruption within the Cardinal Council has put her life in danger. Lumachina believes that Diablo, who saved her, is God.

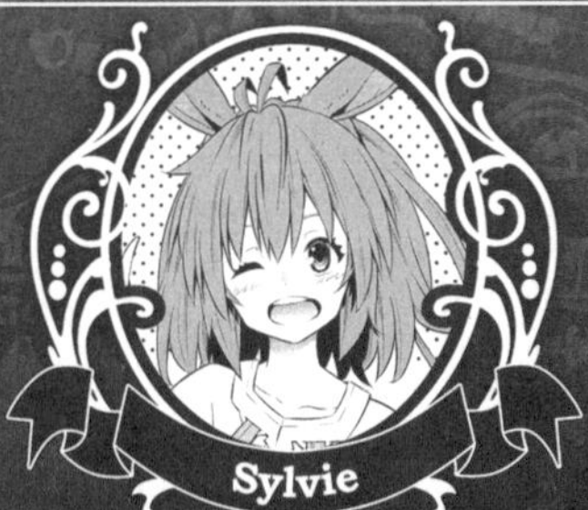
Sylvie

Race: Grasswalker
Guildmaster of the Faltra City Adventurers Guild. Contrary to appearances, she's sharp and capable and far from straightforward.

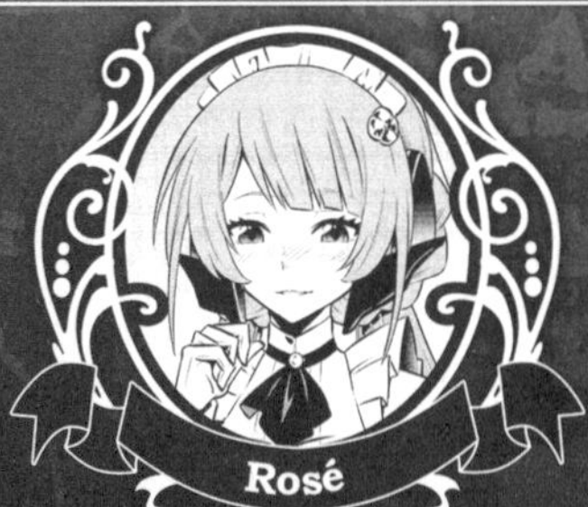
Rosé

The Magimatic Maid who manages Diablo's dungeon, waiting with bated breath for her master's return. In combat, she summons gigantic weapons.

HOW NOT TO SUMMON A DEMON LORD

15

CONTENTS

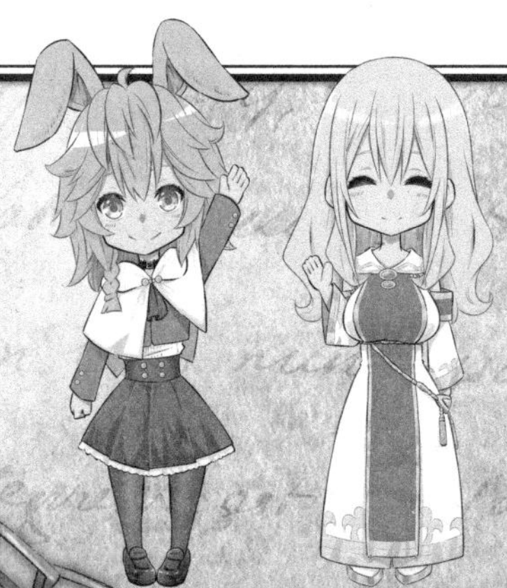

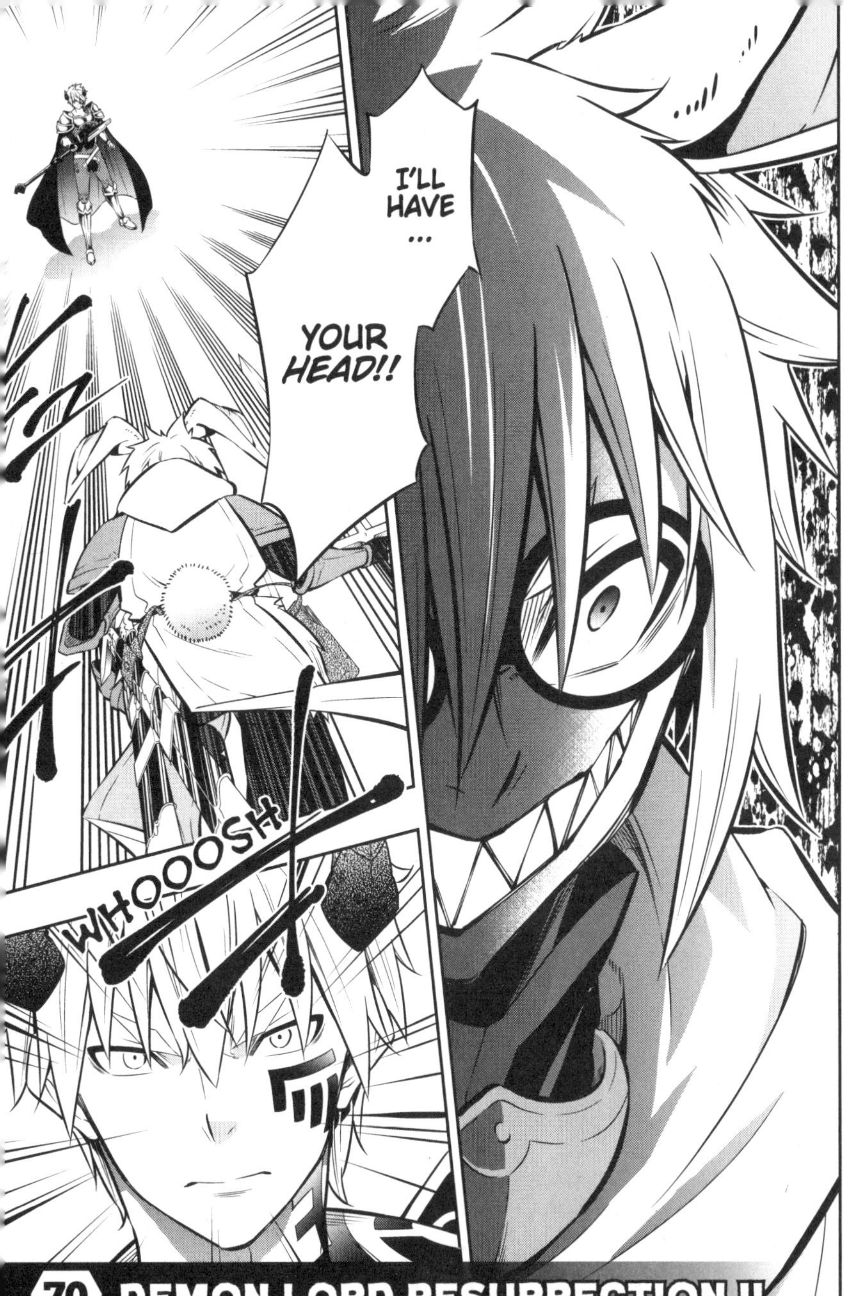
I'LL HAVE ...
YOUR HEAD!!
WHOOOOSH

70 DEMON LORD RESURRECTION II

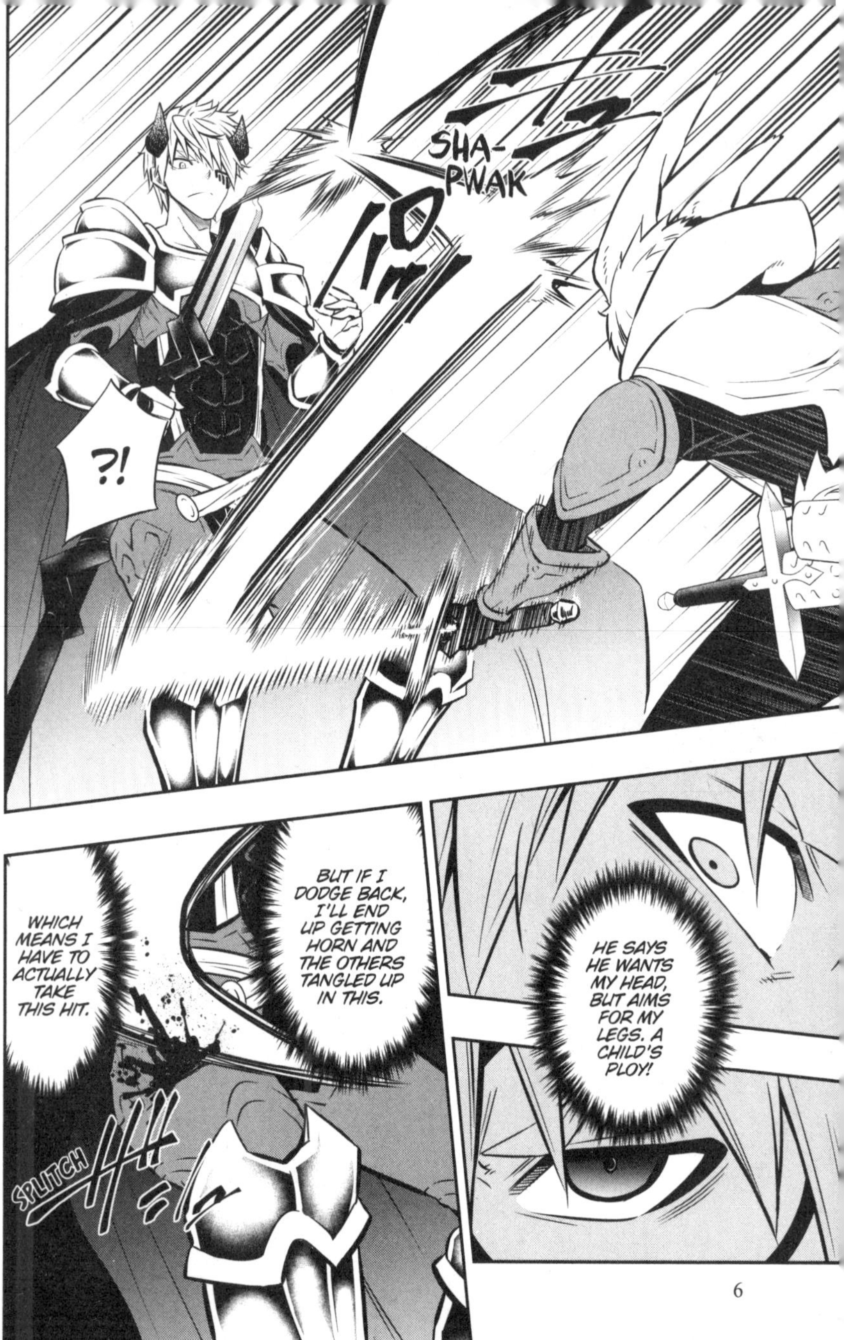
SHA-PWAK
?!
HE SAYS HE WANTS MY HEAD, BUT AIMS FOR MY LEGS. A CHILD'S PLOY!
BUT IF I DODGE BACK, I'LL END UP GETTING HORN AND THE OTHERS TANGLED UP IN THIS.
WHICH MEANS I HAVE TO ACTUALLY TAKE THIS HIT.
SPLITCH

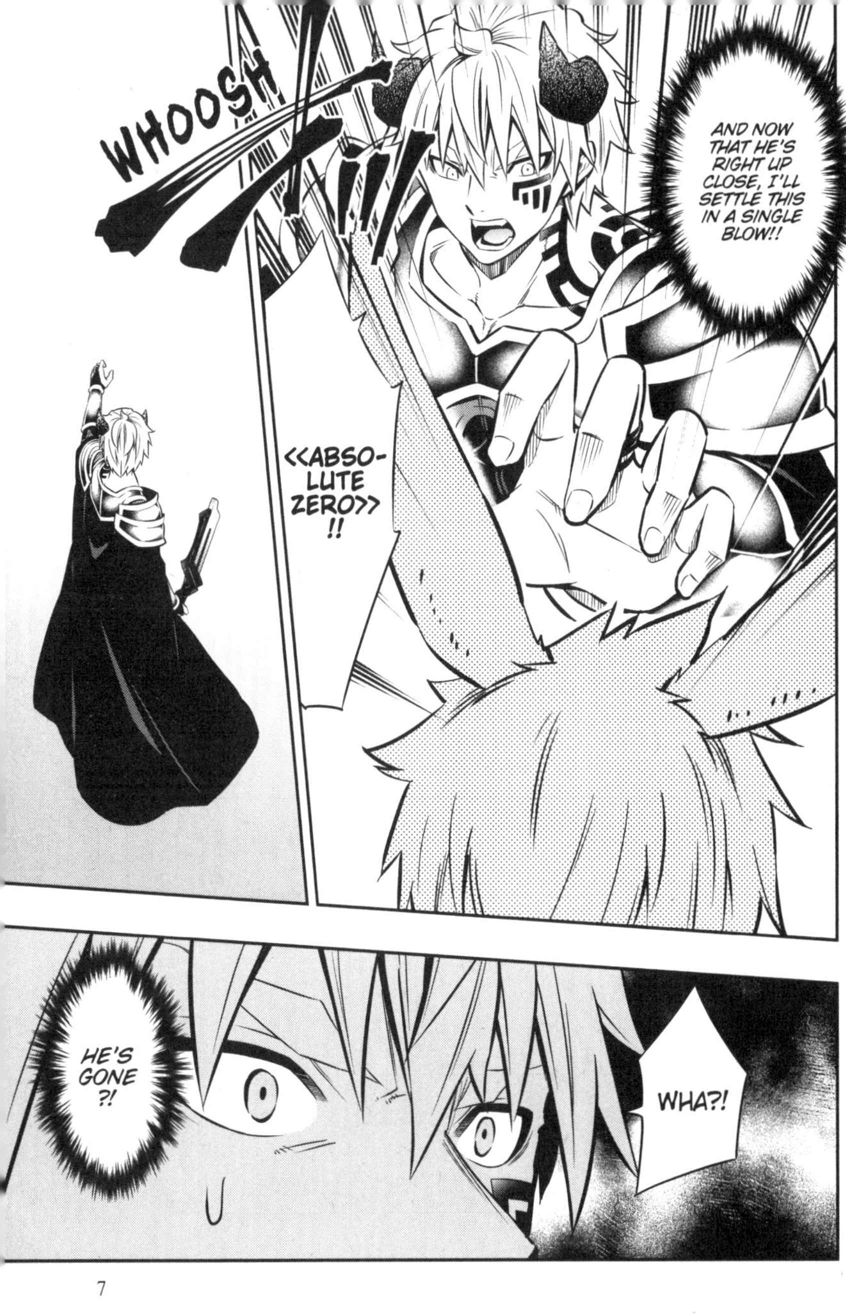
AND NOW THAT HE'S RIGHT UP CLOSE, I'LL SETTLE THIS IN A SINGLE BLOW!!
WHOOSH
<<ABSOLUTE ZERO>>!!
WHA?!
HE'S GONE?!

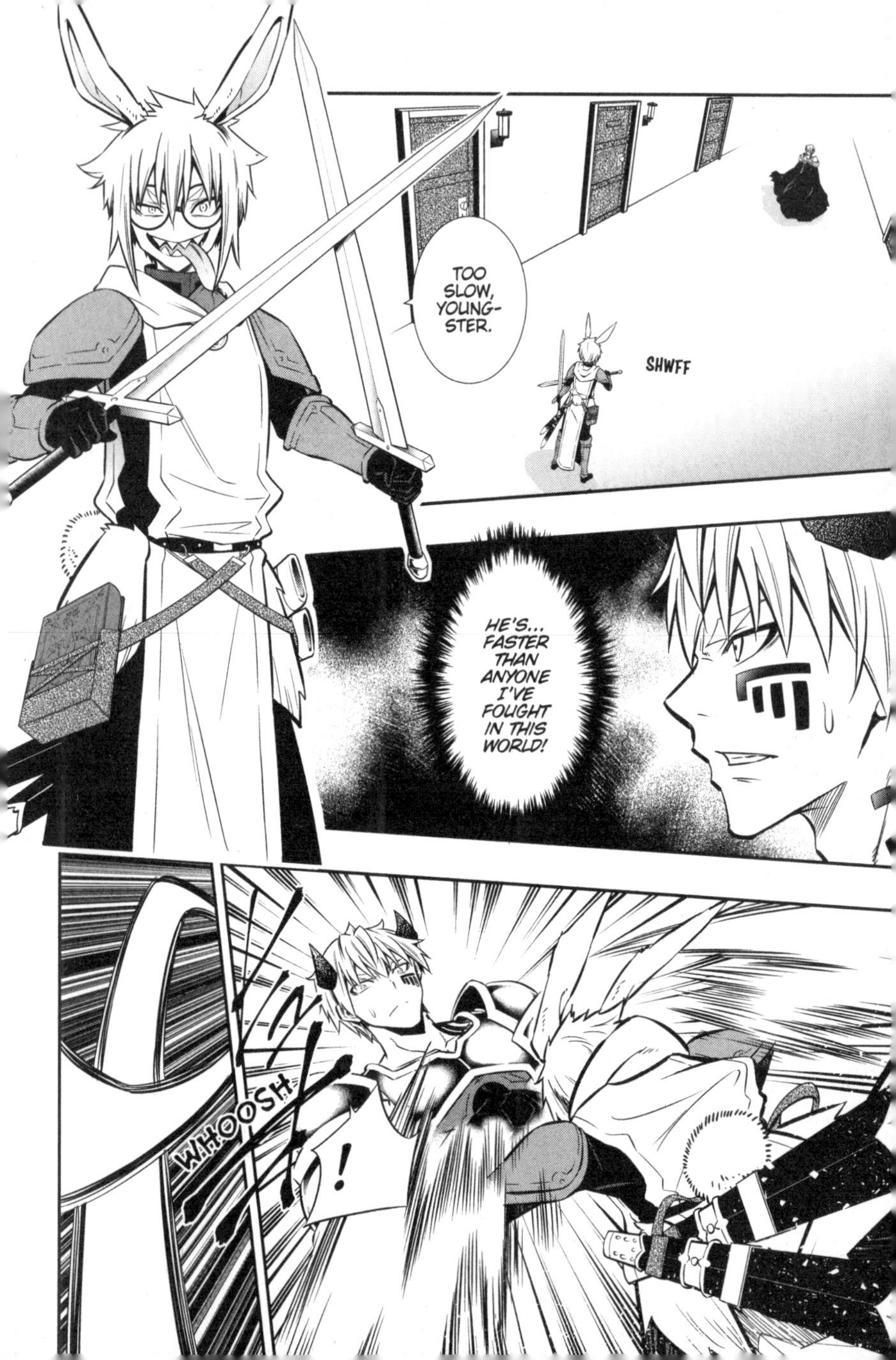
TOO SLOW, YOUNG-STER.
SHWFF
HE'S... FASTER THAN ANYONE I'VE FOUGHT IN THIS WORLD!
WHOOSH
!

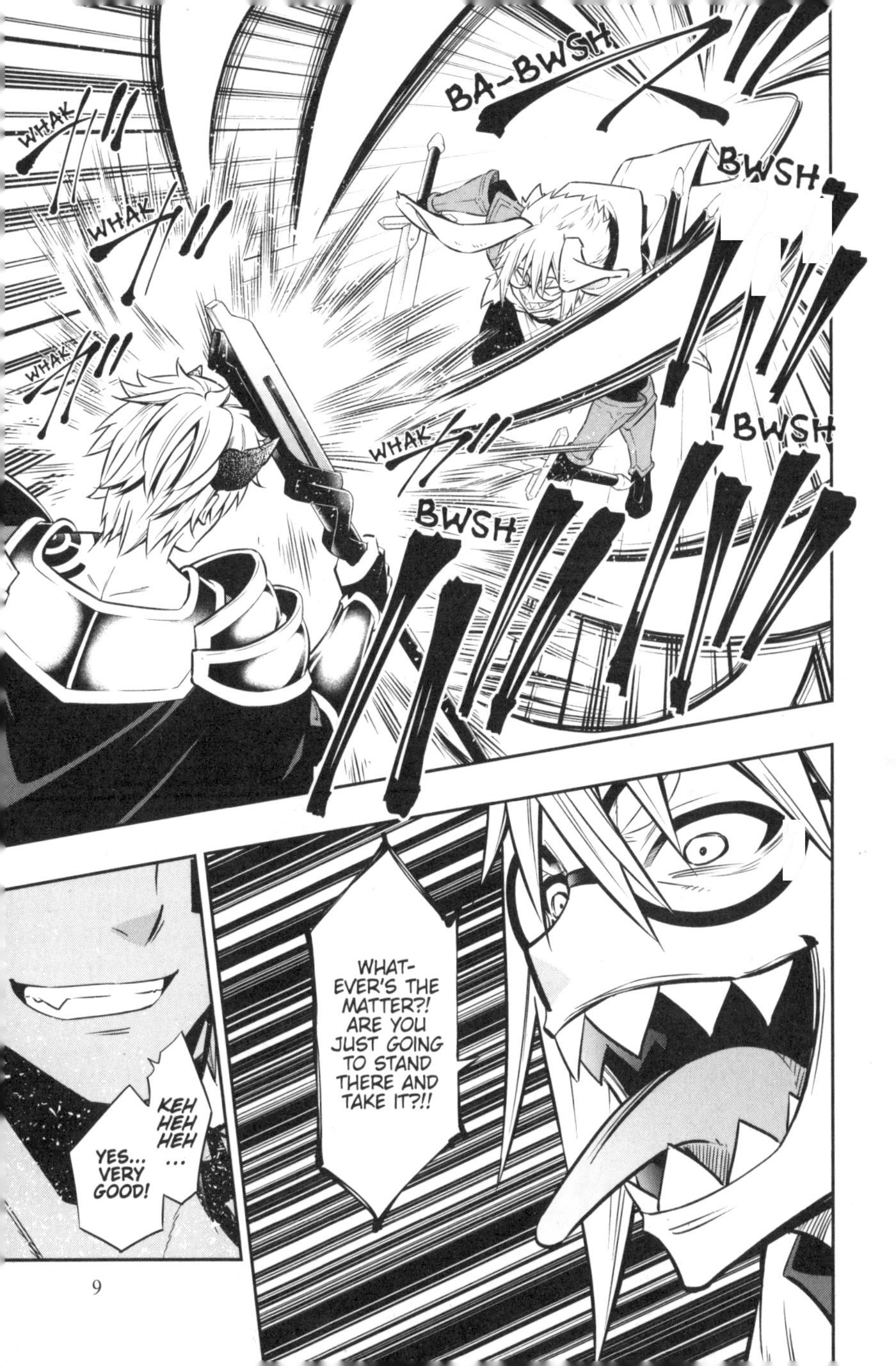
BA-BWSH
BWSH
BWSH
BWSH
WHAK
WHAK
WHAK
WHAK
WHAT-EVER'S THE MATTER?! ARE YOU JUST GOING TO STAND THERE AND TAKE IT?!!
KEH HEH HEH...
YES... VERY GOOD!

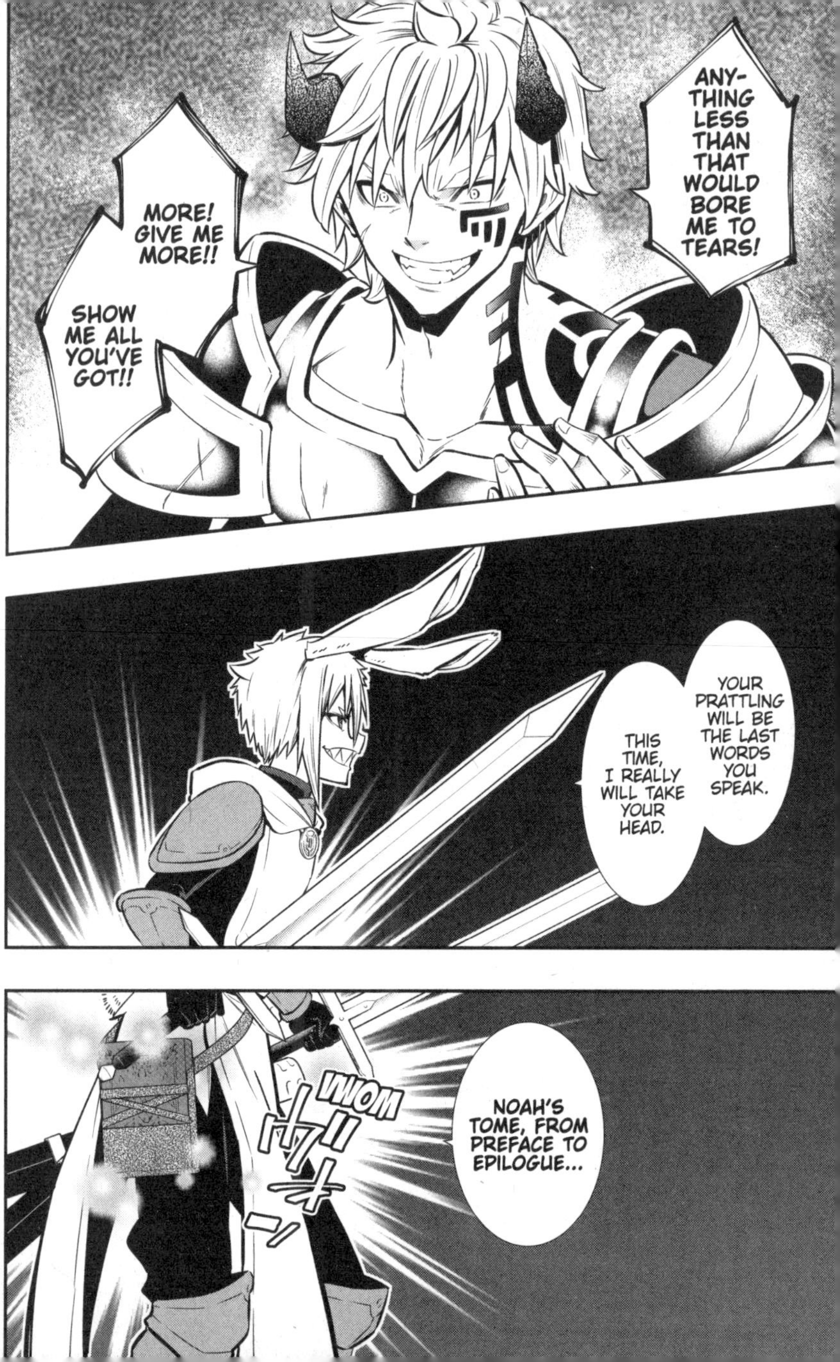
ANYTHING LESS THAN THAT WOULD BORE ME TO TEARS!
MORE! GIVE ME MORE!!
SHOW ME ALL YOU'VE GOT!!
YOUR PRATTLING WILL BE THE LAST WORDS YOU SPEAK.
THIS TIME, I REALLY WILL TAKE YOUR HEAD.
NOAH'S TOME, FROM PREFACE TO EPILOGUE...

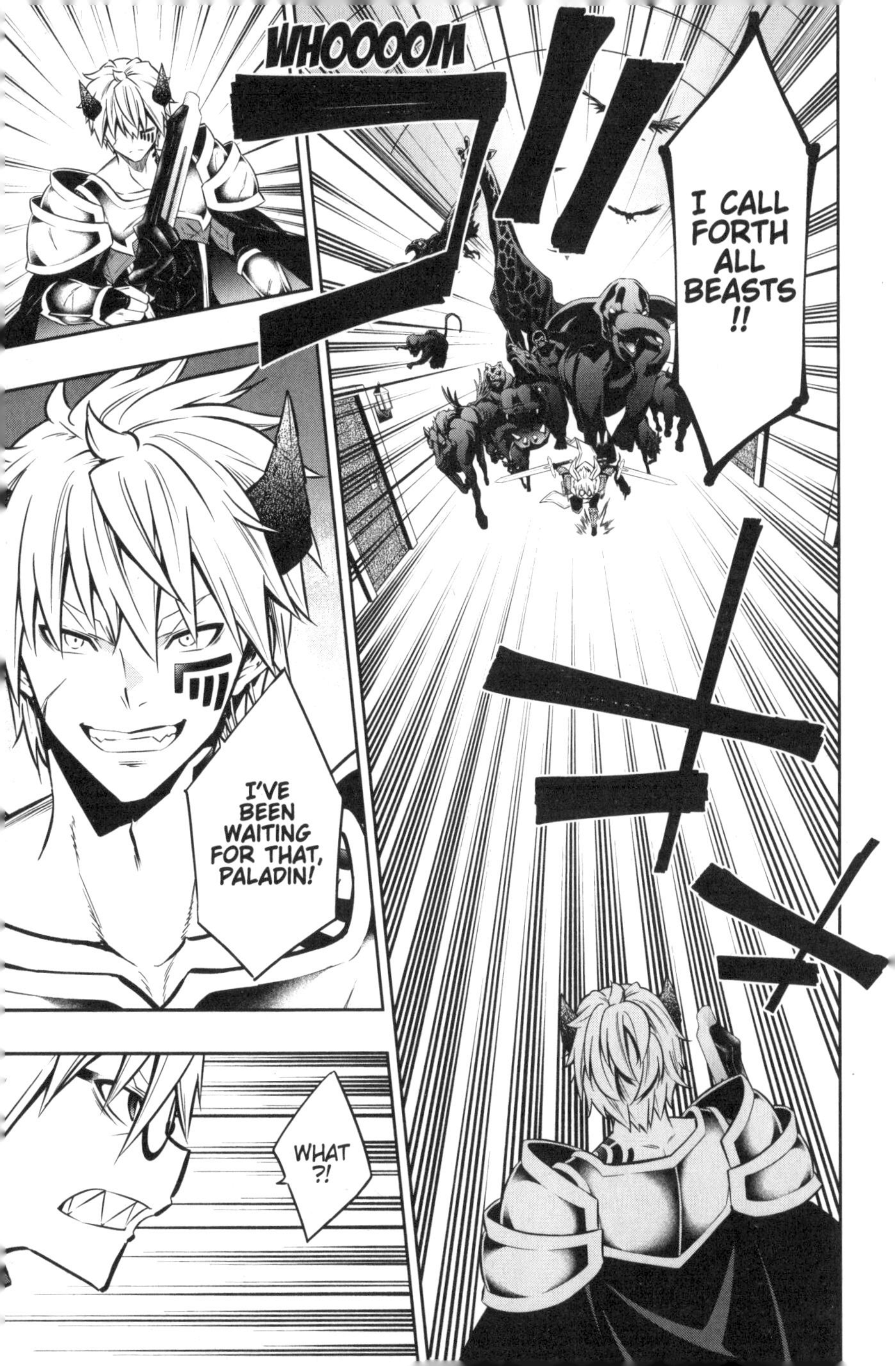
WHOOOOM
I CALL FORTH ALL BEASTS!!
I'VE BEEN WAITING FOR THAT, PALADIN!
WHAT?!

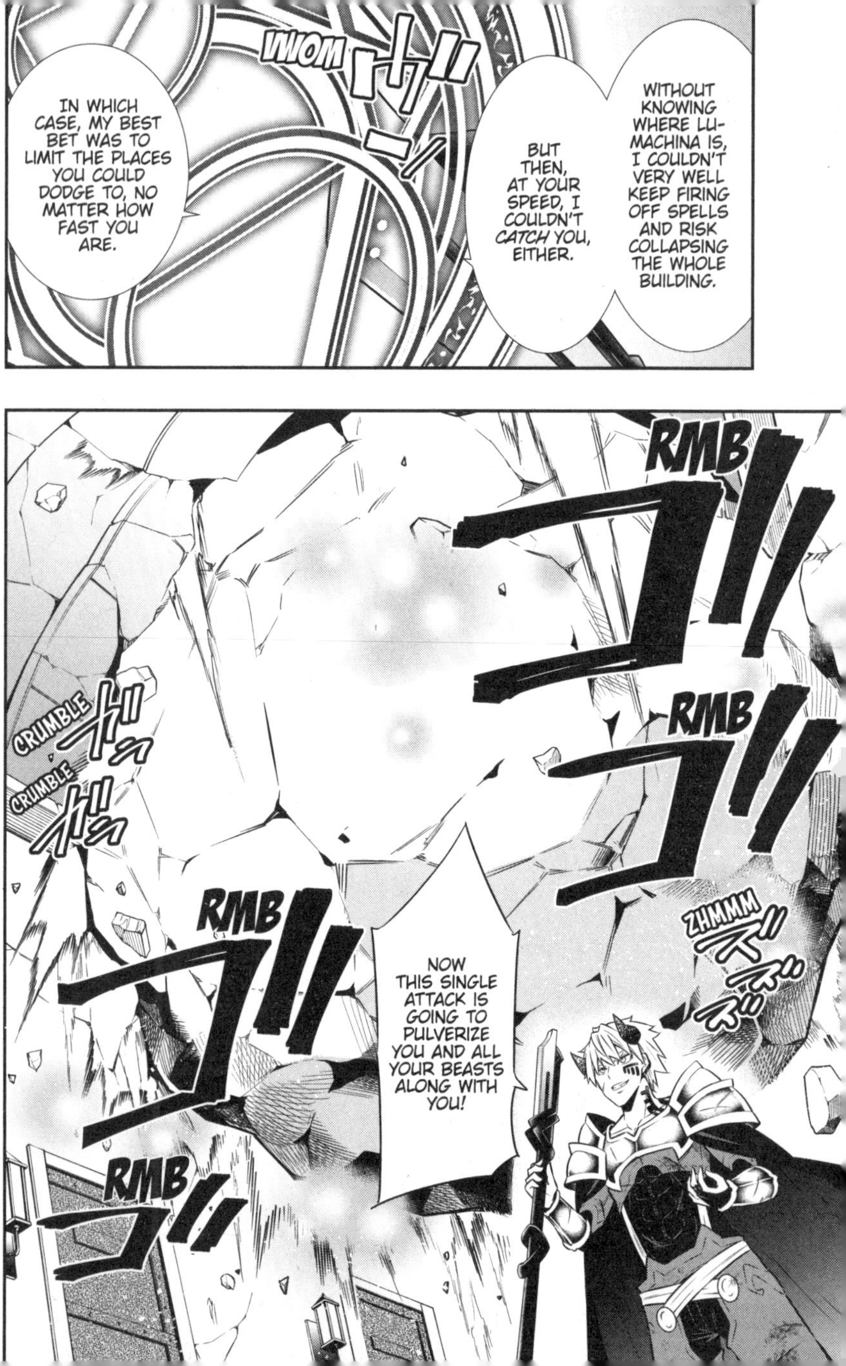
WITHOUT KNOWING WHERE LU-MACHINA IS, I COULDN'T VERY WELL KEEP FIRING OFF SPELLS AND RISK COLLAPSING THE WHOLE BUILDING.
BUT THEN, AT YOUR SPEED, I COULDN'T *CATCH* YOU, EITHER.
VWOM
IN WHICH CASE, MY BEST BET WAS TO LIMIT THE PLACES YOU COULD DODGE TO, NO MATTER HOW FAST YOU ARE.
RMB
RMB
ZHMMM
NOW THIS SINGLE ATTACK IS GOING TO PULVERIZE YOU AND ALL YOUR BEASTS ALONG WITH YOU!
RMB
CRUMBLE
CRUMBLE
RMB

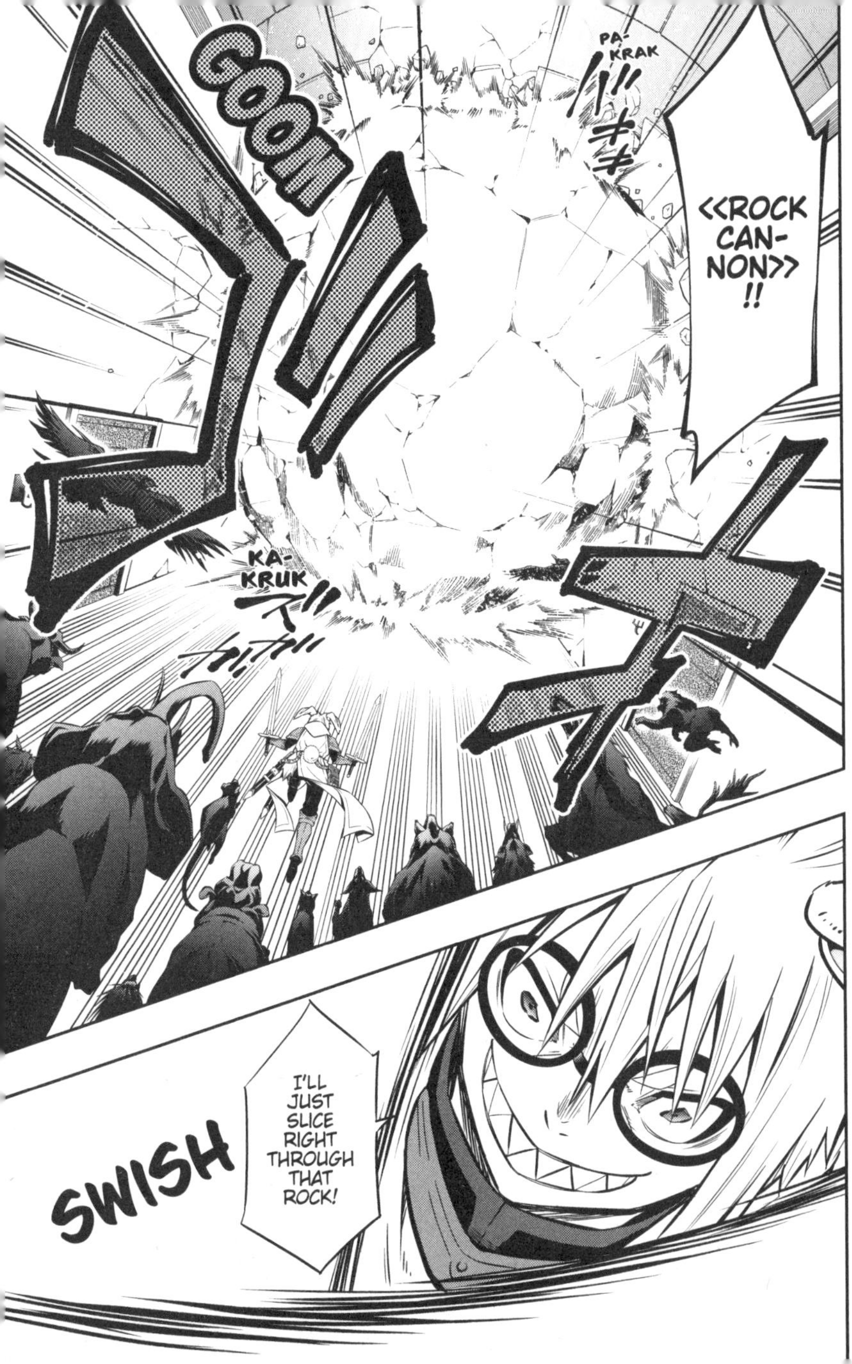
PA-KRAK
<<ROCK CANNON>>!!
GOOO!!
KA-KRUK
I'LL JUST SLICE RIGHT THROUGH THAT ROCK!
SWISH

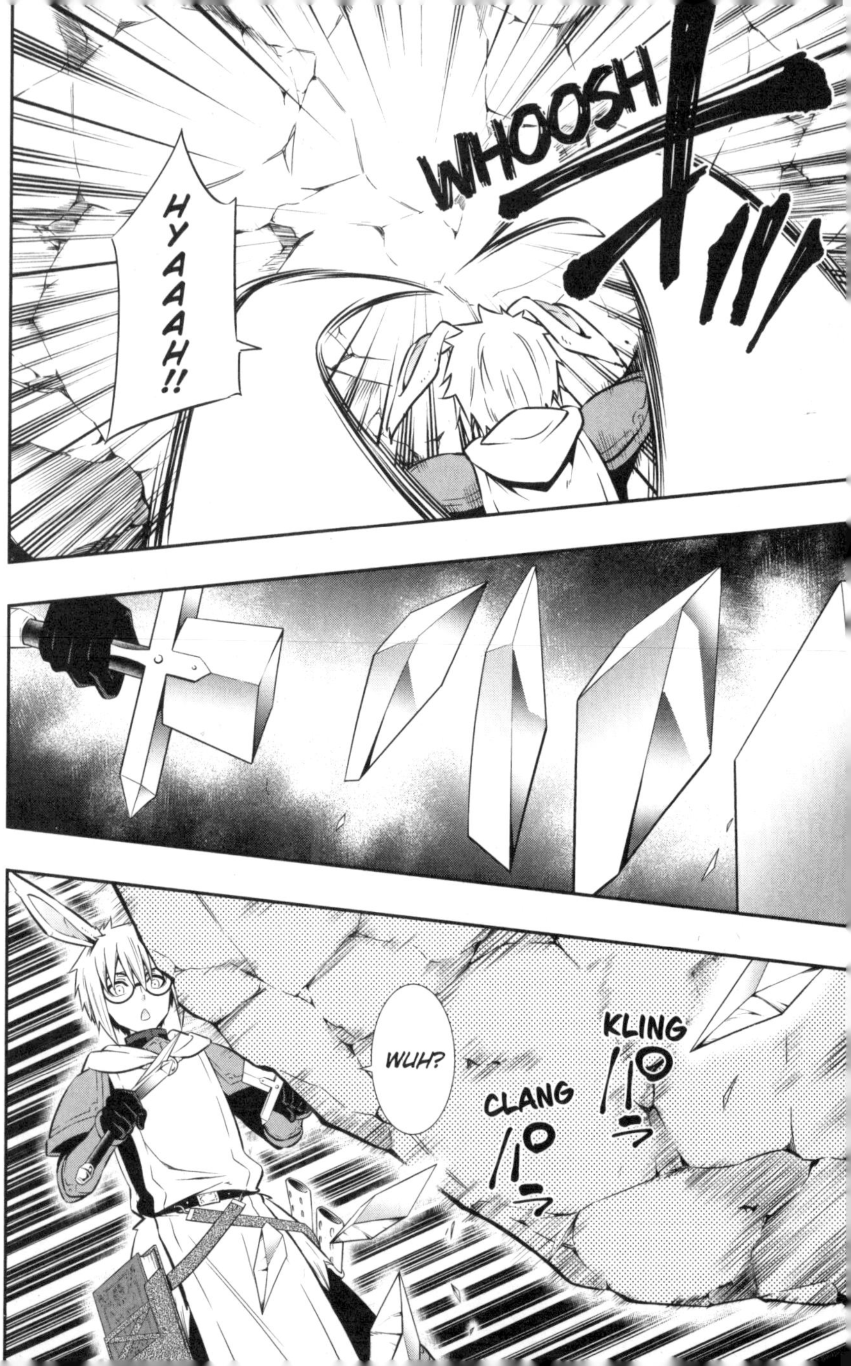
WHOOSH
HYAAAAH!!
KLING
CLANG
WUH?

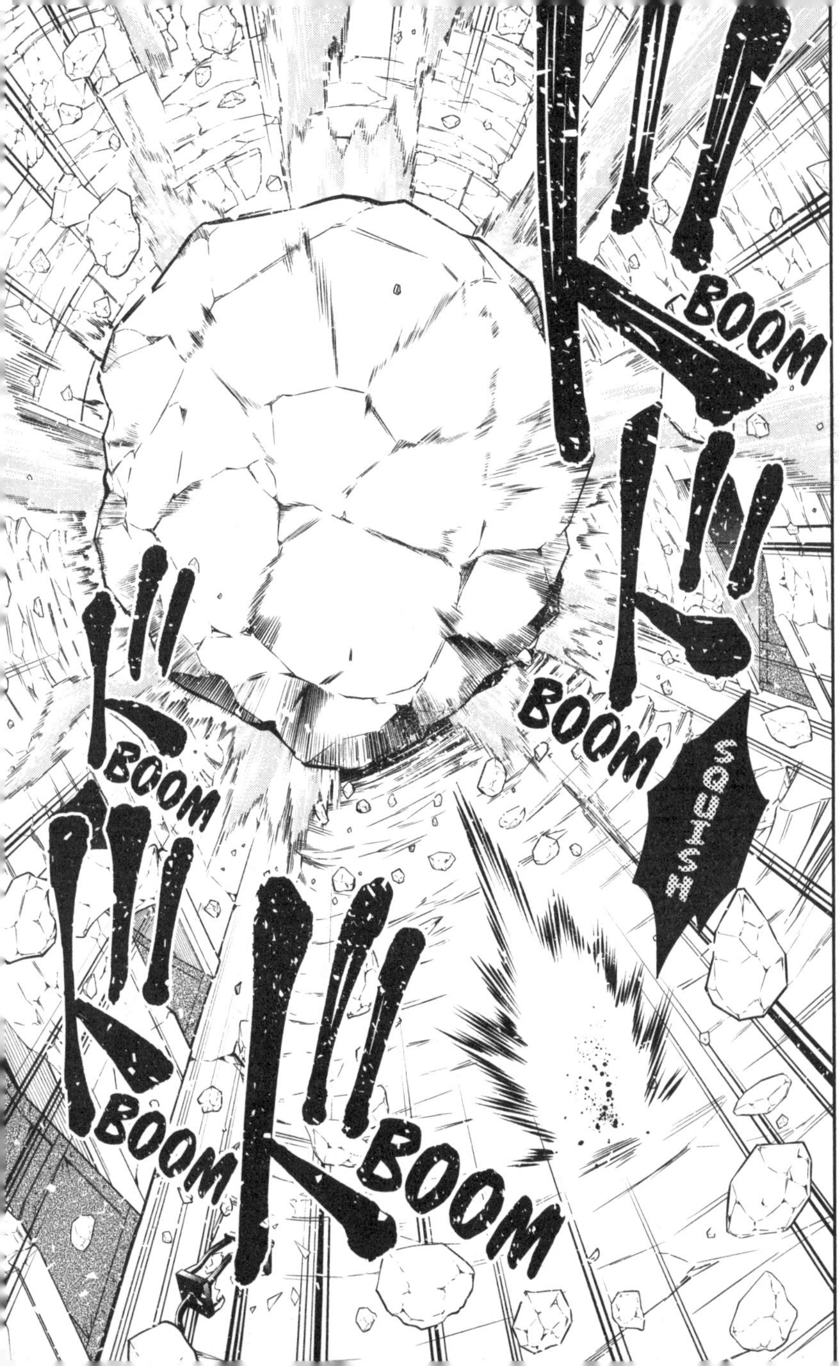
BOOM
BOOM
SWISH
BOOM
BOOM
BOOM

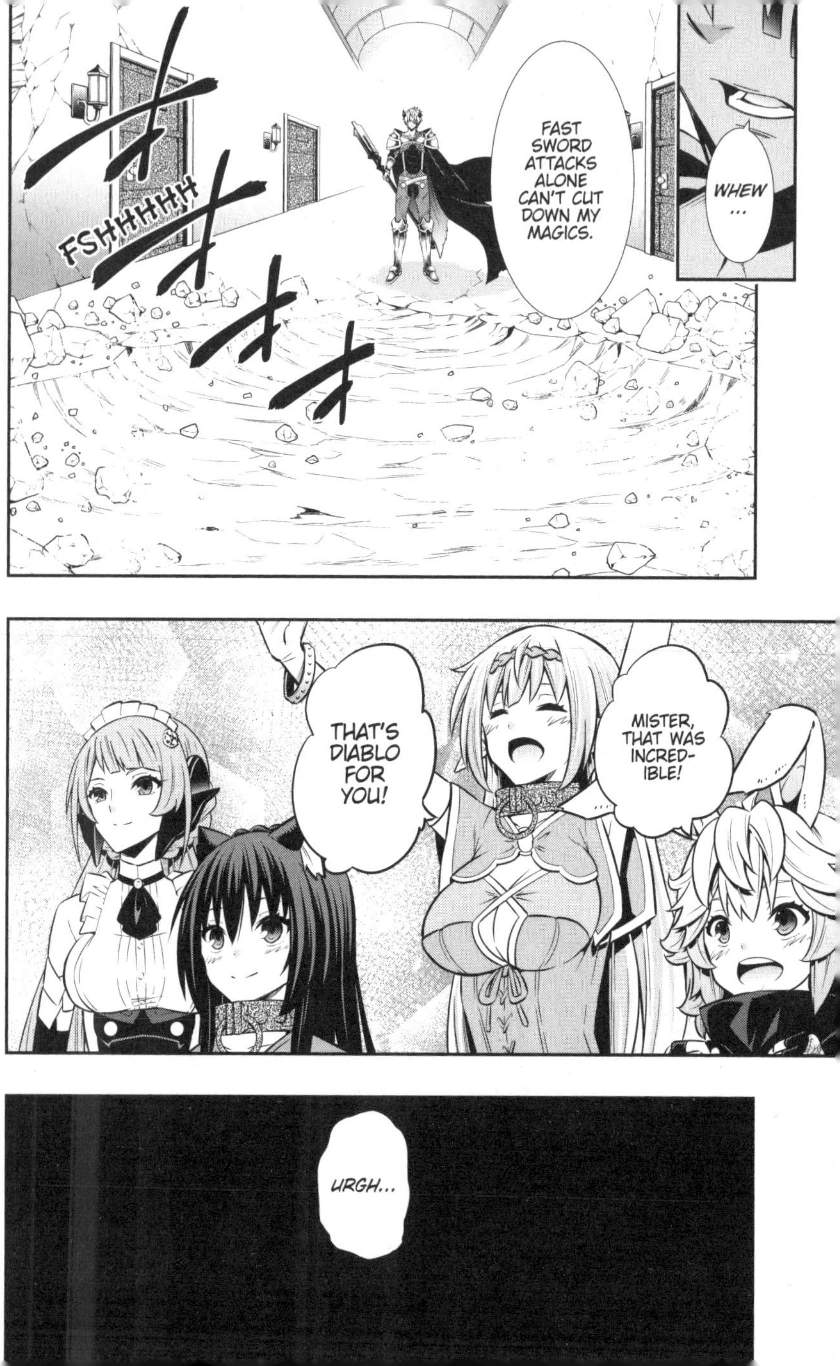
WHEW...
FAST SWORD ATTACKS ALONE CAN'T CUT DOWN MY MAGICS.
FSHHHHHH
MISTER, THAT WAS INCRED-IBLE!
THAT'S DIABLO FOR YOU!
URGH...

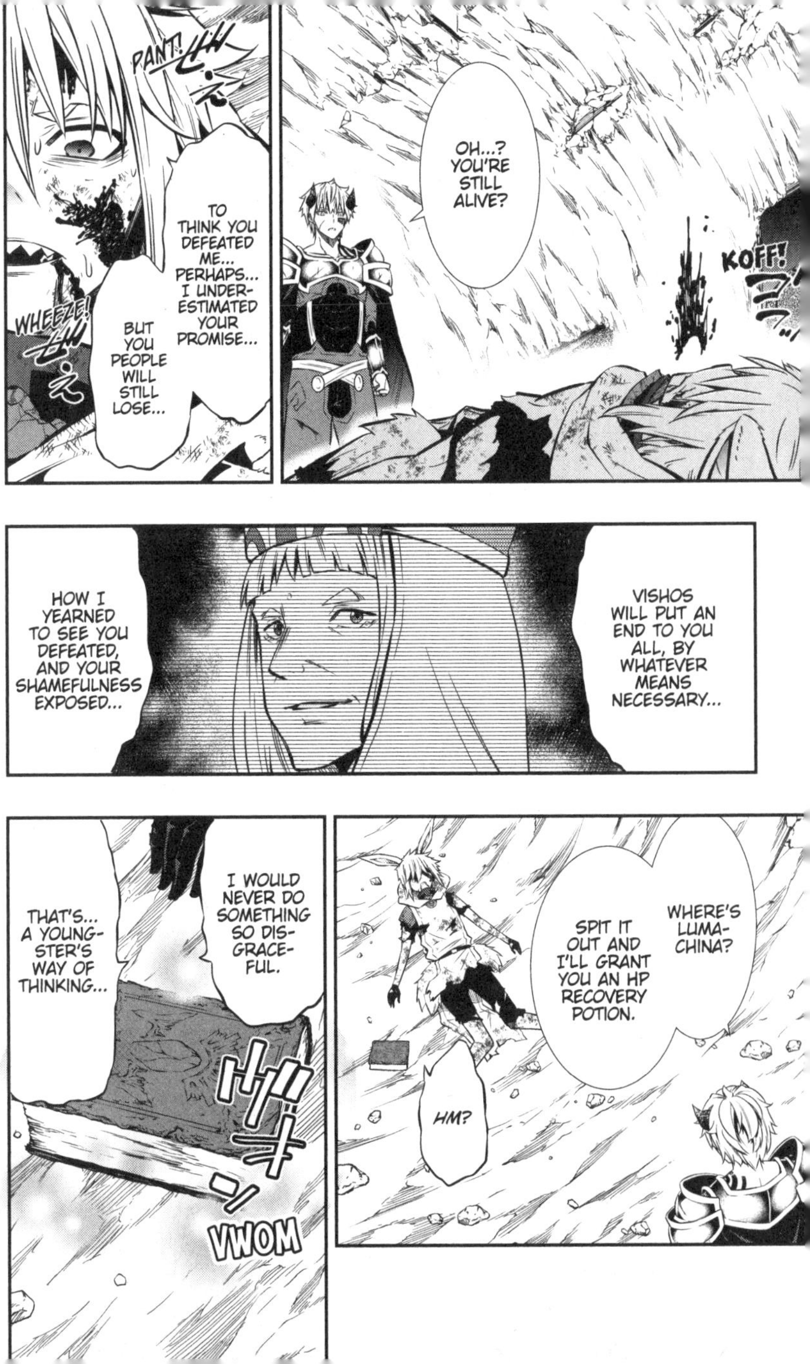
OH...? YOU'RE STILL ALIVE?
KOFF!
PANT!
TO THINK YOU DEFEATED ME... PERHAPS... I UNDER-ESTIMATED YOUR PROMISE...
BUT YOU PEOPLE WILL STILL LOSE...
WHEEZE!
VISHOS WILL PUT AN END TO YOU ALL, BY WHATEVER MEANS NECESSARY...
HOW I YEARNED TO SEE YOU DEFEATED, AND YOUR SHAMEFULNESS EXPOSED...
WHERE'S LUMA-CHINA?
SPIT IT OUT AND I'LL GRANT YOU AN HP RECOVERY POTION.
HM?
I WOULD NEVER DO SOMETHING SO DIS-GRACE-FUL.
THAT'S... A YOUNG-STER'S WAY OF THINKING...
VWOM

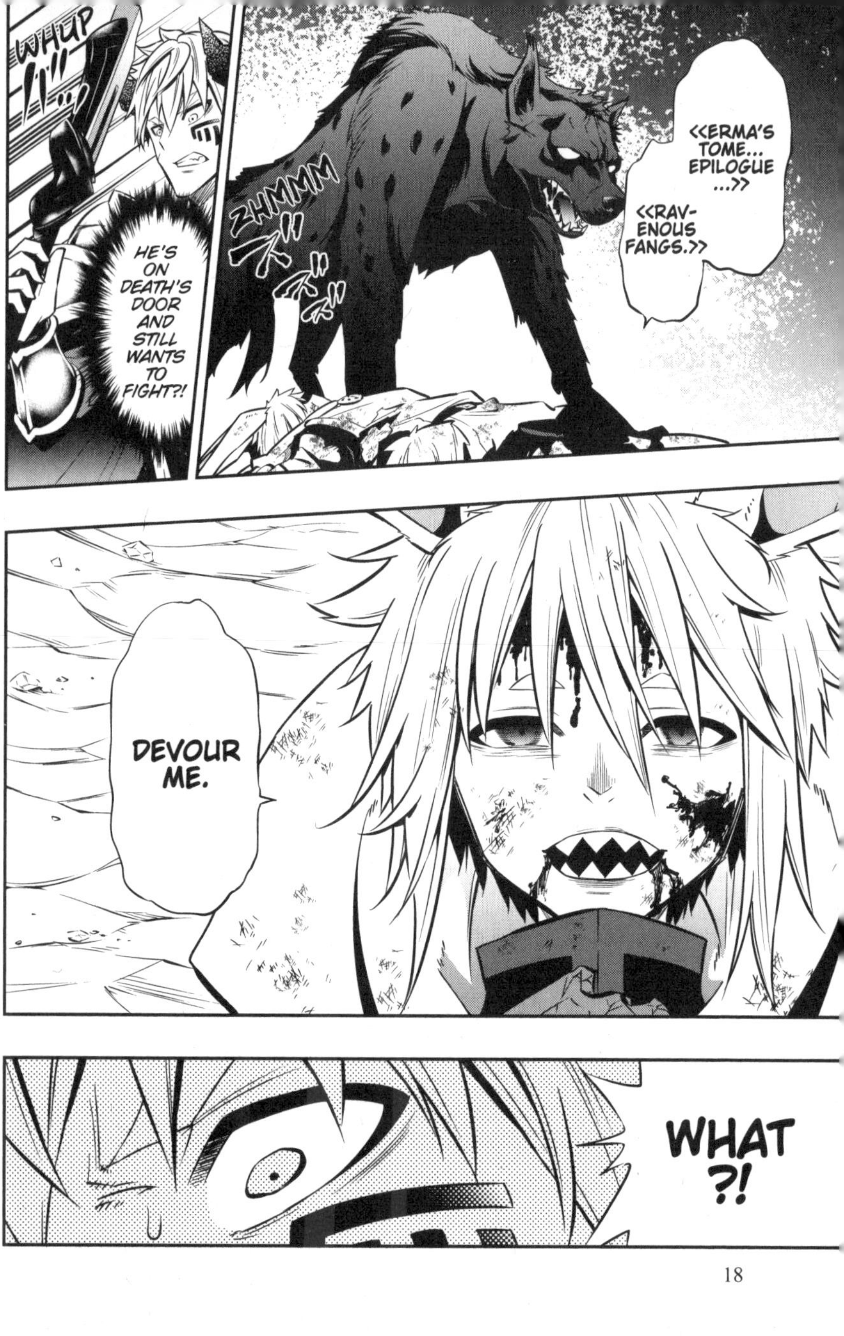
<<ERMA'S TOME... EPILOGUE ...>>
<<RAV-ENOUS FANGS.>>
ZHMMMM
WHUP
HE'S ON DEATH'S DOOR AND STILL WANTS TO FIGHT?!
DEVOUR ME.
WHAT ?!

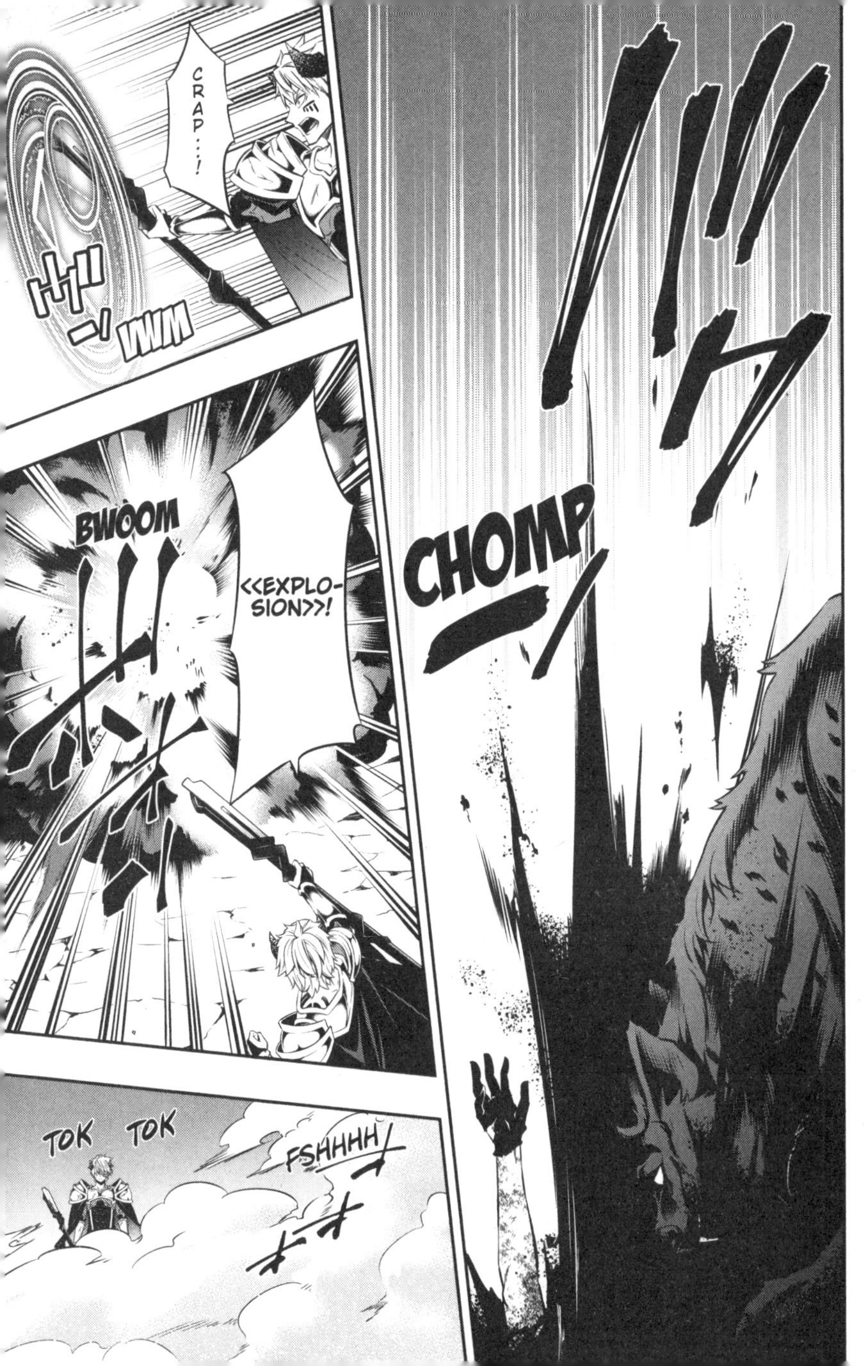
CHOMP
CRAP...!
VWM
<<EXPLOSION>>!
BWOOM
FSHHHH!
TOK TOK

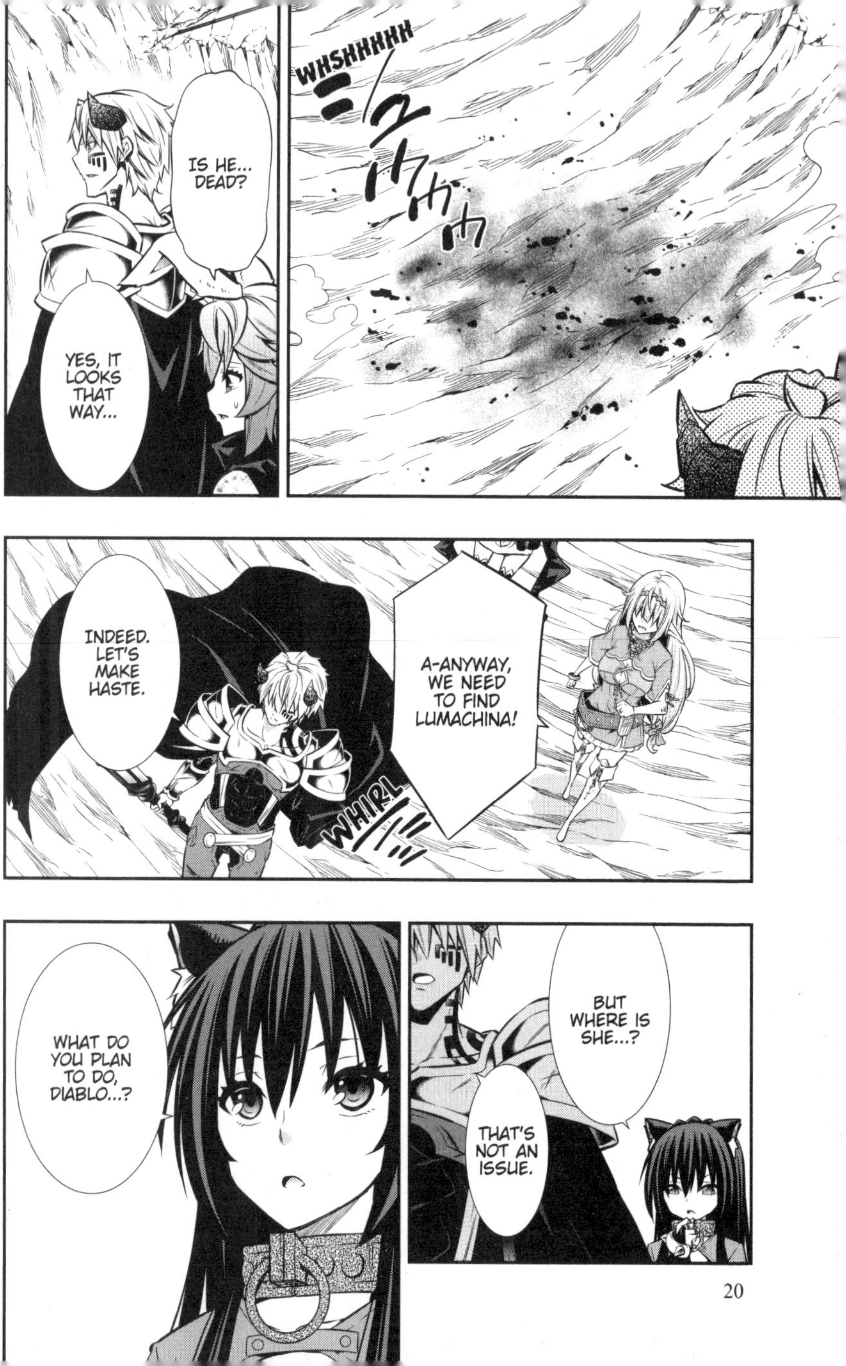
WHSHHHHH
IS HE... DEAD?
YES, IT LOOKS THAT WAY...
A-ANYWAY, WE NEED TO FIND LUMACHINA!
INDEED. LET'S MAKE HASTE.
WHIRL
BUT WHERE IS SHE...?
THAT'S NOT AN ISSUE.
WHAT DO YOU PLAN TO DO, DIABLO...?

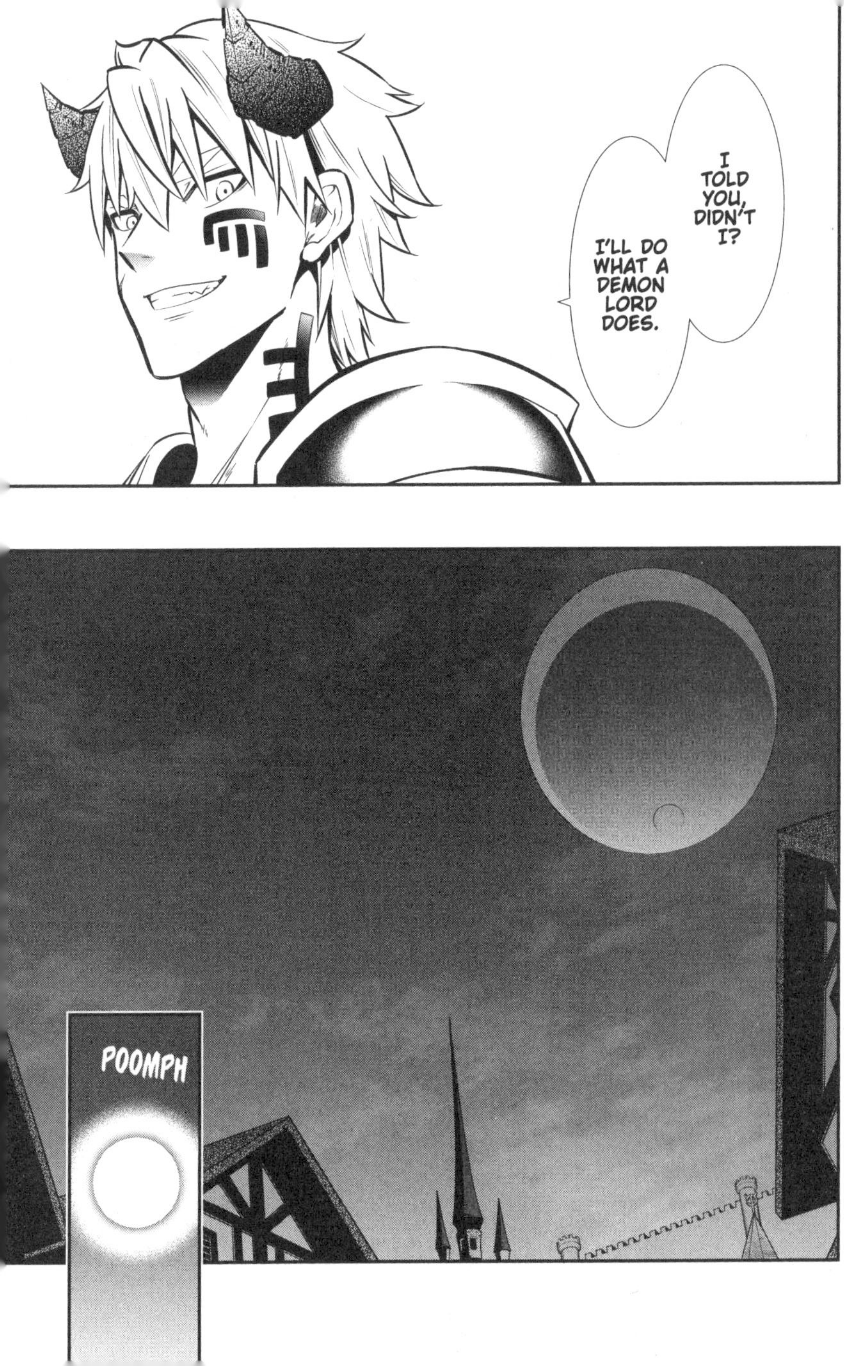
I TOLD YOU, DIDN'T I?
I'LL DO WHAT A DEMON LORD DOES.
POOMPH

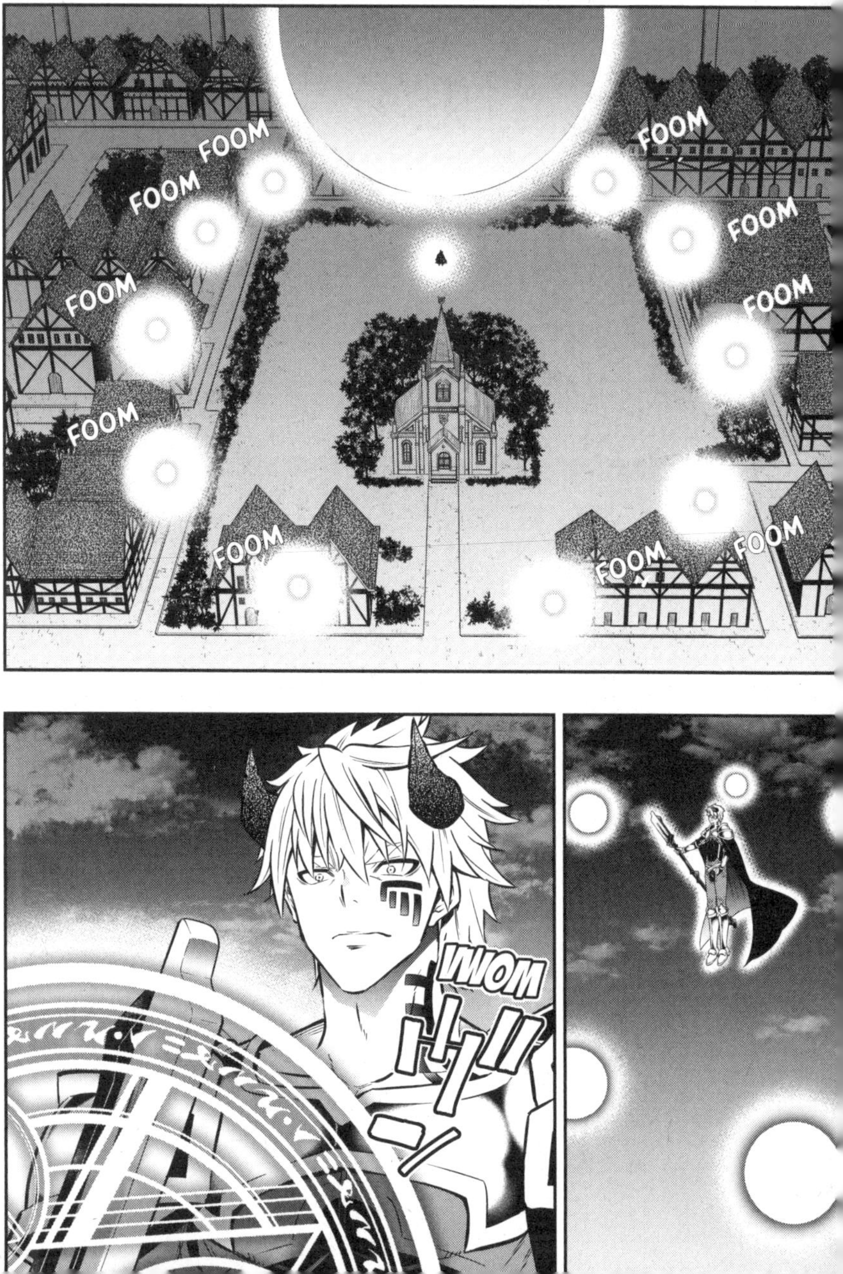
FOOM
FOOM
FOOM
FOOM
FOOM
FOOM
FOOM
FOOM
FOOM
FOOM
FOOM
VWOM

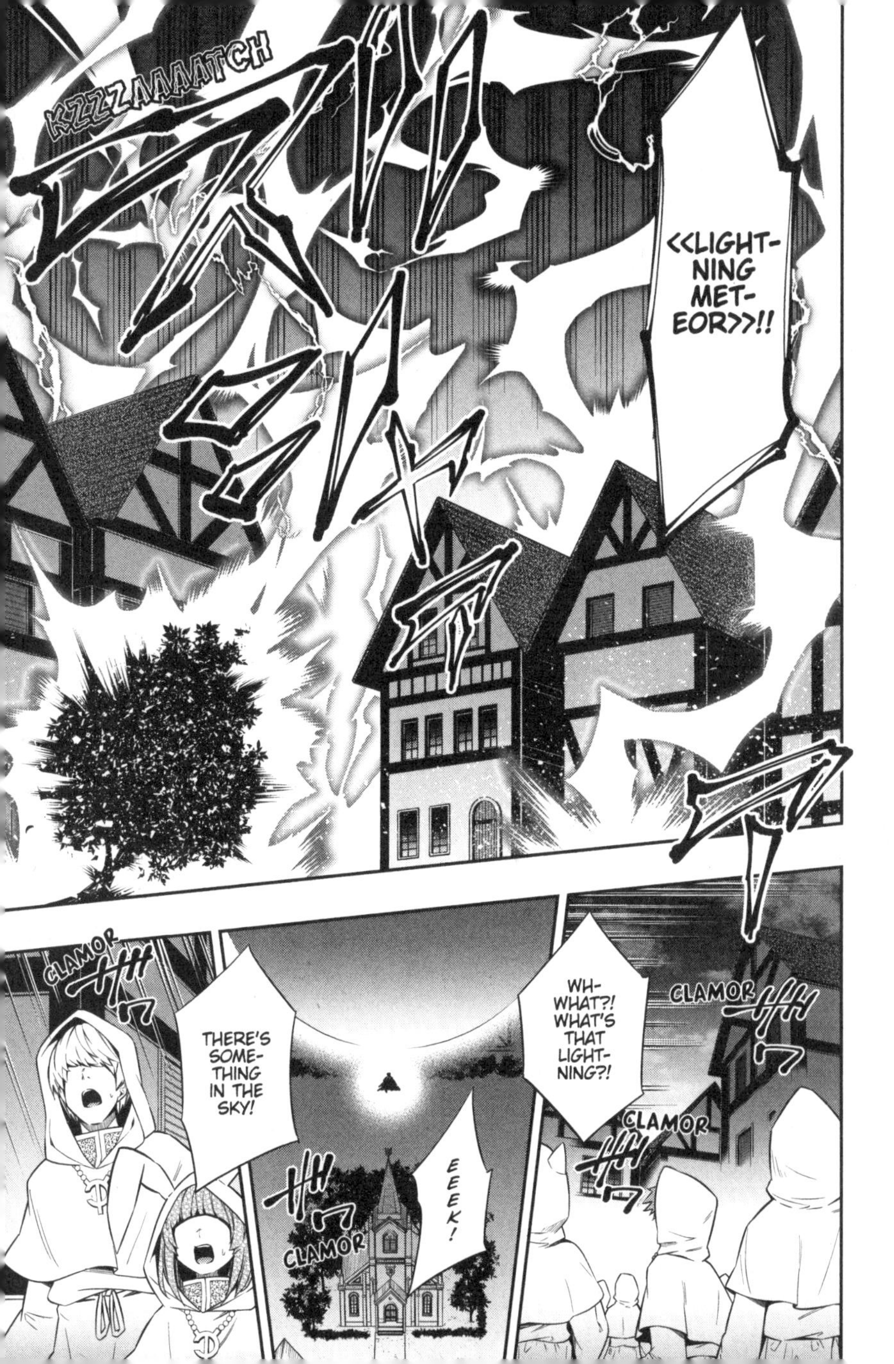

<<LIGHTNING METEOR>>!!
KRZZZAAAATCH
CLAMOR
WH-WHAT?! WHAT'S THAT LIGHTNING?!
CLAMOR
EEEK!
CLAMOR
CLAMOR
THERE'S SOMETHING IN THE SKY!

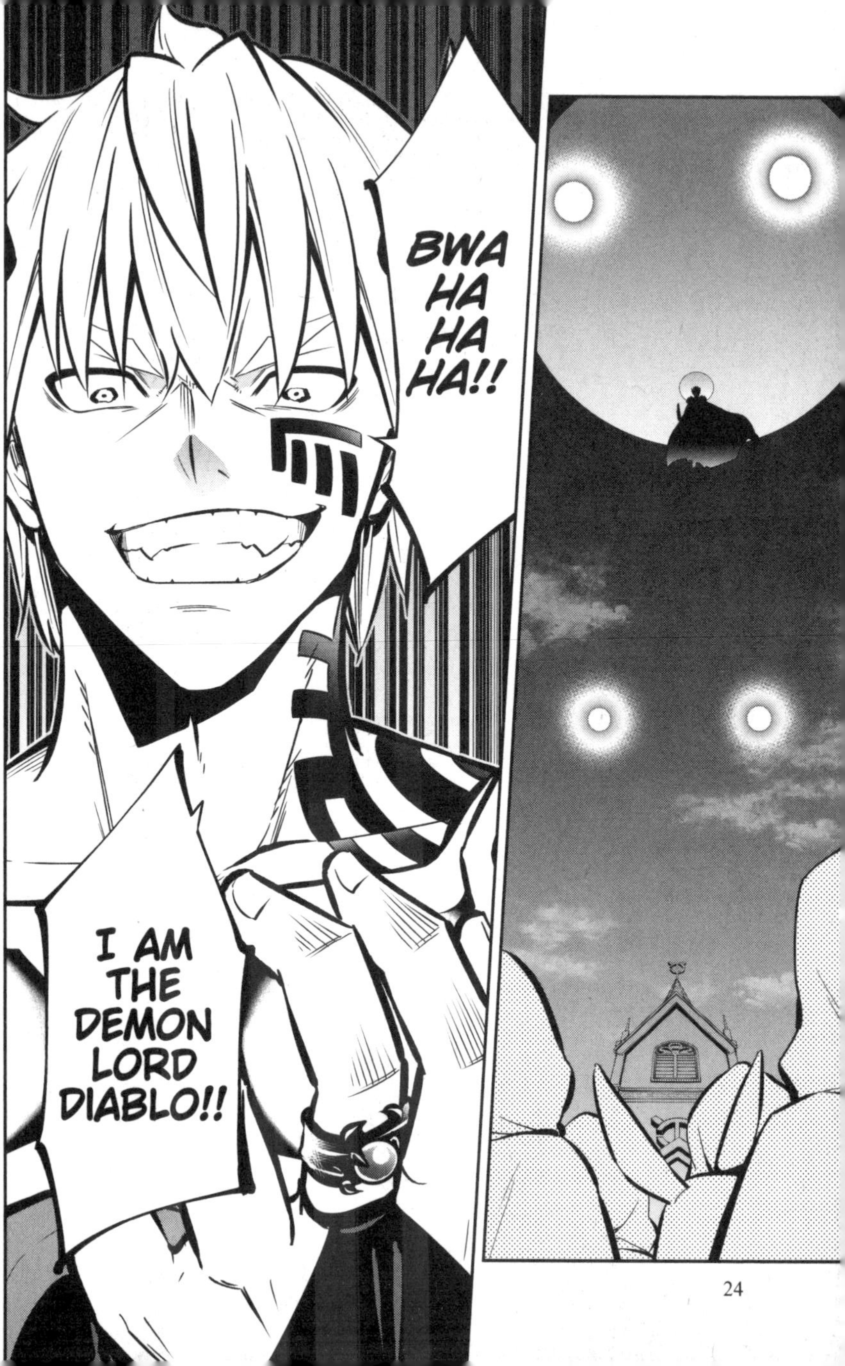
BWA HA HA HA!!
I AM THE DEMON LORD DIABLO!!

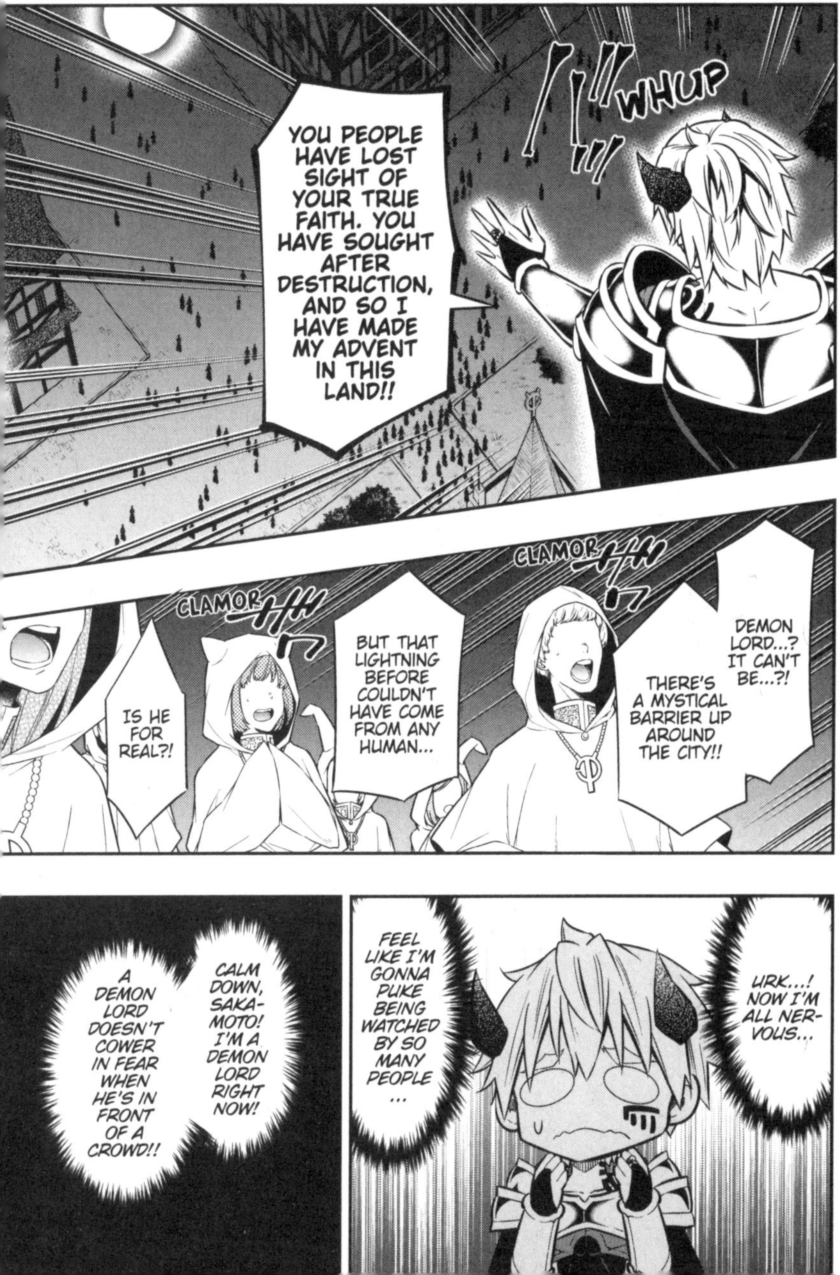
WHUP
YOU PEOPLE HAVE LOST SIGHT OF YOUR TRUE FAITH. YOU HAVE SOUGHT AFTER DESTRUCTION, AND SO I HAVE MADE MY ADVENT IN THIS LAND!!
CLAMOR
DEMON LORD...? IT CAN'T BE...?!
THERE'S A MYSTICAL BARRIER UP AROUND THE CITY!!
CLAMOR
BUT THAT LIGHTNING BEFORE COULDN'T HAVE COME FROM ANY HUMAN...
IS HE FOR REAL?!
URK...! NOW I'M ALL NERVOUS...
FEEL LIKE I'M GONNA PUKE BEING WATCHED BY SO MANY PEOPLE ...
CALM DOWN, SAKAMOTO! I'M A DEMON LORD RIGHT NOW!
A DEMON LORD DOESN'T COWER IN FEAR WHEN HE'S IN FRONT OF A CROWD!!

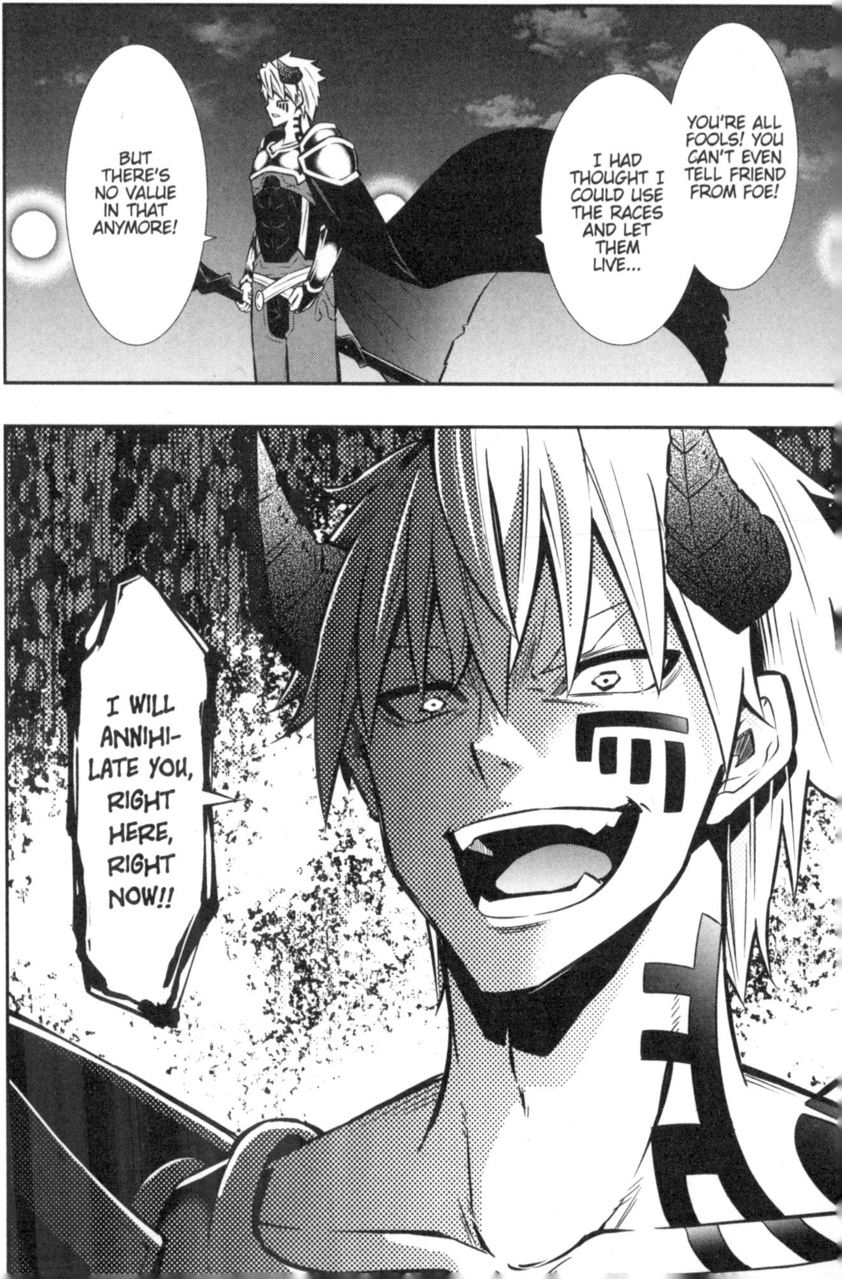
YOU'RE ALL FOOLS! YOU CAN'T EVEN TELL FRIEND FROM FOE!
I HAD THOUGHT I COULD USE THE RACES AND LET THEM LIVE...
BUT THERE'S NO VALUE IN THAT ANYMORE!
I WILL ANNIHI-LATE YOU, RIGHT HERE, RIGHT NOW!!

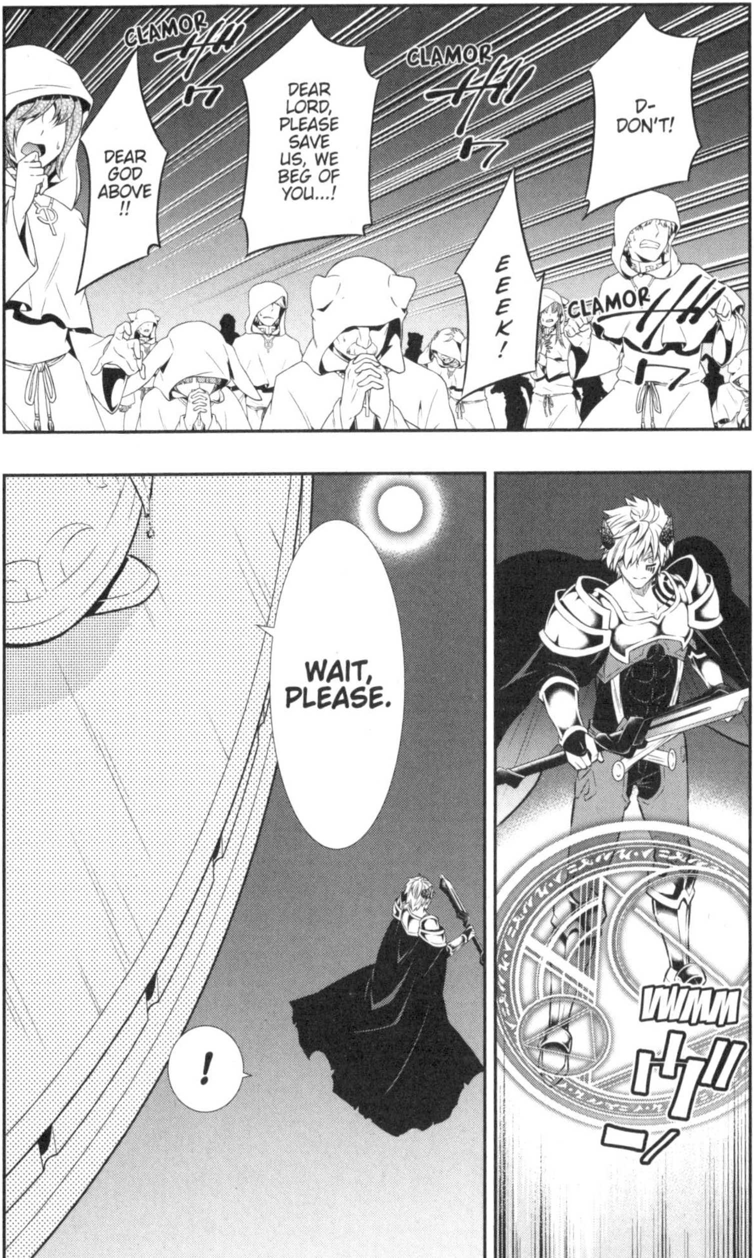
D-DON'T!
CLAMOR
EEEK!
CLAMOR
DEAR LORD, PLEASE SAVE US, WE BEG OF YOU...!
CLAMOR
DEAR GOD ABOVE!!
VWMM
WAIT, PLEASE.
!

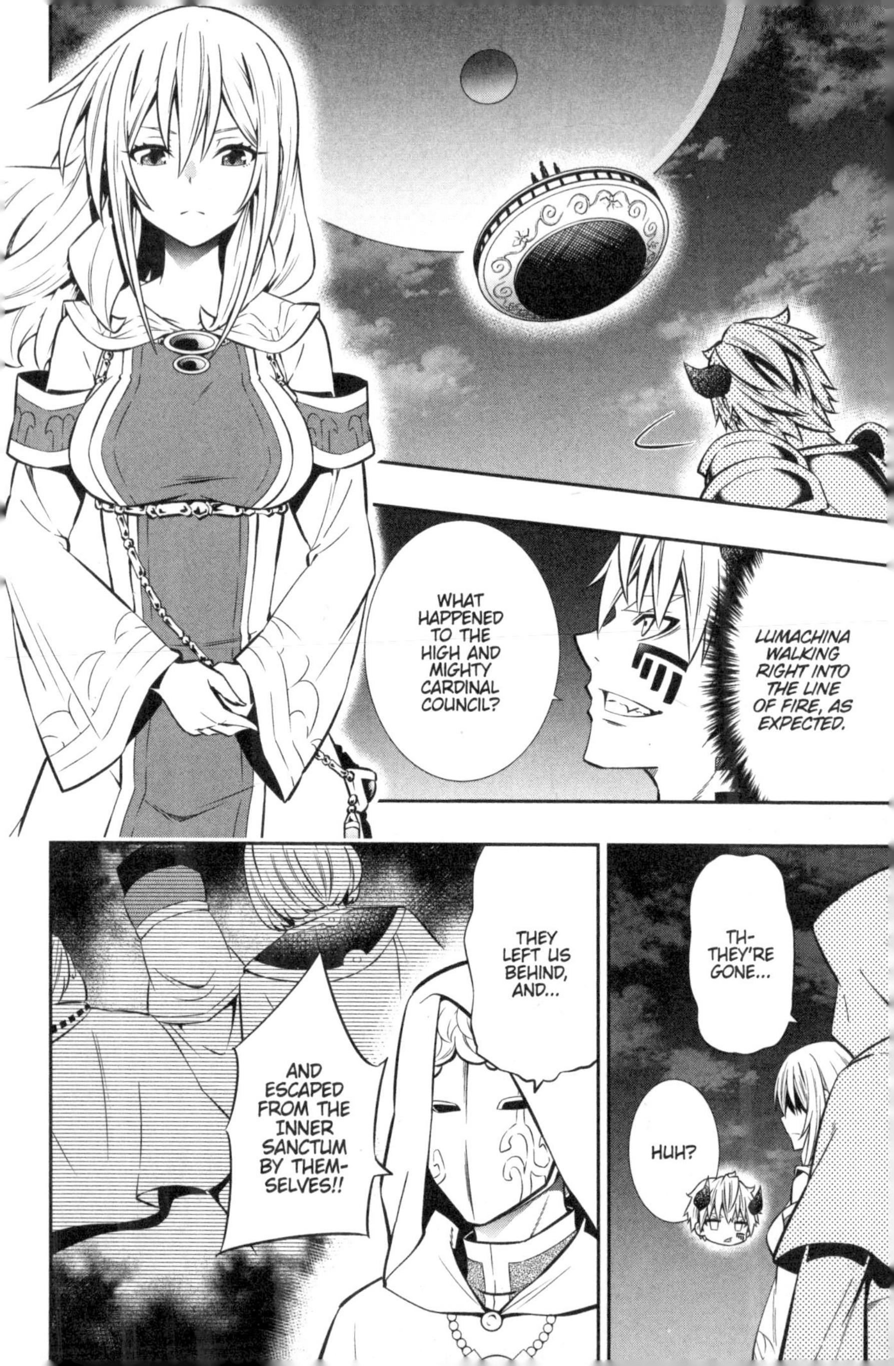
LUMACHINA WALKING RIGHT INTO THE LINE OF FIRE, AS EXPECTED.
WHAT HAPPENED TO THE HIGH AND MIGHTY CARDINAL COUNCIL?
TH- THEY'RE GONE...
HUH?
THEY LEFT US BEHIND, AND...
AND ESCAPED FROM THE INNER SANCTUM BY THEM-SELVES!!

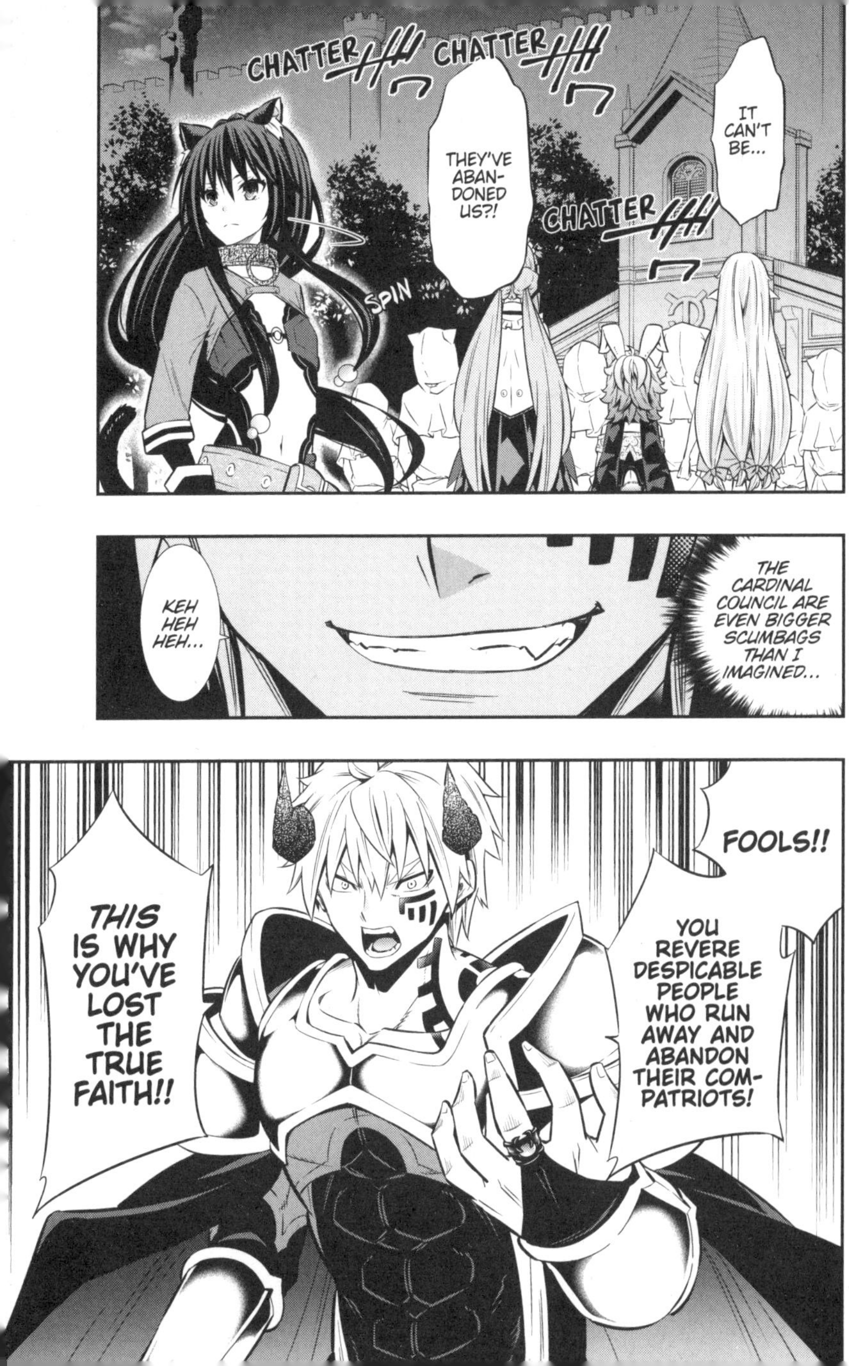
CHATTER
CHATTER
IT CAN'T BE...
CHATTER
CHATTER
THEY'VE ABAN-DONED US?!
SPIN
THE CARDINAL COUNCIL ARE EVEN BIGGER SCUMBAGS THAN I IMAGINED...
KEH HEH HEH...
FOOLS!!
YOU REVERE DESPICABLE PEOPLE WHO RUN AWAY AND ABANDON THEIR COM-PATRIOTS!
THIS IS WHY YOU'VE LOST THE TRUE FAITH!!

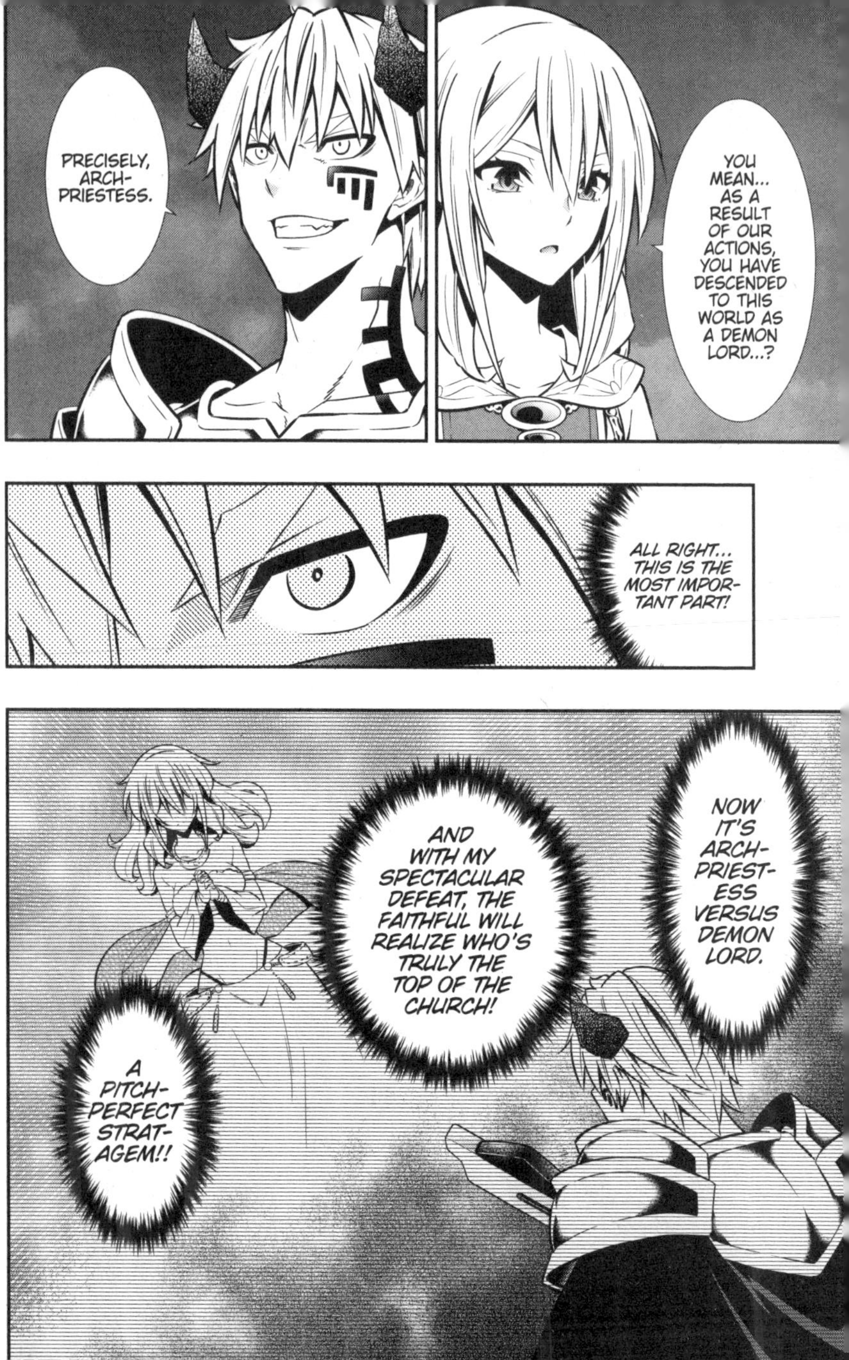
YOU MEAN... AS A RESULT OF OUR ACTIONS, YOU HAVE DESCENDED TO THIS WORLD AS A DEMON LORD...?
PRECISELY, ARCH-PRIESTESS.
ALL RIGHT... THIS IS THE MOST IMPOR-TANT PART!
NOW IT'S ARCH-PRIEST-ESS VERSUS DEMON LORD.
AND WITH MY SPECTACULAR DEFEAT, THE FAITHFUL WILL REALIZE WHO'S TRULY THE TOP OF THE CHURCH!
A PITCH-PERFECT STRAT-AGEM!!

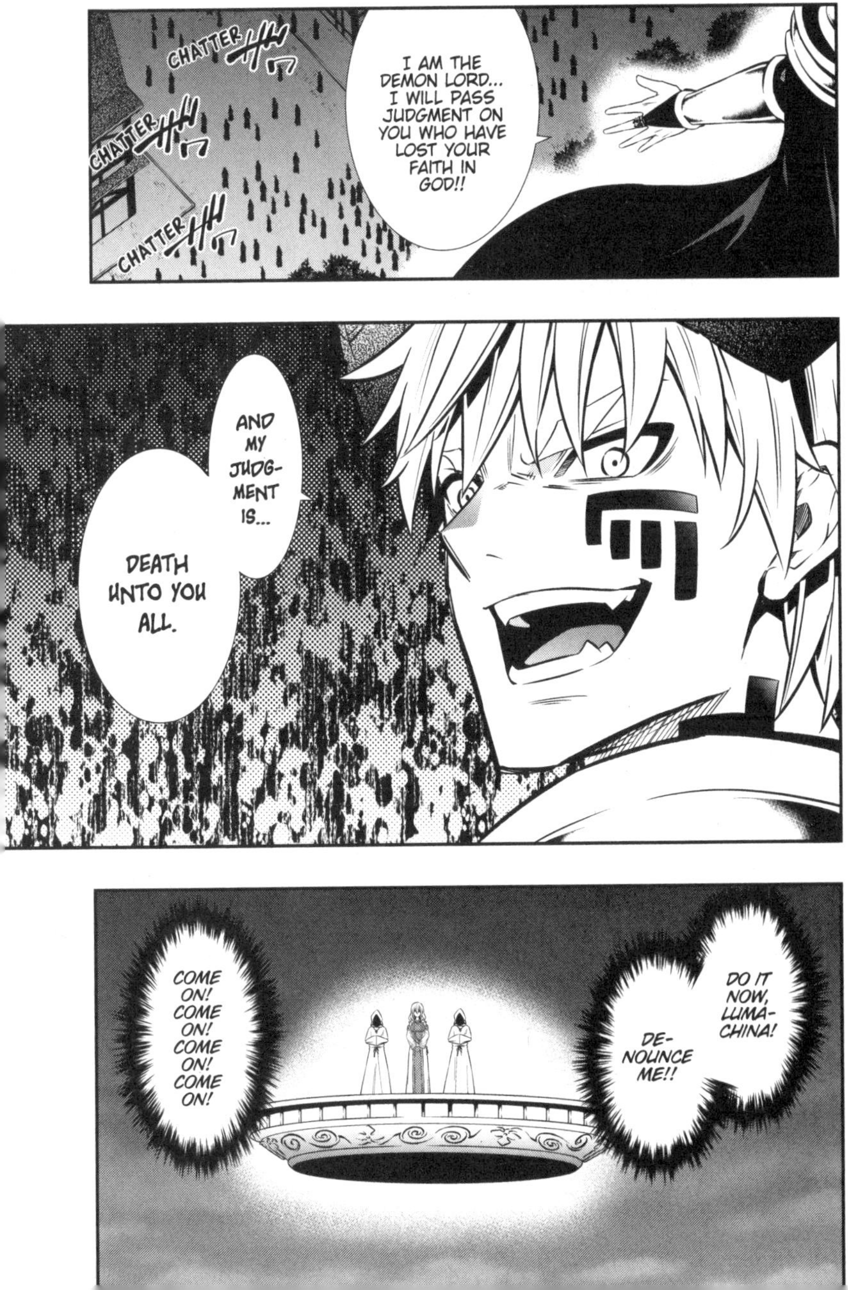
I AM THE DEMON LORD... I WILL PASS JUDGMENT ON YOU WHO HAVE LOST YOUR FAITH IN GOD!!
CHATTER
CHATTER
CHATTER
AND MY JUDGMENT IS...
DEATH UNTO YOU ALL.
DO IT NOW, LUMACHINA!
DENOUNCE ME!!
COME ON! COME ON! COME ON! COME ON!

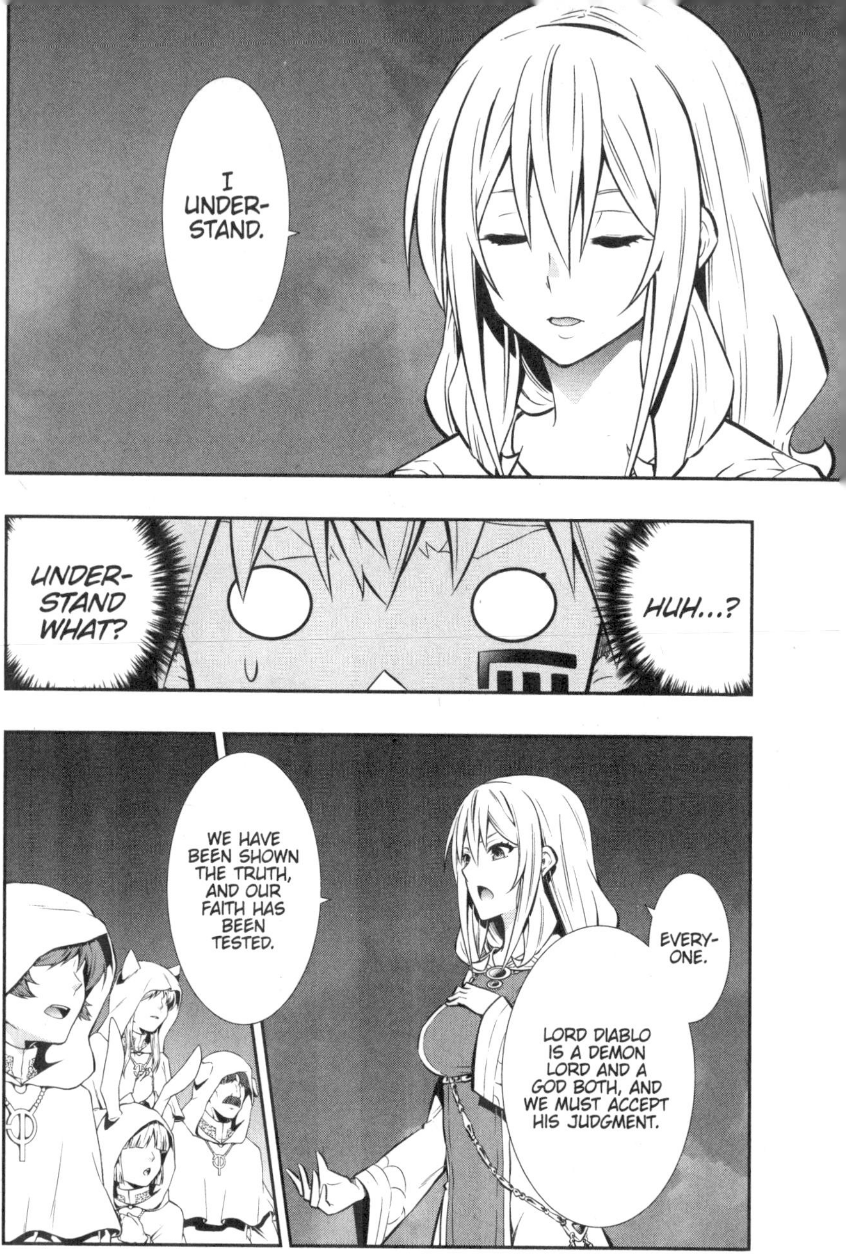
I UNDER-STAND.
HUH...?
UNDER-STAND WHAT?
EVERY-ONE.
LORD DIABLO IS A DEMON LORD AND A GOD BOTH, AND WE MUST ACCEPT HIS JUDGMENT.
WE HAVE BEEN SHOWN THE TRUTH, AND OUR FAITH HAS BEEN TESTED.

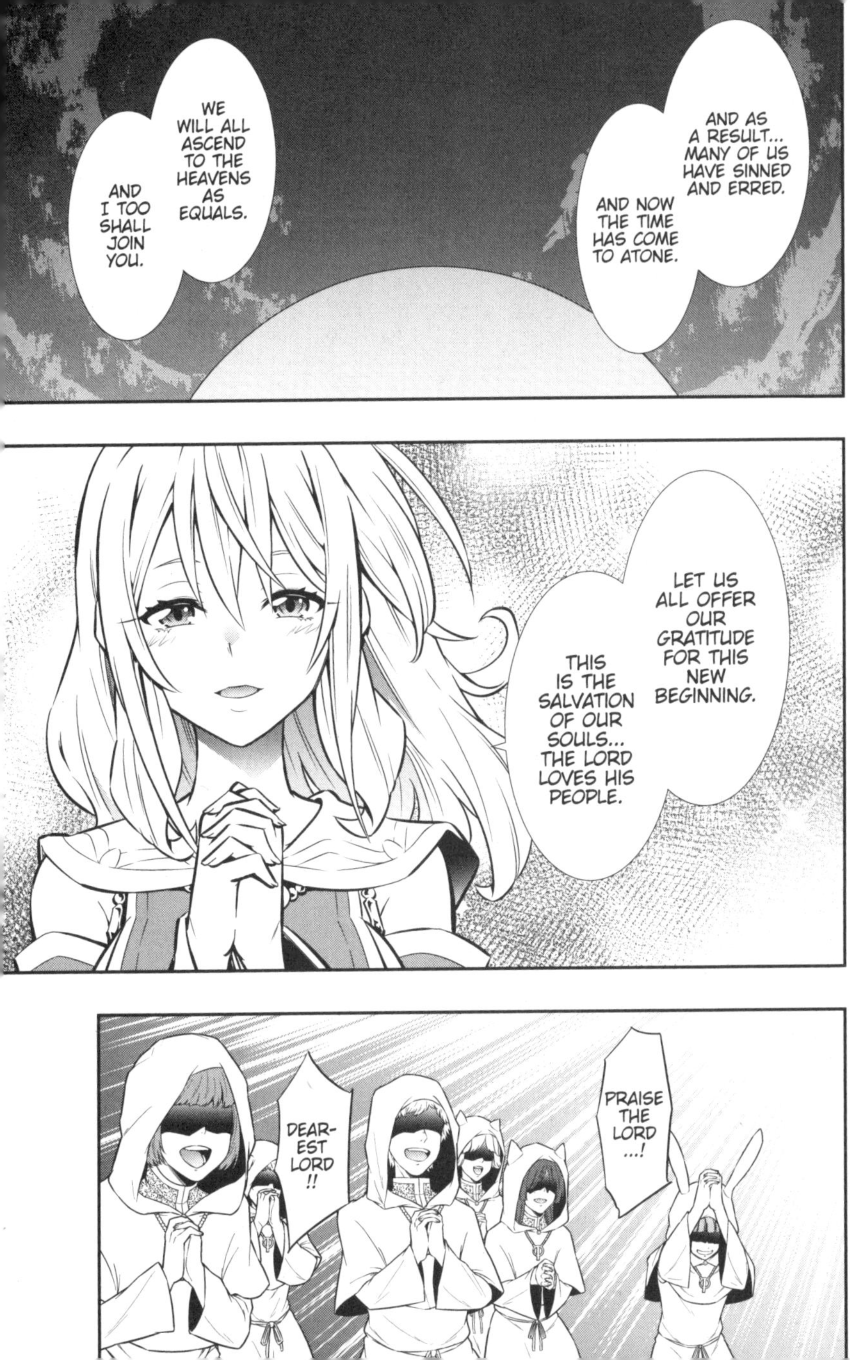
AND AS A RESULT... MANY OF US HAVE SINNED AND ERRED.
AND NOW THE TIME HAS COME TO ATONE.
WE WILL ALL ASCEND TO THE HEAVENS AS EQUALS.
AND I TOO SHALL JOIN YOU.
LET US ALL OFFER OUR GRATITUDE FOR THIS NEW BEGINNING.
THIS IS THE SALVATION OF OUR SOULS... THE LORD LOVES HIS PEOPLE.
PRAISE THE LORD ...!
DEAR-EST LORD !!

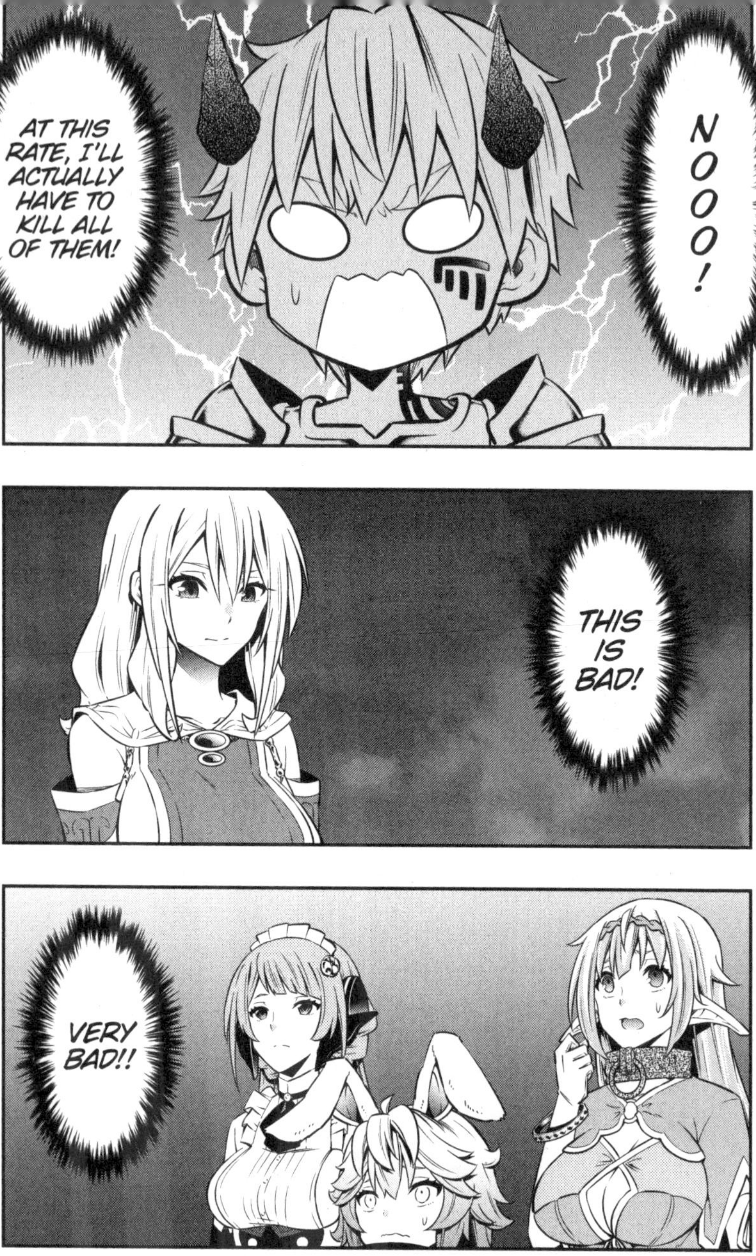
NOOOO!
AT THIS RATE, I'LL ACTUALLY HAVE TO KILL ALL OF THEM!
THIS IS BAD!
VERY BAD!!

REALLY
BAD!!!

YOUR
SEN-
TENCE...

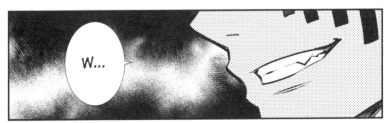

W...

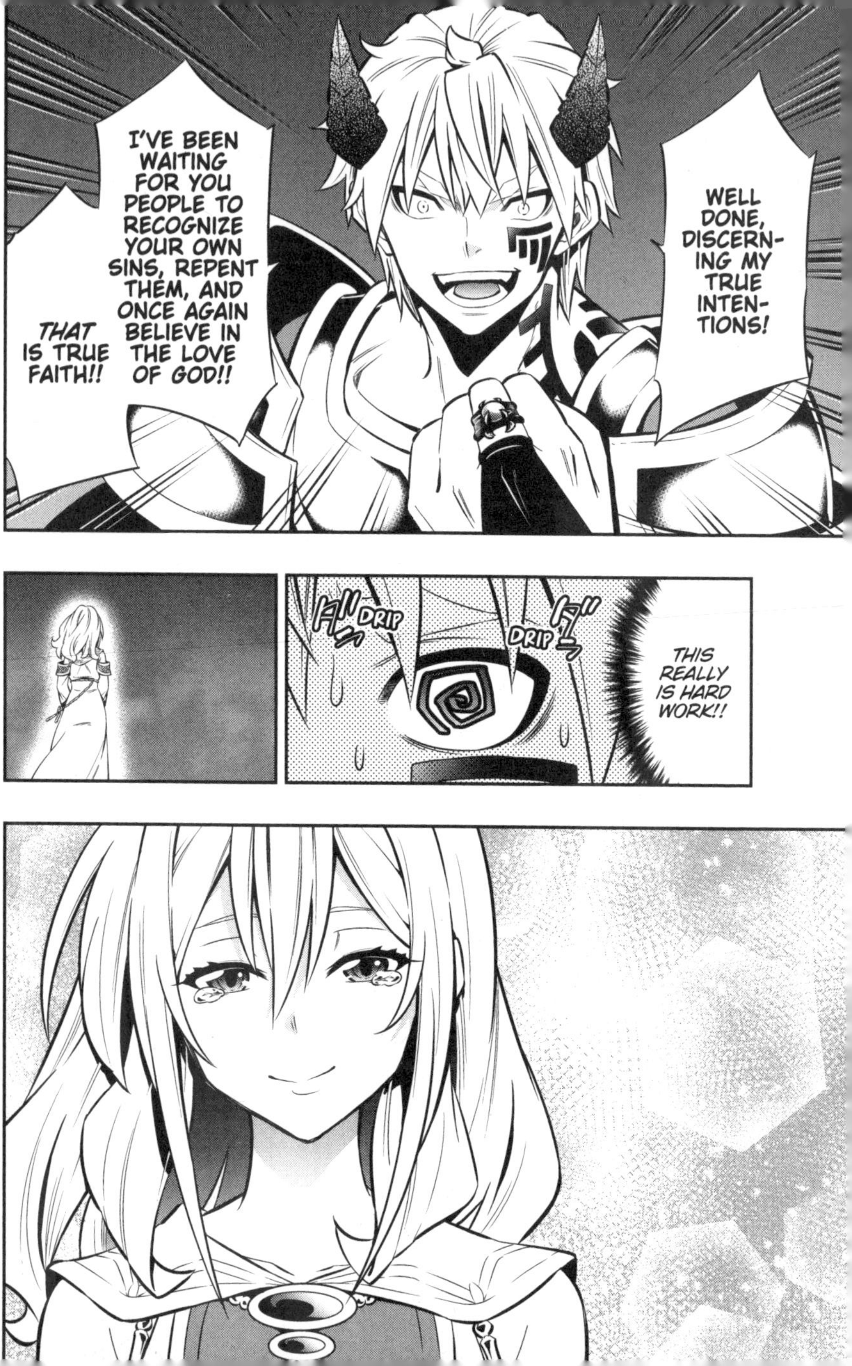
WELL DONE, DISCERNING MY TRUE INTENTIONS!
I'VE BEEN WAITING FOR YOU PEOPLE TO RECOGNIZE YOUR OWN SINS, REPENT THEM, AND ONCE AGAIN BELIEVE IN THE LOVE OF GOD!!
THAT IS TRUE FAITH!!
DRIP
DRIP
THIS REALLY IS HARD WORK!!

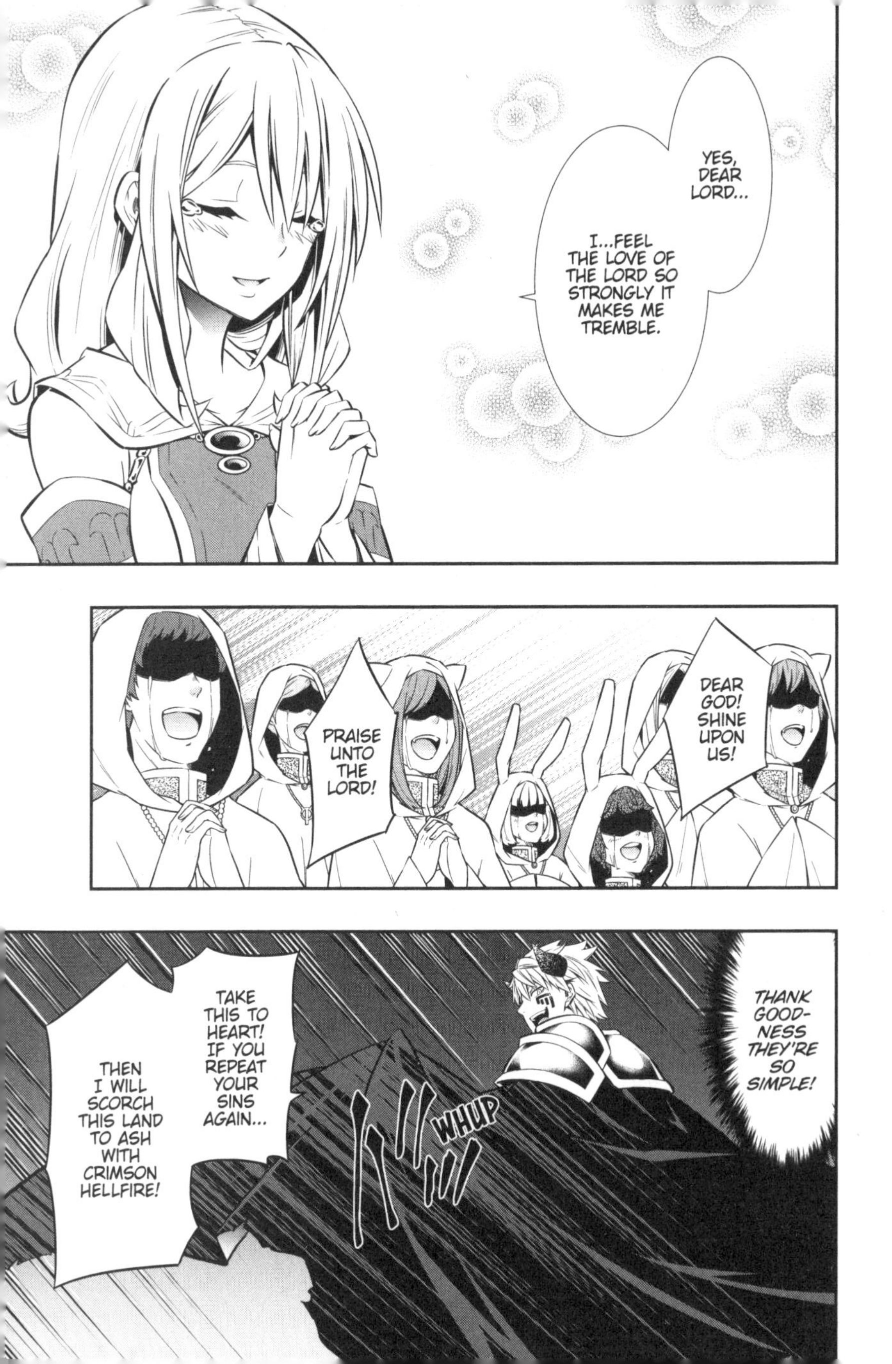
YES, DEAR LORD...
I...FEEL THE LOVE OF THE LORD SO STRONGLY IT MAKES ME TREMBLE.
DEAR GOD! SHINE UPON US!
PRAISE UNTO THE LORD!
THANK GOODNESS THEY'RE SO SIMPLE!
TAKE THIS TO HEART! IF YOU REPEAT YOUR SINS AGAIN...
THEN I WILL SCORCH THIS LAND TO ASH WITH CRIMSON HELLFIRE!
WHUP

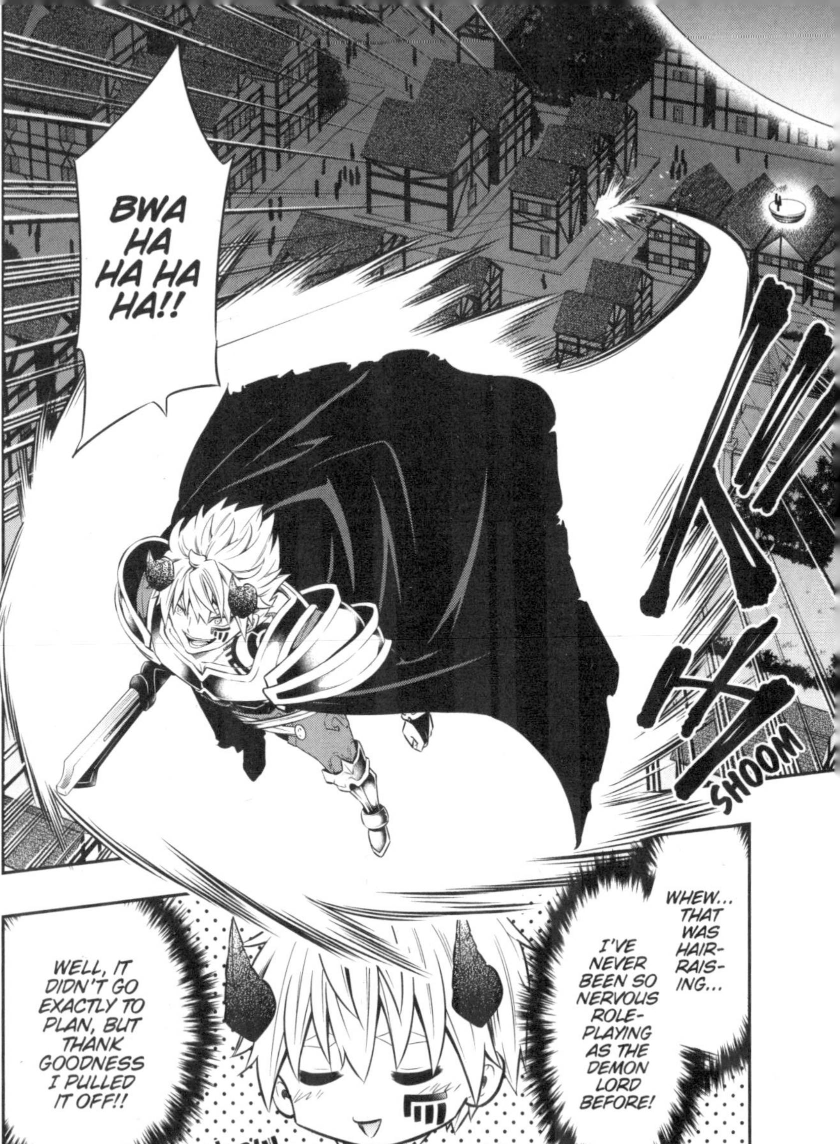
BWA HA HA HA HA HA!!
SHOOM
WHEW... THAT WAS HAIR-RAISING...
I'VE NEVER BEEN SO NERVOUS ROLE-PLAYING AS THE DEMON LORD BEFORE!
WELL, IT DIDN'T GO EXACTLY TO PLAN, BUT THANK GOODNESS I PULLED IT OFF!!
Whew..

HOW NOT TO SUMMON A DEMON LORD

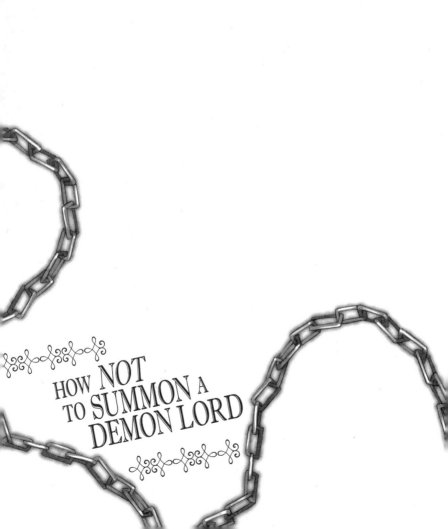

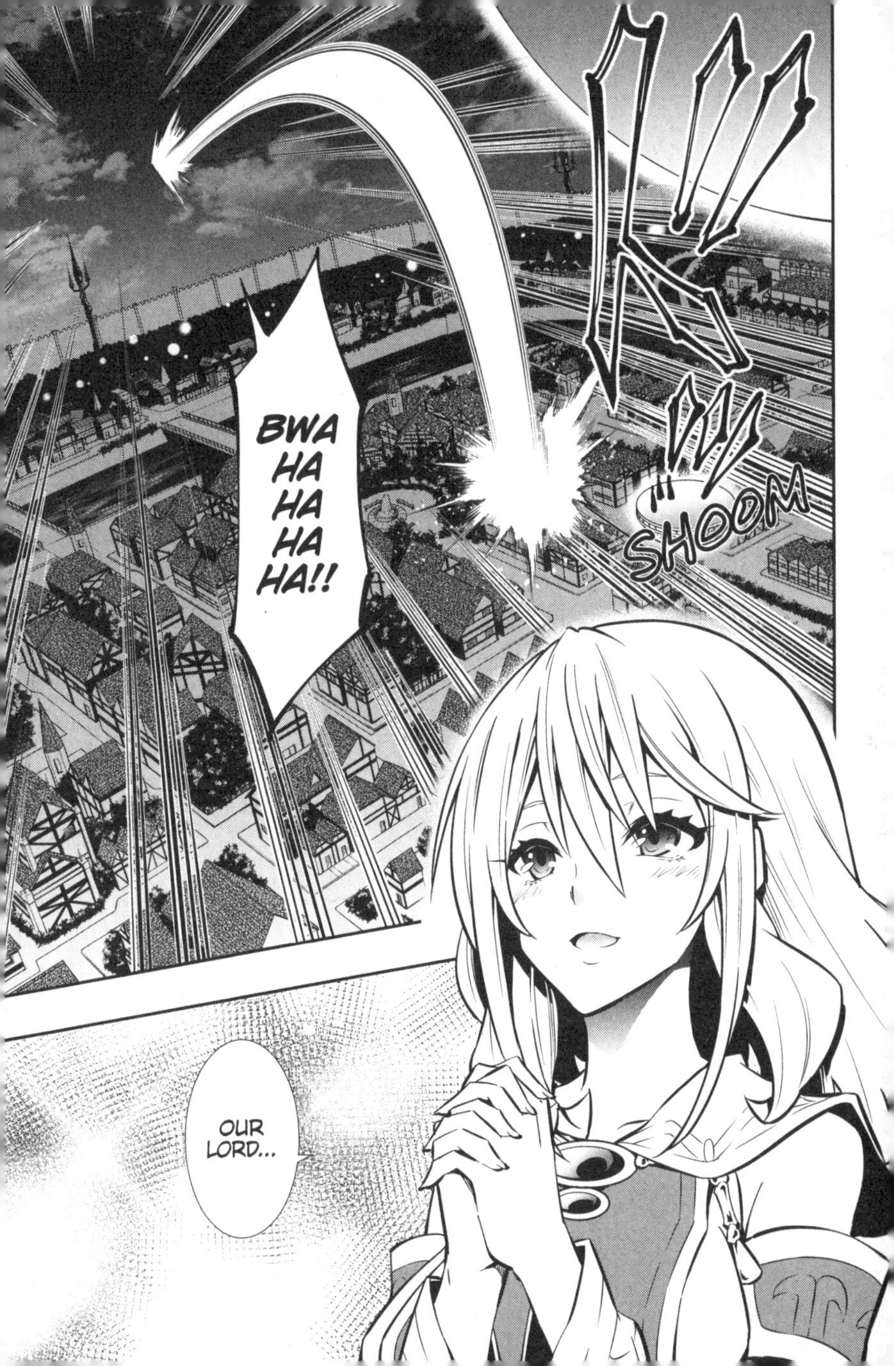
SHOOM
BWA HA HA HA HA!!
OUR LORD...

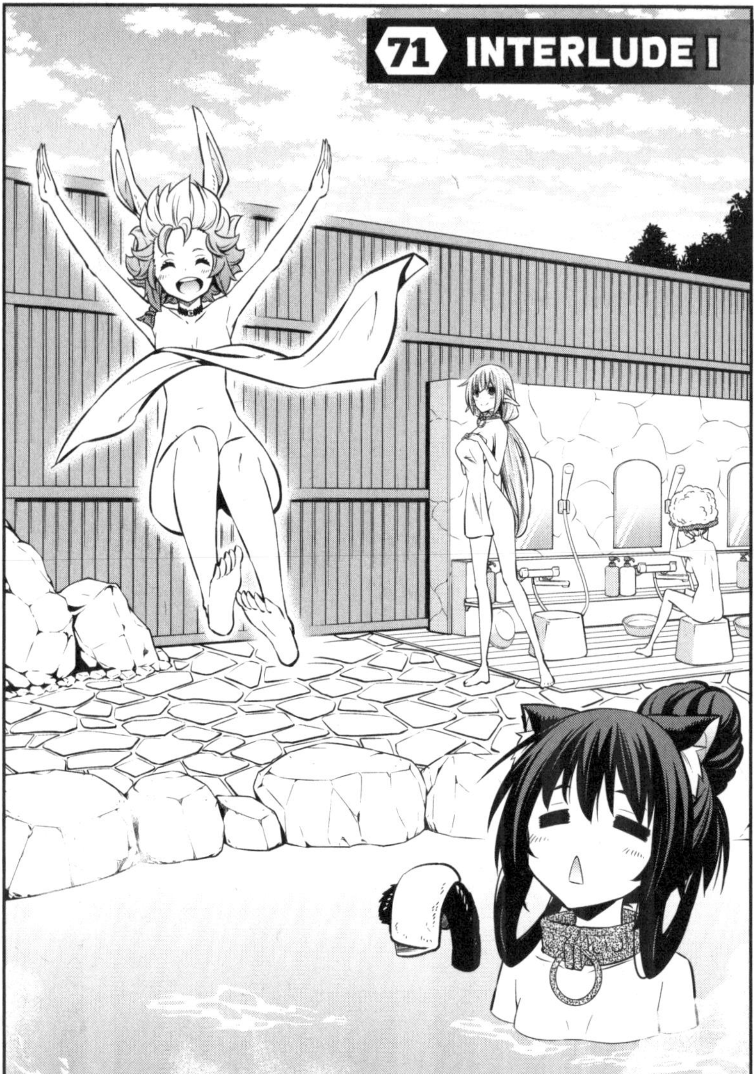
71 INTERLUDE I

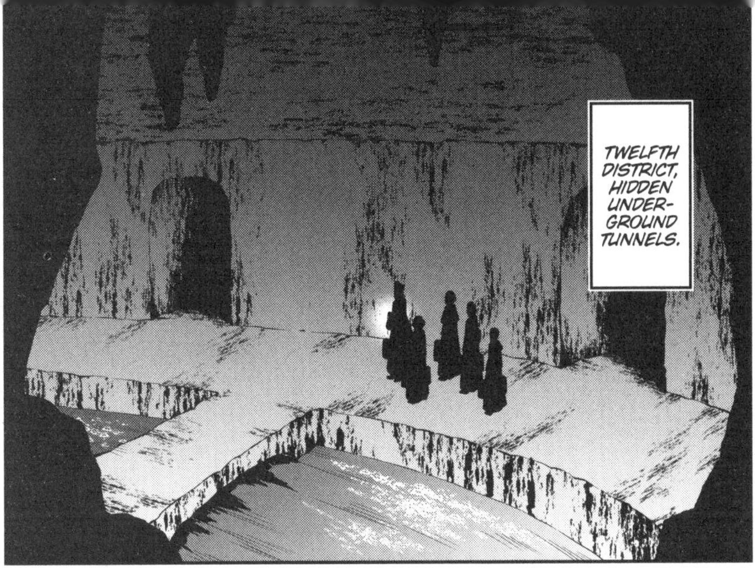
TWELFTH DISTRICT, HIDDEN UNDER-GROUND TUNNELS.

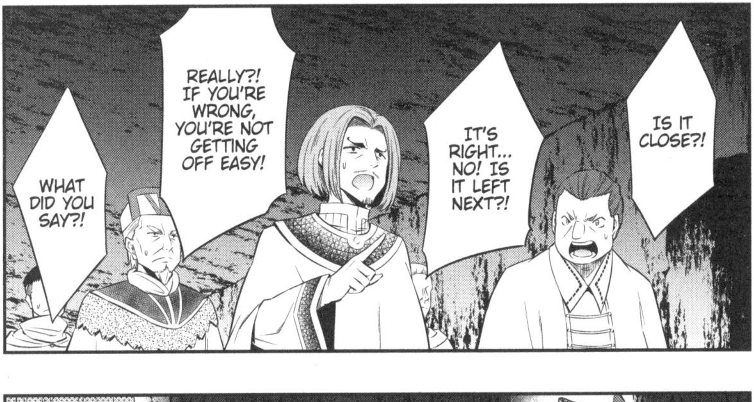
IS IT CLOSE?!
IT'S RIGHT... NO! IS IT LEFT NEXT?!
REALLY?! IF YOU'RE WRONG, YOU'RE NOT GETTING OFF EASY!
WHAT DID YOU SAY?!

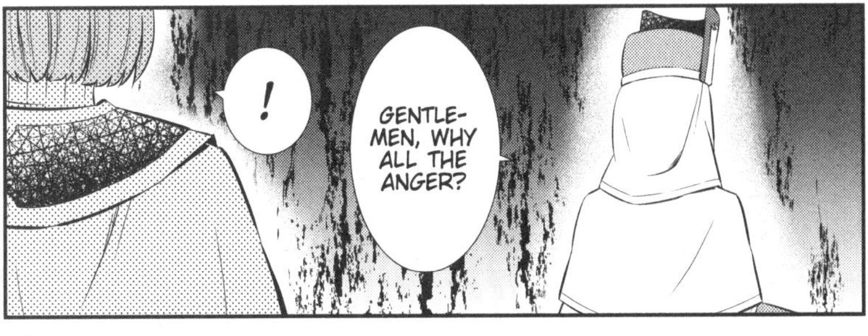
GENTLE-MEN, WHY ALL THE ANGER?
!

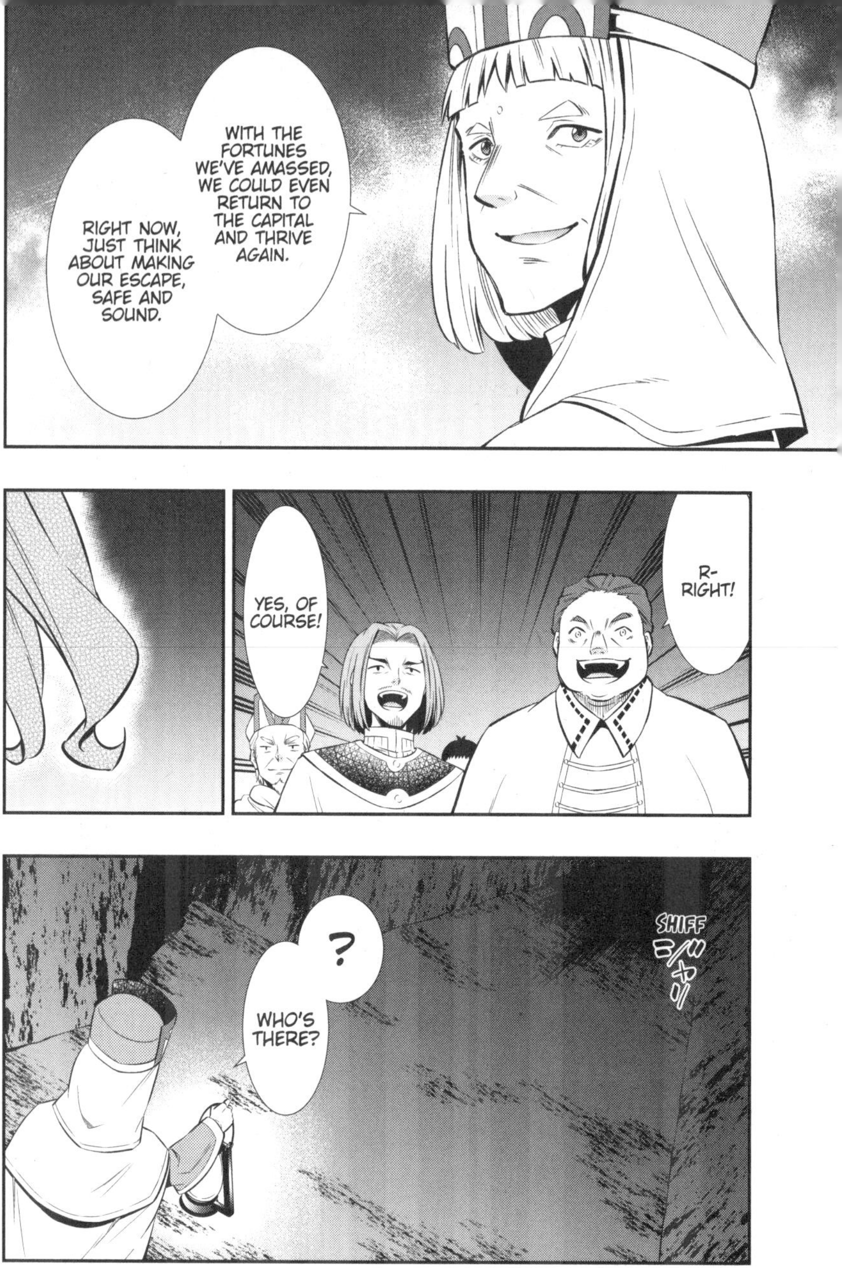
WITH THE FORTUNES WE'VE AMASSED, WE COULD EVEN RETURN TO THE CAPITAL AND THRIVE AGAIN.
RIGHT NOW, JUST THINK ABOUT MAKING OUR ESCAPE, SAFE AND SOUND.
R- RIGHT!
YES, OF COURSE!
SHIFF
?
WHO'S THERE?

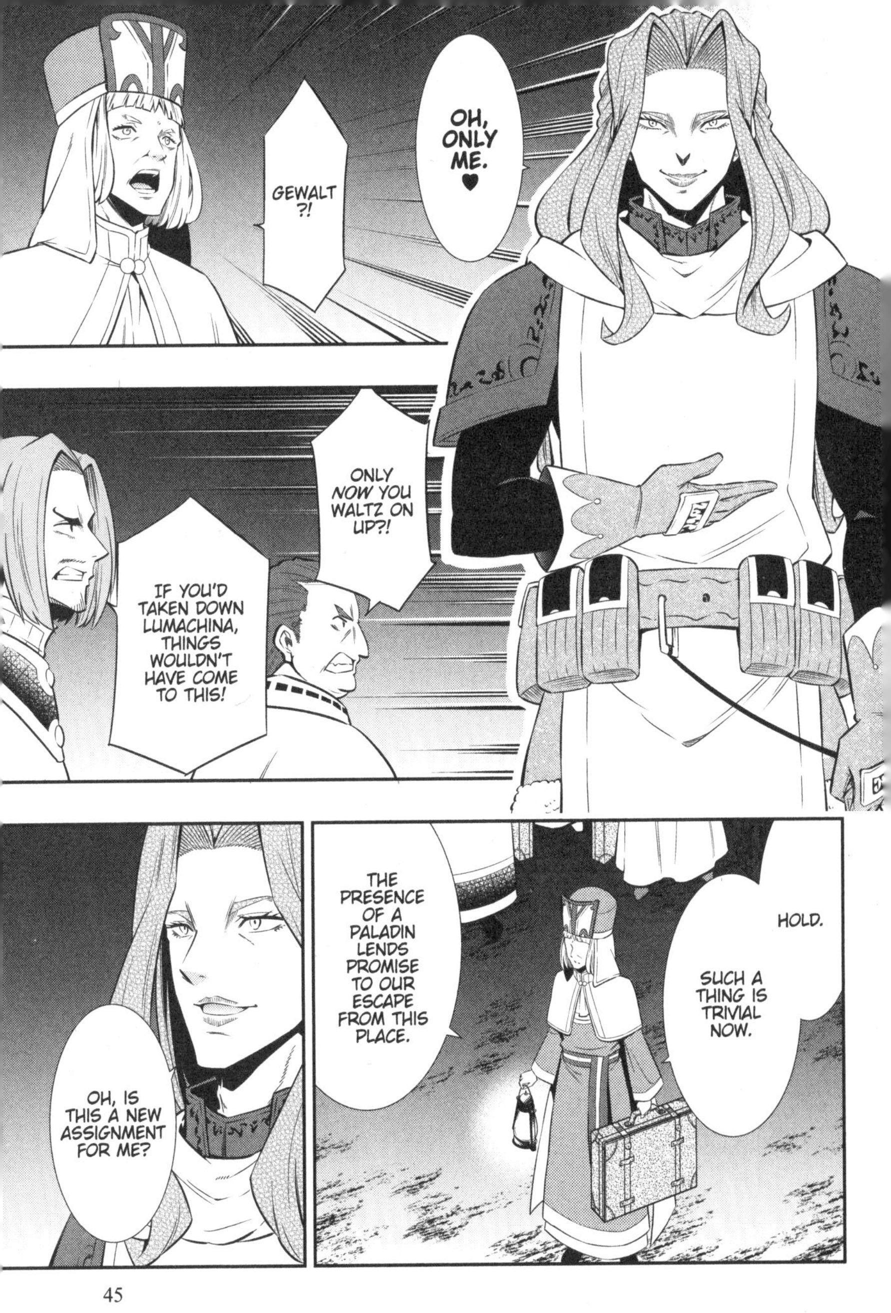
OH, ONLY ME. ♥
GEWALT?!
ONLY *NOW* YOU WALTZ ON UP?!
IF YOU'D TAKEN DOWN LUMACHINA, THINGS WOULDN'T HAVE COME TO THIS!
HOLD.
SUCH A THING IS TRIVIAL NOW.
THE PRESENCE OF A PALADIN LENDS PROMISE TO OUR ESCAPE FROM THIS PLACE.
OH, IS THIS A NEW ASSIGNMENT FOR ME?

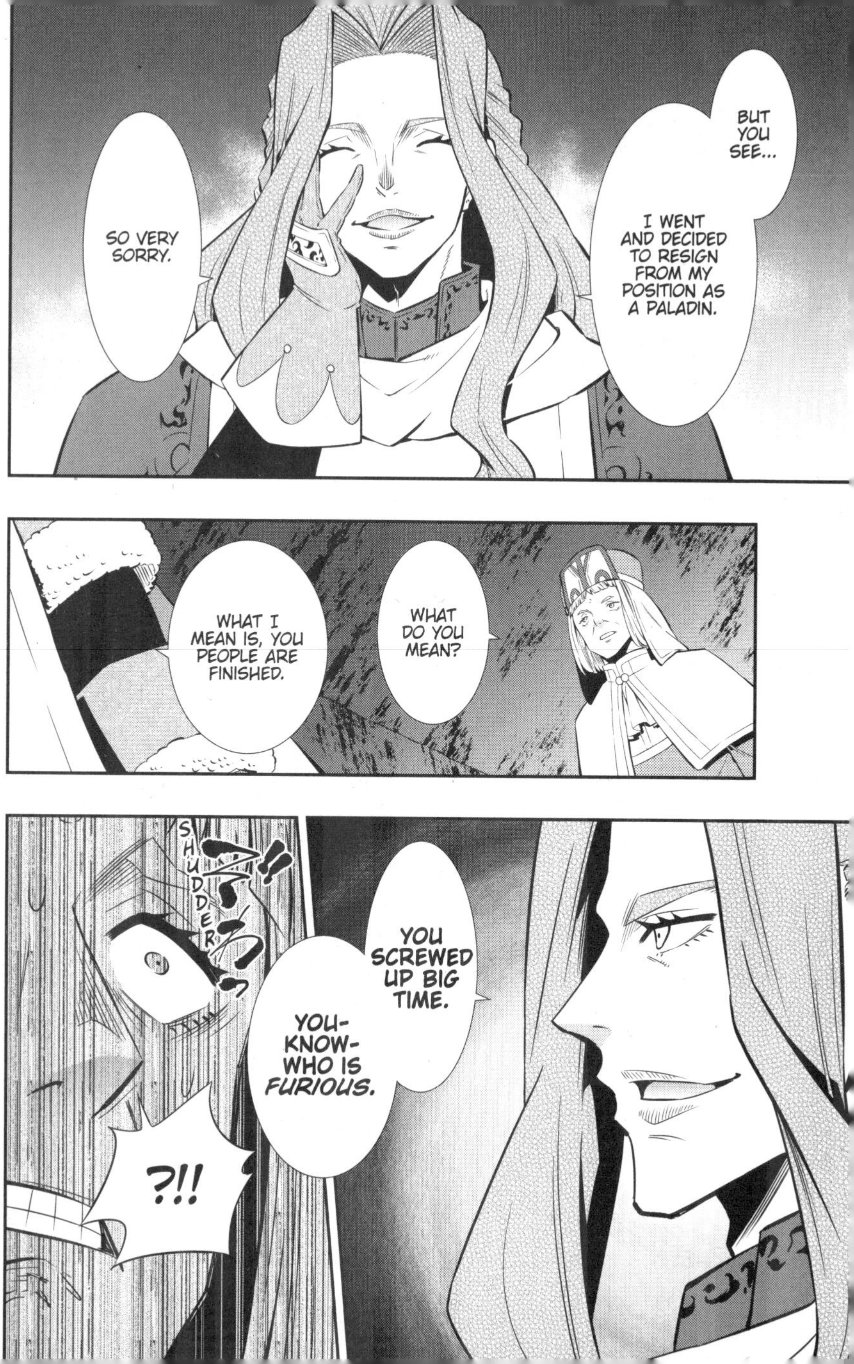
BUT YOU SEE...
I WENT AND DECIDED TO RESIGN FROM MY POSITION AS A PALADIN.
SO VERY SORRY.
WHAT DO YOU MEAN?
WHAT I MEAN IS, YOU PEOPLE ARE FINISHED.
YOU SCREWED UP BIG TIME.
YOU-KNOW-WHO IS *FURIOUS.*
SHUDDER
?!!

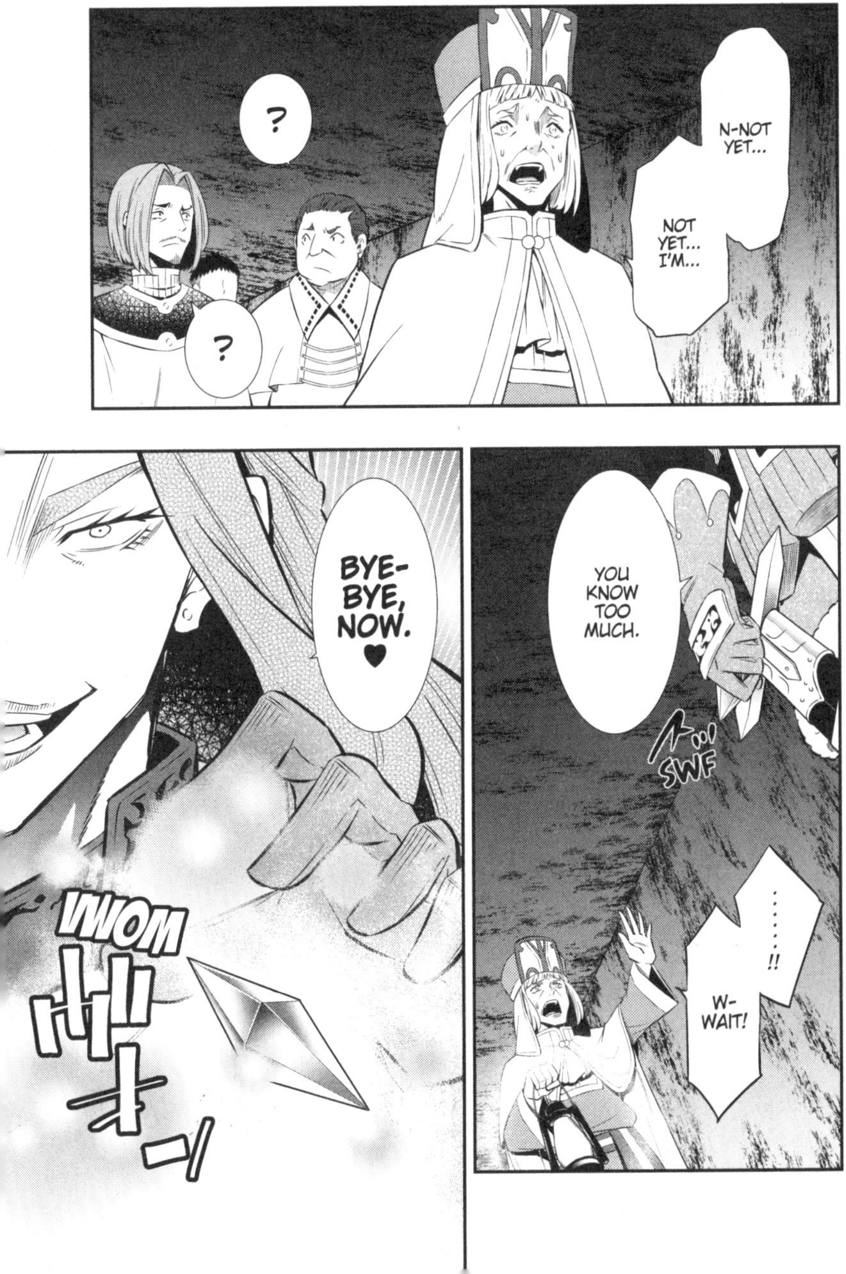
N-NOT YET...
NOT YET... I'M...
?
?
YOU KNOW TOO MUCH.
SWF
......!!
W-WAIT!
BYE-BYE, NOW. ♥
VWOM

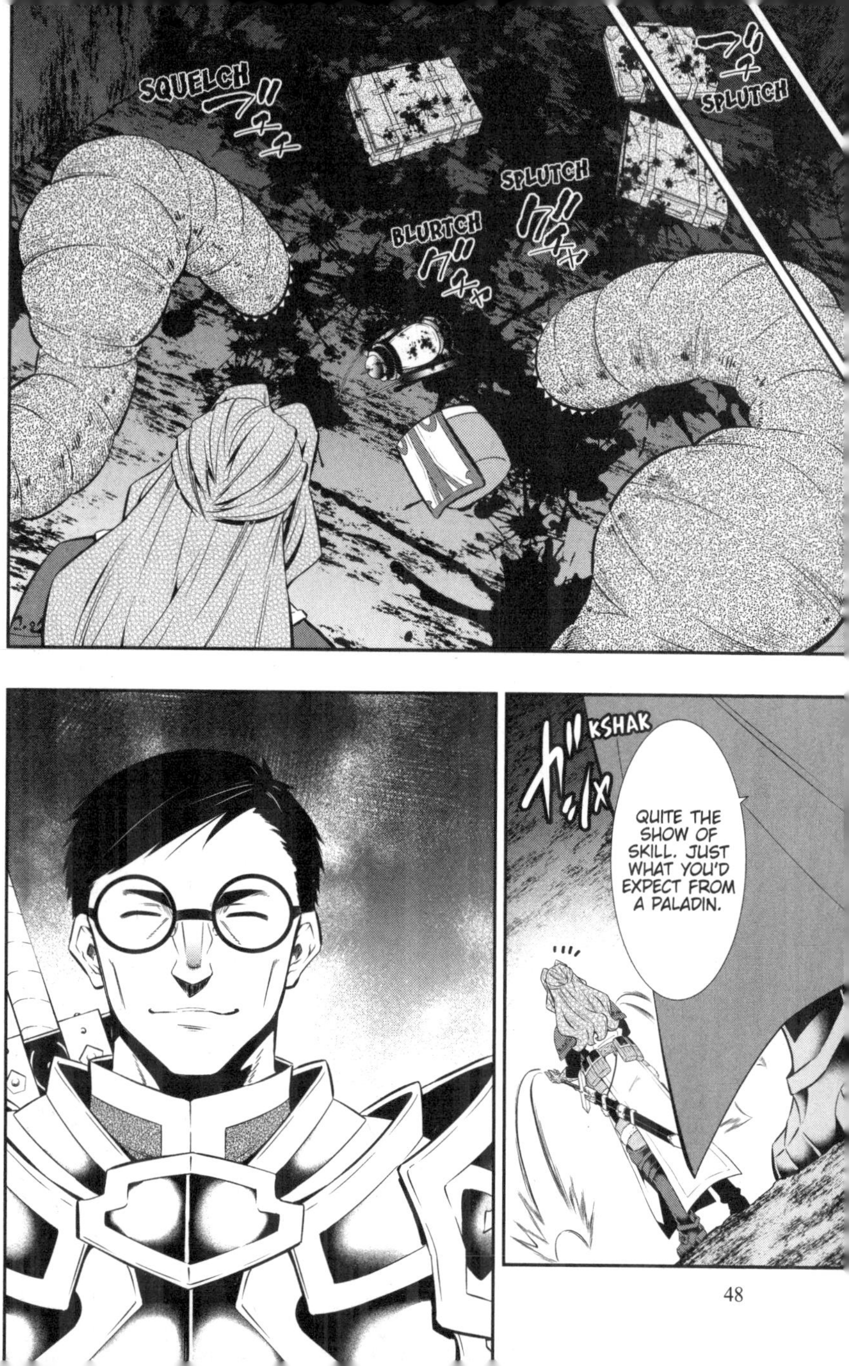
SPLUTCH
SPLUTCH
BLURTCH
SQUELCH
KSHAK
QUITE THE SHOW OF SKILL. JUST WHAT YOU'D EXPECT FROM A PALADIN.

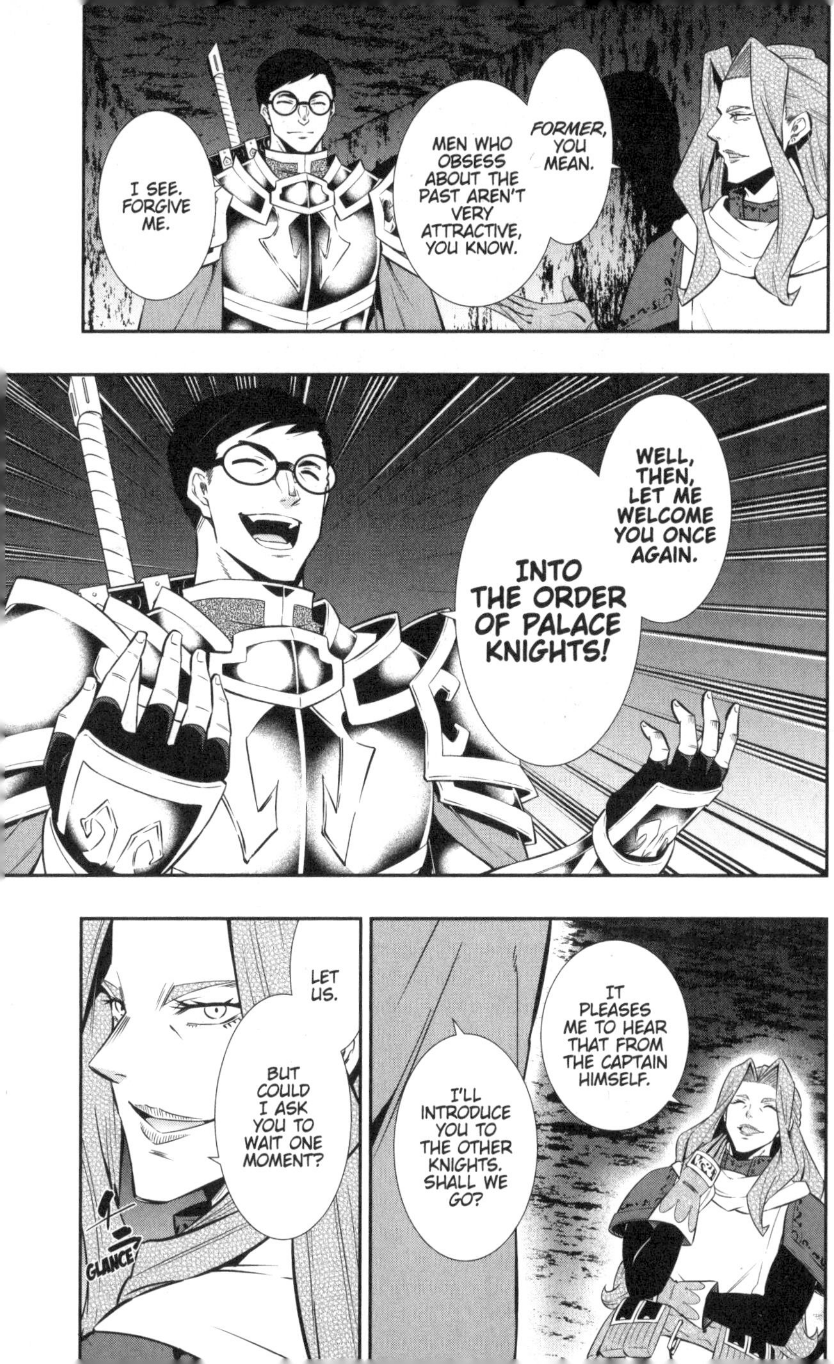
FORMER, YOU MEAN.
MEN WHO OBSESS ABOUT THE PAST AREN'T VERY ATTRACTIVE, YOU KNOW.
I SEE. FORGIVE ME.
WELL, THEN, LET ME WELCOME YOU ONCE AGAIN.
INTO THE ORDER OF PALACE KNIGHTS!
IT PLEASES ME TO HEAR THAT FROM THE CAPTAIN HIMSELF.
I'LL INTRODUCE YOU TO THE OTHER KNIGHTS. SHALL WE GO?
LET US.
BUT COULD I ASK YOU TO WAIT ONE MOMENT?
GLANCE

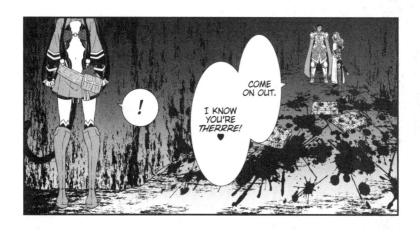

COME ON OUT.

I KNOW YOU'RE *THERRRE!* ♥

!

SHFF

YOU KILLED THE CARDINAL COUNCIL.

WAS IT YOUR NEW EMPLOYER'S INTENTION TO SILENCE THEM?

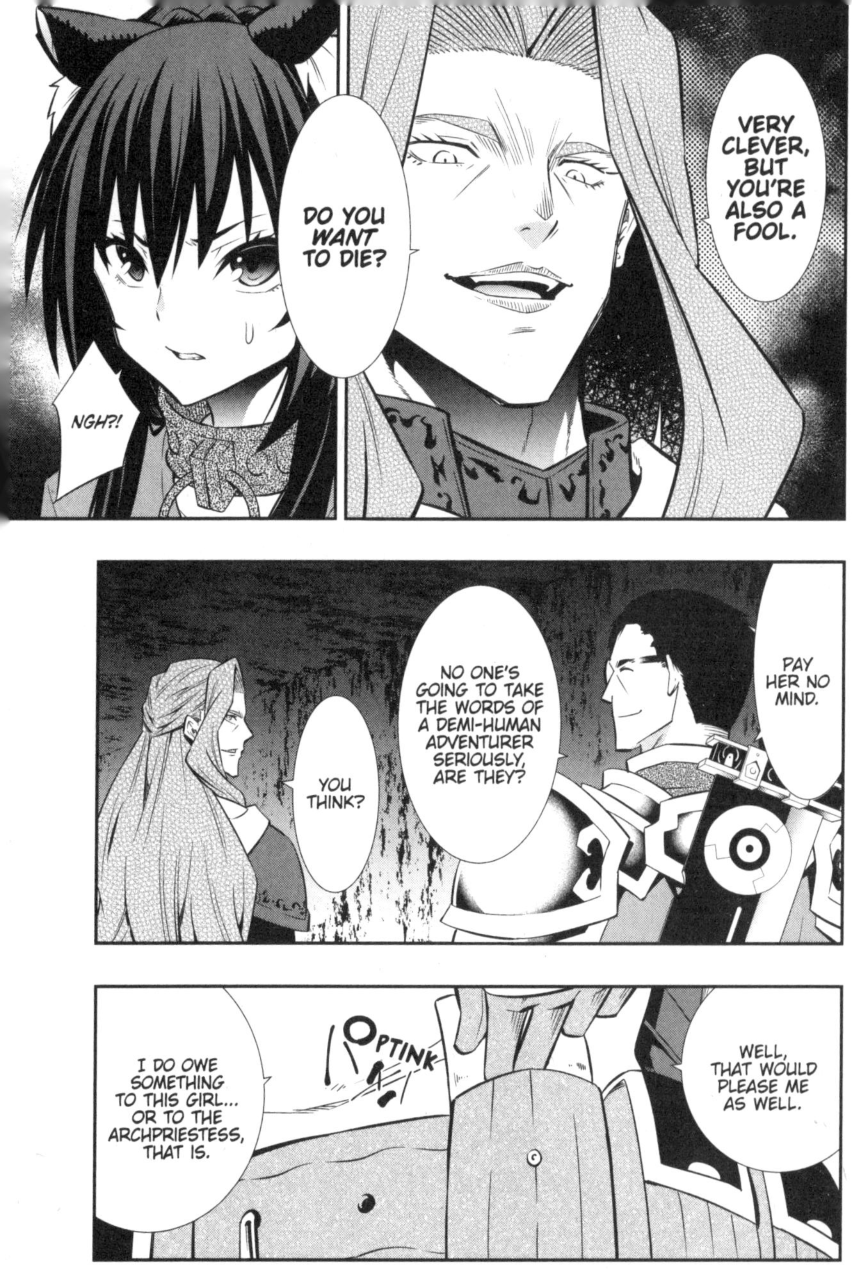
VERY CLEVER, BUT YOU'RE ALSO A FOOL.
DO YOU WANT TO DIE?
NGH?!
PAY HER NO MIND.
NO ONE'S GOING TO TAKE THE WORDS OF A DEMI-HUMAN ADVENTURER SERIOUSLY, ARE THEY?
YOU THINK?
WELL, THAT WOULD PLEASE ME AS WELL.
OPTINK
I DO OWE SOMETHING TO THIS GIRL... OR TO THE ARCHPRIESTESS, THAT IS.

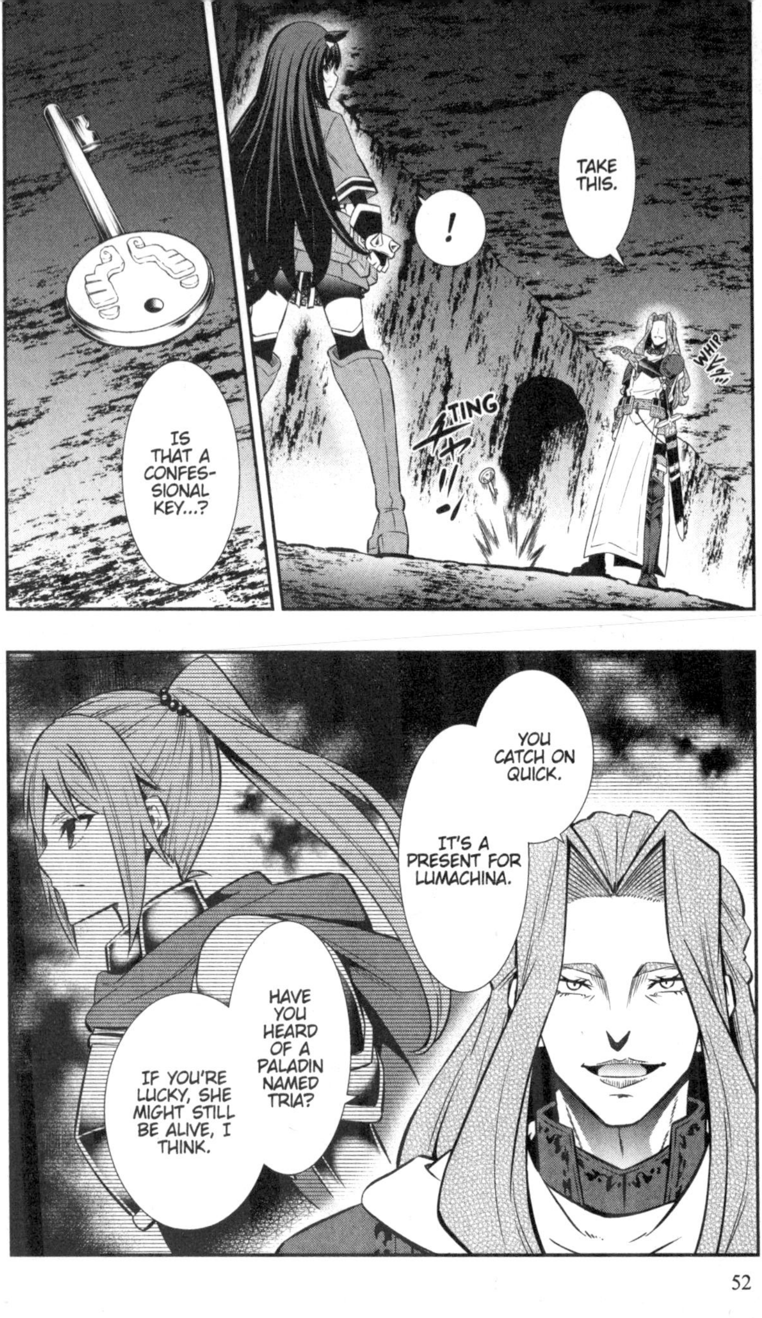
TAKE THIS.
!
WHIP
TING
IS THAT A CONFES-SIONAL KEY...?
YOU CATCH ON QUICK.
IT'S A PRESENT FOR LUMACHINA.
HAVE YOU HEARD OF A PALADIN NAMED TRIA?
IF YOU'RE LUCKY, SHE MIGHT STILL BE ALIVE, I THINK.

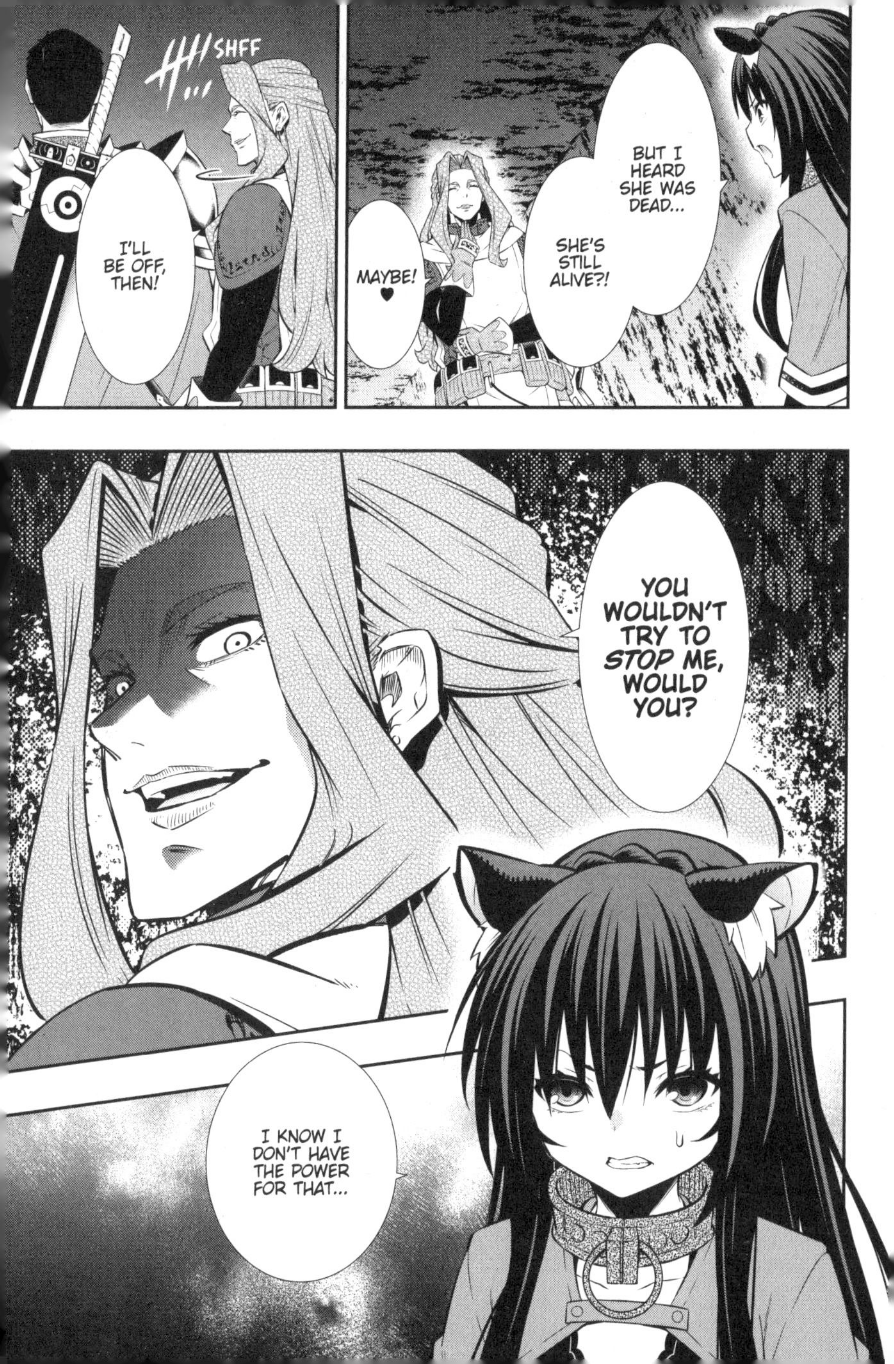
BUT I HEARD SHE WAS DEAD...
SHE'S STILL ALIVE?!
MAYBE! ♥
SHFF
I'LL BE OFF, THEN!
YOU WOULDN'T TRY TO *STOP* ME, WOULD YOU?
I KNOW I DON'T HAVE THE POWER FOR THAT...

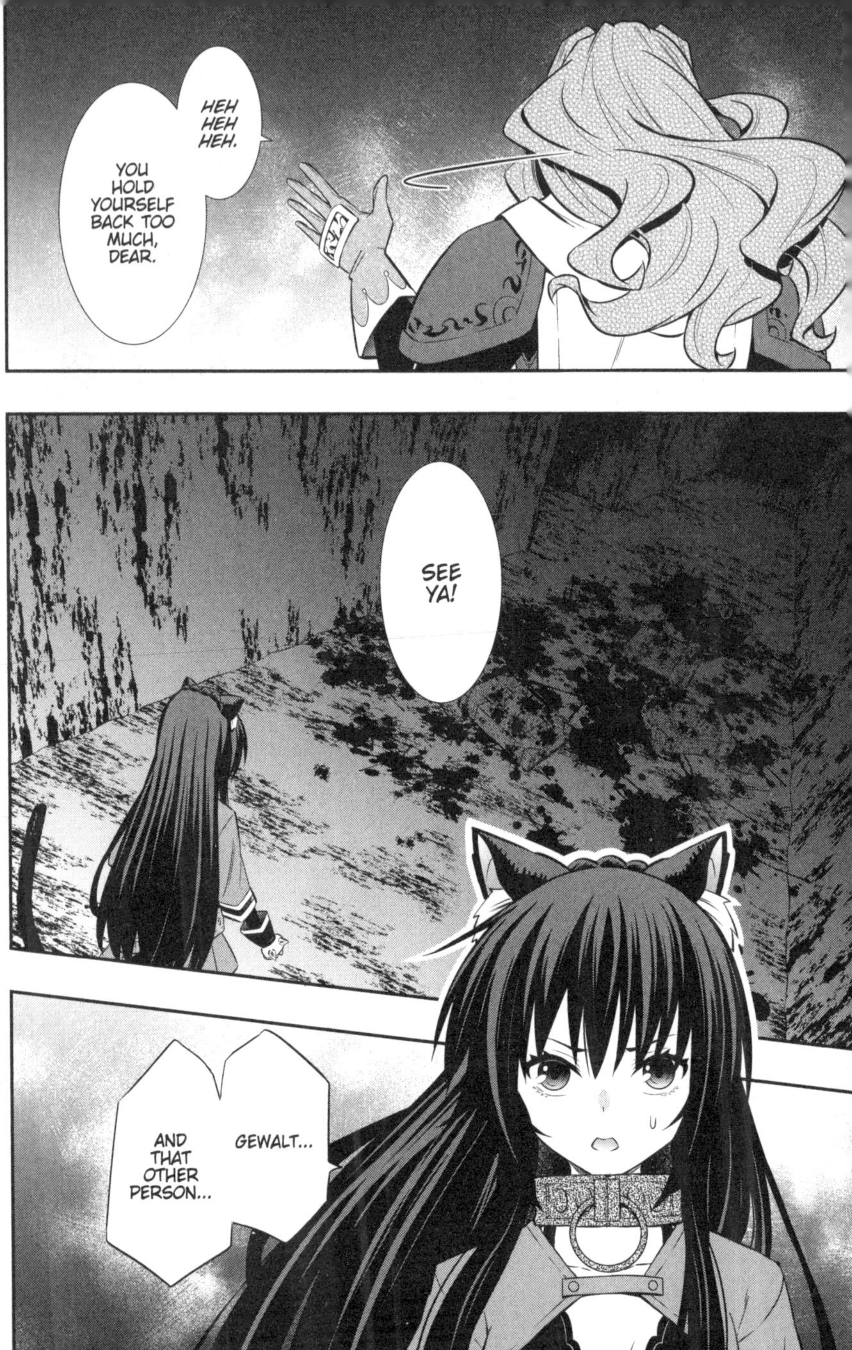
HEH HEH HEH.
YOU HOLD YOURSELF BACK TOO MUCH, DEAR.
SEE YA!
GEWALT...
AND THAT OTHER PERSON...

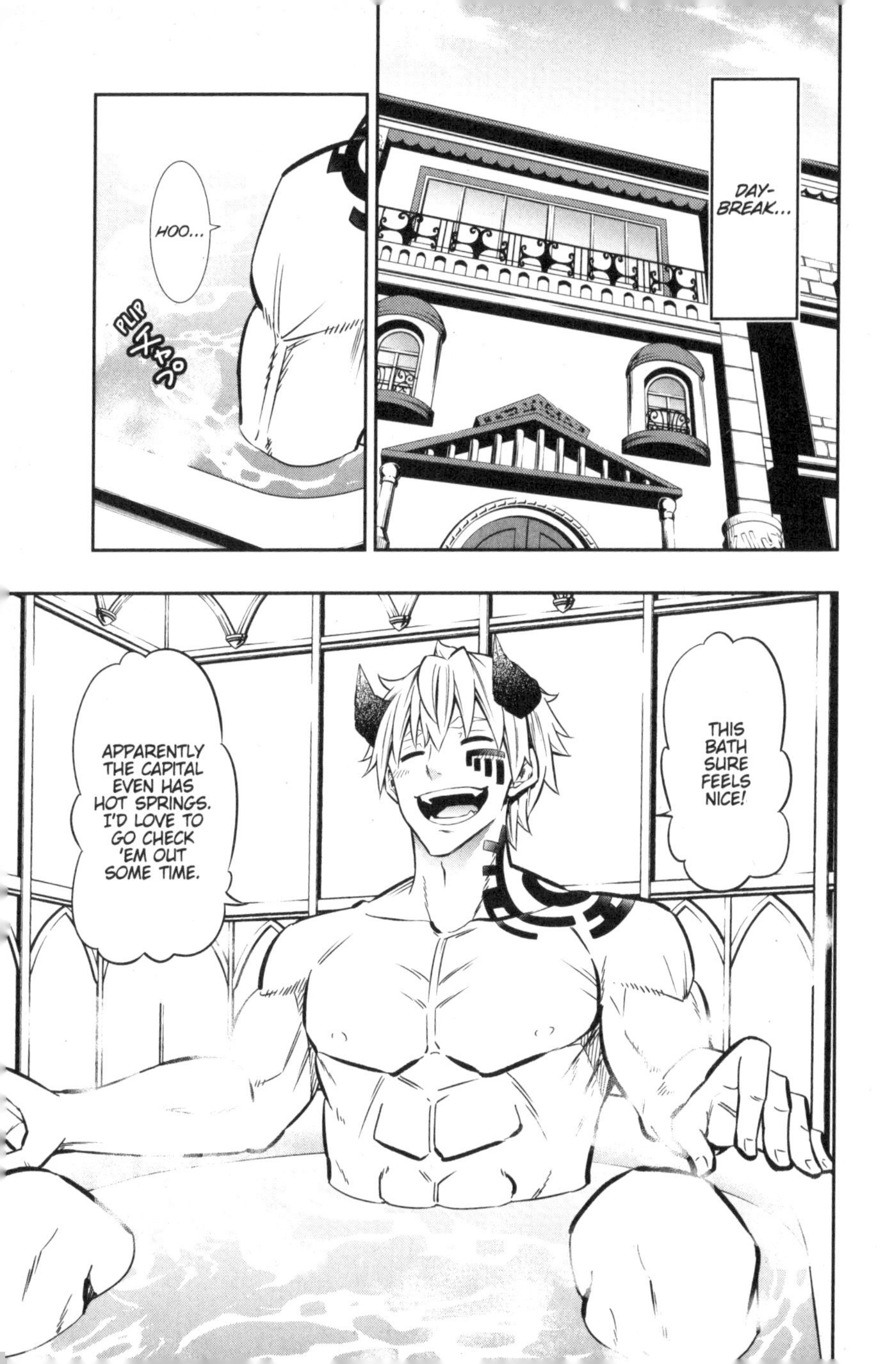
DAY-BREAK...
HOO...
PLIP
THIS BATH SURE FEELS NICE!
APPARENTLY THE CAPITAL EVEN HAS HOT SPRINGS. I'D LOVE TO GO CHECK 'EM OUT SOME TIME.

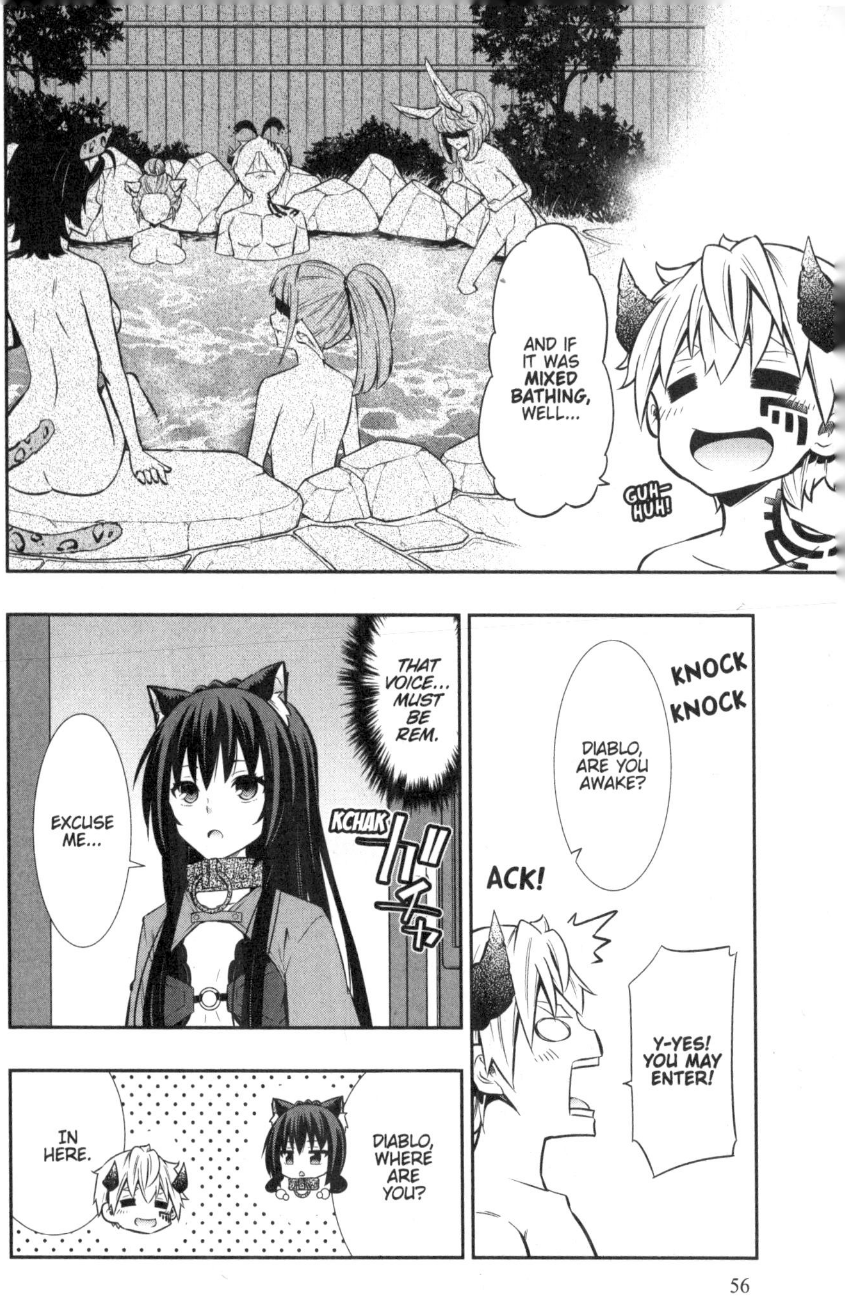
AND IF IT WAS MIXED BATHING, WELL...
GUH-HUH!
KNOCK KNOCK
DIABLO, ARE YOU AWAKE?
ACK!
Y-YES! YOU MAY ENTER!
THAT VOICE... MUST BE REM.
KCHAK
EXCUSE ME...
DIABLO, WHERE ARE YOU?
IN HERE.

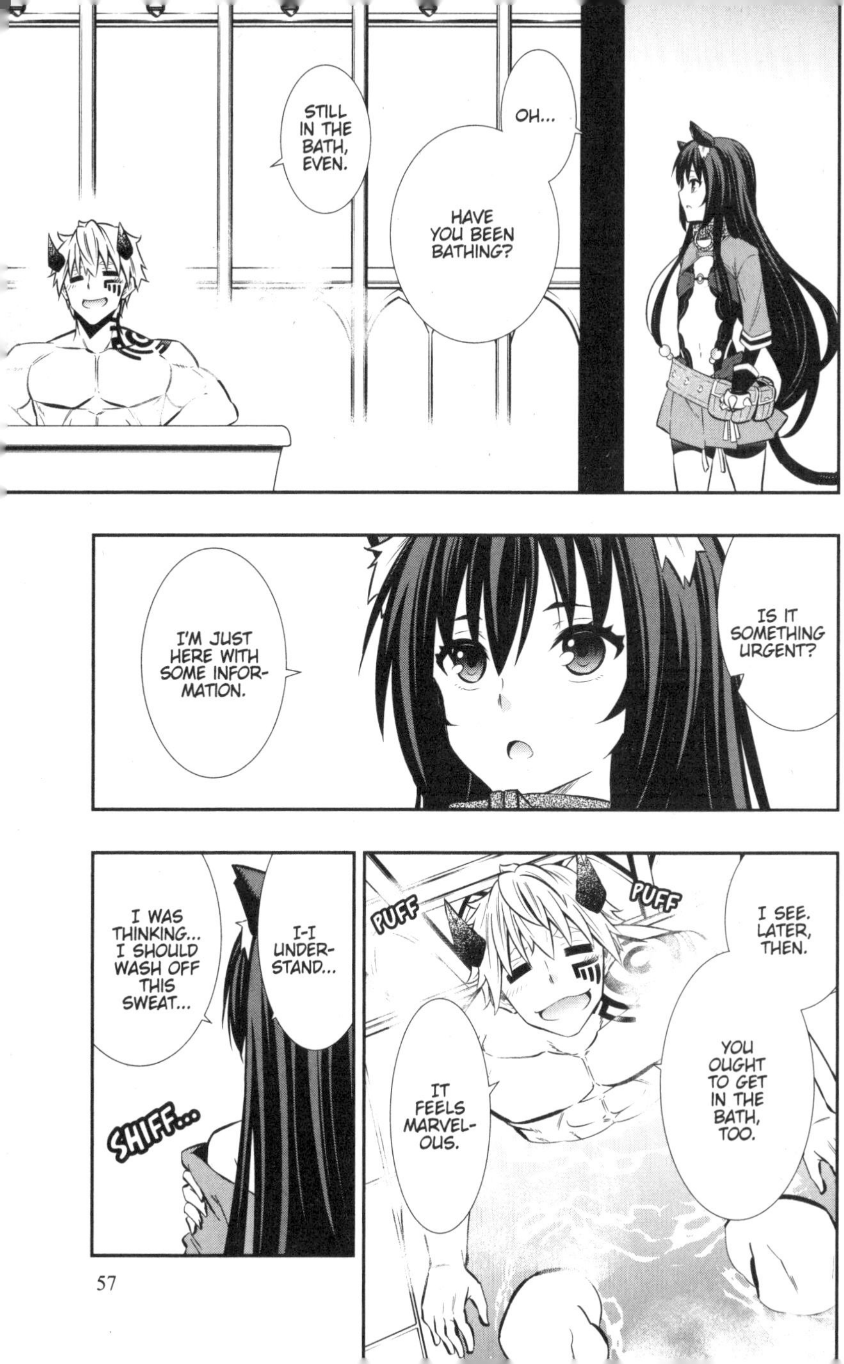
OH...
HAVE YOU BEEN BATHING?
STILL IN THE BATH, EVEN.
IS IT SOMETHING URGENT?
I'M JUST HERE WITH SOME INFOR-MATION.
PUFF
I SEE. LATER, THEN.
YOU OUGHT TO GET IN THE BATH, TOO.
IT FEELS MARVEL-OUS.
PUFF
I-I UNDER-STAND...
I WAS THINKING... I SHOULD WASH OFF THIS SWEAT...
SHIFF...

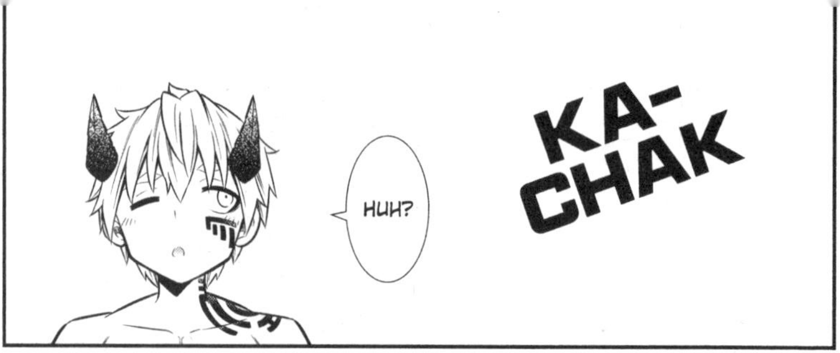
KA-
CHAK
HUH?

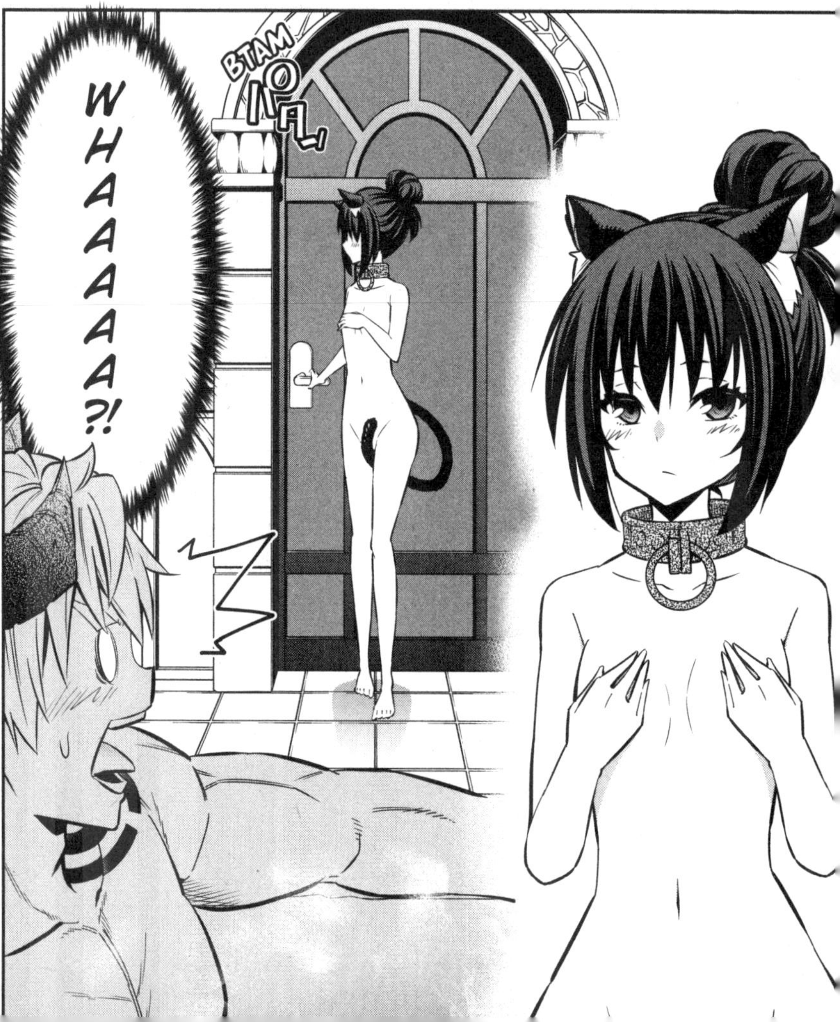
BTAM
WHAAAAA?!

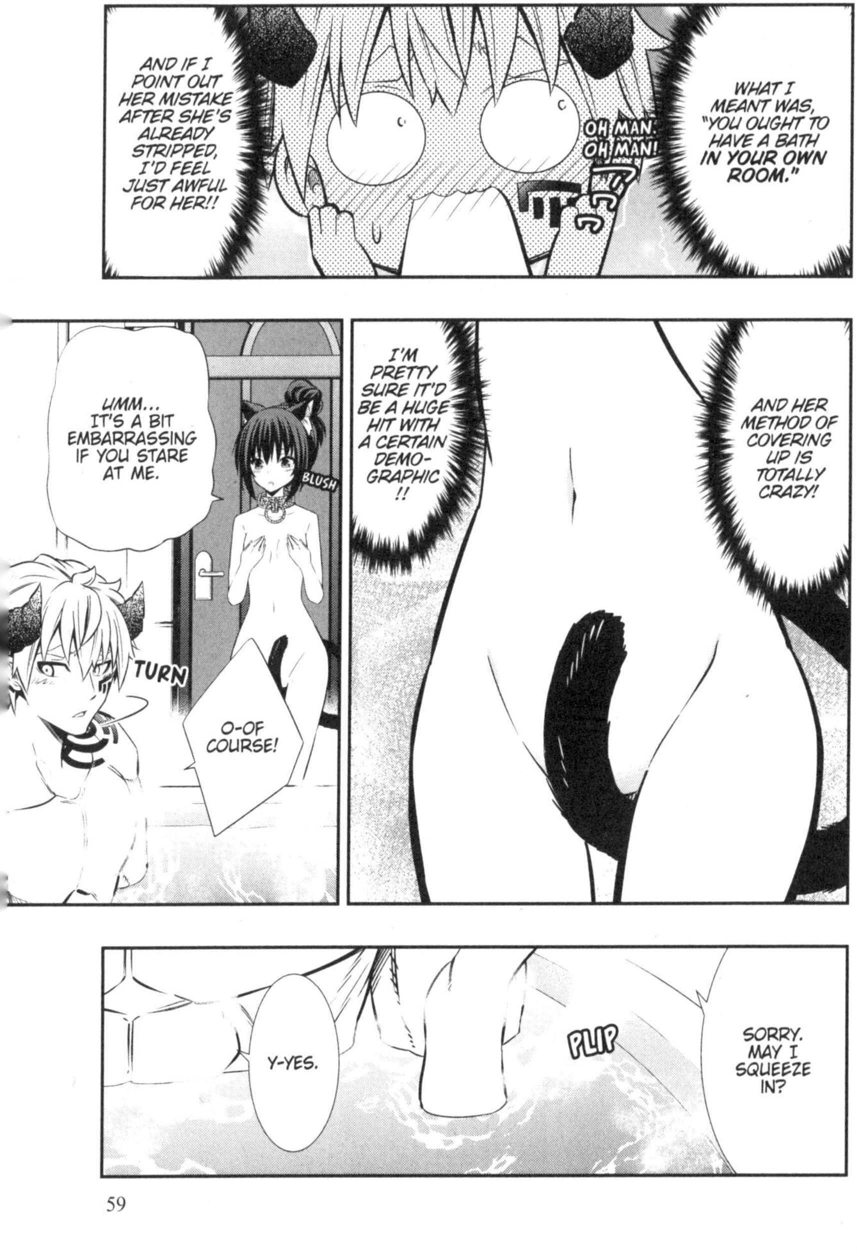
WHAT I MEANT WAS, "YOU OUGHT TO HAVE A BATH IN YOUR OWN ROOM."
OH MAN. OH MAN!
AND IF I POINT OUT HER MISTAKE AFTER SHE'S ALREADY STRIPPED, I'D FEEL JUST AWFUL FOR HER!!
AND HER METHOD OF COVERING UP IS TOTALLY CRAZY!
I'M PRETTY SURE IT'D BE A HUGE HIT WITH A CERTAIN DEMO-GRAPHIC!!
UMM... IT'S A BIT EMBARRASSING IF YOU STARE AT ME.
BLUSH
TURN
O-OF COURSE!
SORRY. MAY I SQUEEZE IN?
PLIP
Y-YES.

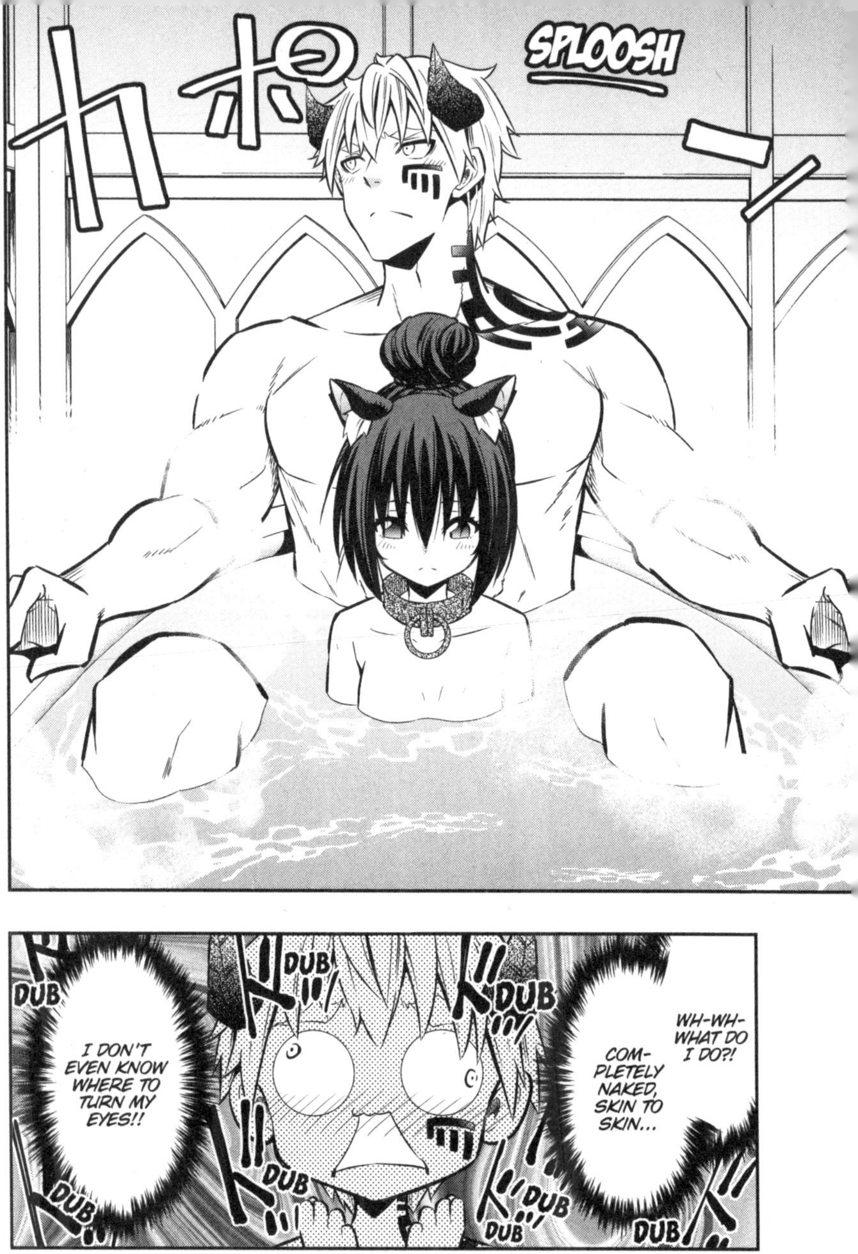
SPLOOSH
WH-WH-WHAT DO I DO?!
COMPLETELY NAKED, SKIN TO SKIN...
I DON'T EVEN KNOW WHERE TO TURN MY EYES!!
DUB DUB DUB DUB DUB DUB DUB DUB DUB

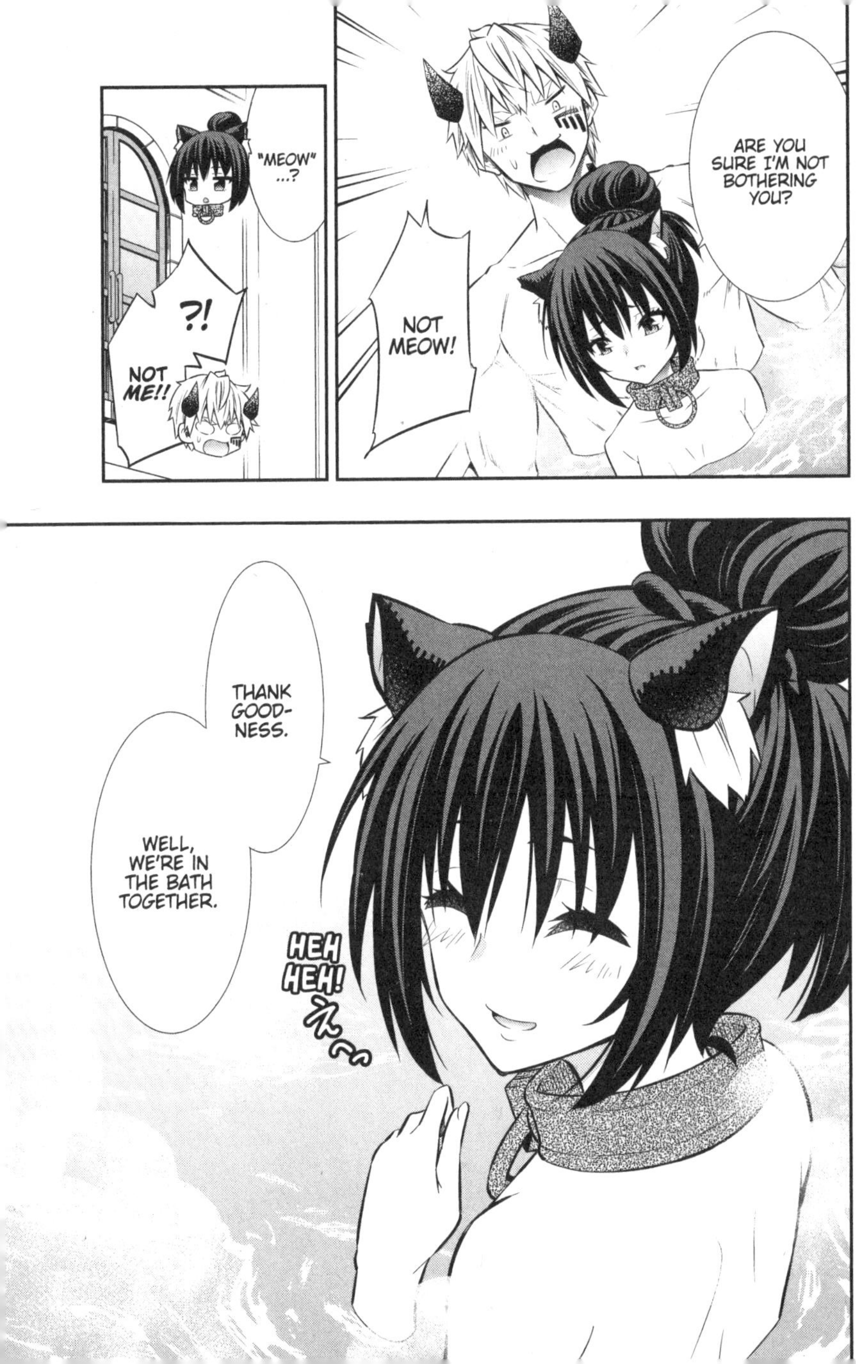
ARE YOU SURE I'M NOT BOTHERING YOU?
NOT MEOW!
"MEOW" ...?
?!
NOT ME!!
THANK GOOD-NESS.
WELL, WE'RE IN THE BATH TOGETHER.
HEH HEH!

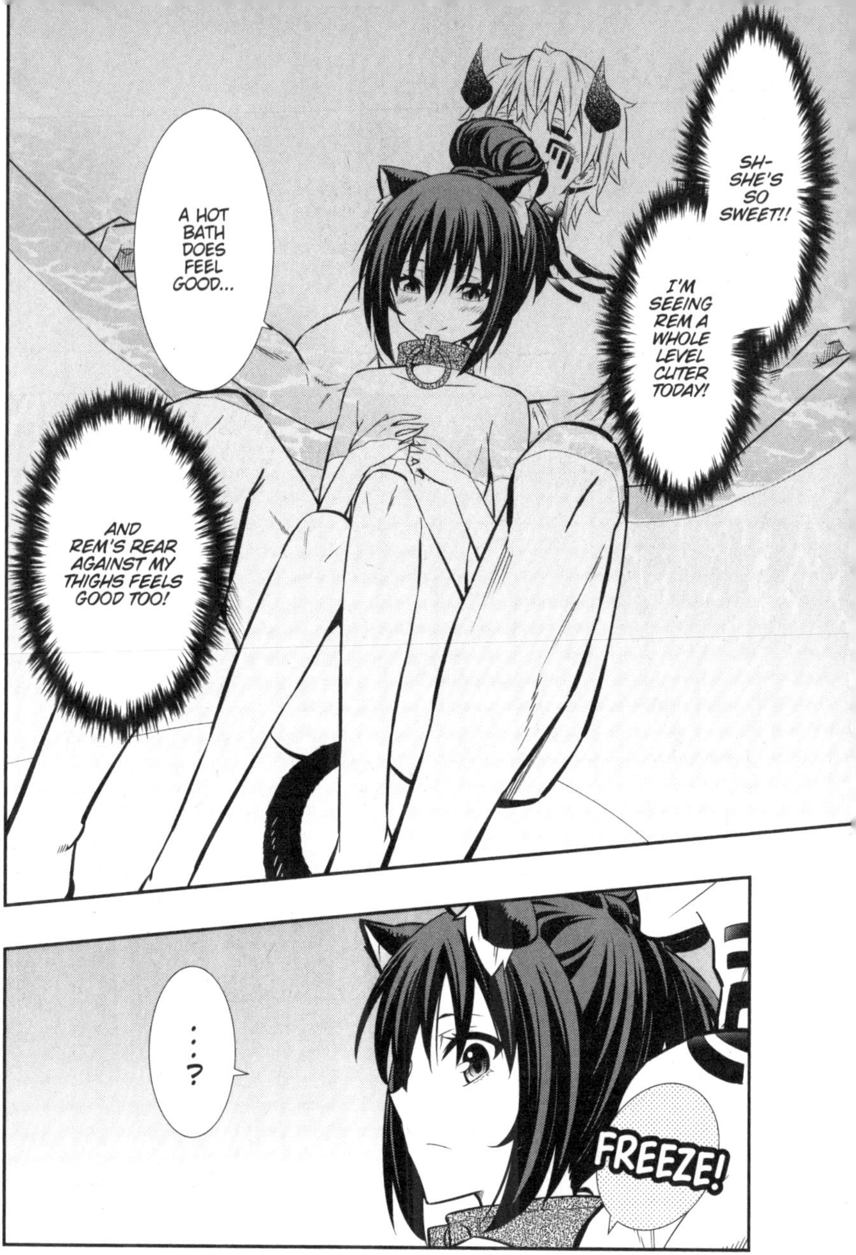
SH- SHE'S SO SWEET!!
I'M SEEING REM A WHOLE LEVEL CUTER TODAY!
A HOT BATH DOES FEEL GOOD...
AND REM'S REAR AGAINST MY THIGHS FEELS GOOD TOO!
FREEZE!
...?

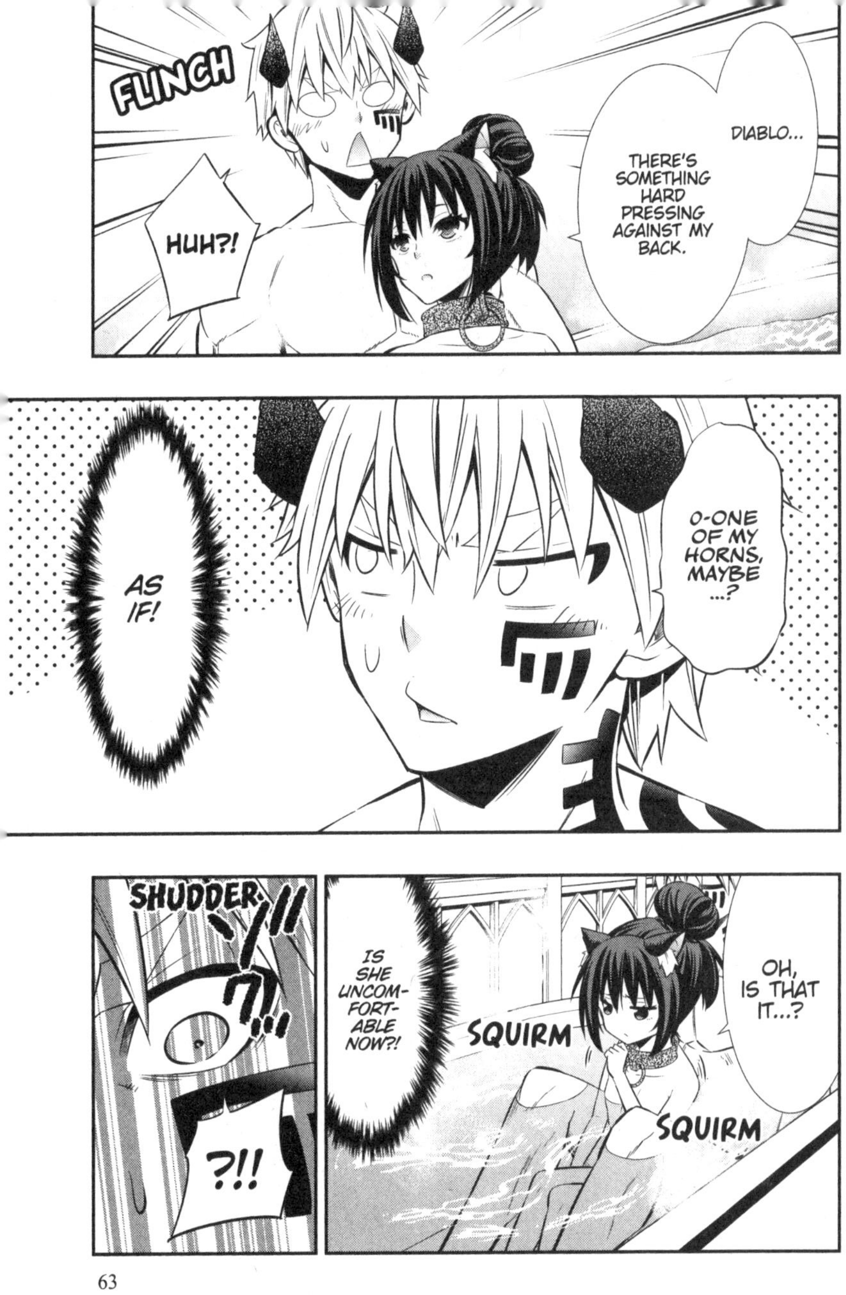
DIABLO... THERE'S SOMETHING HARD PRESSING AGAINST MY BACK.
FLINCH
HUH?!
O-ONE OF MY HORNS, MAYBE ...?
AS IF!
OH, IS THAT IT...?
IS SHE UNCOM-FORT-ABLE NOW?!
SQUIRM
SQUIRM
SHUDDER
?!!

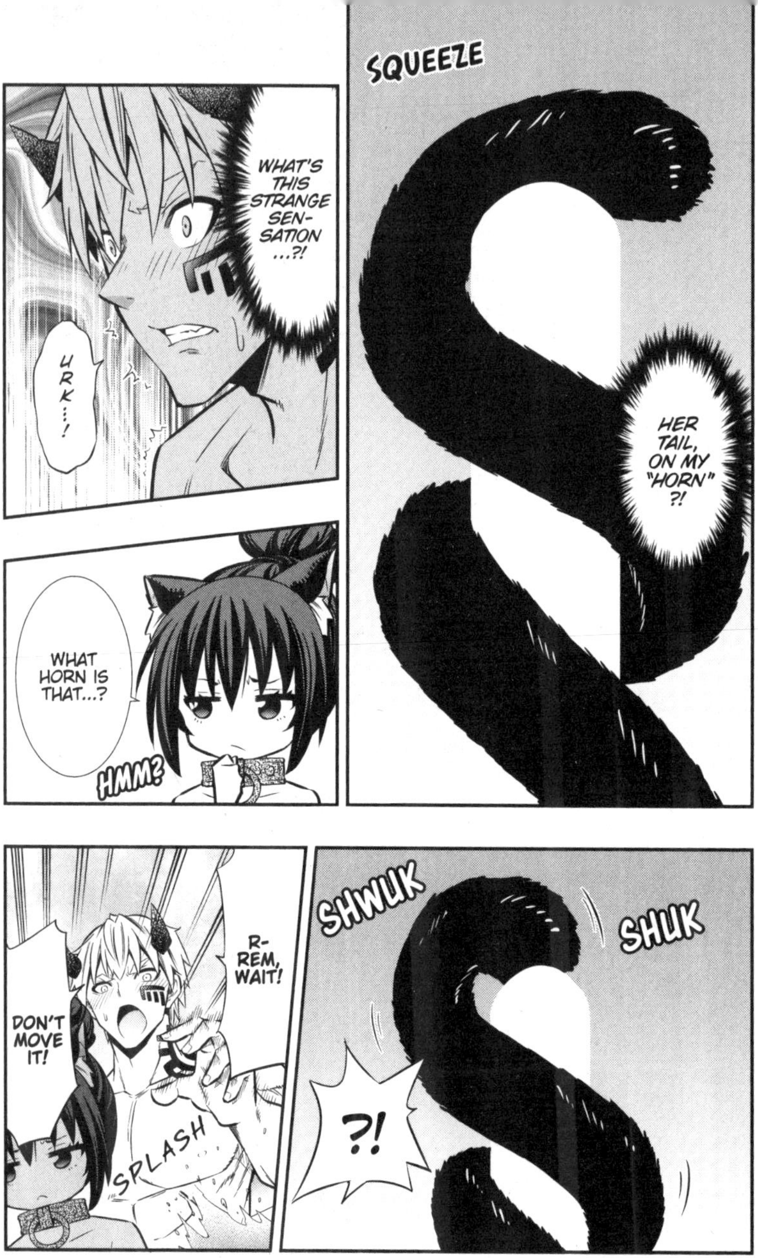
SQUEEZE
HER TAIL, ON MY "HORN"?!
WHAT'S THIS STRANGE SEN-SATION ...?!
URK...!
WHAT HORN IS THAT...?
HMM?
SHWUK
SHUK
?!
R-REM, WAIT!
DON'T MOVE IT!
SPLASH

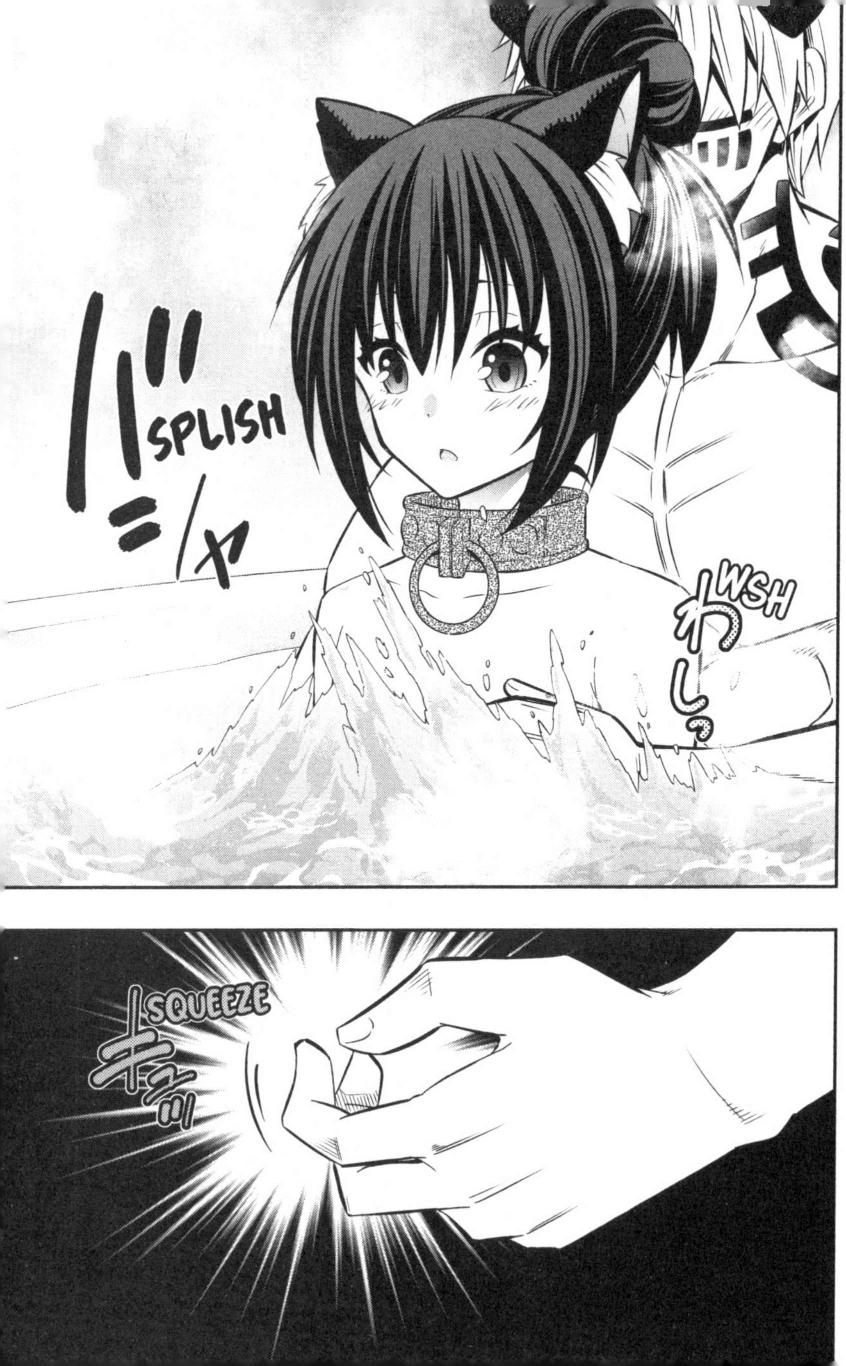
バシャ
SPLISH
わしっ
WSH
キュッ
SQUEEZE

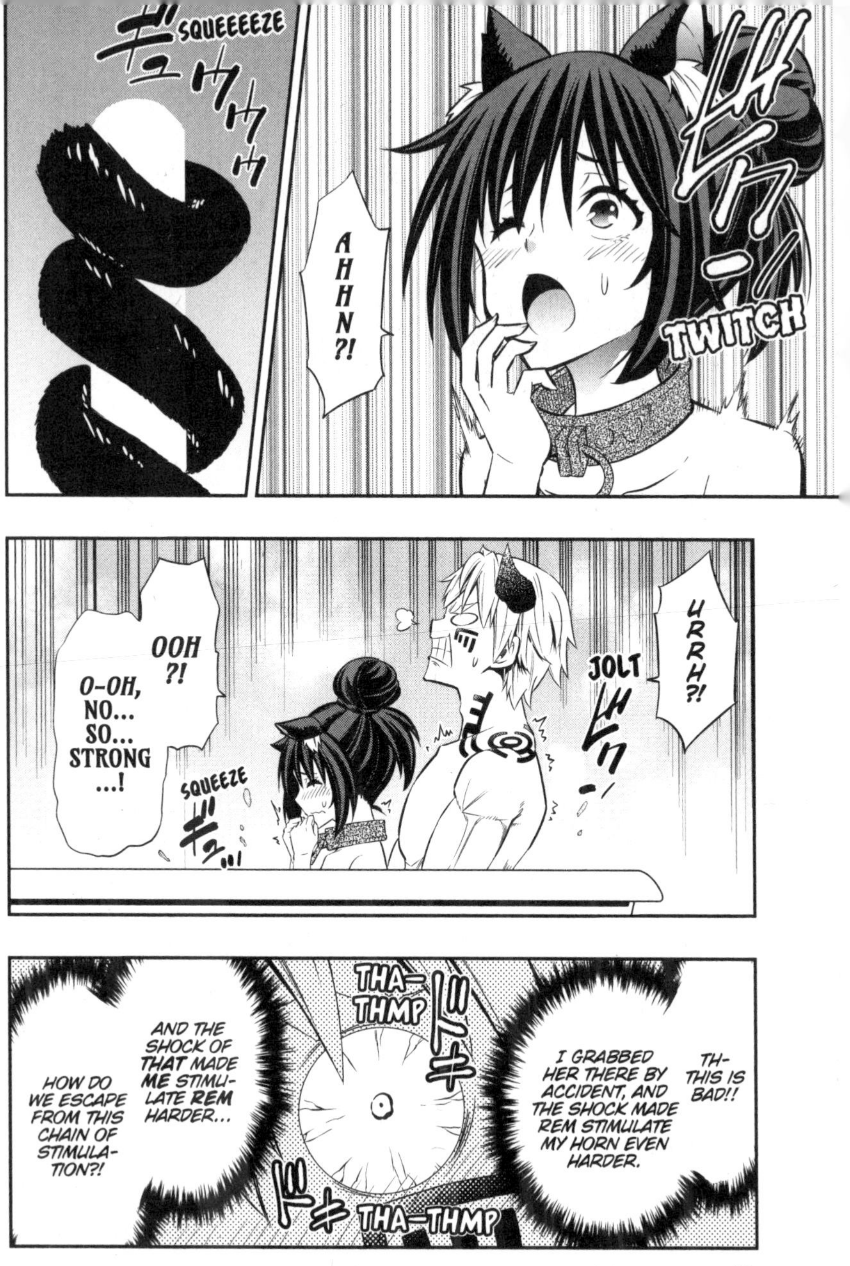

TWITCH
AHHN?!
SQUEEEEEZE
URRH?!
JOLT
OOH?!
O-OH, NO... SO... STRONG...!
SQUEEZE
TH-THIS IS BAD!!
I GRABBED HER THERE BY ACCIDENT, AND THE SHOCK MADE REM STIMULATE MY HORN EVEN HARDER.
THA-THMP
AND THE SHOCK OF THAT MADE ME STIMULATE REM HARDER...
HOW DO WE ESCAPE FROM THIS CHAIN OF STIMULATION?!
THA-THMP

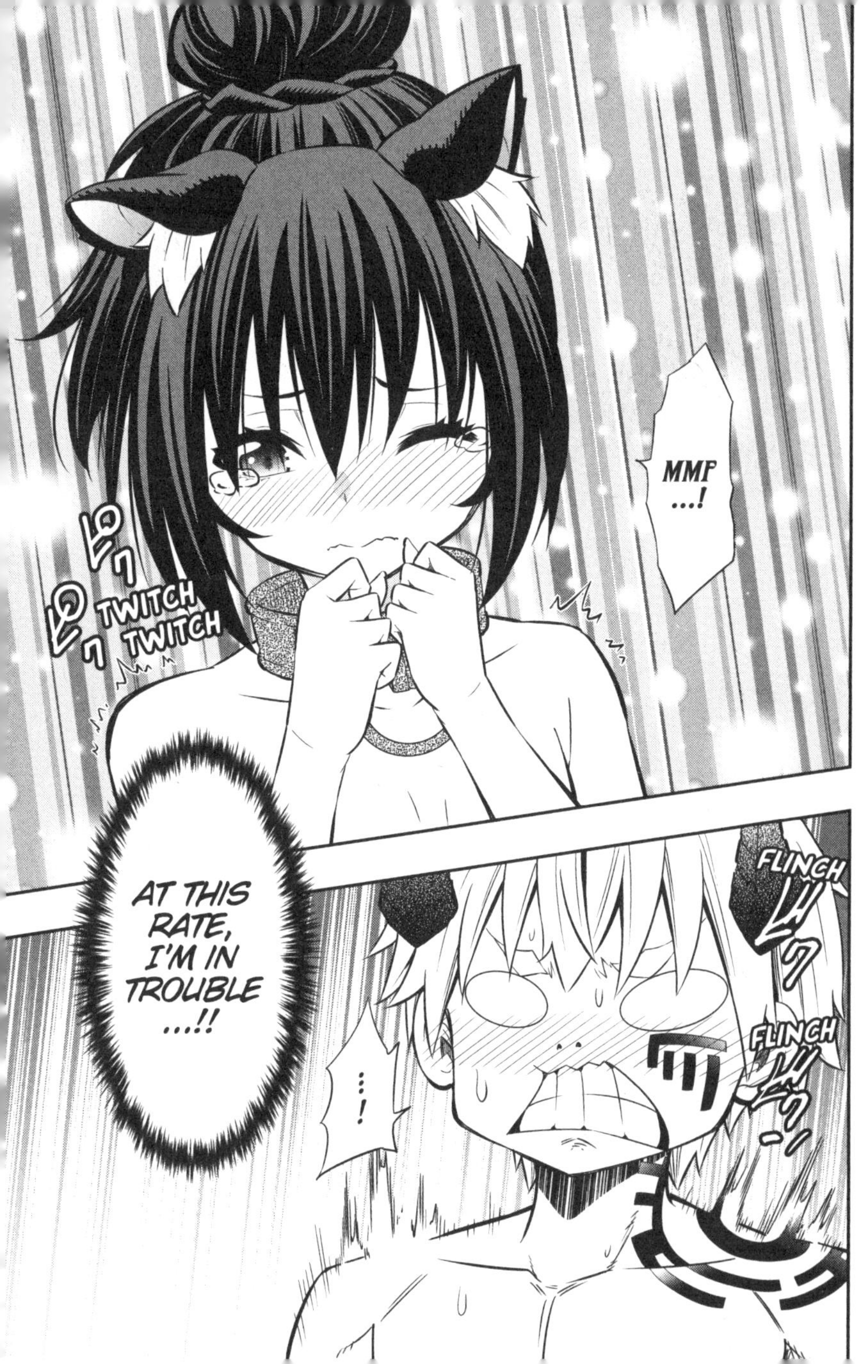
MMF ...!
TWITCH TWITCH
FLINCH FLINCH
...!
AT THIS RATE, I'M IN TROUBLE ...!!

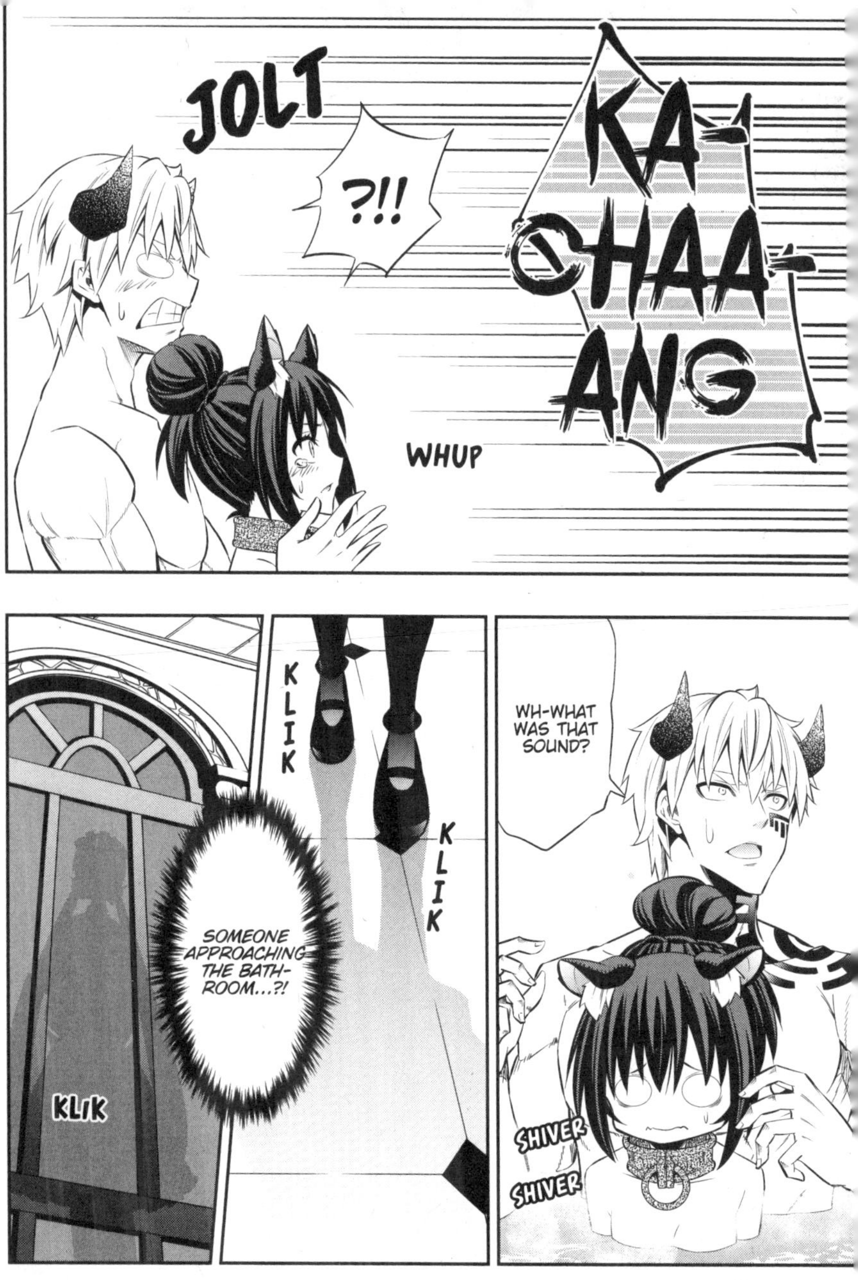
KA-CHAA-ANG
?!!
JOLT
WHUP
WH-WHAT WAS THAT SOUND?
SHIVER
SHIVER
KLIK
KLIK
SOMEONE APPROACHING THE BATH-ROOM...?!
KLIK

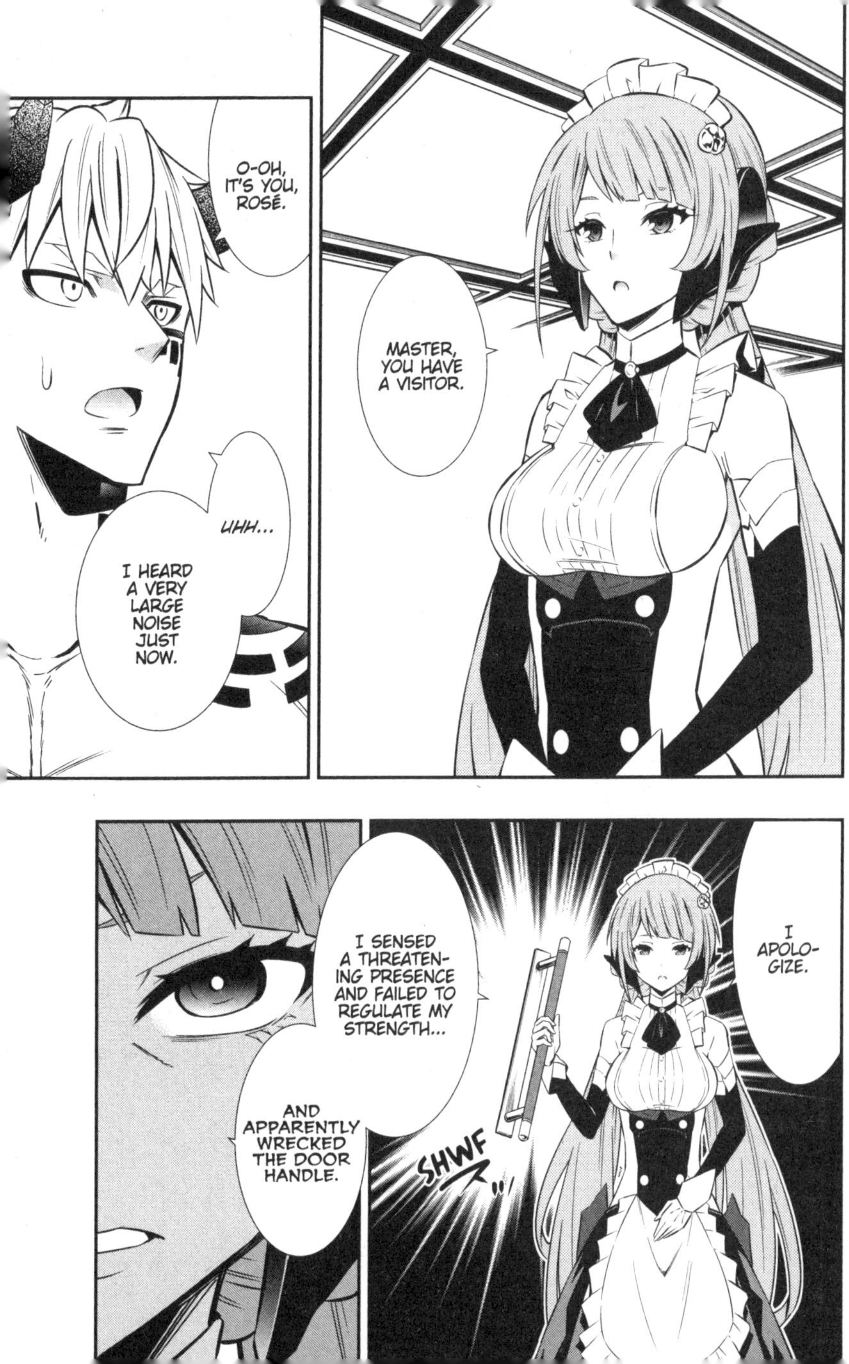
MASTER, YOU HAVE A VISITOR.
O-OH, IT'S YOU, ROSÉ.
UHH...
I HEARD A VERY LARGE NOISE JUST NOW.
I APOLOGIZE.
I SENSED A THREATENING PRESENCE AND FAILED TO REGULATE MY STRENGTH...
SHWF
AND APPARENTLY WRECKED THE DOOR HANDLE.

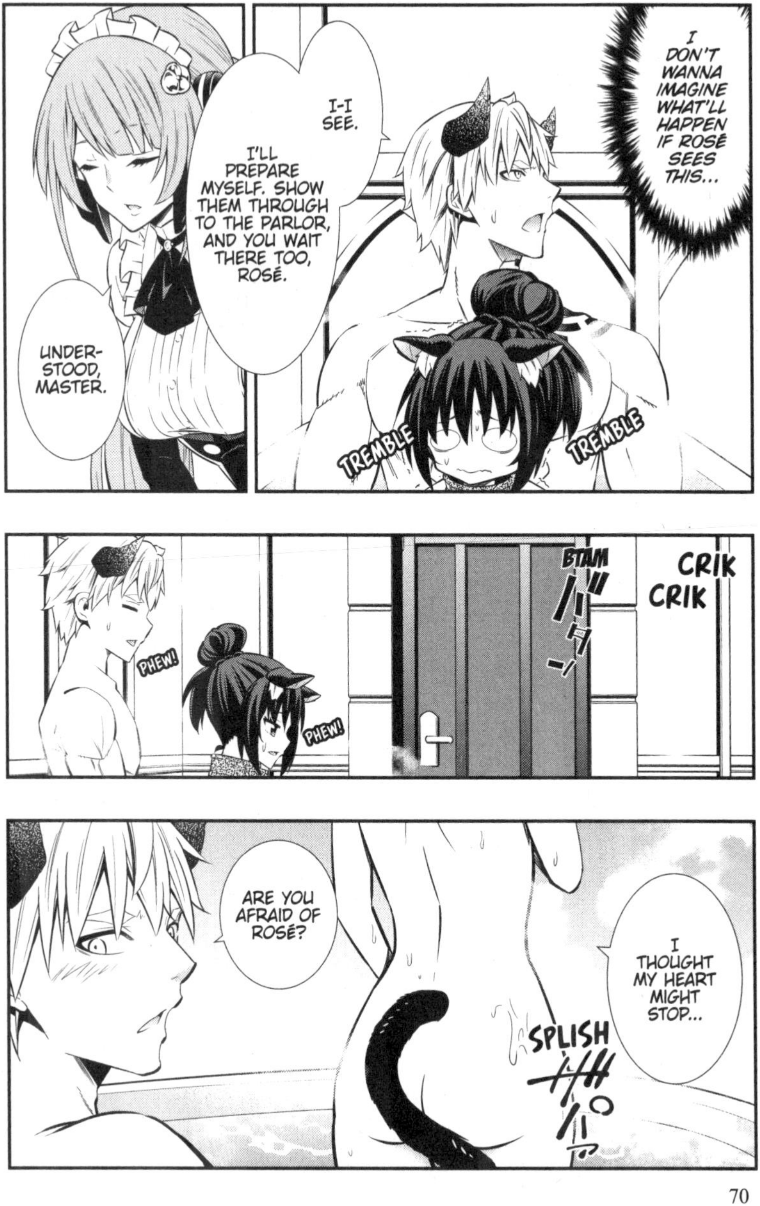
I DON'T WANNA IMAGINE WHAT'LL HAPPEN IF ROSÉ SEES THIS...
I-I SEE.
I'LL PREPARE MYSELF. SHOW THEM THROUGH TO THE PARLOR, AND YOU WAIT THERE TOO, ROSÉ.
TREMBLE
TREMBLE
UNDER-STOOD, MASTER.
CRIK CRIK
BTAM
PHEW!
PHEW!
I THOUGHT MY HEART MIGHT STOP...
SPLISH
ARE YOU AFRAID OF ROSÉ?

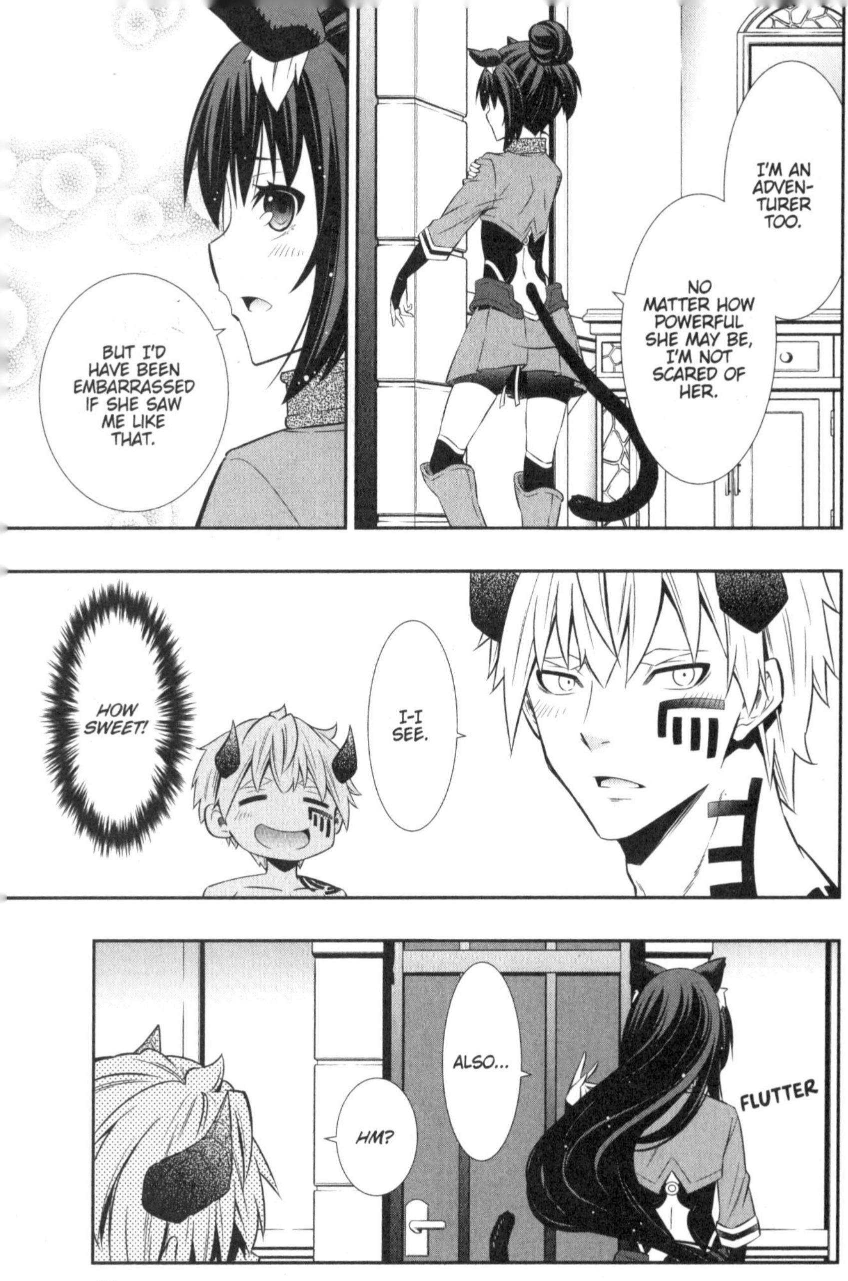
I'M AN ADVENTURER TOO.
NO MATTER HOW POWERFUL SHE MAY BE, I'M NOT SCARED OF HER.
BUT I'D HAVE BEEN EMBARRASSED IF SHE SAW ME LIKE THAT.
I-I SEE.
HOW SWEET!
FLUTTER
ALSO...
HM?

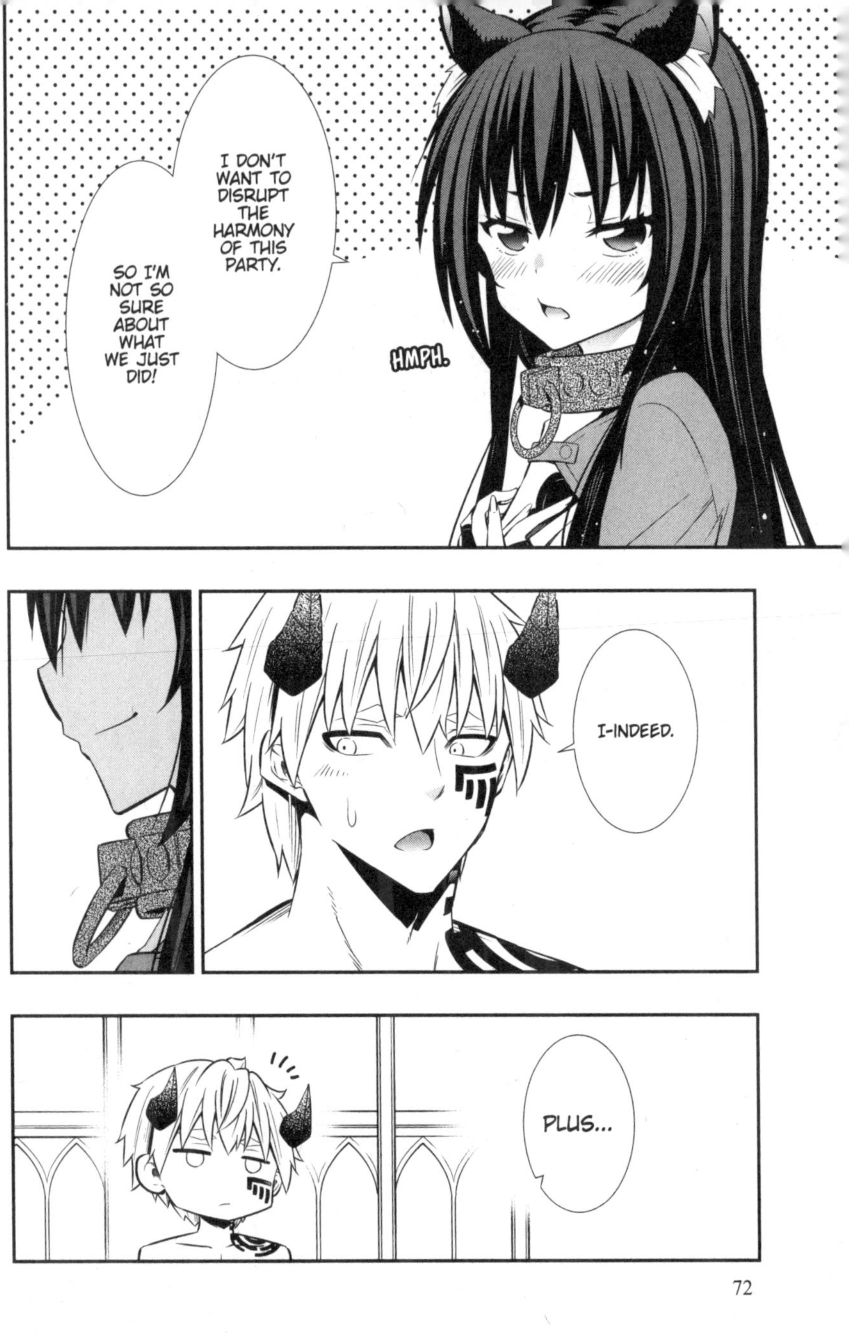
I DON'T WANT TO DISRUPT THE HARMONY OF THIS PARTY.
SO I'M NOT SO SURE ABOUT WHAT WE JUST DID!
HMPH.
I-INDEED.
PLUS...

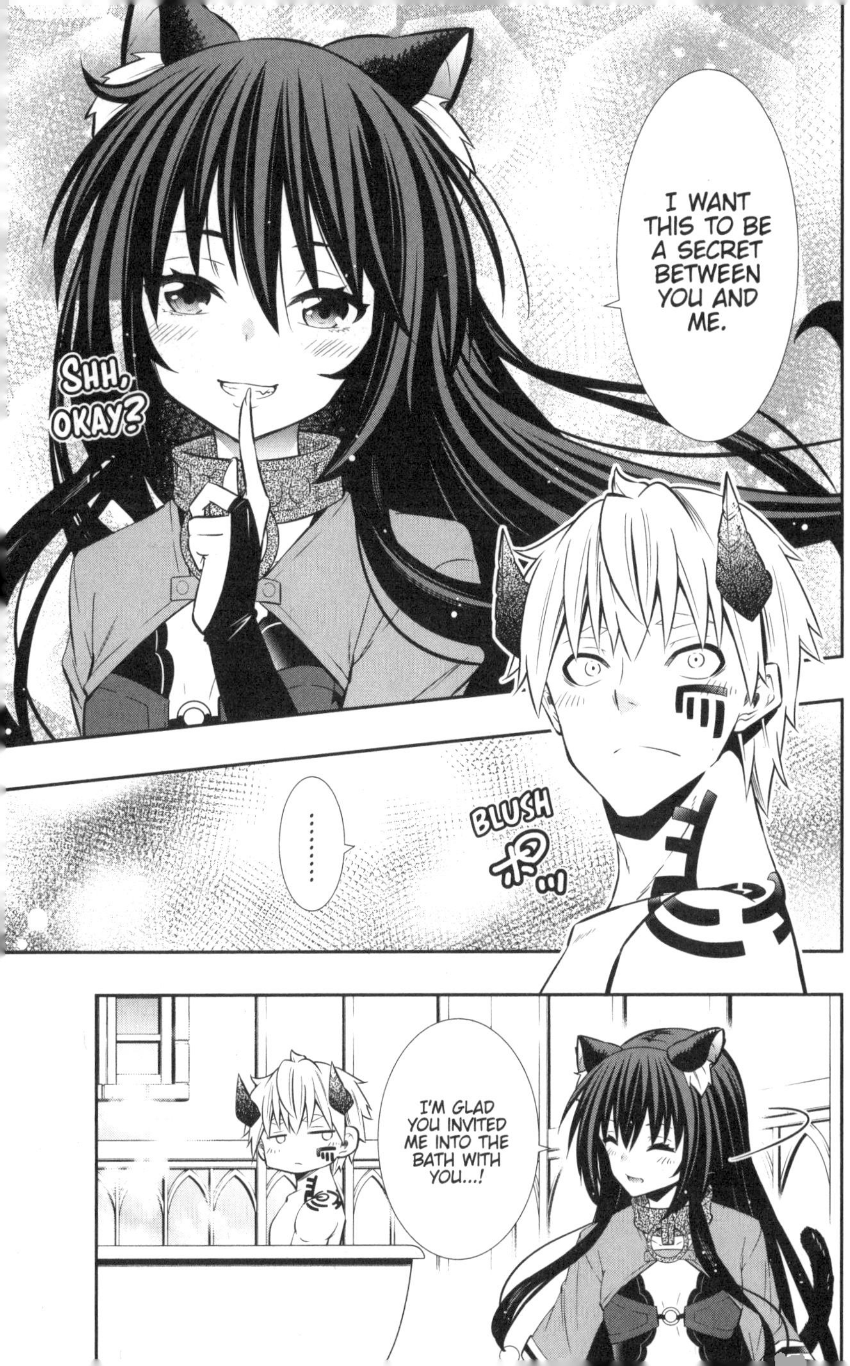
I WANT THIS TO BE A SECRET BETWEEN YOU AND ME.
SHH, OKAY?
......
BLUSH
ポッ
I'M GLAD YOU INVITED ME INTO THE BATH WITH YOU...!

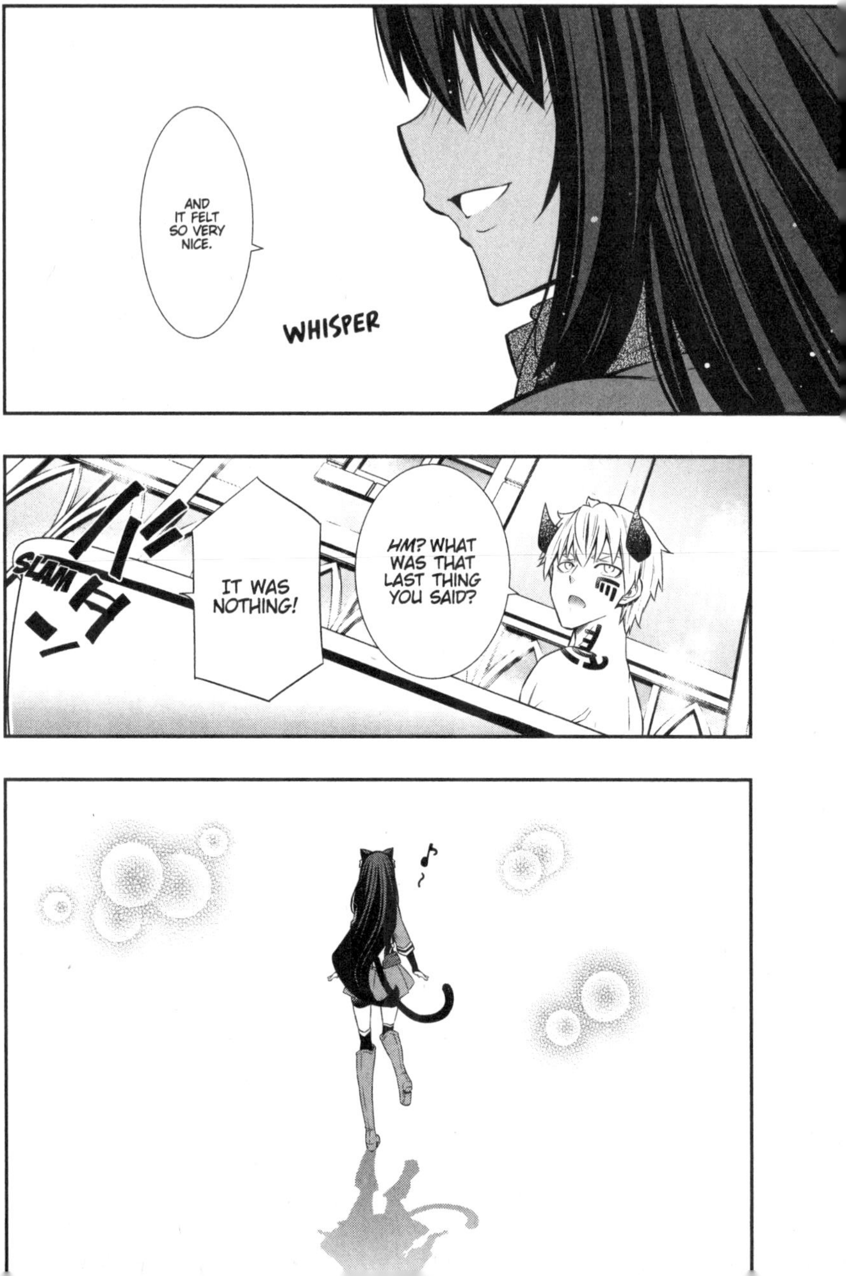
AND IT FELT SO VERY NICE.
WHISPER
HM? WHAT WAS THAT LAST THING YOU SAID?
IT WAS NOTHING!
SLAM

HOW NOT TO SUMMON A DEMON LORD

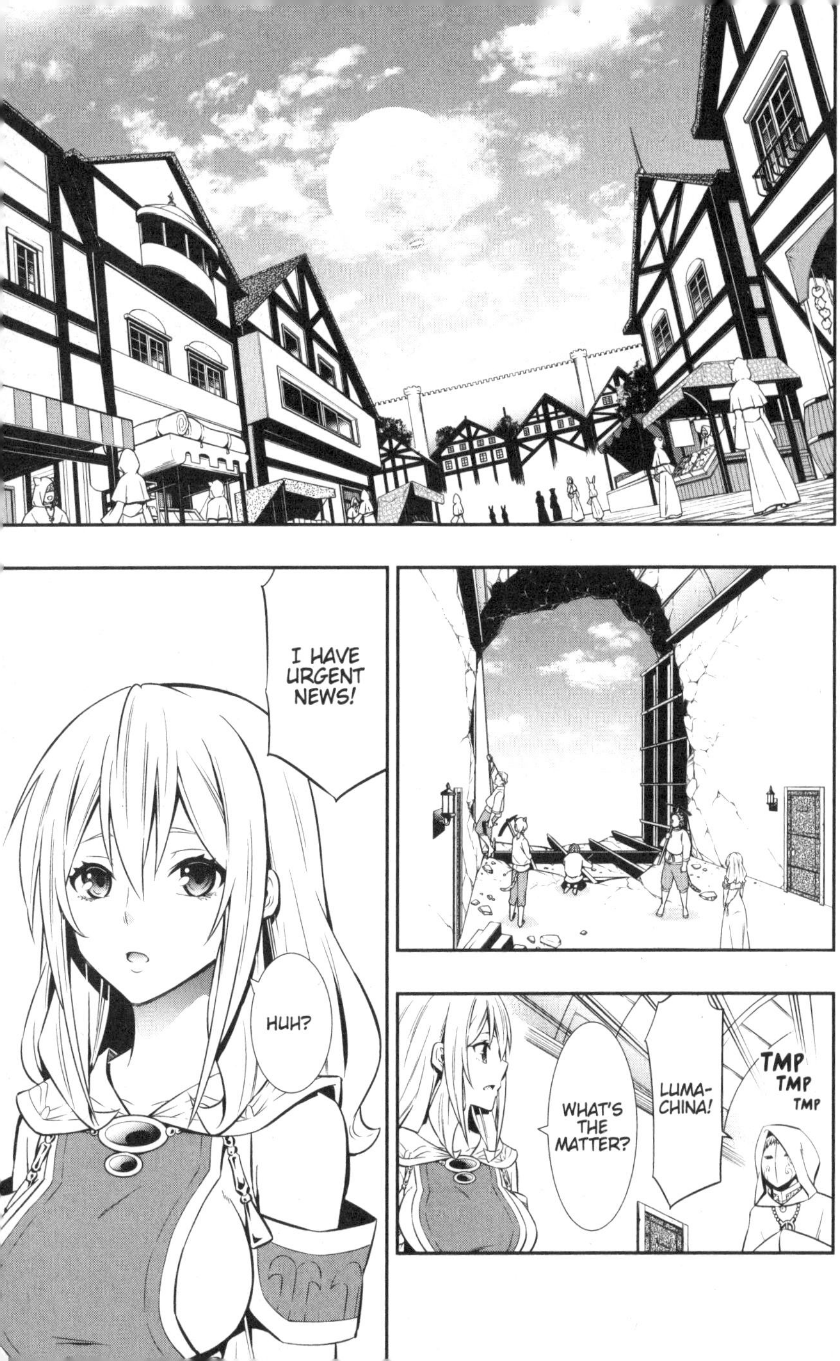
TMP TMP TMP
LUMA-CHINA!
WHAT'S THE MATTER?
I HAVE URGENT NEWS!
HUH?

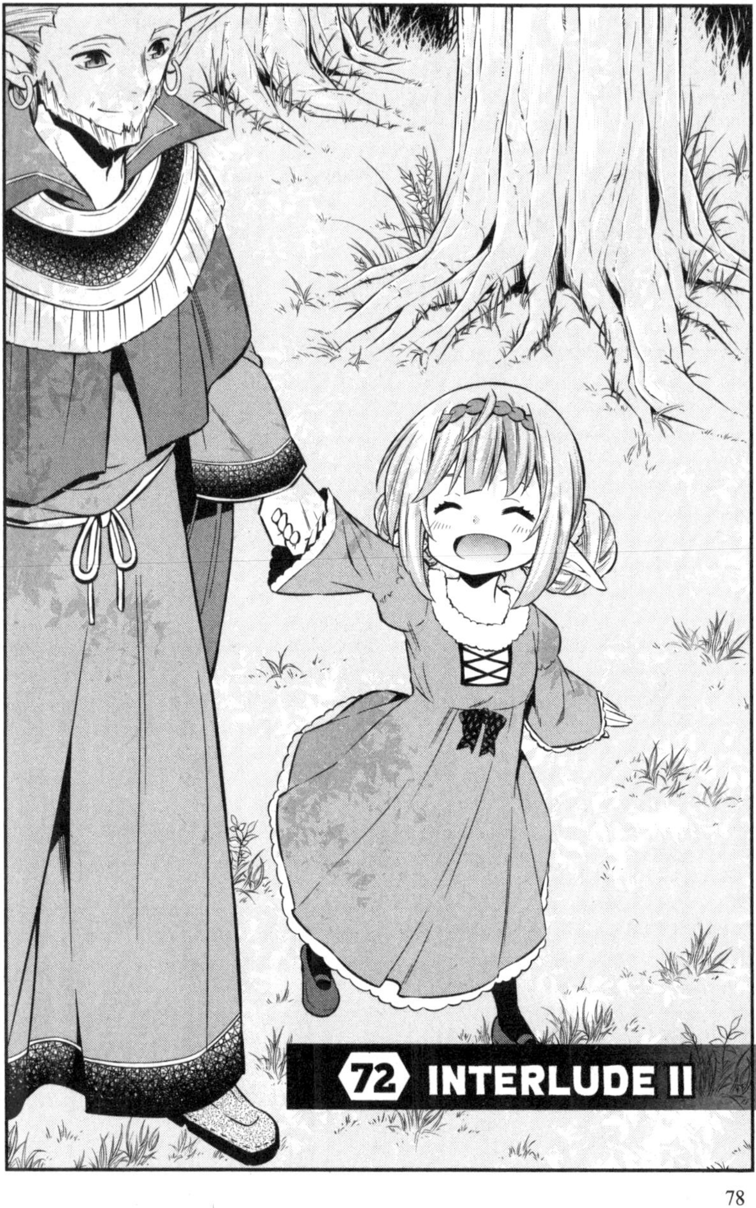
72 INTERLUDE II

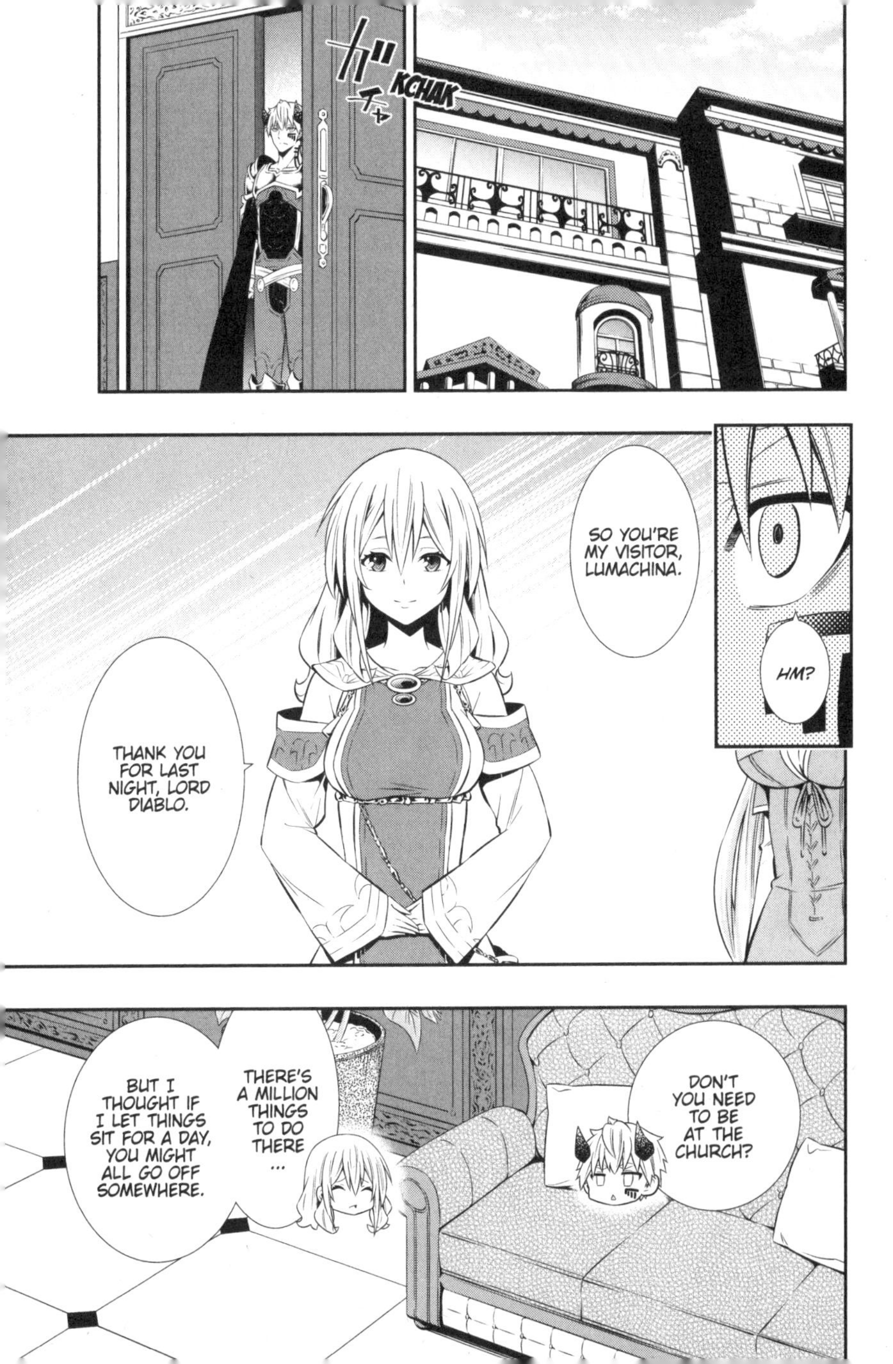
KCHAK
HM?
SO YOU'RE MY VISITOR, LUMACHINA.
THANK YOU FOR LAST NIGHT, LORD DIABLO.
DON'T YOU NEED TO BE AT THE CHURCH?
THERE'S A MILLION THINGS TO DO THERE ...
BUT I THOUGHT IF I LET THINGS SIT FOR A DAY, YOU MIGHT ALL GO OFF SOMEWHERE.

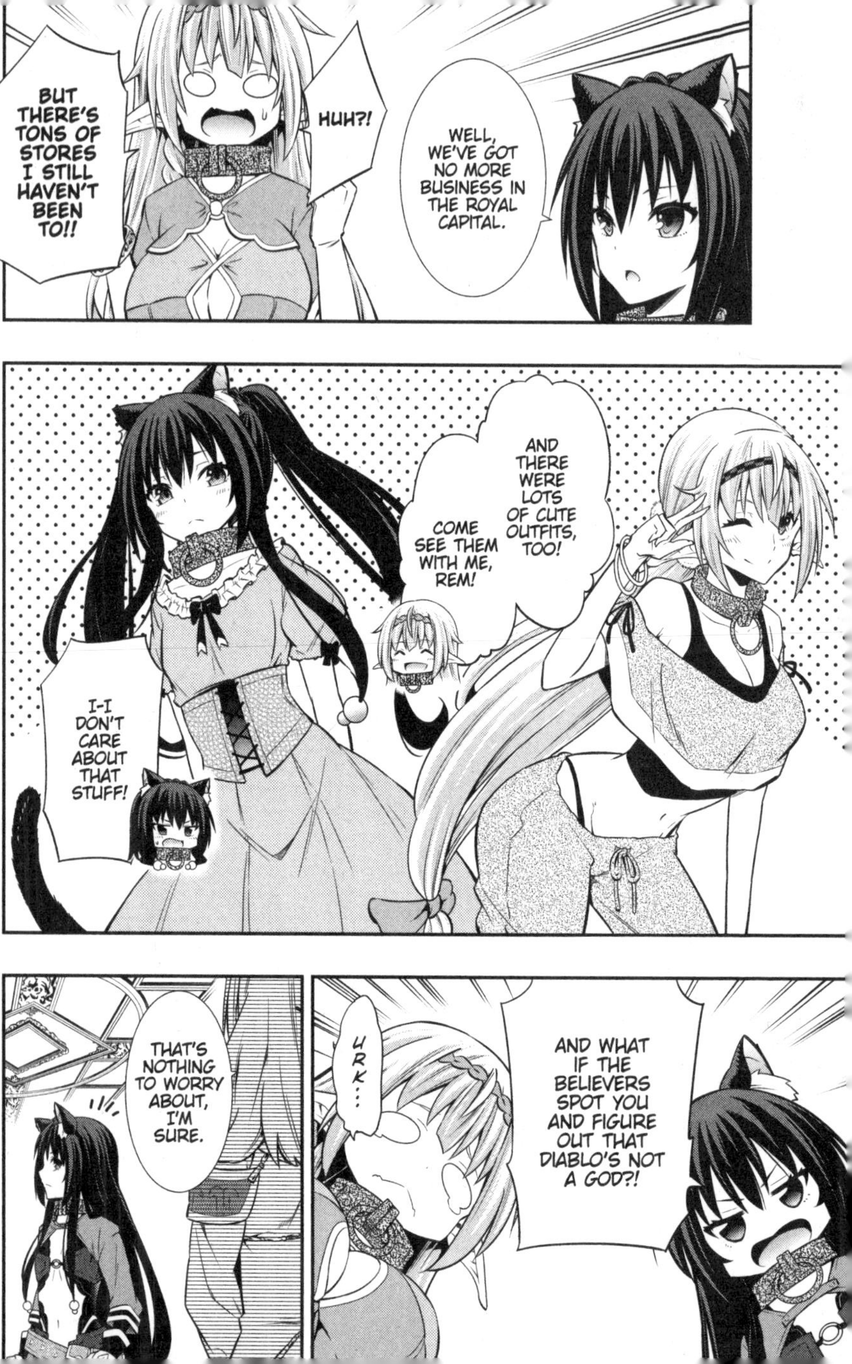
WELL, WE'VE GOT NO MORE BUSINESS IN THE ROYAL CAPITAL.
HUH?!
BUT THERE'S TONS OF STORES I STILL HAVEN'T BEEN TO!!
AND THERE WERE LOTS OF CUTE OUTFITS, TOO!
COME SEE THEM WITH ME, REM!
I-I DON'T CARE ABOUT THAT STUFF!
AND WHAT IF THE BELIEVERS SPOT YOU AND FIGURE OUT THAT DIABLO'S NOT A GOD?!
URK...
THAT'S NOTHING TO WORRY ABOUT, I'M SURE.

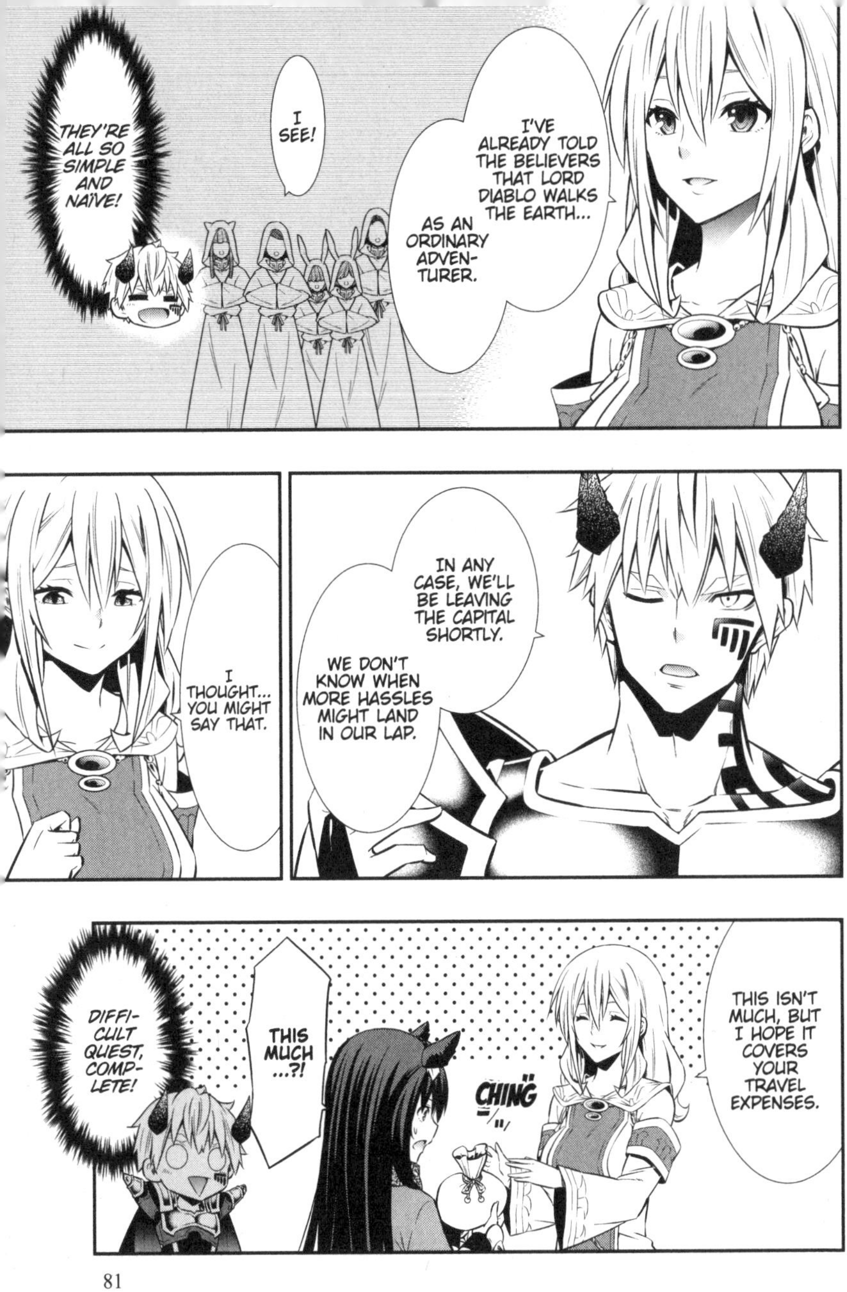
I'VE ALREADY TOLD THE BELIEVERS THAT LORD DIABLO WALKS THE EARTH...
AS AN ORDINARY ADVENTURER.
I SEE!
THEY'RE ALL SO SIMPLE AND NAÏVE!
IN ANY CASE, WE'LL BE LEAVING THE CAPITAL SHORTLY.
WE DON'T KNOW WHEN MORE HASSLES MIGHT LAND IN OUR LAP.
I THOUGHT... YOU MIGHT SAY THAT.
THIS ISN'T MUCH, BUT I HOPE IT COVERS YOUR TRAVEL EXPENSES.
CHING
THIS MUCH...?!
DIFFICULT QUEST, COMPLETE!

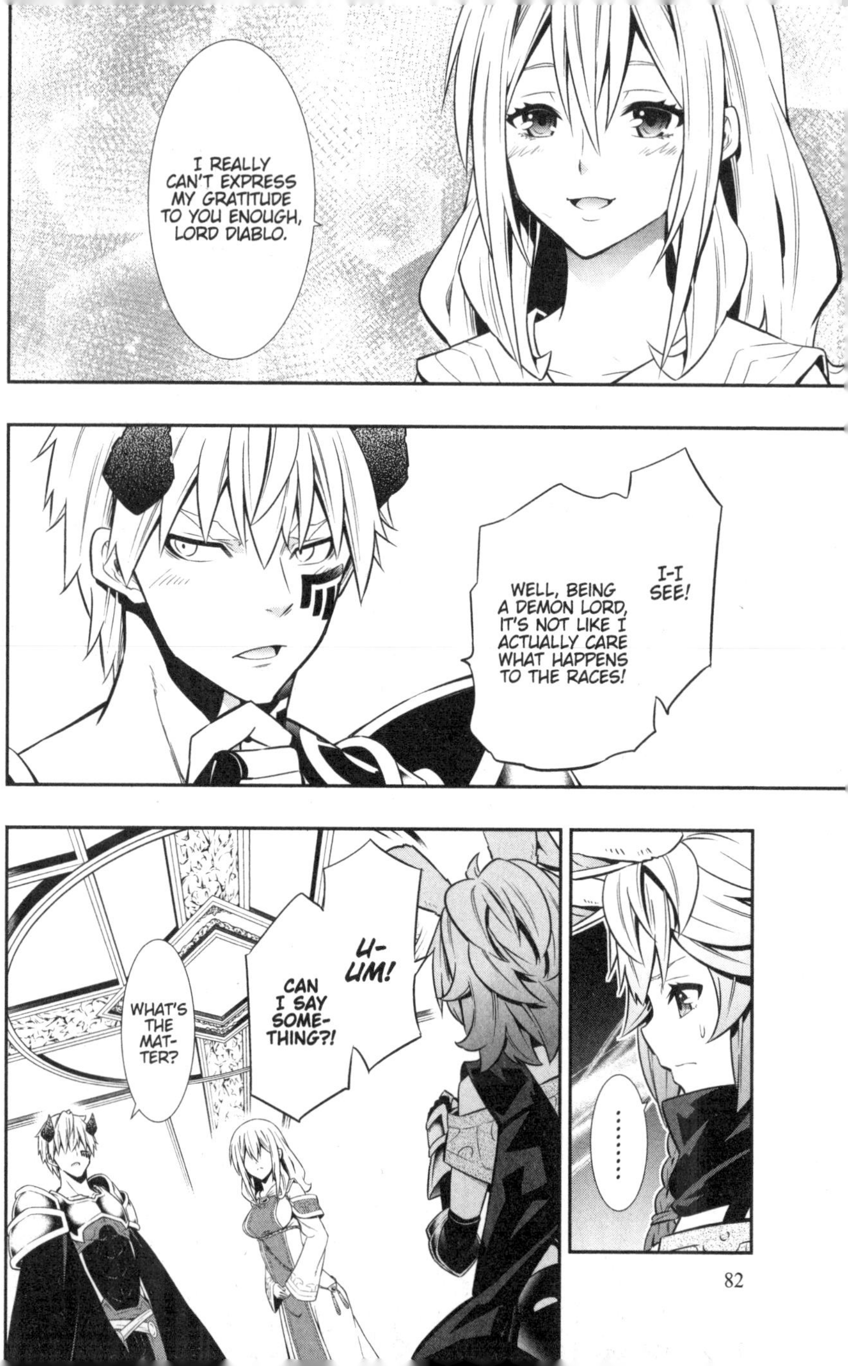
I REALLY CAN'T EXPRESS MY GRATITUDE TO YOU ENOUGH, LORD DIABLO.
I-I SEE!
WELL, BEING A DEMON LORD, IT'S NOT LIKE I ACTUALLY CARE WHAT HAPPENS TO THE RACES!
....
U-UM!
CAN I SAY SOME-THING?!
WHAT'S THE MAT-TER?

WHAM

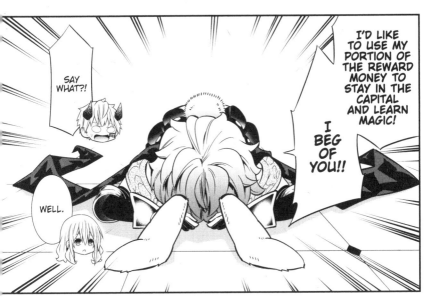

I'D LIKE TO USE MY PORTION OF THE REWARD MONEY TO STAY IN THE CAPITAL AND LEARN MAGIC!

I BEG OF YOU!!

SAY WHAT?!

WELL.

I-I'M SORRY FOR THE BURDEN I'VE BEEN ON YOU SO FAR...

BUT!!

I WANT TO BECOME A SORCERER LIKE YOU, MISTER!

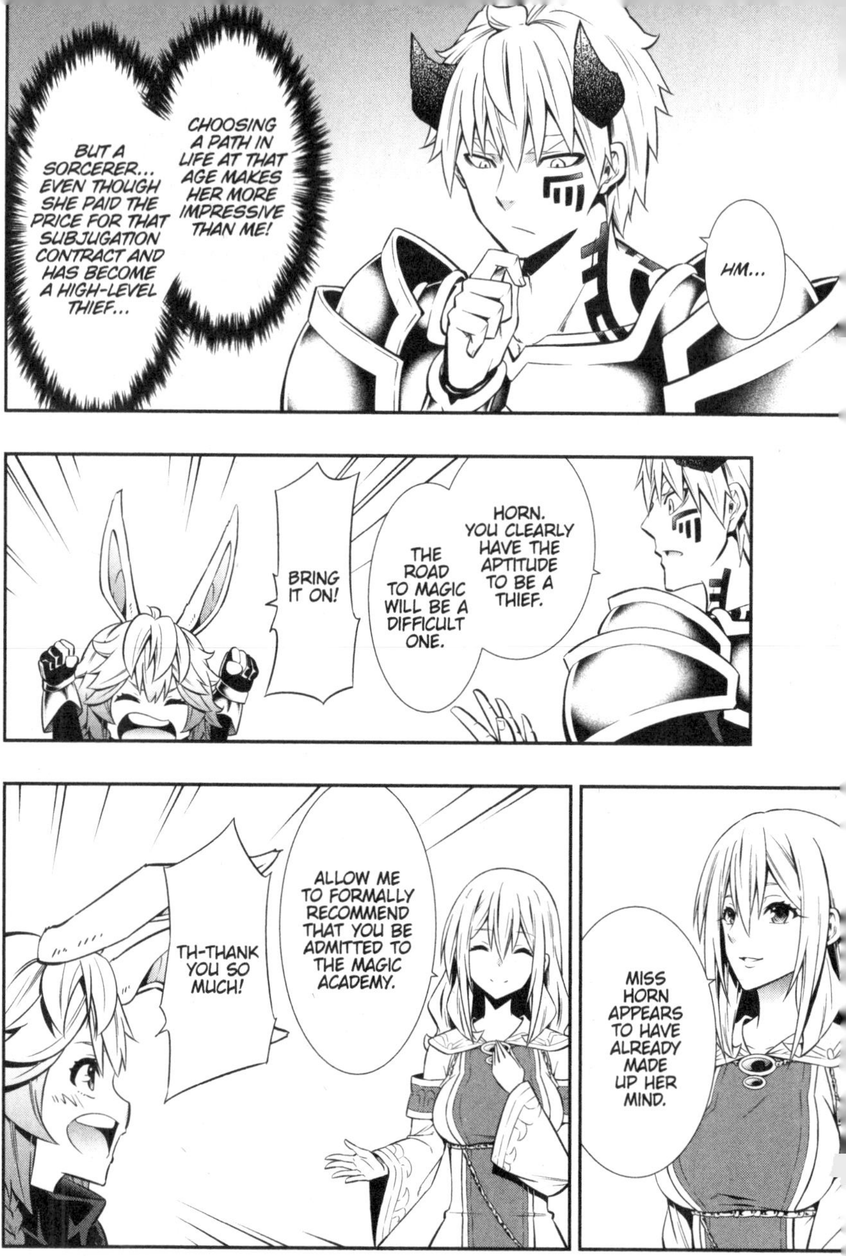
HM...
CHOOSING A PATH IN LIFE AT THAT AGE MAKES HER MORE IMPRESSIVE THAN ME!
BUT A SORCERER... EVEN THOUGH SHE PAID THE PRICE FOR THAT SUBJUGATION CONTRACT AND HAS BECOME A HIGH-LEVEL THIEF...
HORN. YOU CLEARLY HAVE THE APTITUDE TO BE A THIEF.
THE ROAD TO MAGIC WILL BE A DIFFICULT ONE.
BRING IT ON!
MISS HORN APPEARS TO HAVE ALREADY MADE UP HER MIND.
ALLOW ME TO FORMALLY RECOMMEND THAT YOU BE ADMITTED TO THE MAGIC ACADEMY.
TH-THANK YOU SO MUCH!

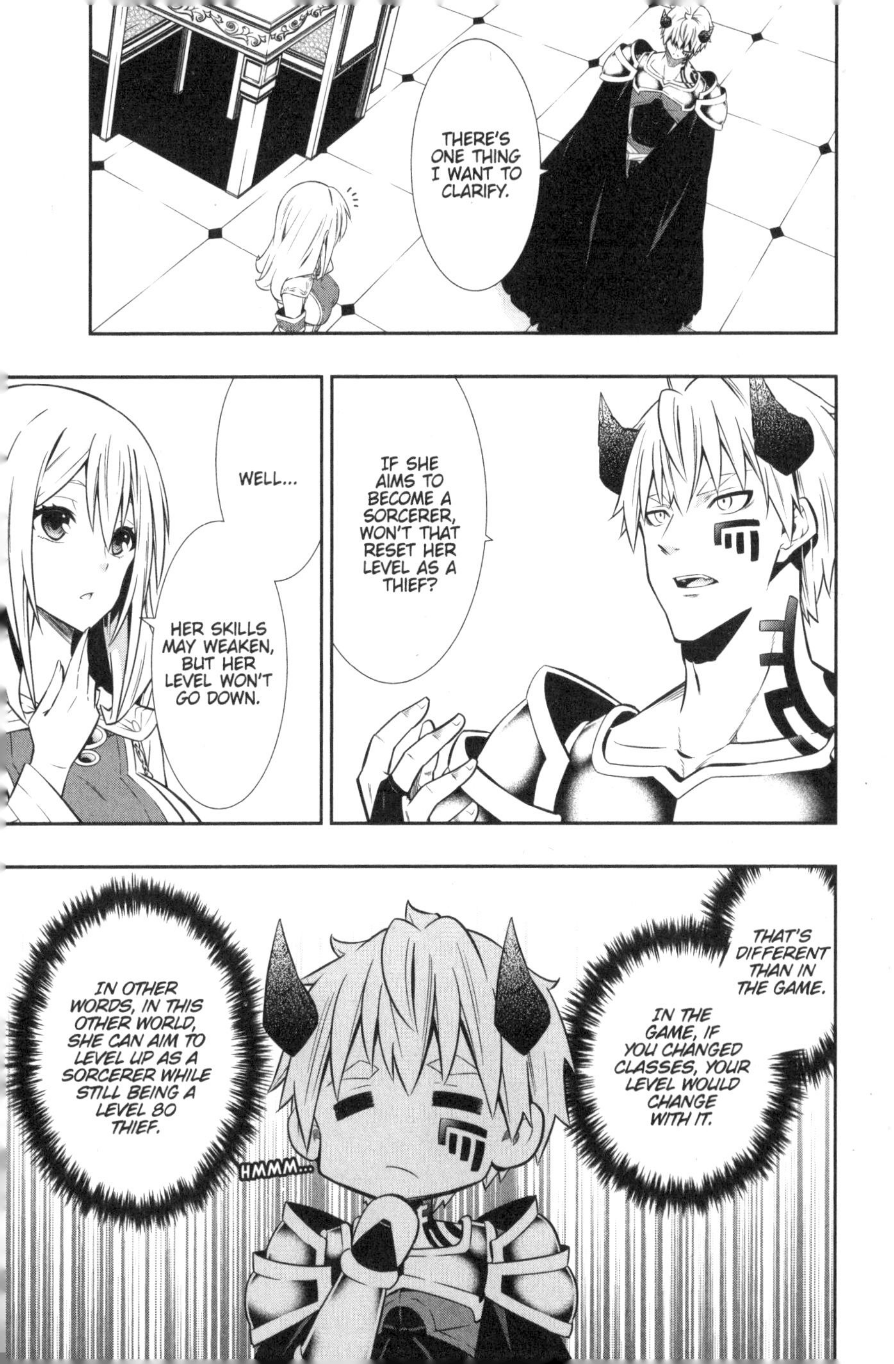
THERE'S ONE THING I WANT TO CLARIFY.
IF SHE AIMS TO BECOME A SORCERER, WON'T THAT RESET HER LEVEL AS A THIEF?
WELL...
HER SKILLS MAY WEAKEN, BUT HER LEVEL WON'T GO DOWN.
THAT'S DIFFERENT THAN IN THE GAME.
IN THE GAME, IF YOU CHANGED CLASSES, YOUR LEVEL WOULD CHANGE WITH IT.
HMMM...
IN OTHER WORDS, IN THIS OTHER WORLD, SHE CAN AIM TO LEVEL UP AS A SORCERER WHILE STILL BEING A LEVEL 80 THIEF.

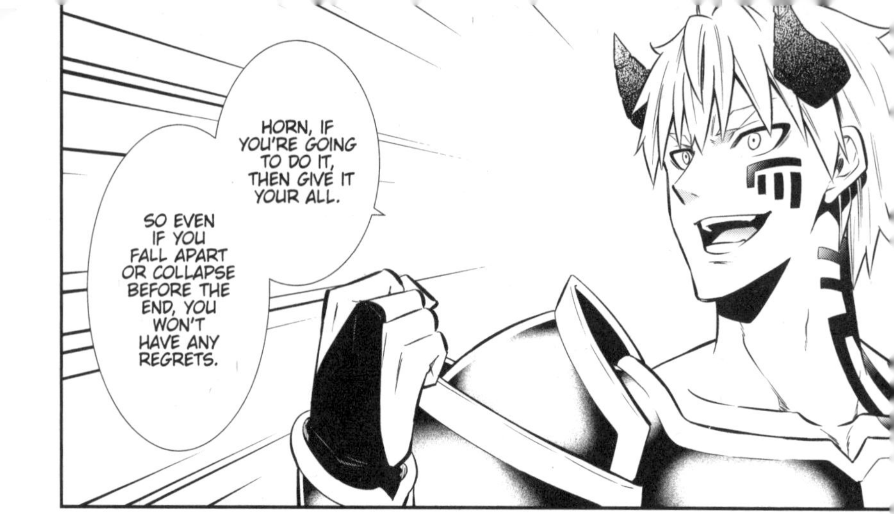
HORN, IF YOU'RE GOING TO DO IT, THEN GIVE IT YOUR ALL.
SO EVEN IF YOU FALL APART OR COLLAPSE BEFORE THE END, YOU WON'T HAVE ANY REGRETS.

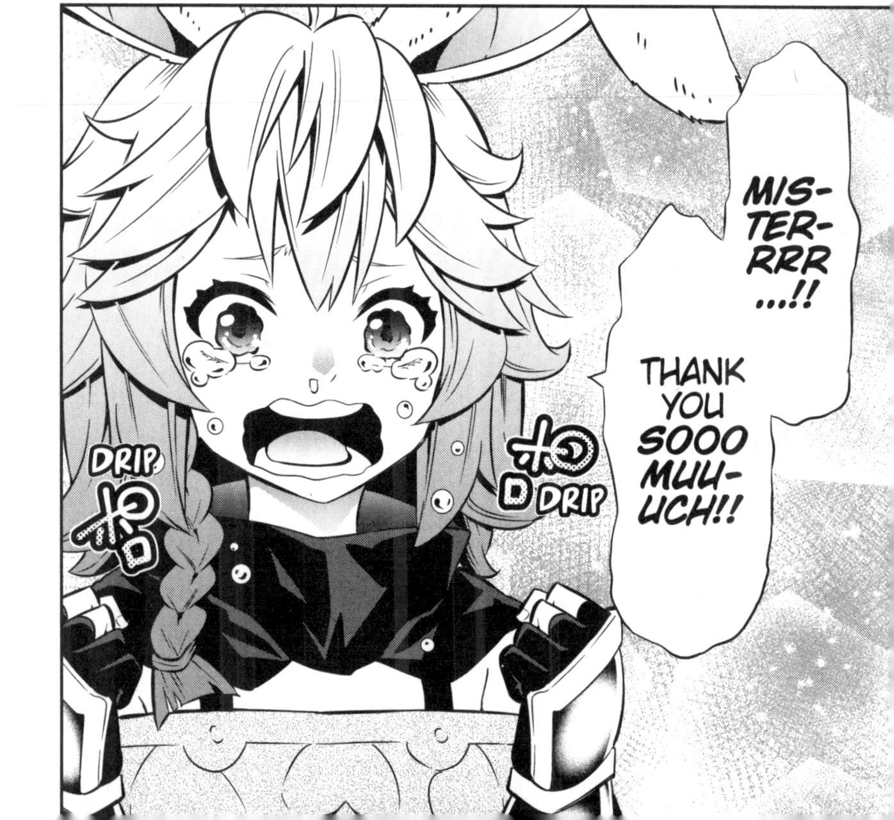
MIS-TER-RRR...!!
THANK YOU SOOO MUU-UCH!!
D DRIP
DRIP

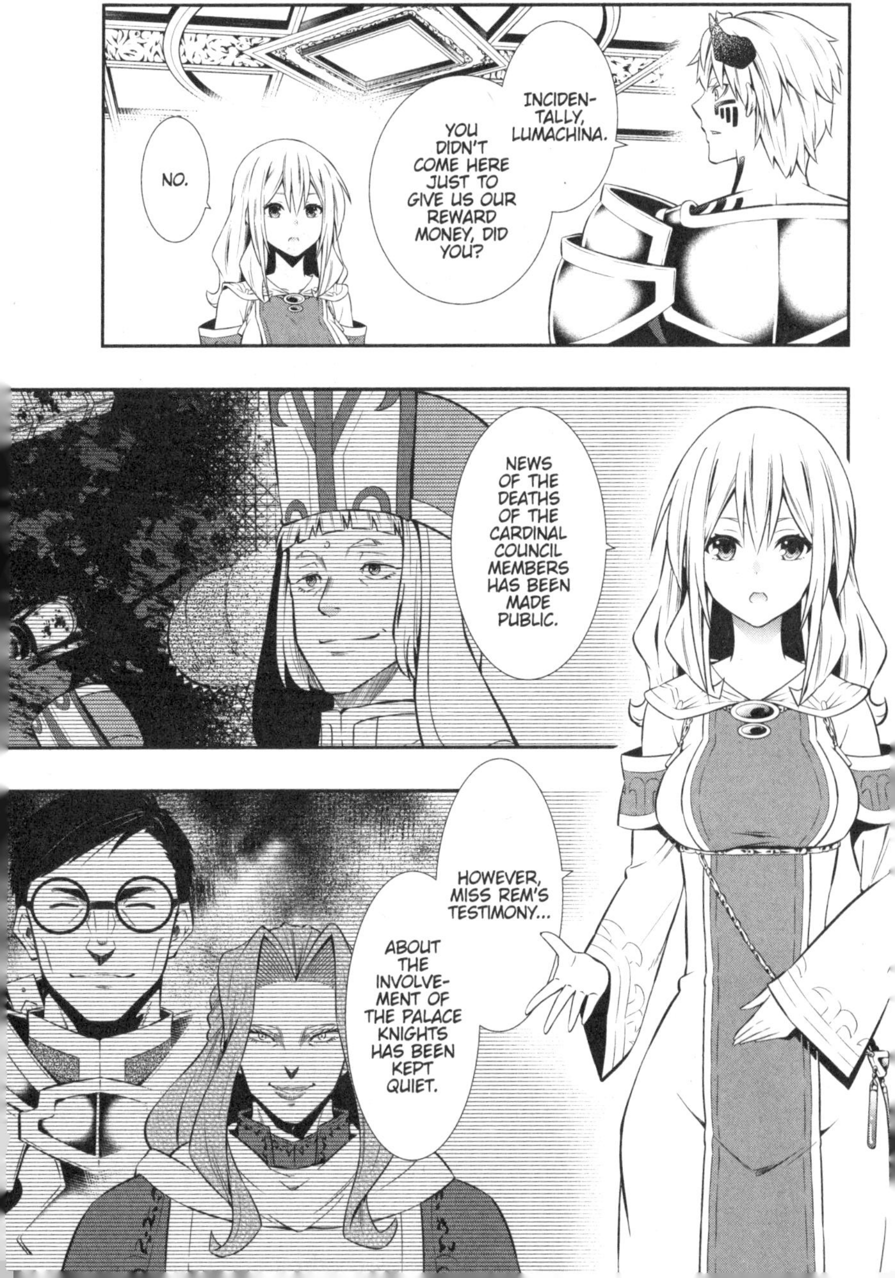
INCIDEN-TALLY, LUMACHINA.
YOU DIDN'T COME HERE JUST TO GIVE US OUR REWARD MONEY, DID YOU?
NO.
NEWS OF THE DEATHS OF THE CARDINAL COUNCIL MEMBERS HAS BEEN MADE PUBLIC.
HOWEVER, MISS REM'S TESTIMONY...
ABOUT THE INVOLVE-MENT OF THE PALACE KNIGHTS HAS BEEN KEPT QUIET.

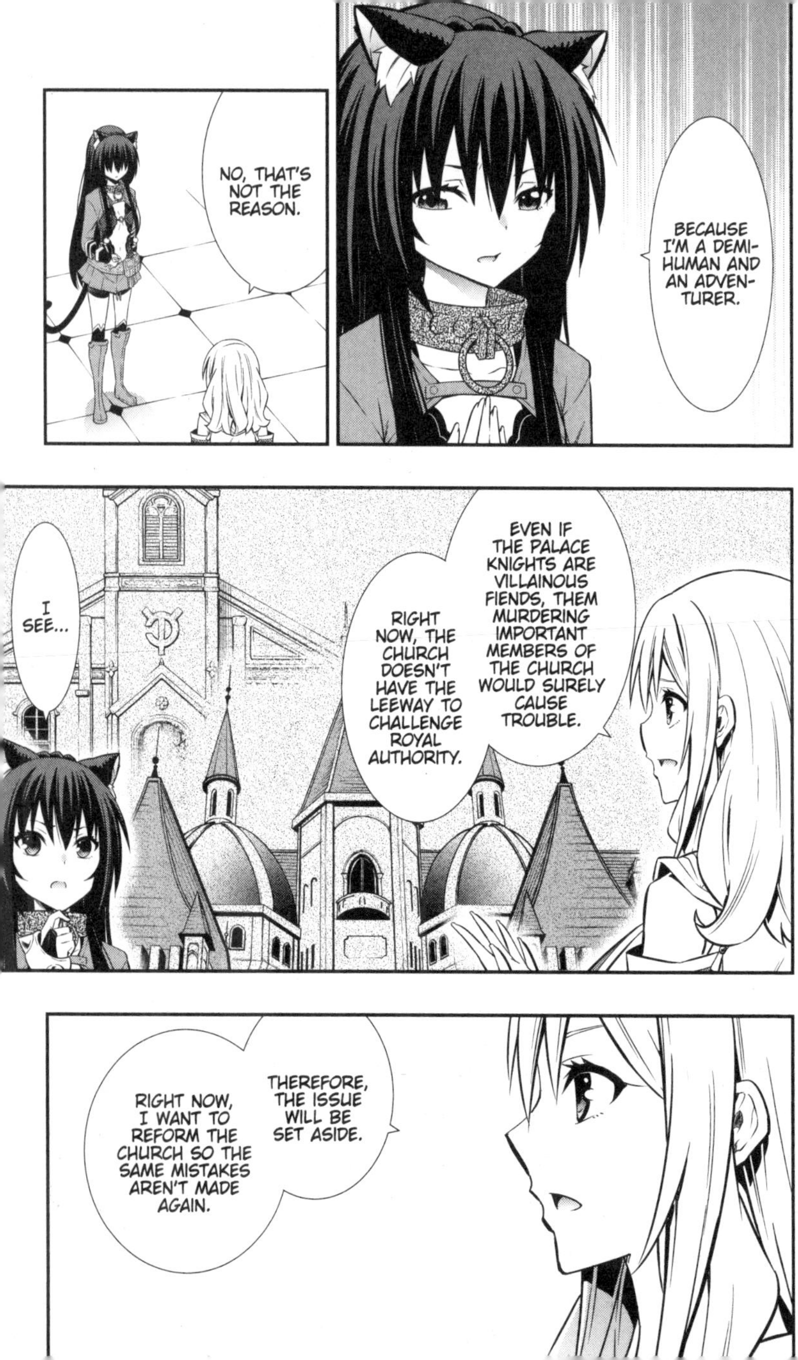
BECAUSE I'M A DEMI-HUMAN AND AN ADVENTURER.
NO, THAT'S NOT THE REASON.
EVEN IF THE PALACE KNIGHTS ARE VILLAINOUS FIENDS, THEM MURDERING IMPORTANT MEMBERS OF THE CHURCH WOULD SURELY CAUSE TROUBLE.
RIGHT NOW, THE CHURCH DOESN'T HAVE THE LEEWAY TO CHALLENGE ROYAL AUTHORITY.
I SEE...
THEREFORE, THE ISSUE WILL BE SET ASIDE.
RIGHT NOW, I WANT TO REFORM THE CHURCH SO THE SAME MISTAKES AREN'T MADE AGAIN.

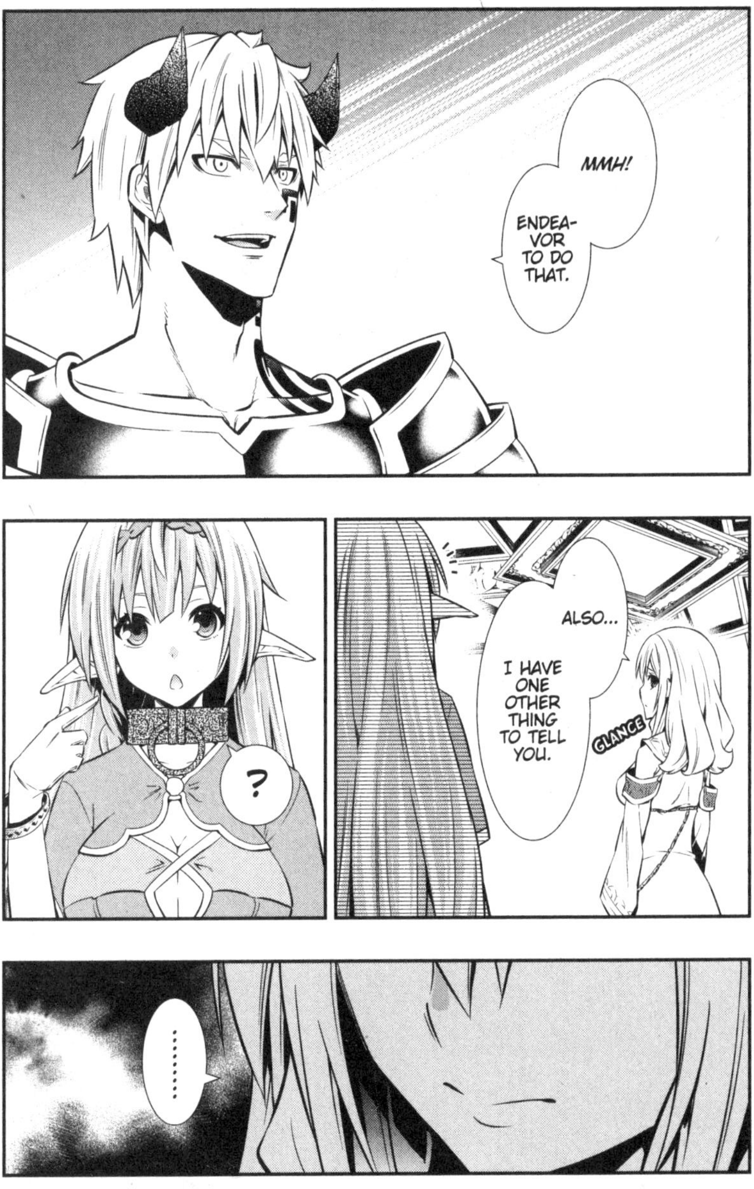
MMH!
ENDEA-VOR TO DO THAT.
ALSO...
I HAVE ONE OTHER THING TO TELL YOU.
GLANCE
?
....

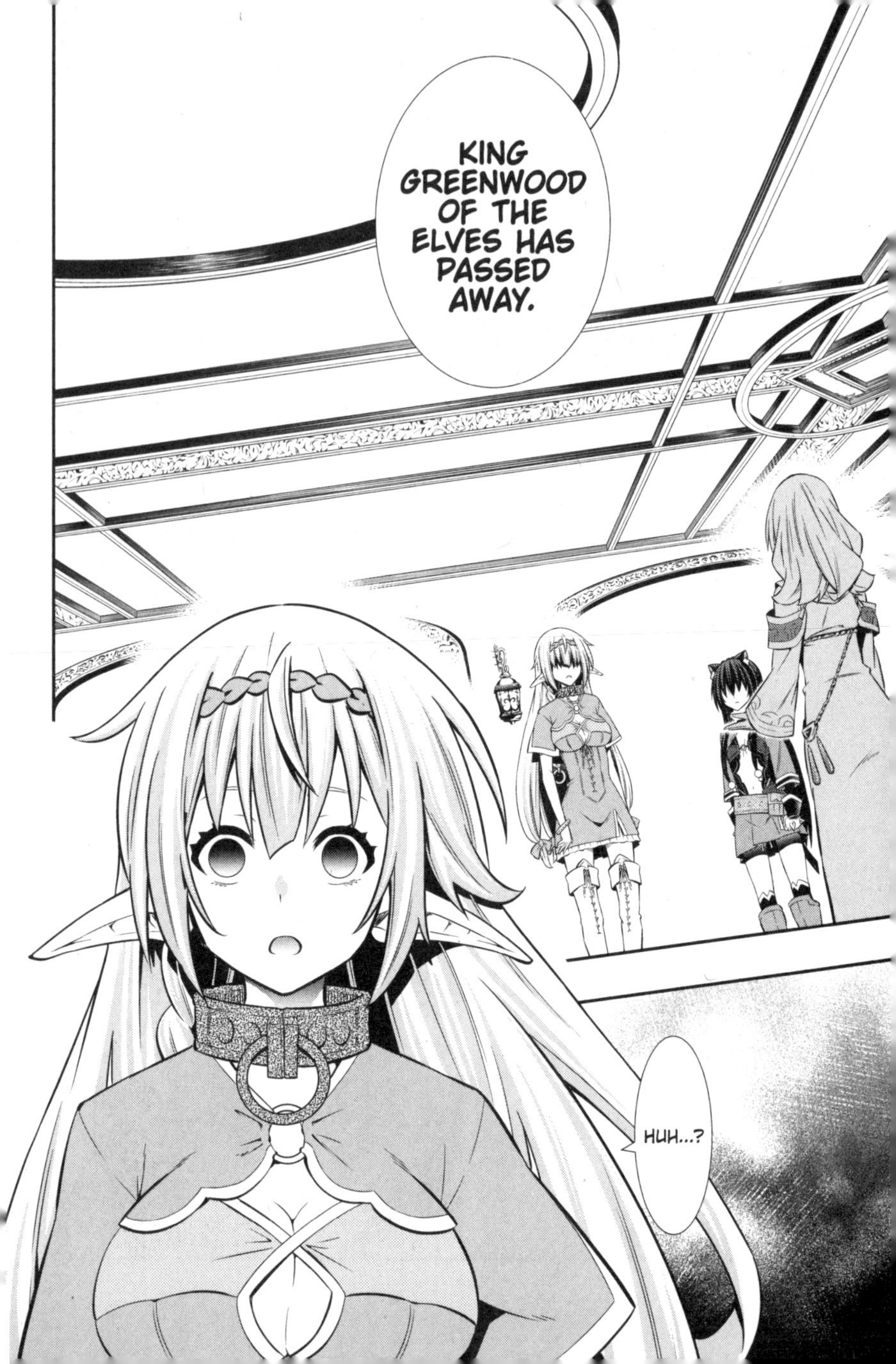
KING GREENWOOD OF THE ELVES HAS PASSED AWAY.
HUH...?

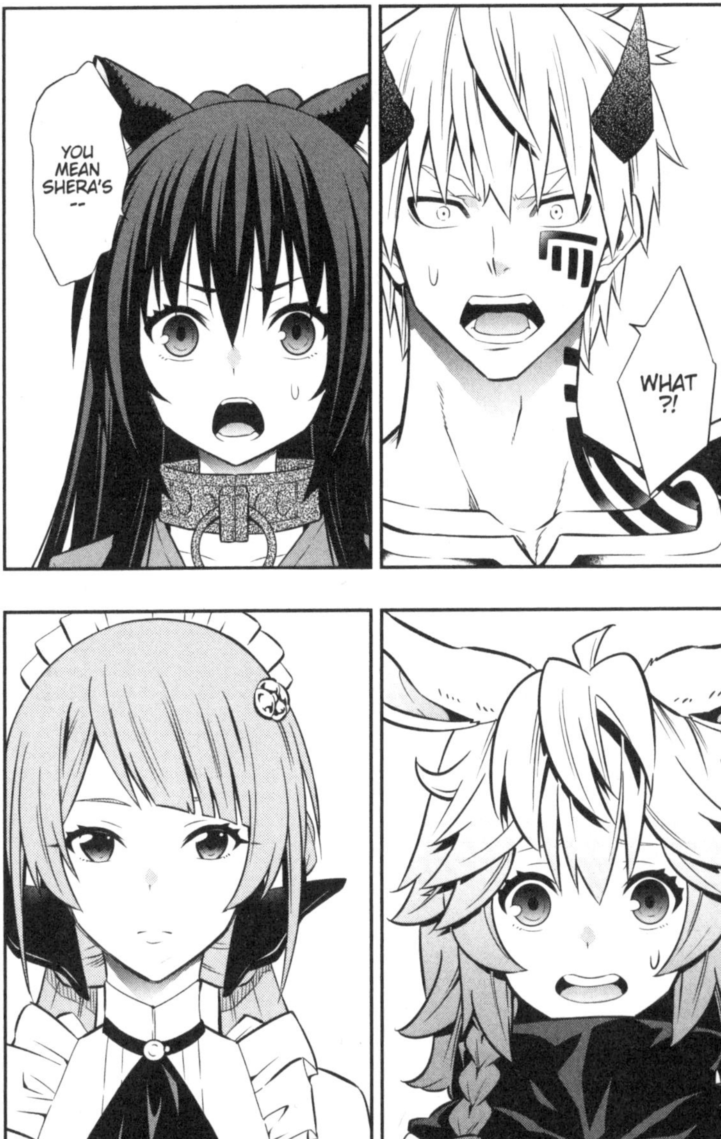
WHAT?!
YOU MEAN SHERA'S --

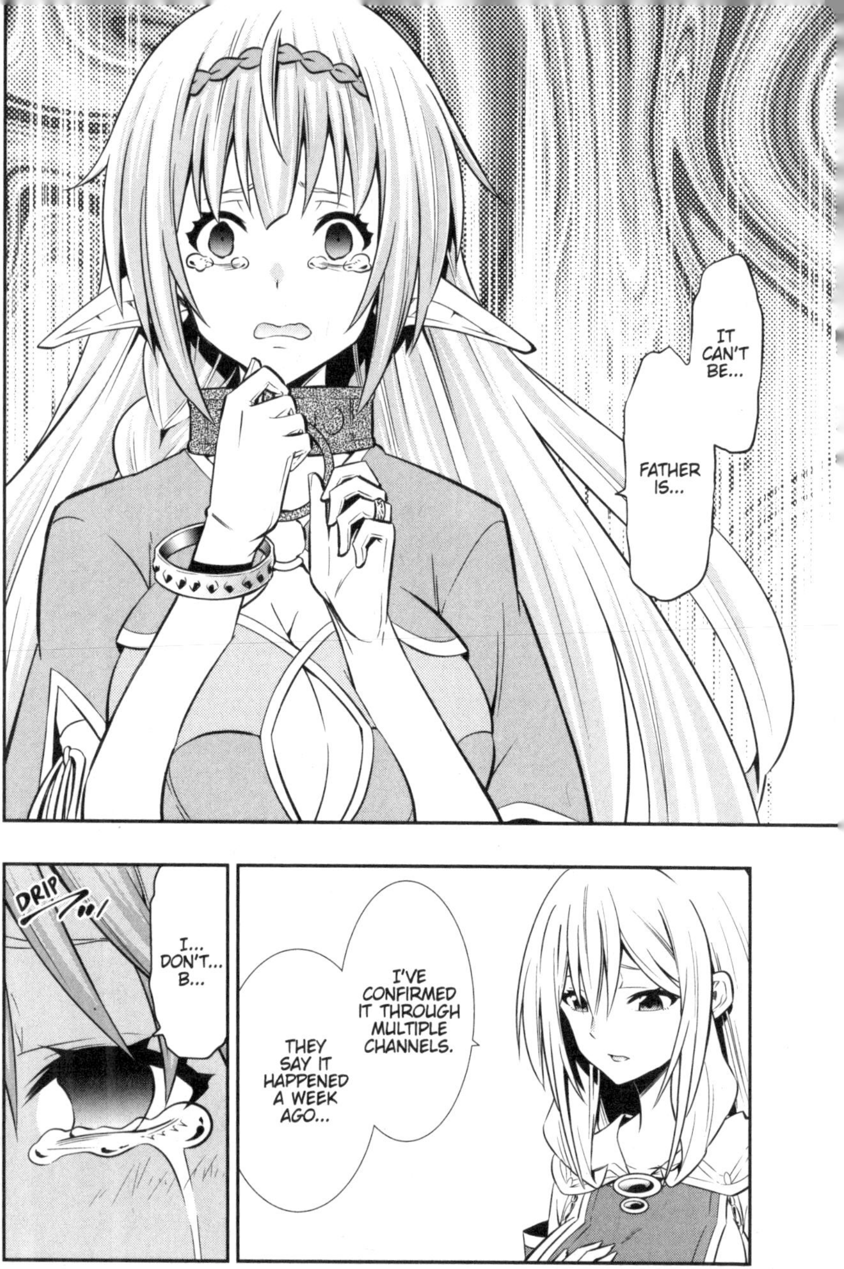
IT CAN'T BE...
FATHER IS...
I'VE CONFIRMED IT THROUGH MULTIPLE CHANNELS.
THEY SAY IT HAPPENED A WEEK AGO...
DRIP
I... DON'T... B...

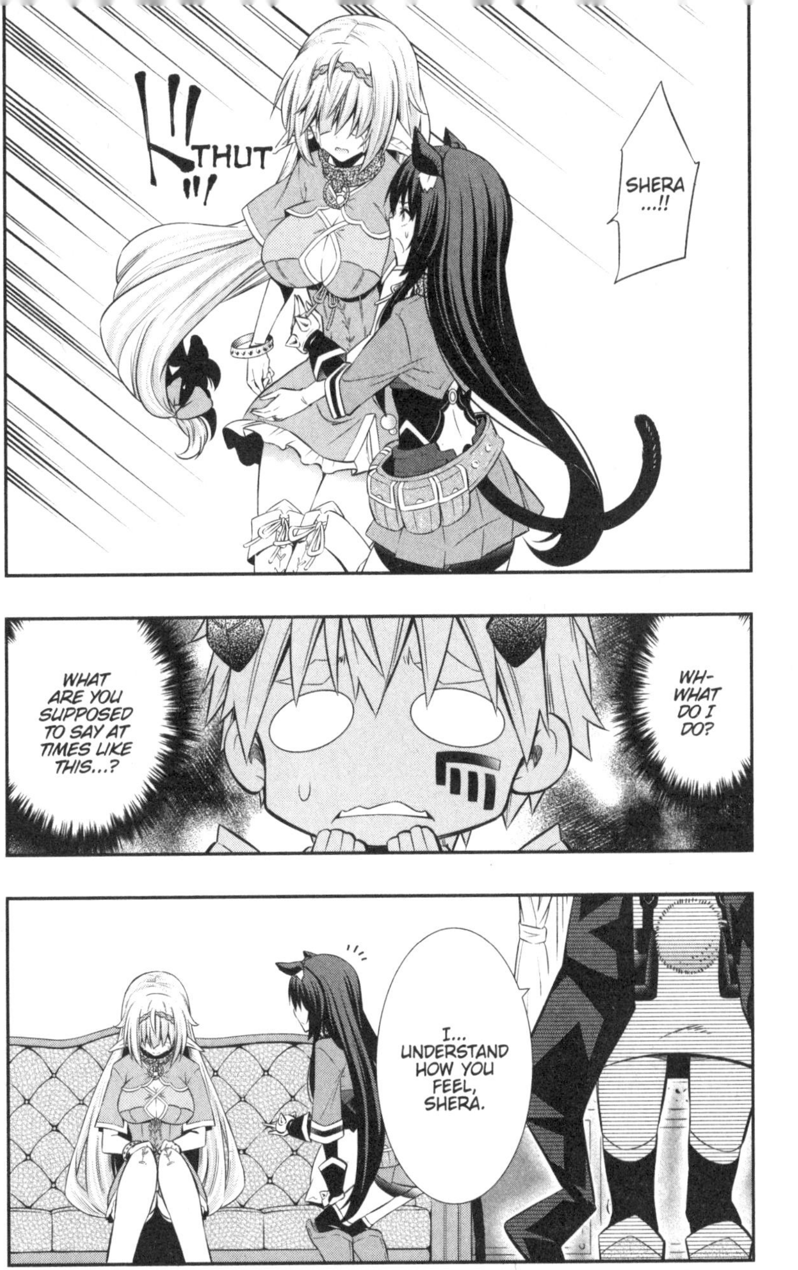
SHERA ...!!
THUT
WH- WHAT DO I DO?
WHAT ARE YOU SUPPOSED TO SAY AT TIMES LIKE THIS...?
I... UNDERSTAND HOW YOU FEEL, SHERA.

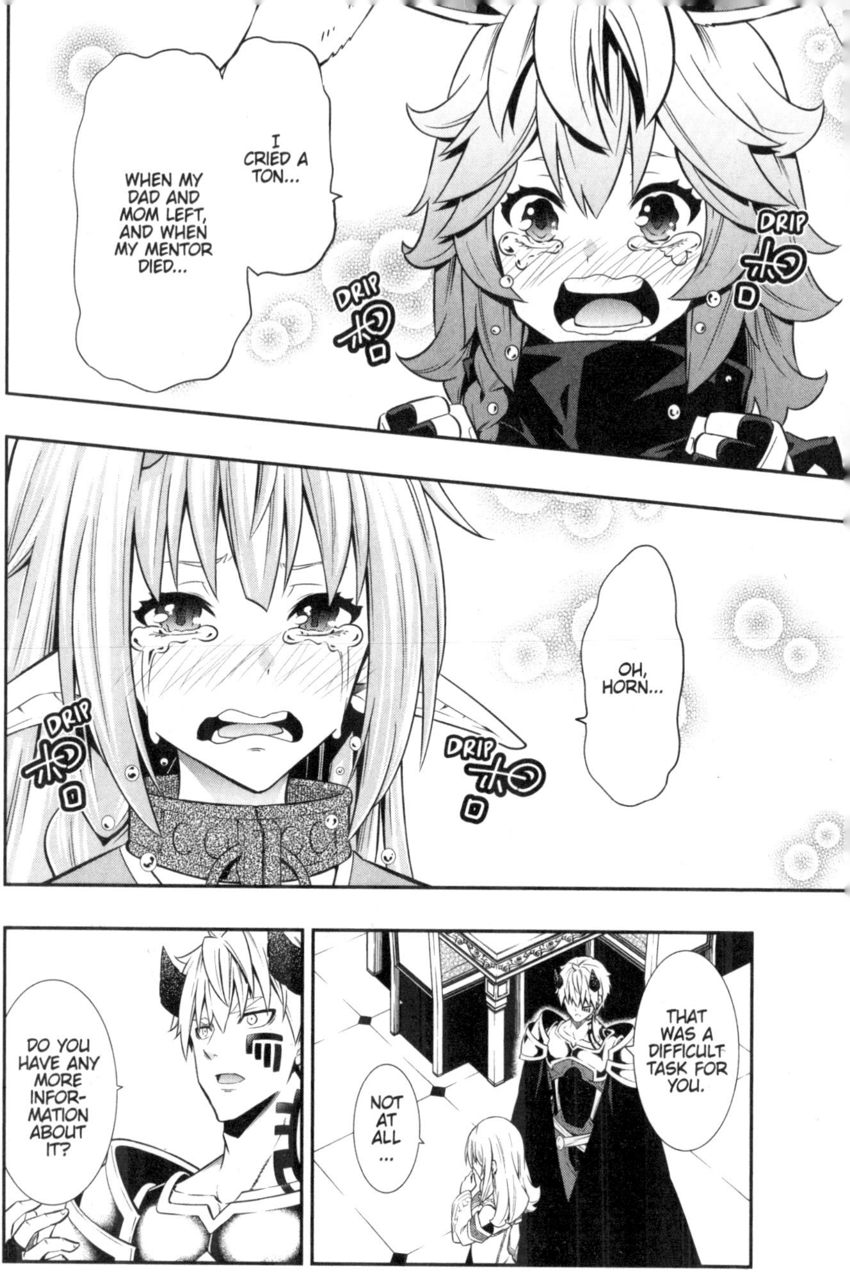
I CRIED A TON...
WHEN MY DAD AND MOM LEFT, AND WHEN MY MENTOR DIED...
DRIP
DRIP
OH, HORN...
DRIP
DRIP
THAT WAS A DIFFICULT TASK FOR YOU.
NOT AT ALL...
DO YOU HAVE ANY MORE INFOR-MATION ABOUT IT?

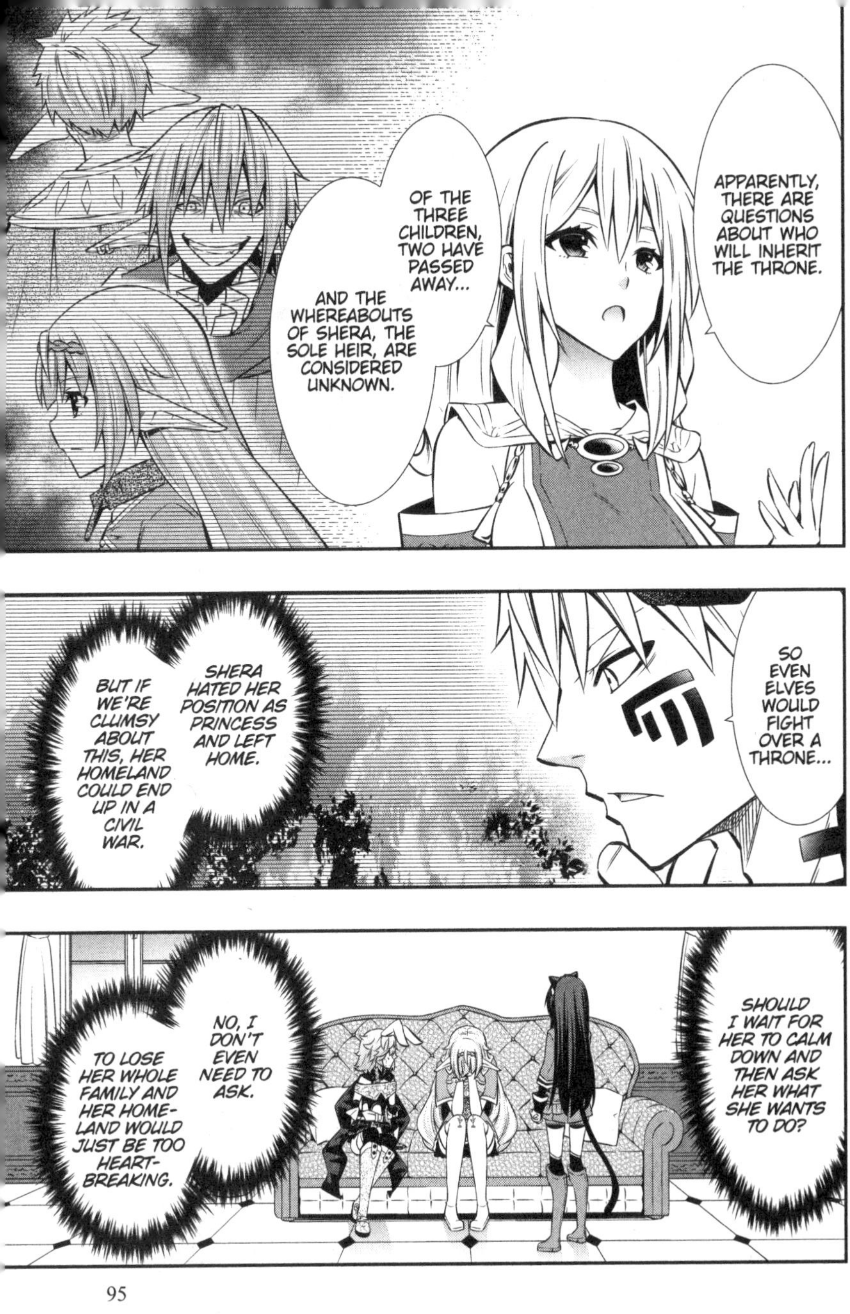
APPARENTLY, THERE ARE QUESTIONS ABOUT WHO WILL INHERIT THE THRONE.
OF THE THREE CHILDREN, TWO HAVE PASSED AWAY...
AND THE WHEREABOUTS OF SHERA, THE SOLE HEIR, ARE CONSIDERED UNKNOWN.
SO EVEN ELVES WOULD FIGHT OVER A THRONE...
SHERA HATED HER POSITION AS PRINCESS AND LEFT HOME.
BUT IF WE'RE CLUMSY ABOUT THIS, HER HOMELAND COULD END UP IN A CIVIL WAR.
SHOULD I WAIT FOR HER TO CALM DOWN AND THEN ASK HER WHAT SHE WANTS TO DO?
NO, I DON'T EVEN NEED TO ASK.
TO LOSE HER WHOLE FAMILY AND HER HOME-LAND WOULD JUST BE TOO HEART-BREAKING.

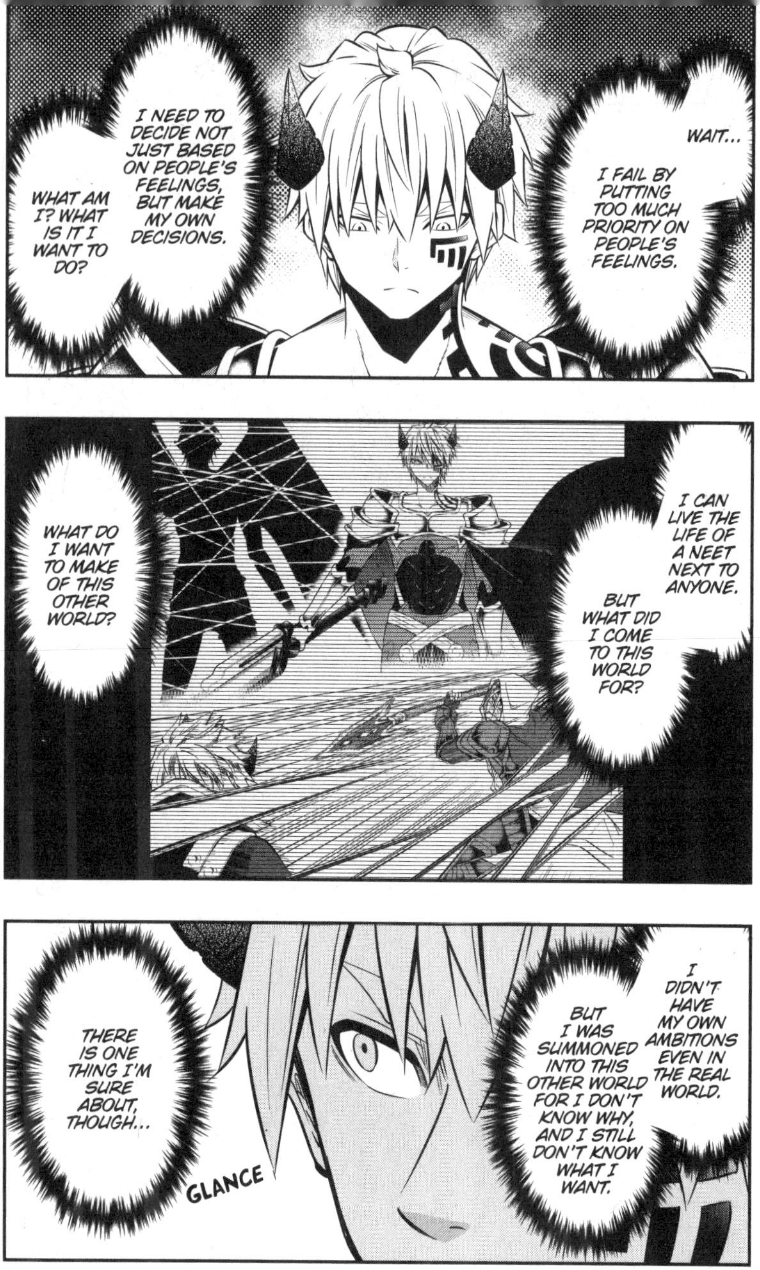
WAIT...
I FAIL BY PUTTING TOO MUCH PRIORITY ON PEOPLE'S FEELINGS.
I NEED TO DECIDE NOT JUST BASED ON PEOPLE'S FEELINGS, BUT MAKE MY OWN DECISIONS.
WHAT AM I? WHAT IS IT I WANT TO DO?
I CAN LIVE THE LIFE OF A NEET NEXT TO ANYONE.
BUT WHAT DID I COME TO THIS WORLD FOR?
WHAT DO I WANT TO MAKE OF THIS OTHER WORLD?
I DIDN'T HAVE MY OWN AMBITIONS EVEN IN THE REAL WORLD.
BUT I WAS SUMMONED INTO THIS OTHER WORLD FOR I DON'T KNOW WHY, AND I STILL DON'T KNOW WHAT I WANT.
THERE IS ONE THING I'M SURE ABOUT, THOUGH...
GLANCE

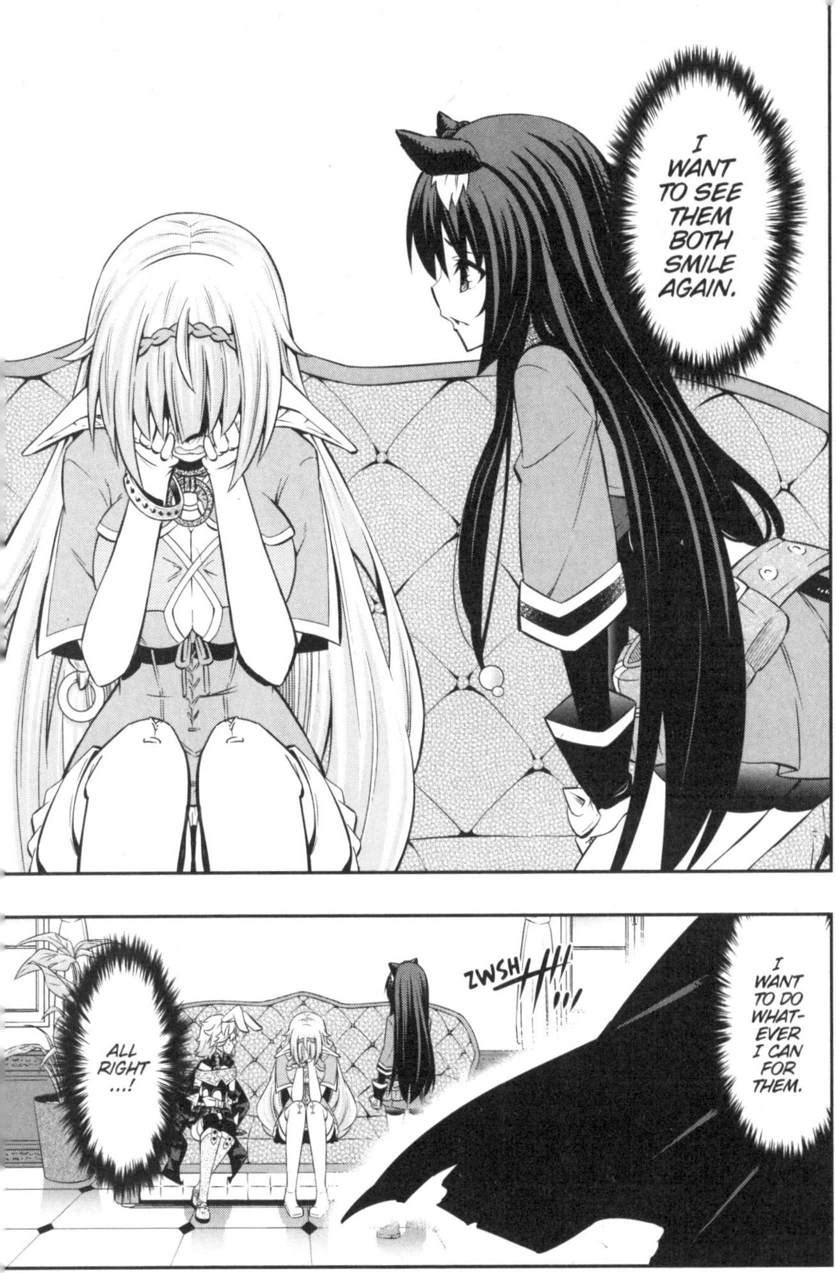
I WANT TO SEE THEM BOTH SMILE AGAIN.
I WANT TO DO WHATEVER I CAN FOR THEM.
ZWSH
ALL RIGHT ...!

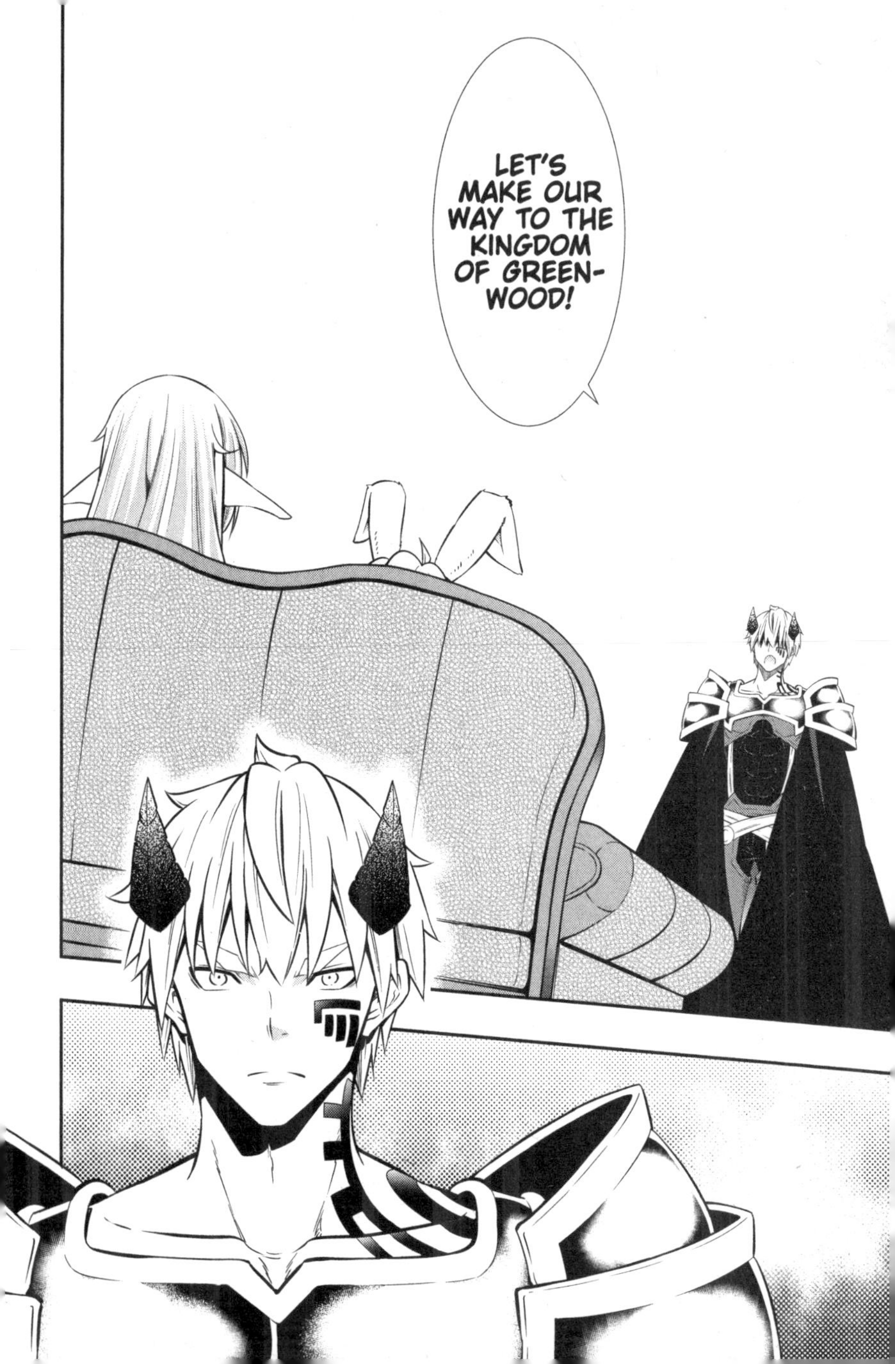
LET'S MAKE OUR WAY TO THE KINGDOM OF GREEN-WOOD!

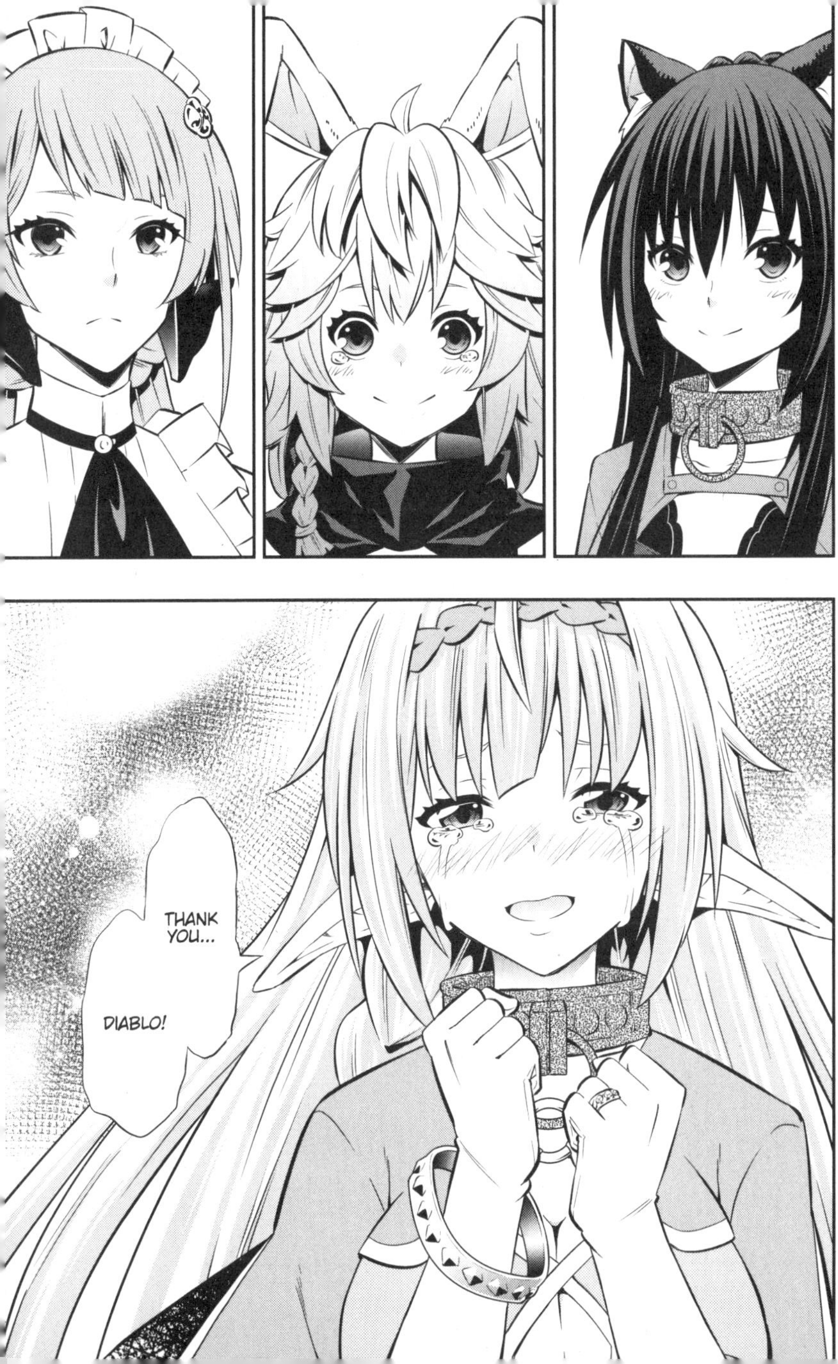
THANK YOU...
DIABLO!

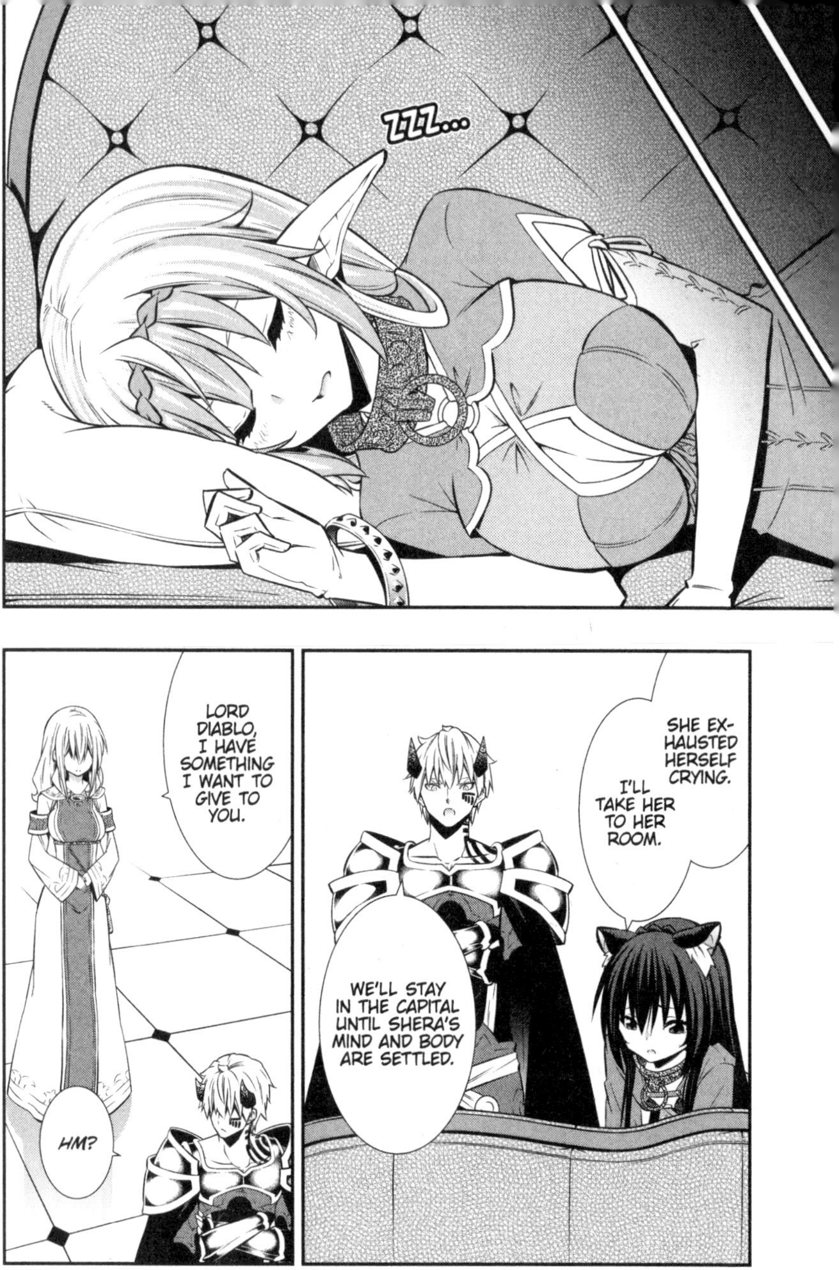
ZZZ...
SHE EX-HAUSTED HERSELF CRYING.
I'LL TAKE HER TO HER ROOM.
WE'LL STAY IN THE CAPITAL UNTIL SHERA'S MIND AND BODY ARE SETTLED.
LORD DIABLO, I HAVE SOMETHING I WANT TO GIVE TO YOU.
HM?

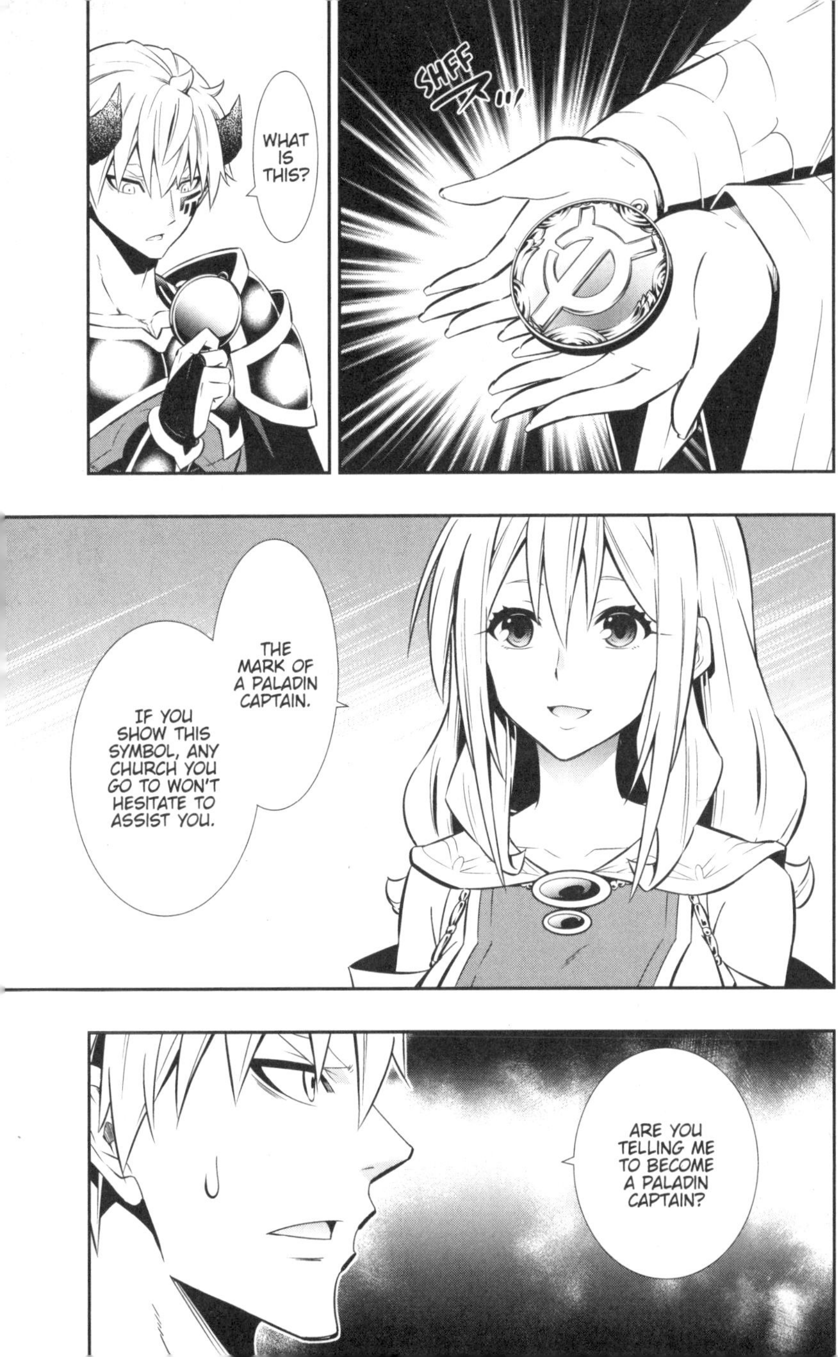
SHFF
WHAT IS THIS?
THE MARK OF A PALADIN CAPTAIN.
IF YOU SHOW THIS SYMBOL, ANY CHURCH YOU GO TO WON'T HESITATE TO ASSIST YOU.
ARE YOU TELLING ME TO BECOME A PALADIN CAPTAIN?

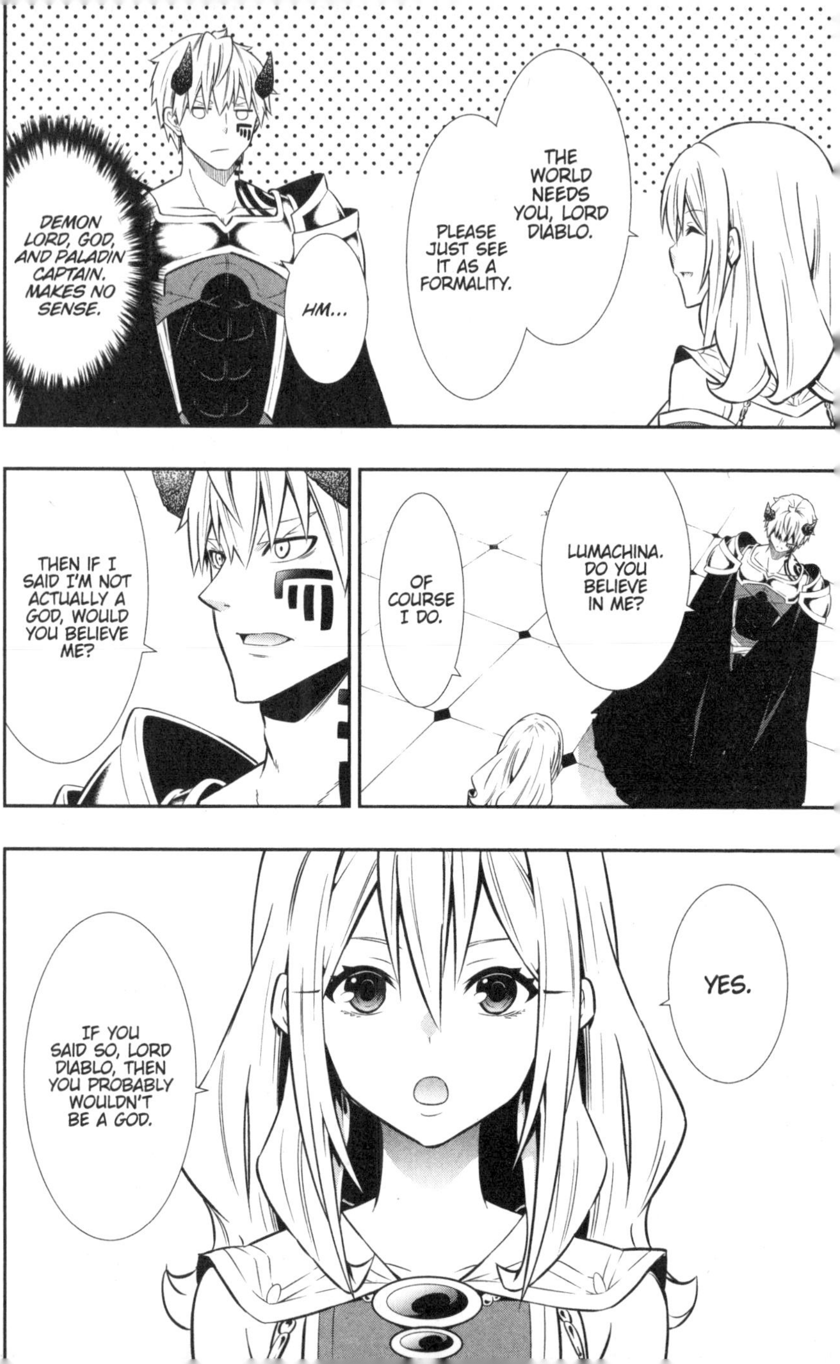
THE WORLD NEEDS YOU, LORD DIABLO.
PLEASE JUST SEE IT AS A FORMALITY.
HM...
DEMON LORD, GOD, AND PALADIN CAPTAIN. MAKES NO SENSE.
LUMACHINA. DO YOU BELIEVE IN ME?
OF COURSE I DO.
THEN IF I SAID I'M NOT ACTUALLY A GOD, WOULD YOU BELIEVE ME?
YES.
IF YOU SAID SO, LORD DIABLO, THEN YOU PROBABLY WOULDN'T BE A GOD.

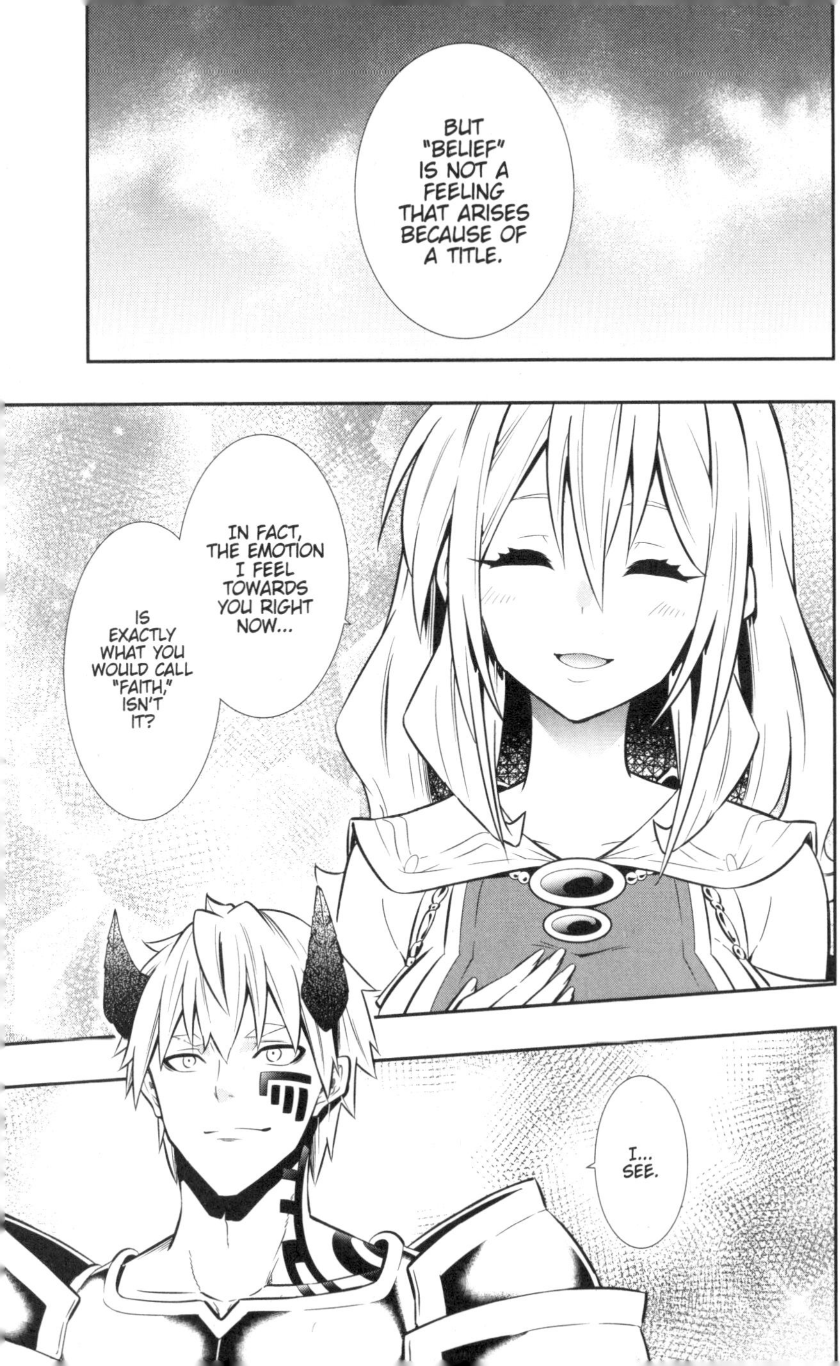
BUT "BELIEF" IS NOT A FEELING THAT ARISES BECAUSE OF A TITLE.
IN FACT, THE EMOTION I FEEL TOWARDS YOU RIGHT NOW...
IS EXACTLY WHAT YOU WOULD CALL "FAITH," ISN'T IT?
I... SEE.

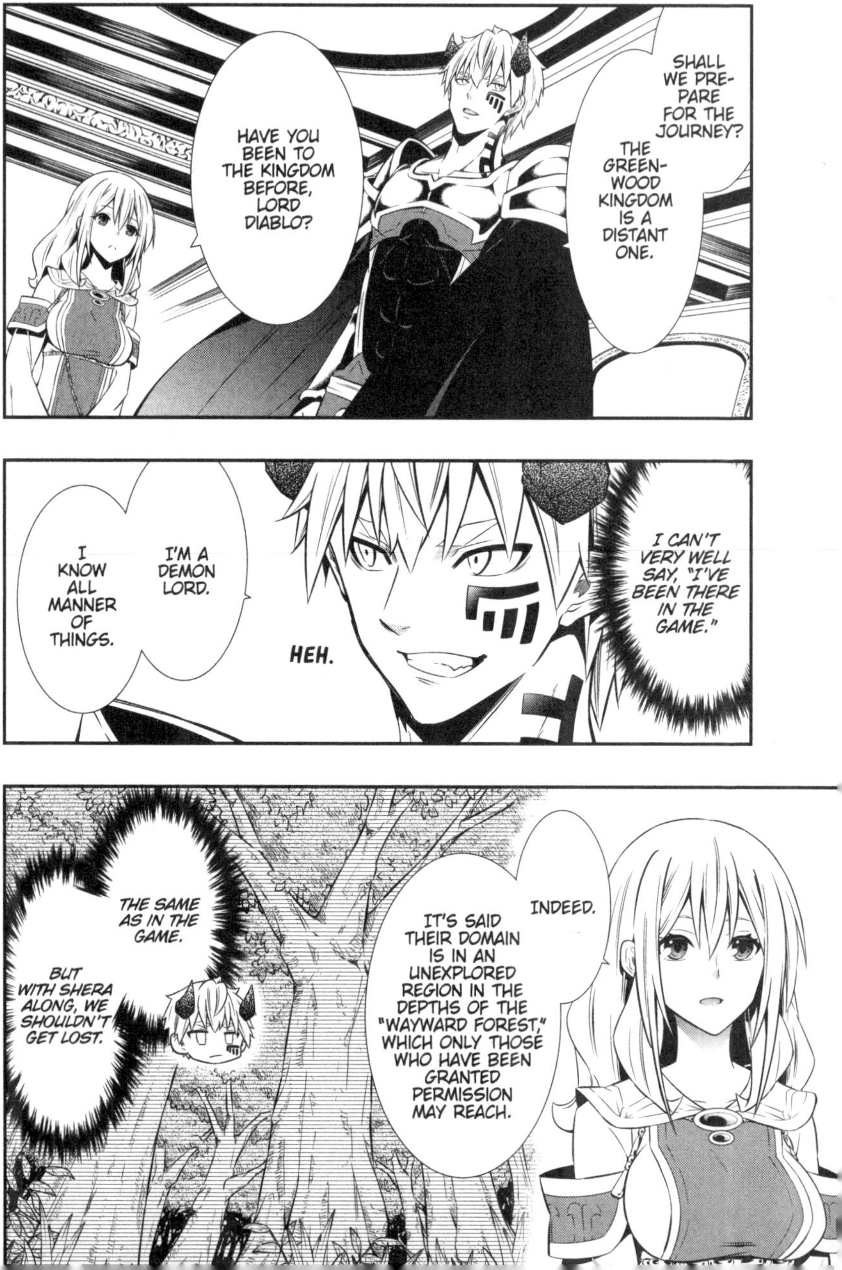
SHALL WE PRE-PARE FOR THE JOURNEY? THE GREEN-WOOD KINGDOM IS A DISTANT ONE.
HAVE YOU BEEN TO THE KINGDOM BEFORE, LORD DIABLO?
I CAN'T VERY WELL SAY, "I'VE BEEN THERE IN THE GAME."
HEH.
I'M A DEMON LORD.
I KNOW ALL MANNER OF THINGS.
INDEED.
IT'S SAID THEIR DOMAIN IS IN AN UNEXPLORED REGION IN THE DEPTHS OF THE "WAYWARD FOREST," WHICH ONLY THOSE WHO HAVE BEEN GRANTED PERMISSION MAY REACH.
THE SAME AS IN THE GAME.
BUT WITH SHERA ALONG, WE SHOULDN'T GET LOST.

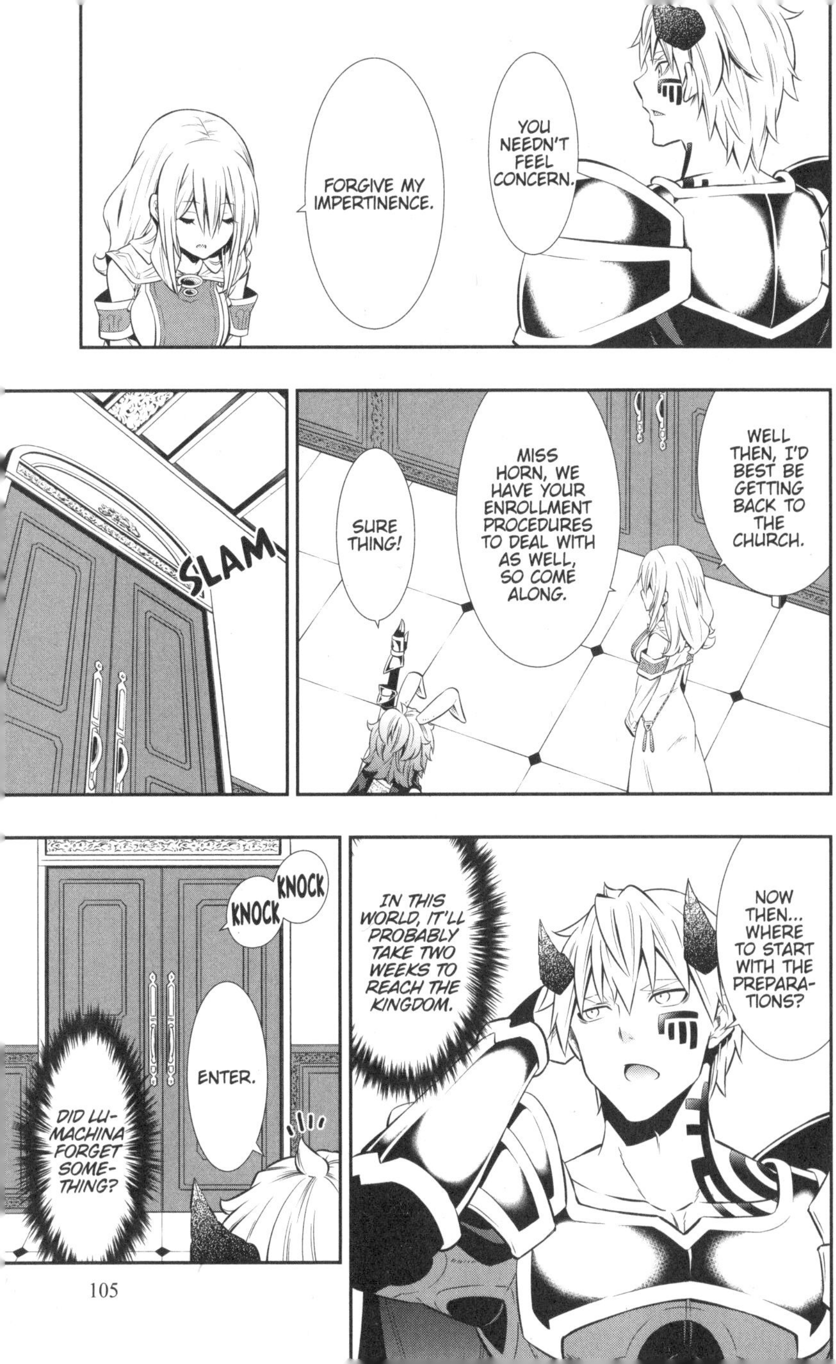
YOU NEEDN'T FEEL CONCERN.
FORGIVE MY IMPERTINENCE.
WELL THEN, I'D BEST BE GETTING BACK TO THE CHURCH.
MISS HORN, WE HAVE YOUR ENROLLMENT PROCEDURES TO DEAL WITH AS WELL, SO COME ALONG.
SURE THING!
SLAM
NOW THEN... WHERE TO START WITH THE PREPARATIONS?
IN THIS WORLD, IT'LL PROBABLY TAKE TWO WEEKS TO REACH THE KINGDOM.
KNOCK
KNOCK
ENTER.
DID LUMACHINA FORGET SOMETHING?

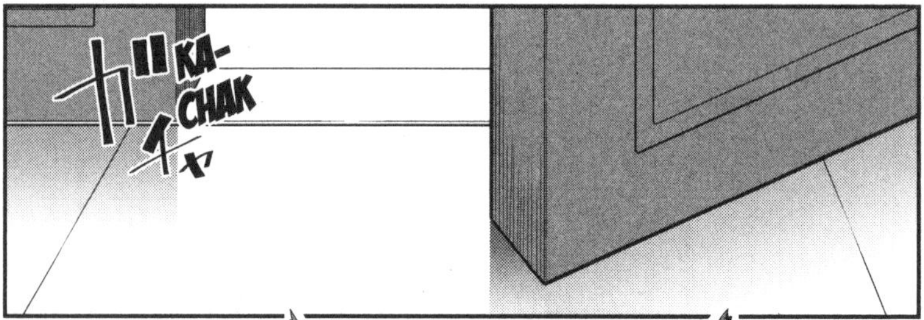
KA-CHAK

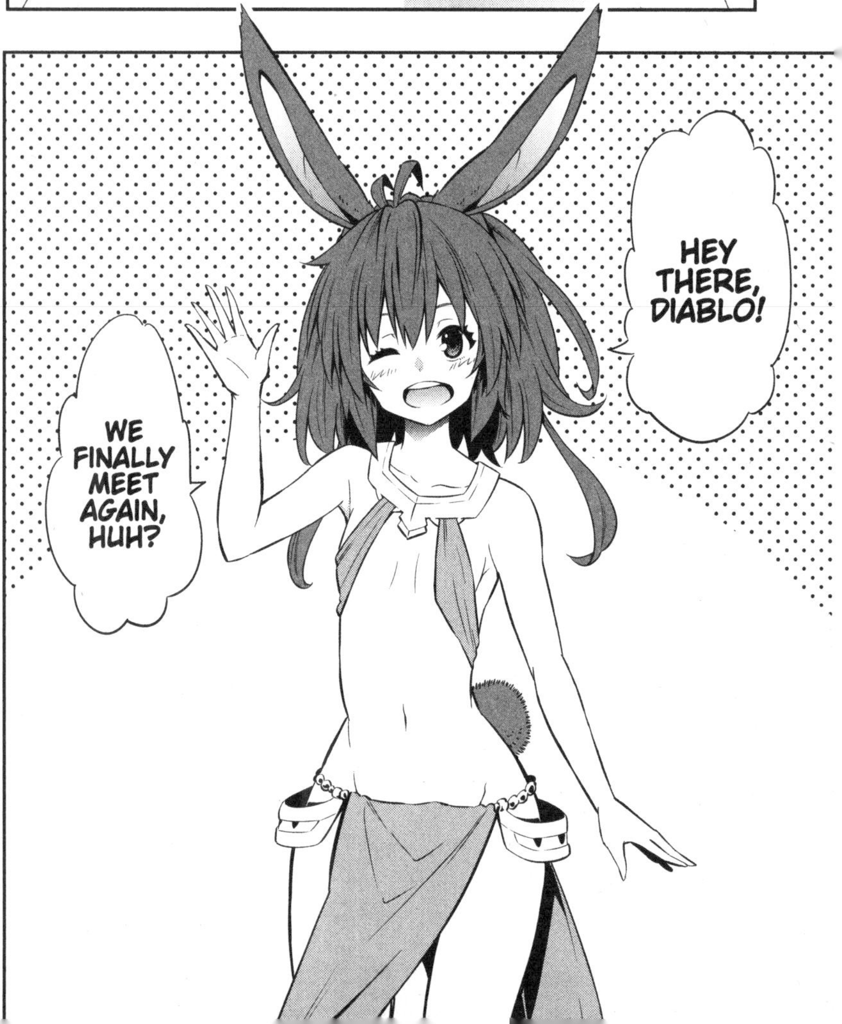
HEY THERE, DIABLO!
WE FINALLY MEET AGAIN, HUH?

HOW NOT
TO SUMMON A
DEMON LORD

73 SYLVIE, ONCE AGAIN

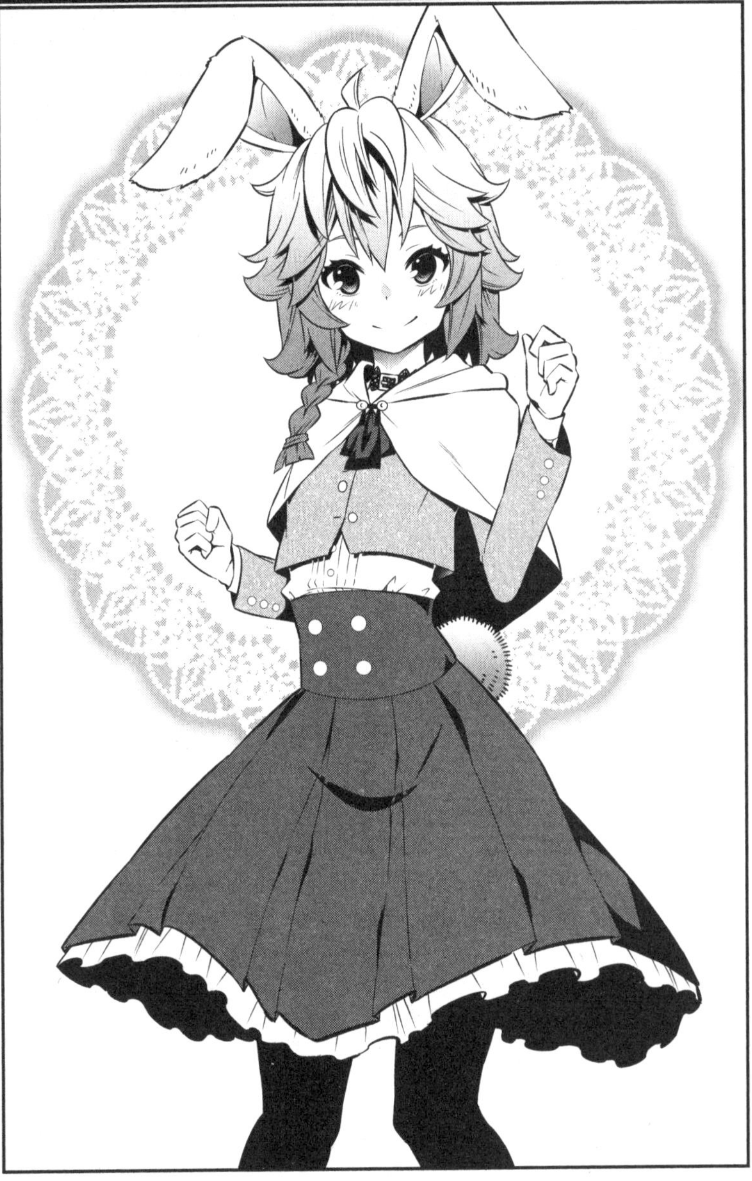

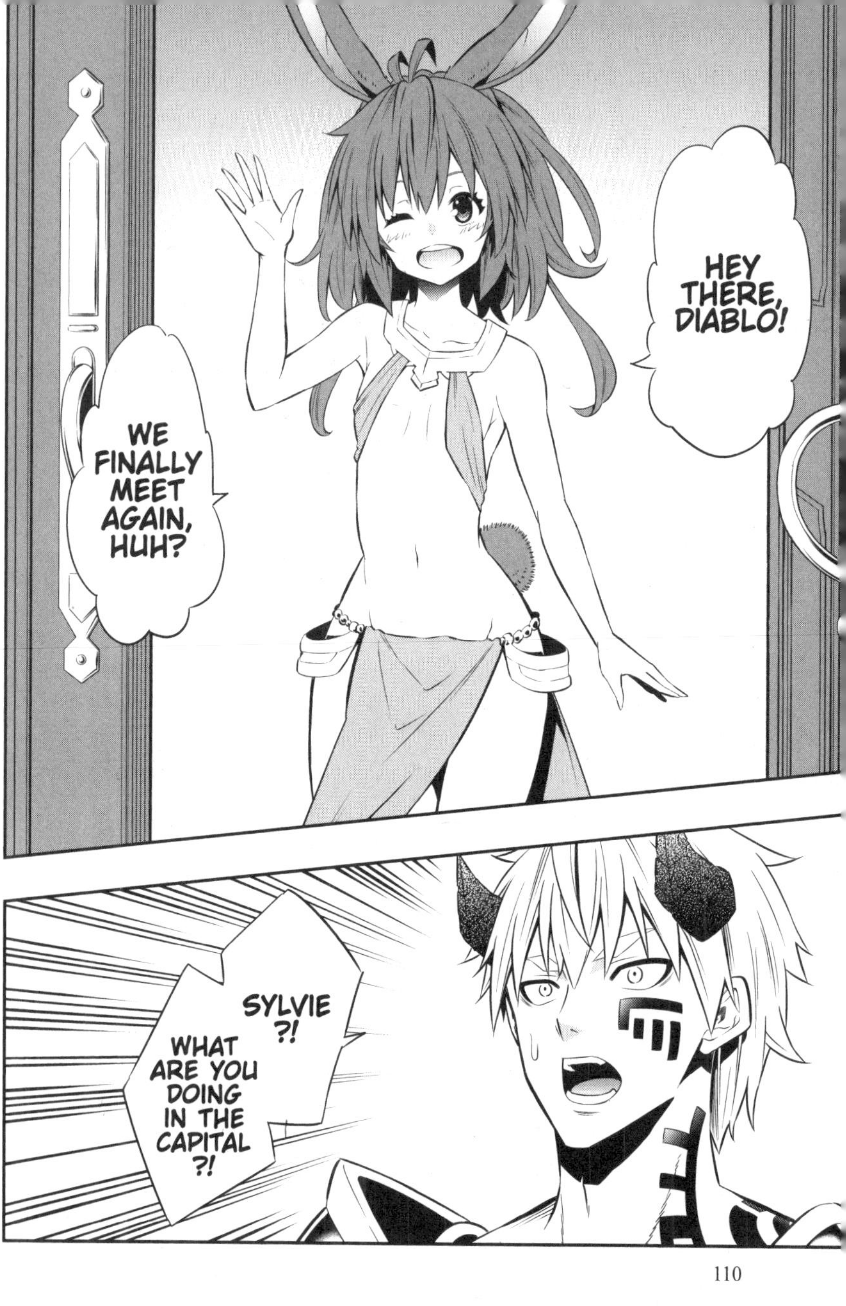
HEY THERE, DIABLO!
WE FINALLY MEET AGAIN, HUH?
SYLVIE?! WHAT ARE YOU DOING IN THE CAPITAL?!

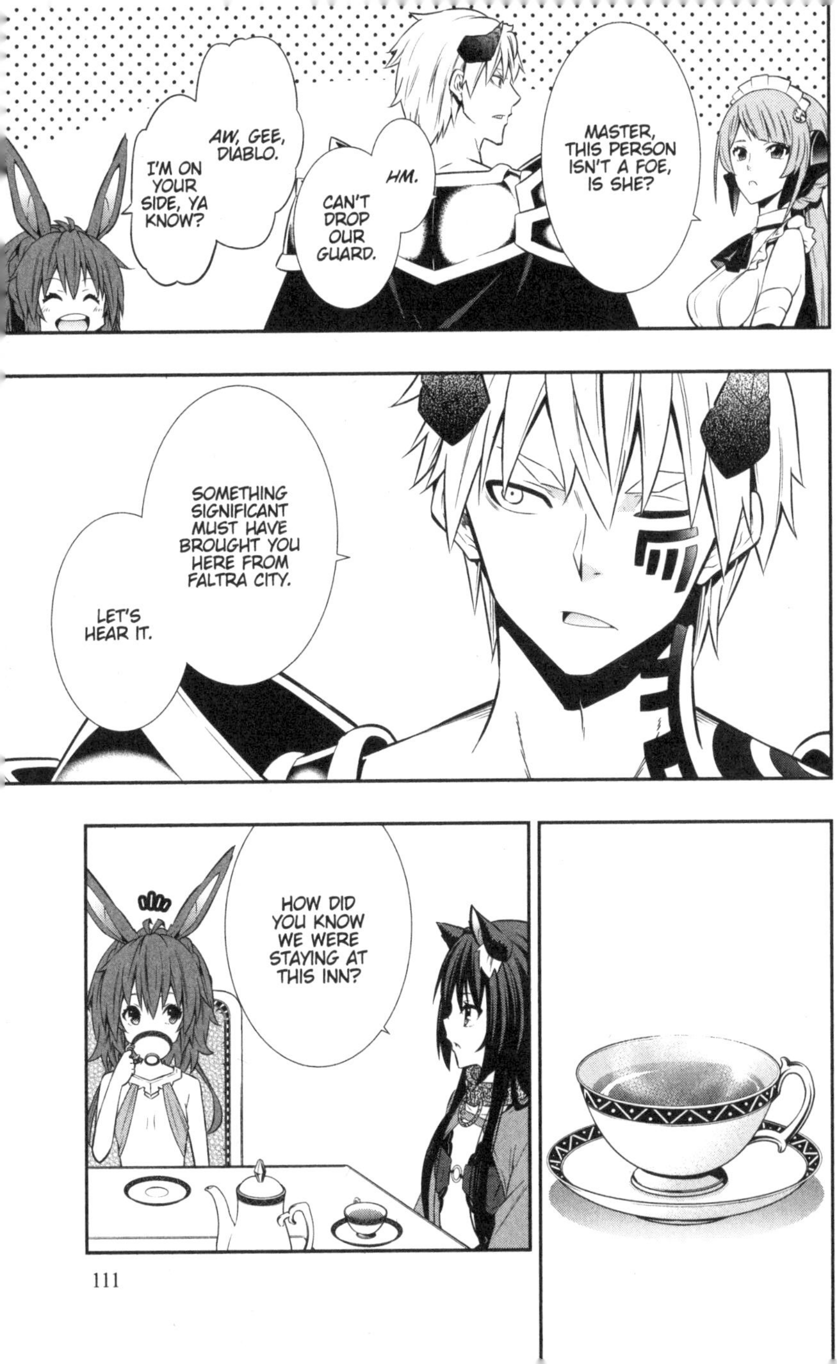
MASTER, THIS PERSON ISN'T A FOE, IS SHE?
HM.
CAN'T DROP OUR GUARD.
AW, GEE, DIABLO.
I'M ON YOUR SIDE, YA KNOW?
SOMETHING SIGNIFICANT MUST HAVE BROUGHT YOU HERE FROM FALTRA CITY.
LET'S HEAR IT.
HOW DID YOU KNOW WE WERE STAYING AT THIS INN?

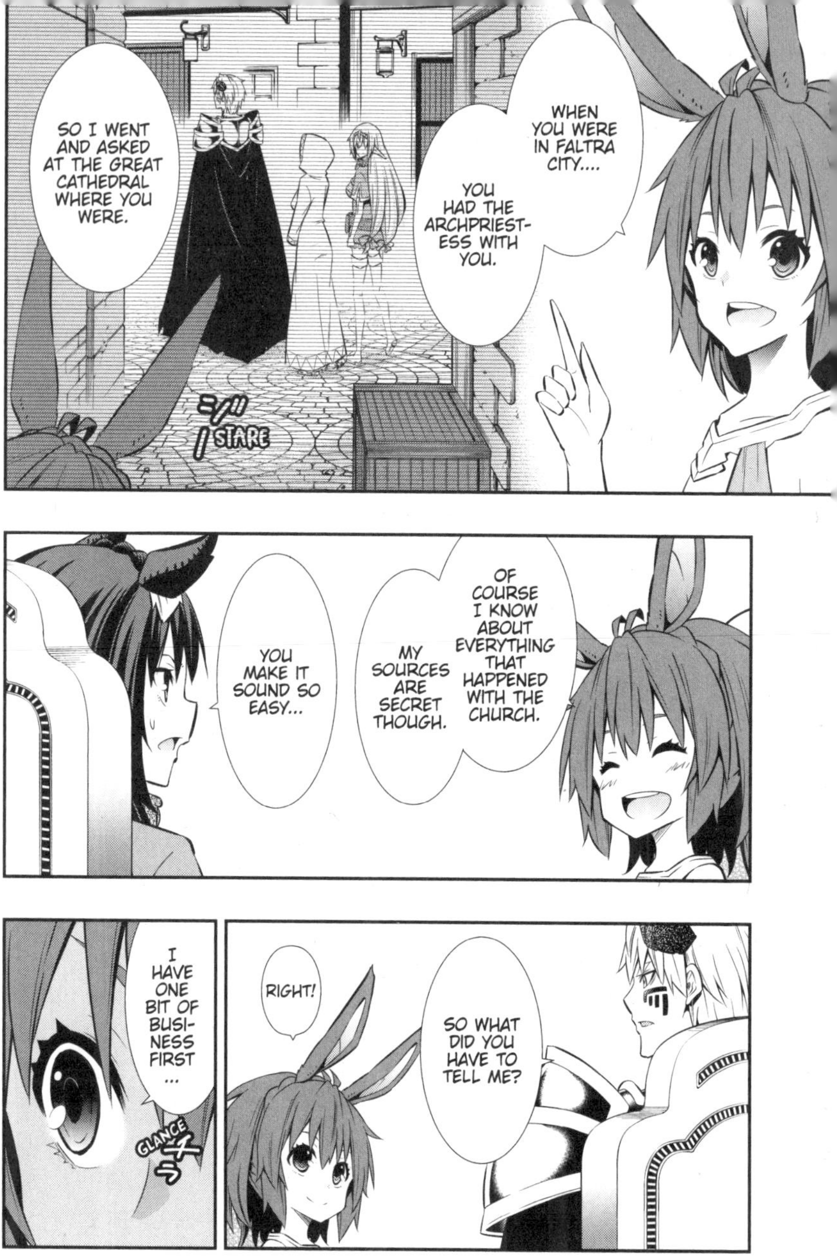
WHEN YOU WERE IN FALTRA CITY....
YOU HAD THE ARCHPRIEST-ESS WITH YOU.
SO I WENT AND ASKED AT THE GREAT CATHEDRAL WHERE YOU WERE.
STARE
OF COURSE I KNOW ABOUT EVERYTHING THAT HAPPENED WITH THE CHURCH.
MY SOURCES ARE SECRET THOUGH.
YOU MAKE IT SOUND SO EASY...
SO WHAT DID YOU HAVE TO TELL ME?
RIGHT!
I HAVE ONE BIT OF BUSI-NESS FIRST ...
GLANCE

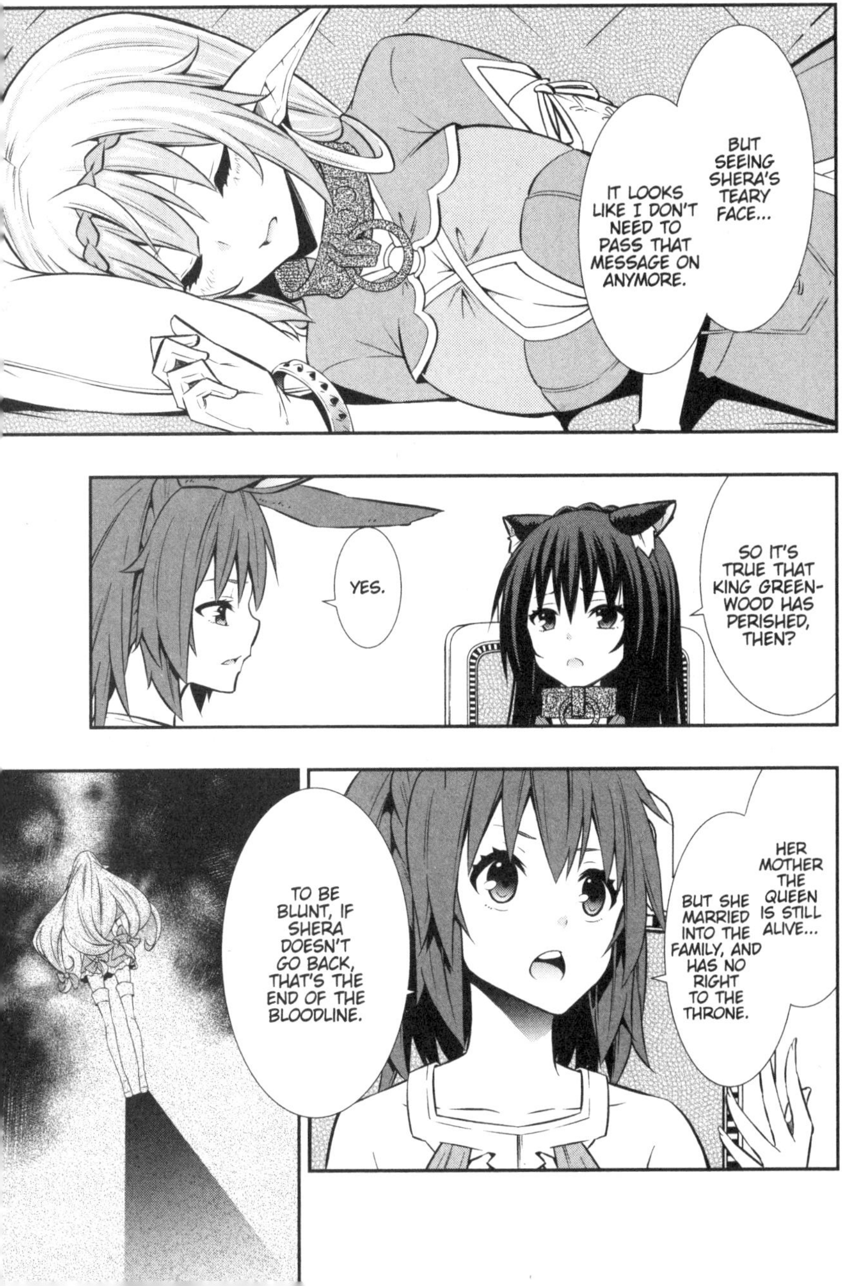
BUT SEEING SHERA'S TEARY FACE...
IT LOOKS LIKE I DON'T NEED TO PASS THAT MESSAGE ON ANYMORE.
SO IT'S TRUE THAT KING GREEN-WOOD HAS PERISHED, THEN?
YES.
HER MOTHER THE QUEEN IS STILL ALIVE...
BUT SHE MARRIED INTO THE FAMILY, AND HAS NO RIGHT TO THE THRONE.
TO BE BLUNT, IF SHERA DOESN'T GO BACK, THAT'S THE END OF THE BLOODLINE.

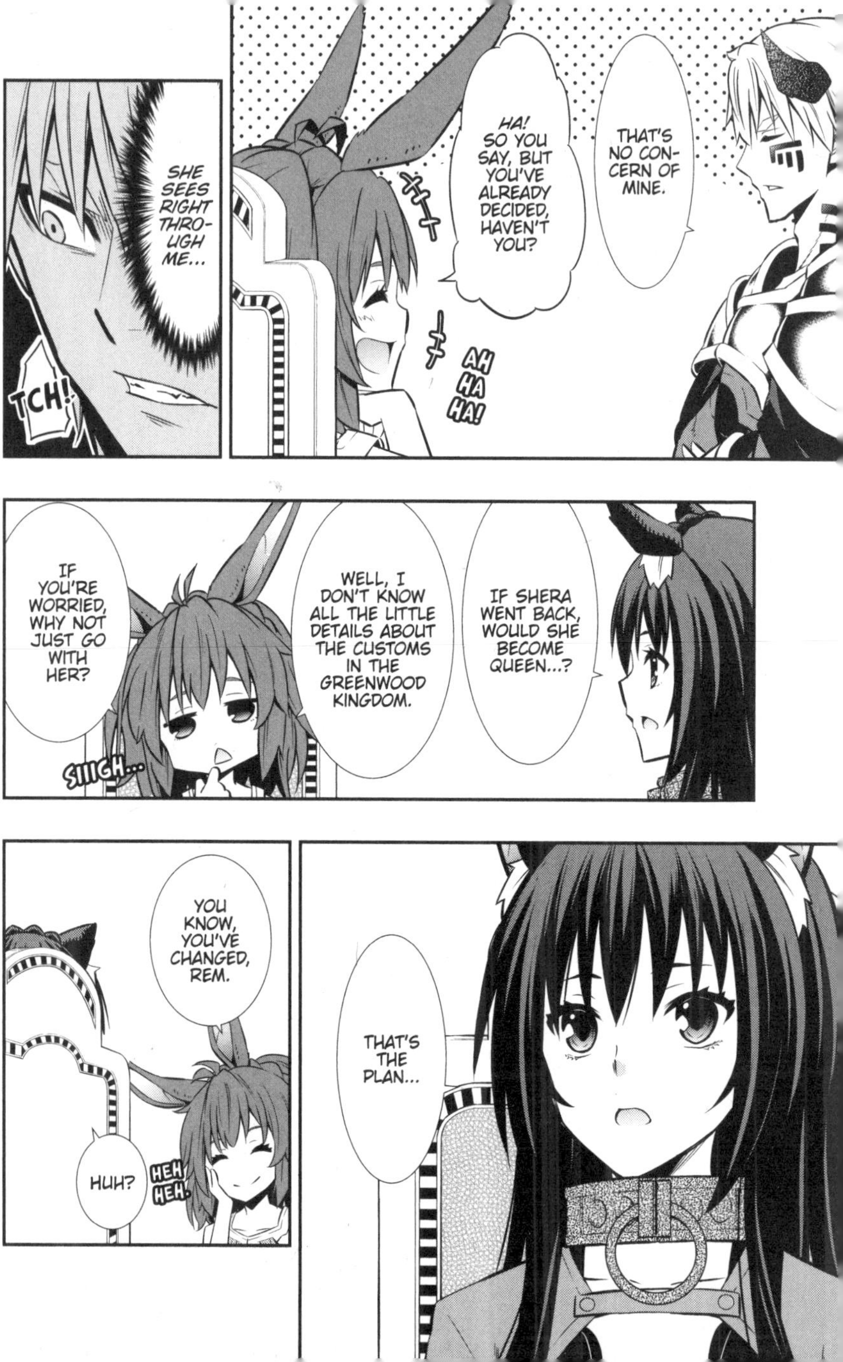
THAT'S NO CONCERN OF MINE.
HA! SO YOU SAY, BUT YOU'VE ALREADY DECIDED, HAVEN'T YOU?
AH HA HA!
SHE SEES RIGHT THROUGH ME...
TCH!
IF SHERA WENT BACK, WOULD SHE BECOME QUEEN...?
WELL, I DON'T KNOW ALL THE LITTLE DETAILS ABOUT THE CUSTOMS IN THE GREENWOOD KINGDOM.
IF YOU'RE WORRIED, WHY NOT JUST GO WITH HER?
SIIIGH...
THAT'S THE PLAN...
YOU KNOW, YOU'VE CHANGED, REM.
HUH?
HEH HEH.

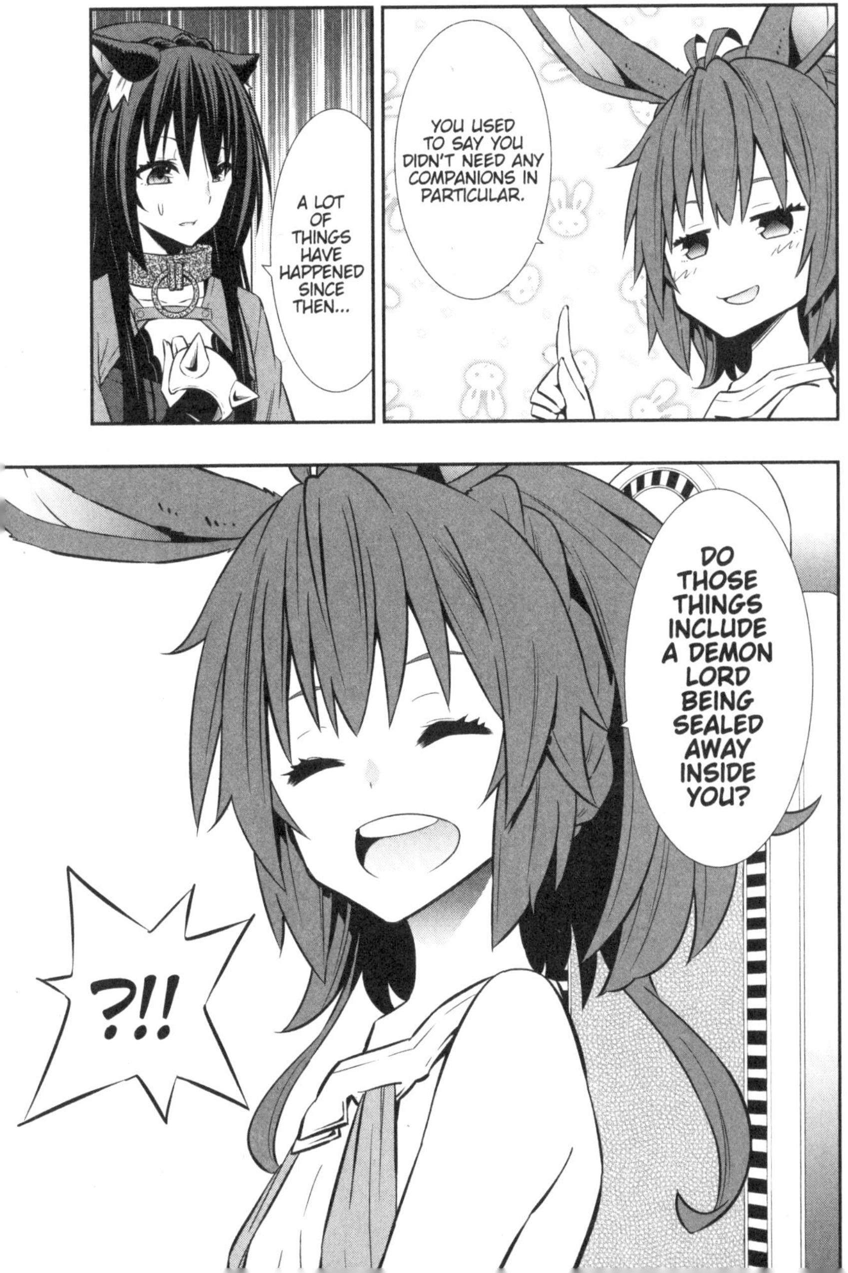

YOU USED TO SAY YOU DIDN'T NEED ANY COMPANIONS IN PARTICULAR.
A LOT OF THINGS HAVE HAPPENED SINCE THEN...
DO THOSE THINGS INCLUDE A DEMON LORD BEING SEALED AWAY INSIDE YOU?
?!!

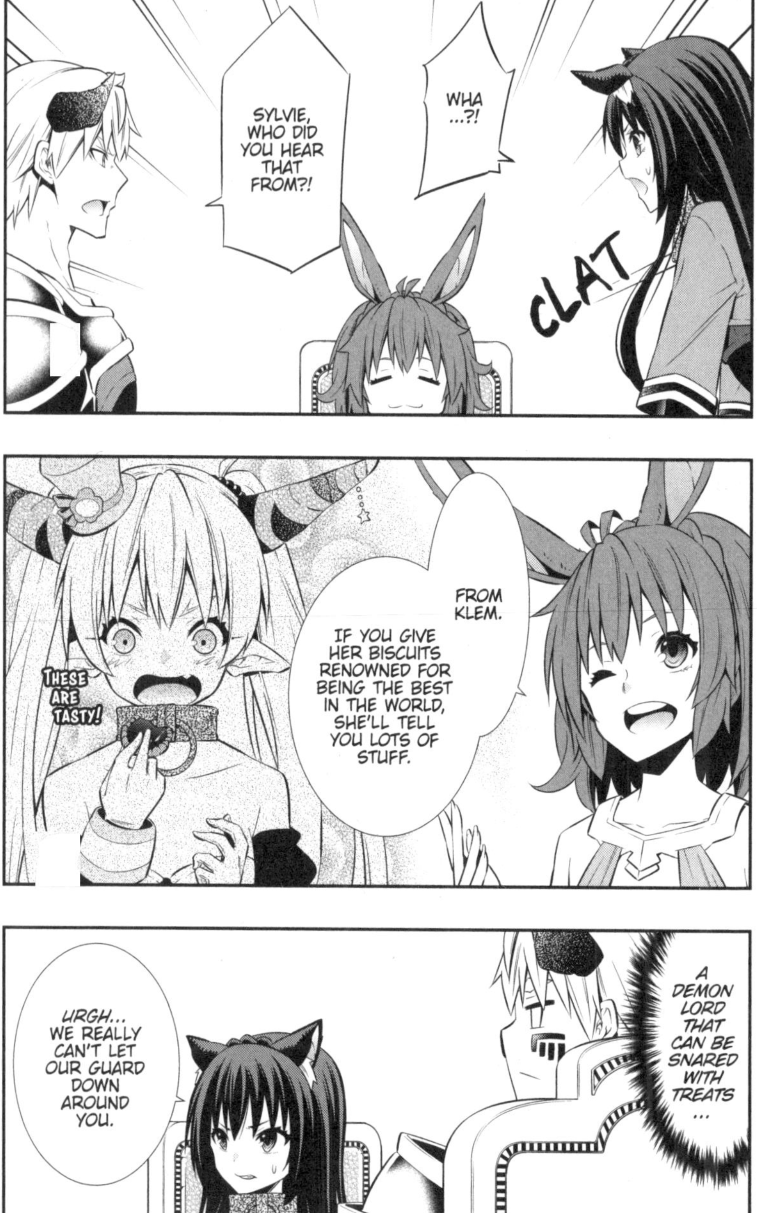
WHA ...?!
SYLVIE, WHO DID YOU HEAR THAT FROM?!
CLAT
FROM KLEM.
IF YOU GIVE HER BISCUITS RENOWNED FOR BEING THE BEST IN THE WORLD, SHE'LL TELL YOU LOTS OF STUFF.
THESE ARE TASTY!
A DEMON LORD THAT CAN BE SNARED WITH TREATS ...
URGH... WE REALLY CAN'T LET OUR GUARD DOWN AROUND YOU.

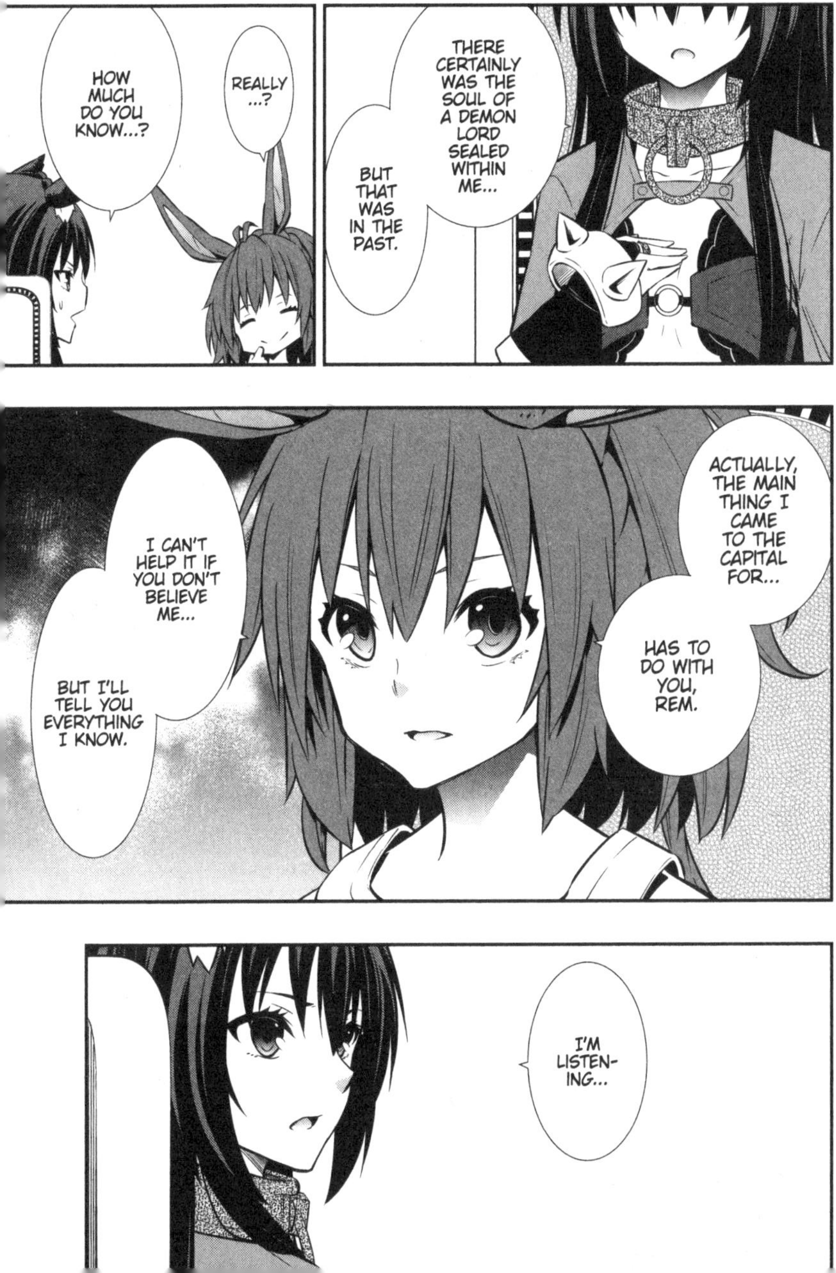
THERE CERTAINLY WAS THE SOUL OF A DEMON LORD SEALED WITHIN ME...
BUT THAT WAS IN THE PAST.
REALLY ...?
HOW MUCH DO YOU KNOW...?
ACTUALLY, THE MAIN THING I CAME TO THE CAPITAL FOR...
HAS TO DO WITH YOU, REM.
I CAN'T HELP IT IF YOU DON'T BELIEVE ME...
BUT I'LL TELL YOU EVERYTHING I KNOW.
I'M LISTEN-ING...

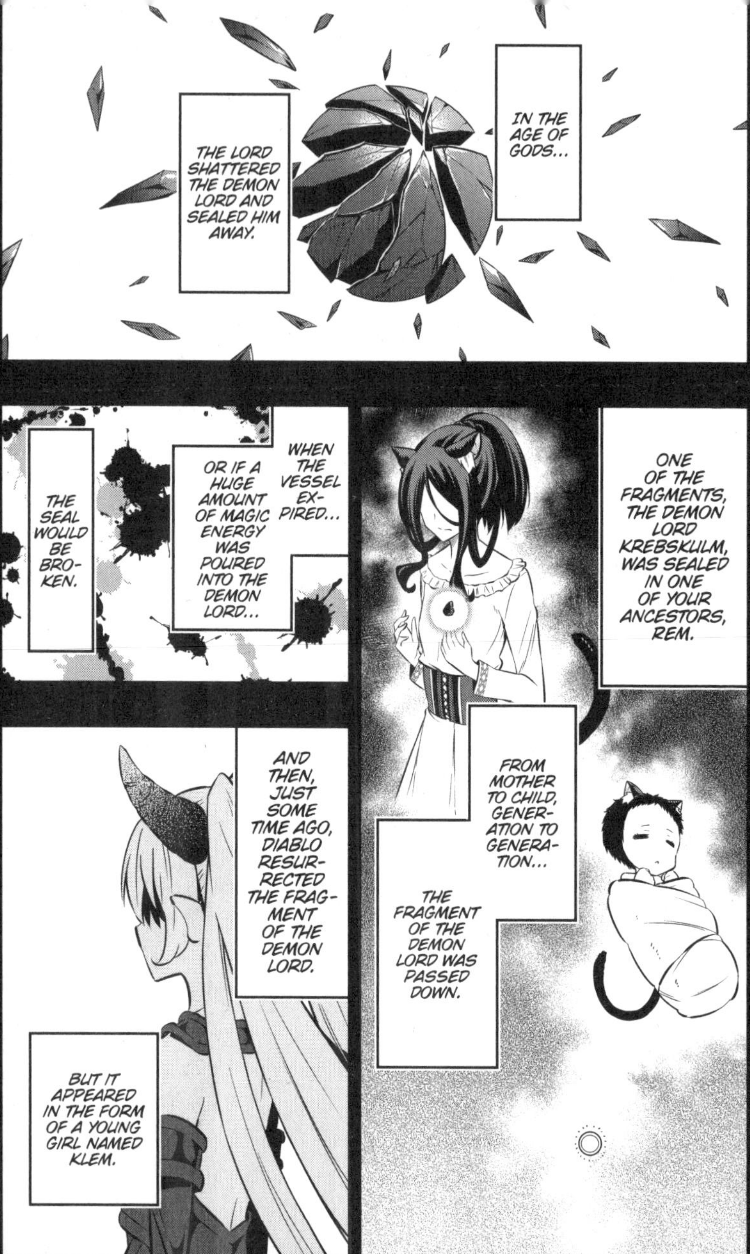

IN THE AGE OF GODS...
THE LORD SHATTERED THE DEMON LORD AND SEALED HIM AWAY.
ONE OF THE FRAGMENTS, THE DEMON LORD KREBSKULM, WAS SEALED IN ONE OF YOUR ANCESTORS, REM.
FROM MOTHER TO CHILD, GENERATION TO GENERATION...
THE FRAGMENT OF THE DEMON LORD WAS PASSED DOWN.
WHEN THE VESSEL EXPIRED...
OR IF A HUGE AMOUNT OF MAGIC ENERGY WAS POURED INTO THE DEMON LORD...
THE SEAL WOULD BE BROKEN.
AND THEN, JUST SOME TIME AGO, DIABLO RESURRECTED THE FRAGMENT OF THE DEMON LORD.
BUT IT APPEARED IN THE FORM OF A YOUNG GIRL NAMED KLEM.

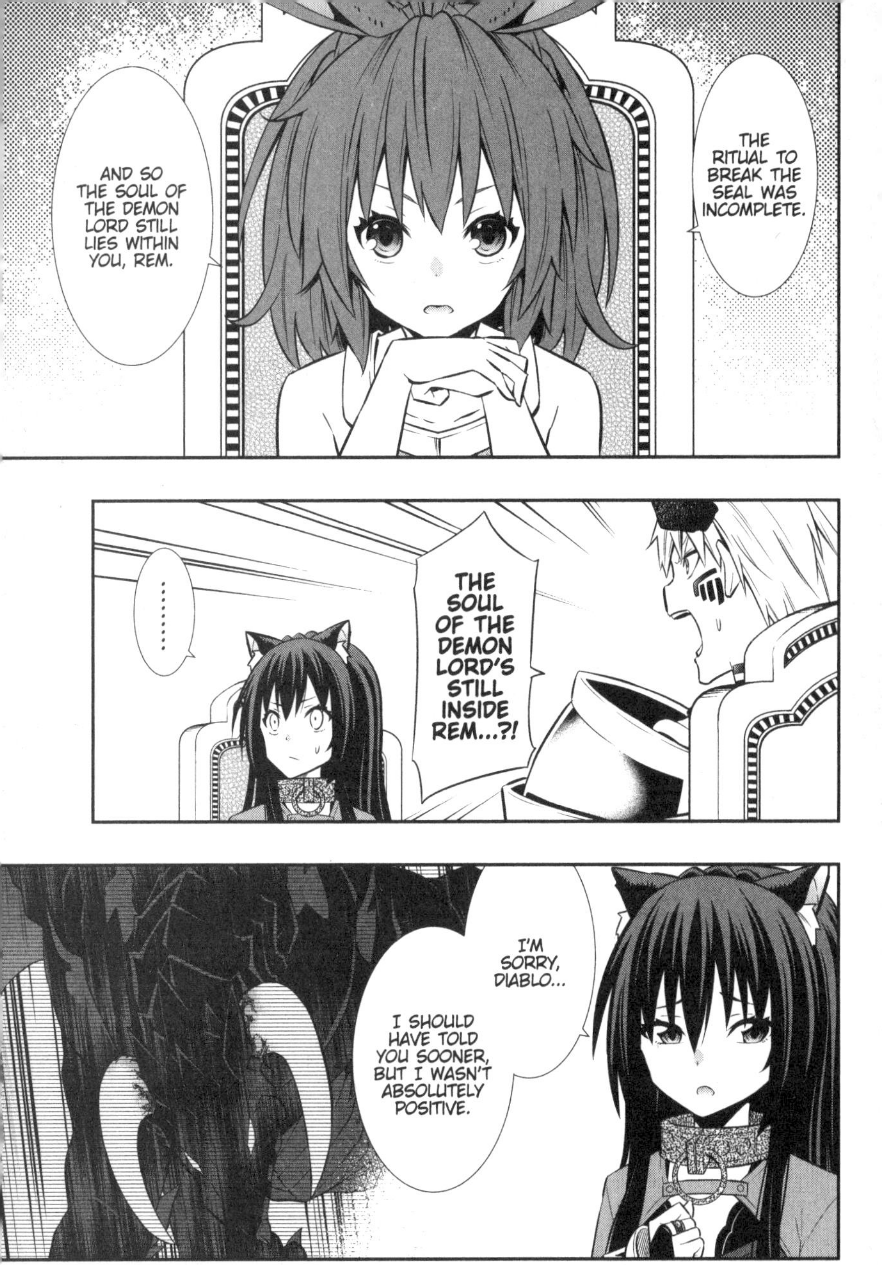
THE RITUAL TO BREAK THE SEAL WAS INCOMPLETE.
AND SO THE SOUL OF THE DEMON LORD STILL LIES WITHIN YOU, REM.
THE SOUL OF THE DEMON LORD'S STILL INSIDE REM...?!
....
I'M SORRY, DIABLO...
I SHOULD HAVE TOLD YOU SOONER, BUT I WASN'T ABSOLUTELY POSITIVE.

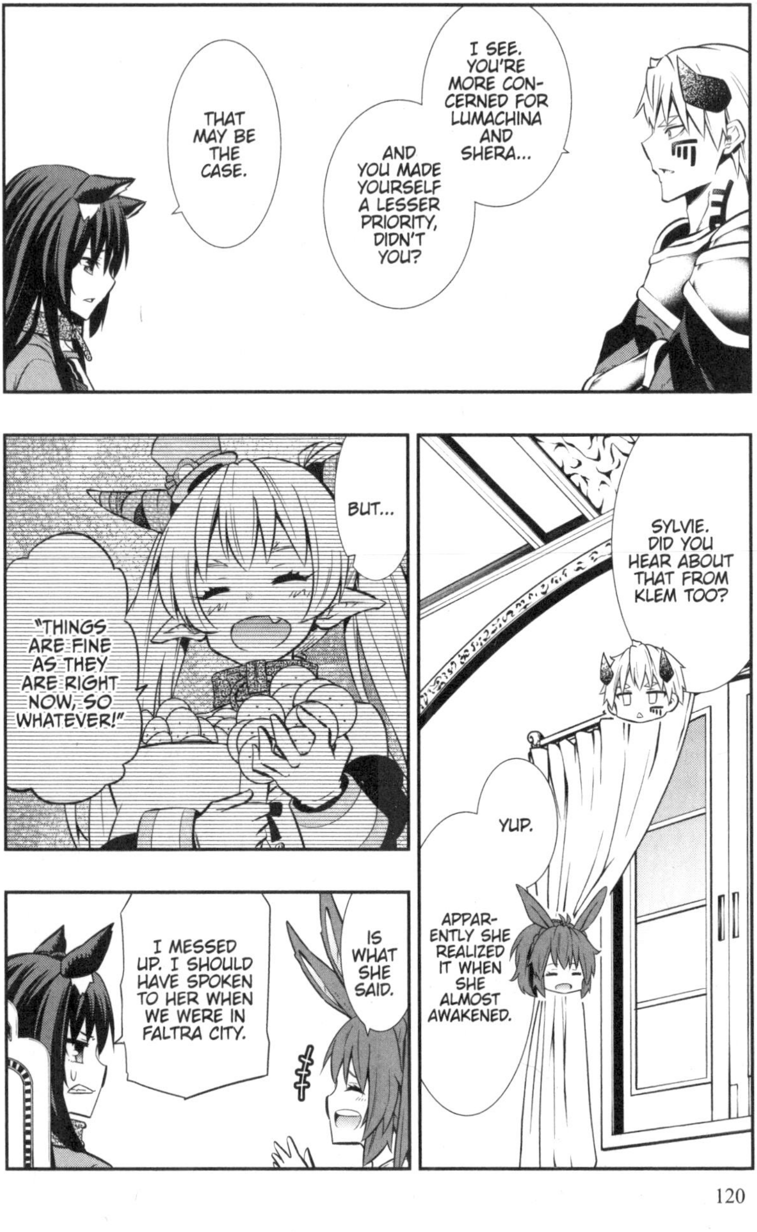
I SEE. YOU'RE MORE CON-CERNED FOR LUMACHINA AND SHERA...
AND YOU MADE YOURSELF A LESSER PRIORITY, DIDN'T YOU?
THAT MAY BE THE CASE.
SYLVIE. DID YOU HEAR ABOUT THAT FROM KLEM TOO?
YUP.
APPAR-ENTLY SHE REALIZED IT WHEN SHE ALMOST AWAKENED.
BUT...
"THINGS ARE FINE AS THEY ARE RIGHT NOW, SO WHATEVER!"
IS WHAT SHE SAID.
I MESSED UP. I SHOULD HAVE SPOKEN TO HER WHEN WE WERE IN FALTRA CITY.

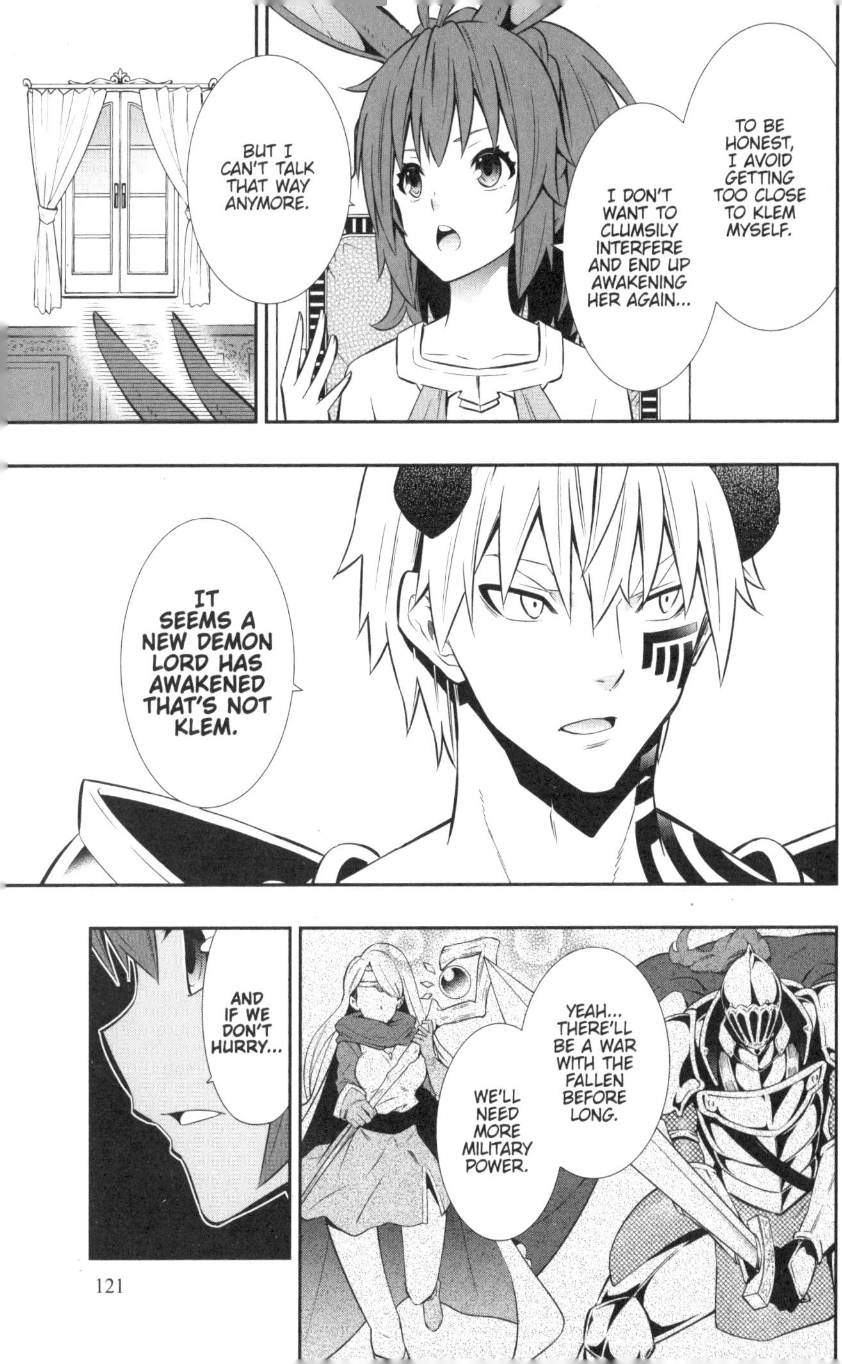
TO BE HONEST, I AVOID GETTING TOO CLOSE TO KLEM MYSELF.
I DON'T WANT TO CLUMSILY INTERFERE AND END UP AWAKENING HER AGAIN...
BUT I CAN'T TALK THAT WAY ANYMORE.
IT SEEMS A NEW DEMON LORD HAS AWAKENED THAT'S NOT KLEM.
YEAH... THERE'LL BE A WAR WITH THE FALLEN BEFORE LONG.
WE'LL NEED MORE MILITARY POWER.
AND IF WE DON'T HURRY...

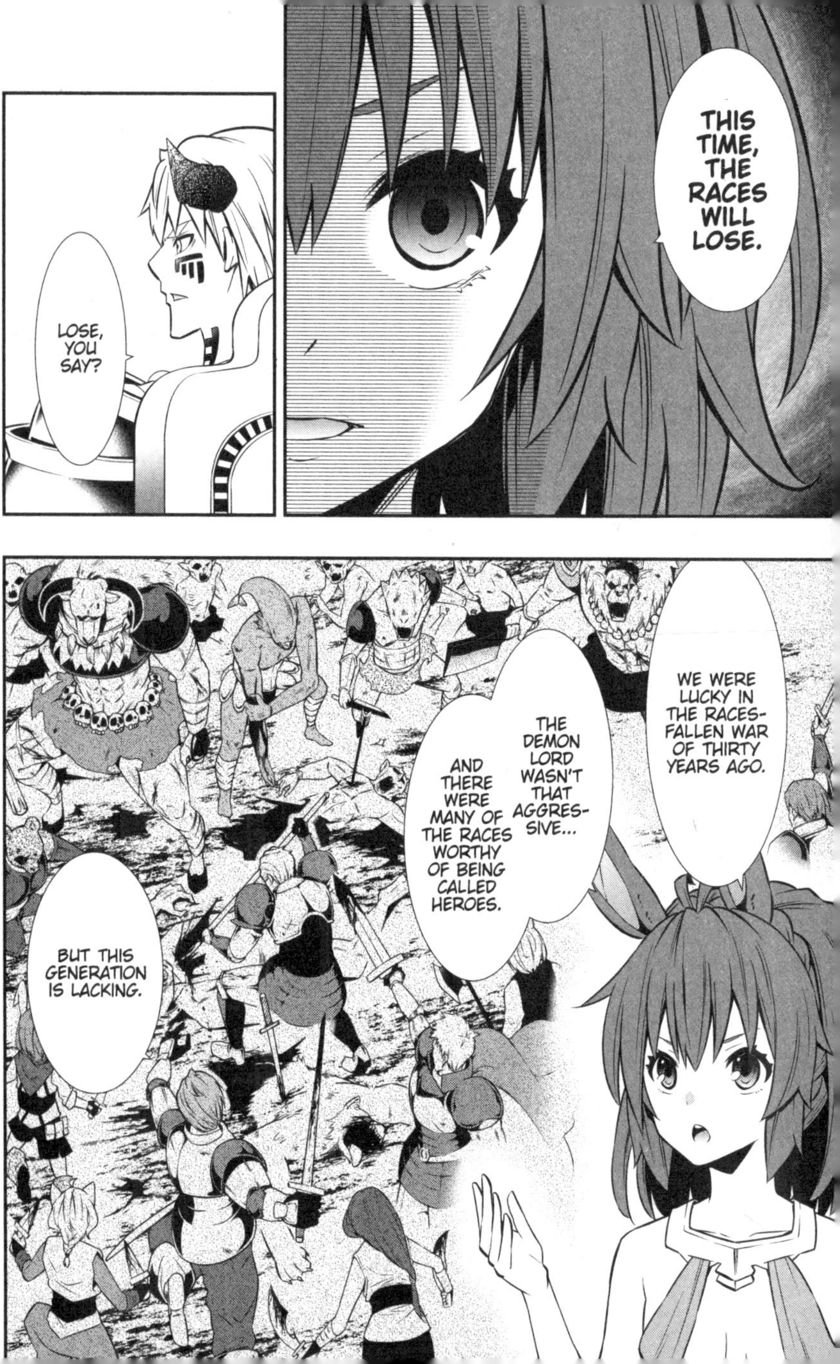
THIS TIME, THE RACES WILL LOSE.
LOSE, YOU SAY?
WE WERE LUCKY IN THE RACES-FALLEN WAR OF THIRTY YEARS AGO.
THE DEMON LORD WASN'T THAT AGGRES-SIVE...
AND THERE WERE MANY OF THE RACES WORTHY OF BEING CALLED HEROES.
BUT THIS GENERATION IS LACKING.

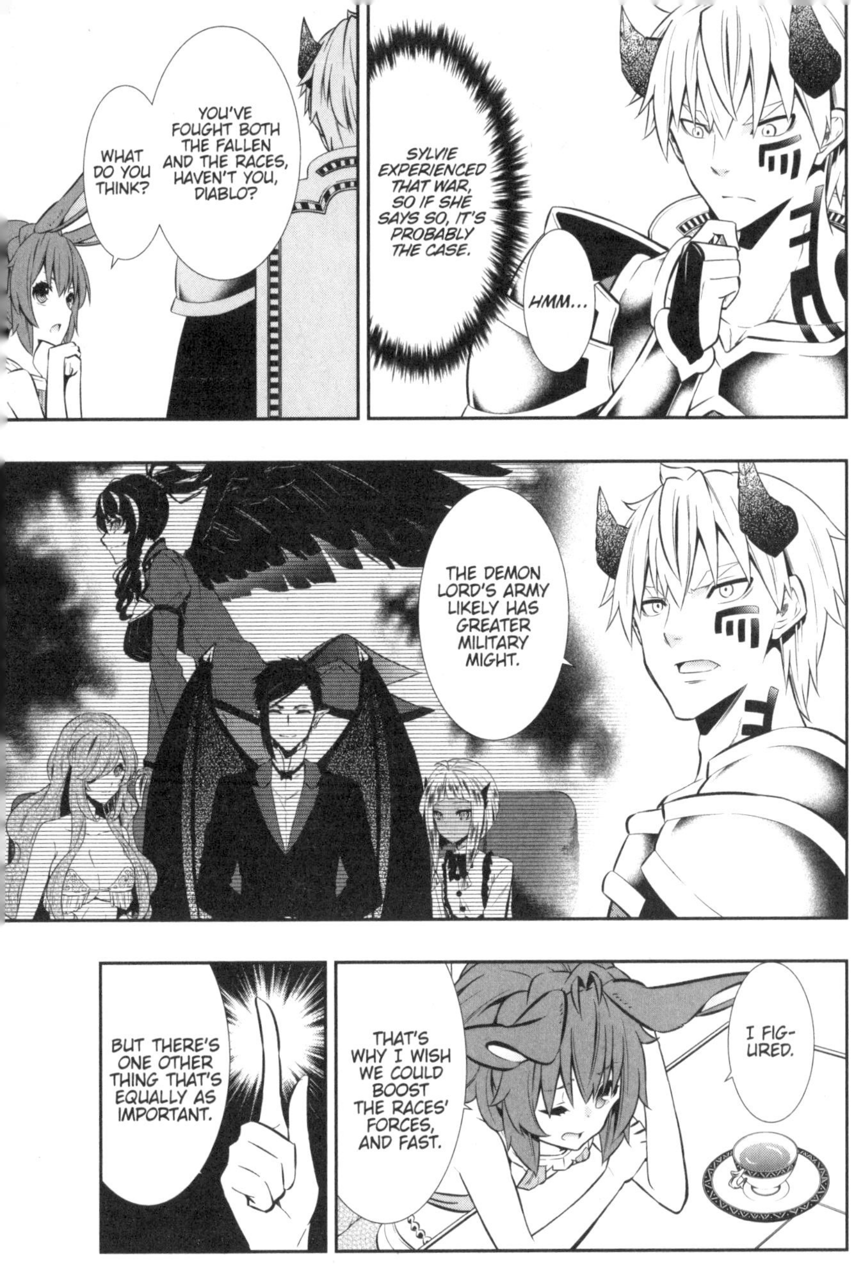
YOU'VE FOUGHT BOTH THE FALLEN AND THE RACES, HAVEN'T YOU, DIABLO?
WHAT DO YOU THINK?
HMM...
SYLVIE EXPERIENCED THAT WAR, SO IF SHE SAYS SO, IT'S PROBABLY THE CASE.
THE DEMON LORD'S ARMY LIKELY HAS GREATER MILITARY MIGHT.
I FIG-URED.
THAT'S WHY I WISH WE COULD BOOST THE RACES' FORCES, AND FAST.
BUT THERE'S ONE OTHER THING THAT'S EQUALLY AS IMPORTANT.

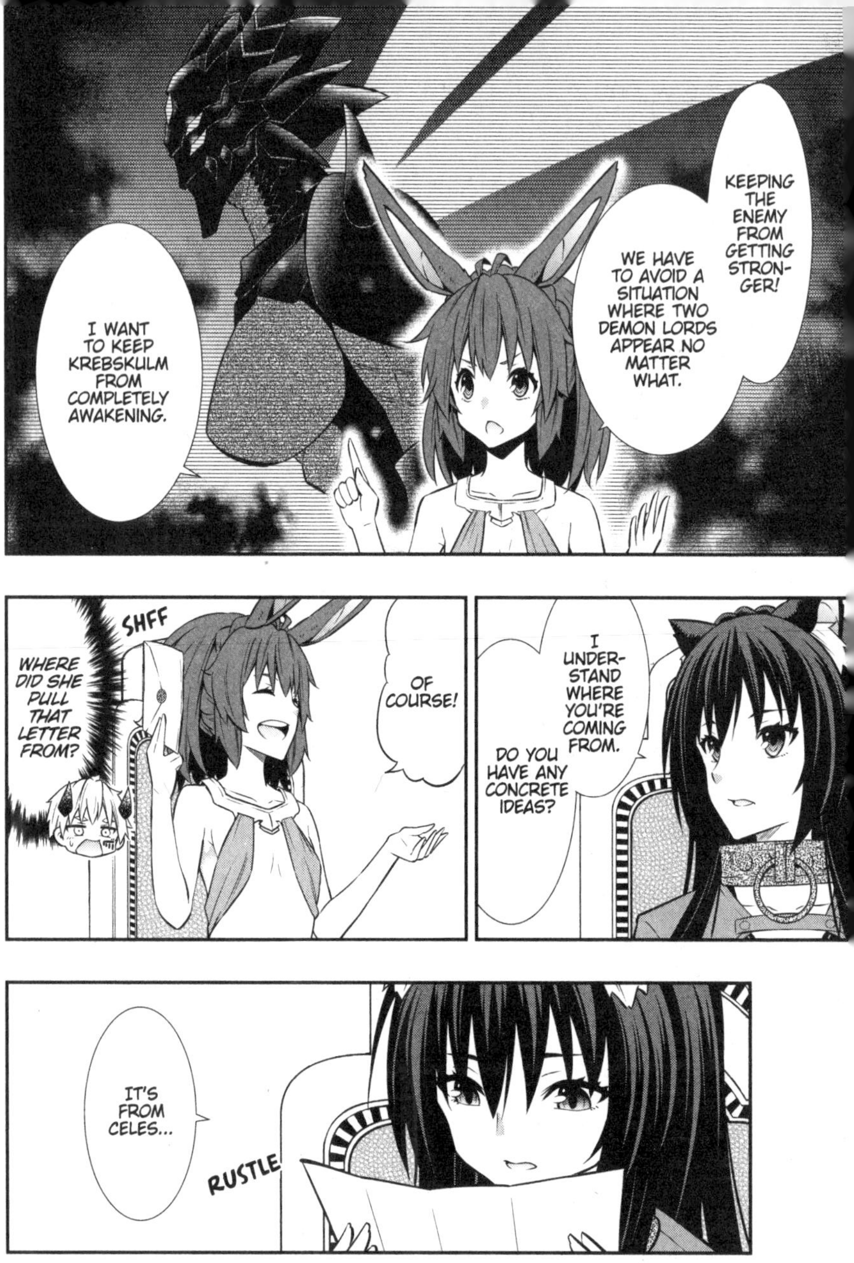
KEEPING THE ENEMY FROM GETTING STRONGER!
WE HAVE TO AVOID A SITUATION WHERE TWO DEMON LORDS APPEAR NO MATTER WHAT.
I WANT TO KEEP KREBSKULM FROM COMPLETELY AWAKENING.
I UNDERSTAND WHERE YOU'RE COMING FROM.
DO YOU HAVE ANY CONCRETE IDEAS?
OF COURSE!
SHFF
WHERE DID SHE PULL THAT LETTER FROM?
IT'S FROM CELES...
RUSTLE

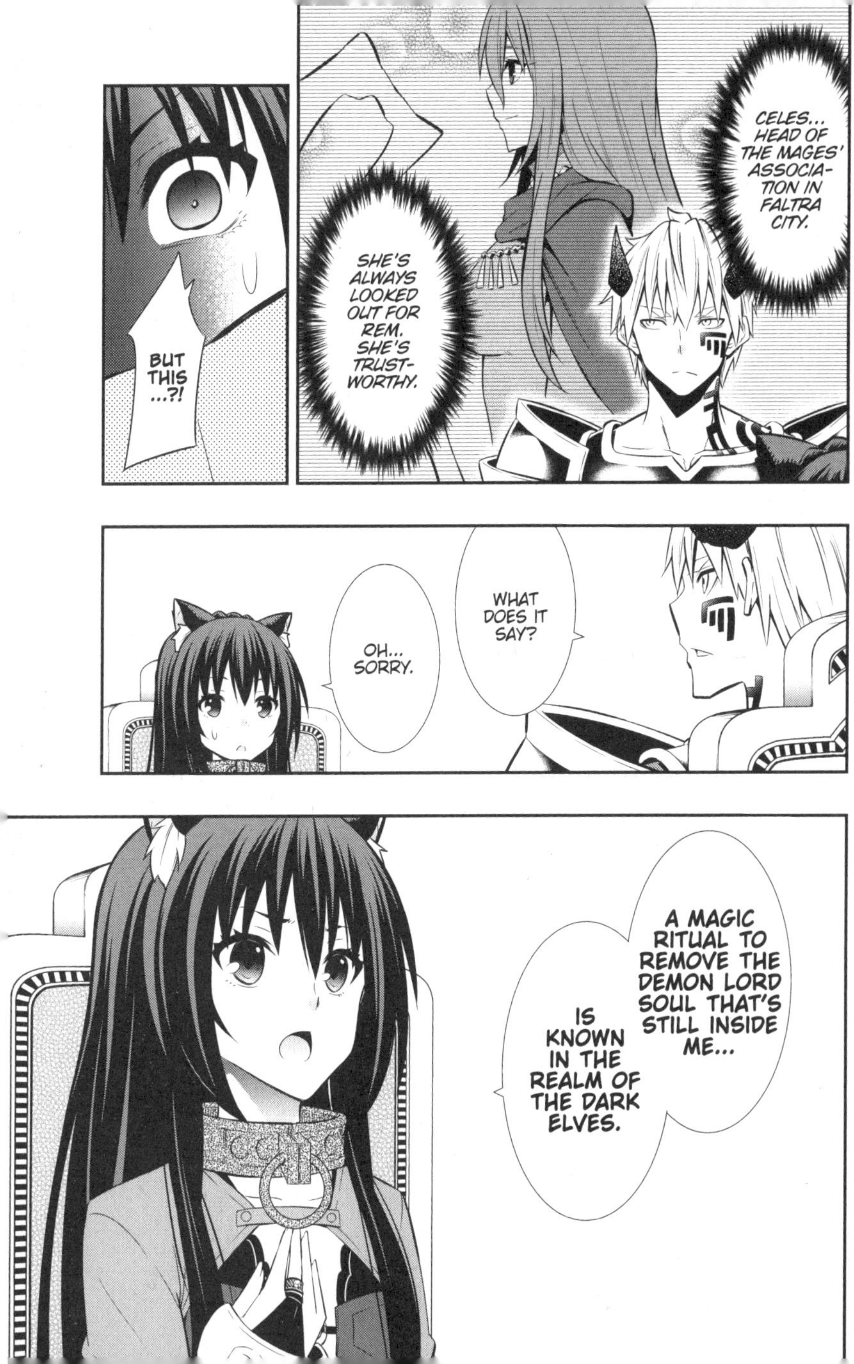
CELES... HEAD OF THE MAGES' ASSOCIATION IN FALTRA CITY.
SHE'S ALWAYS LOOKED OUT FOR REM. SHE'S TRUSTWORTHY.
BUT THIS ...?!
WHAT DOES IT SAY?
OH... SORRY.
A MAGIC RITUAL TO REMOVE THE DEMON LORD SOUL THAT'S STILL INSIDE ME...
IS KNOWN IN THE REALM OF THE DARK ELVES.

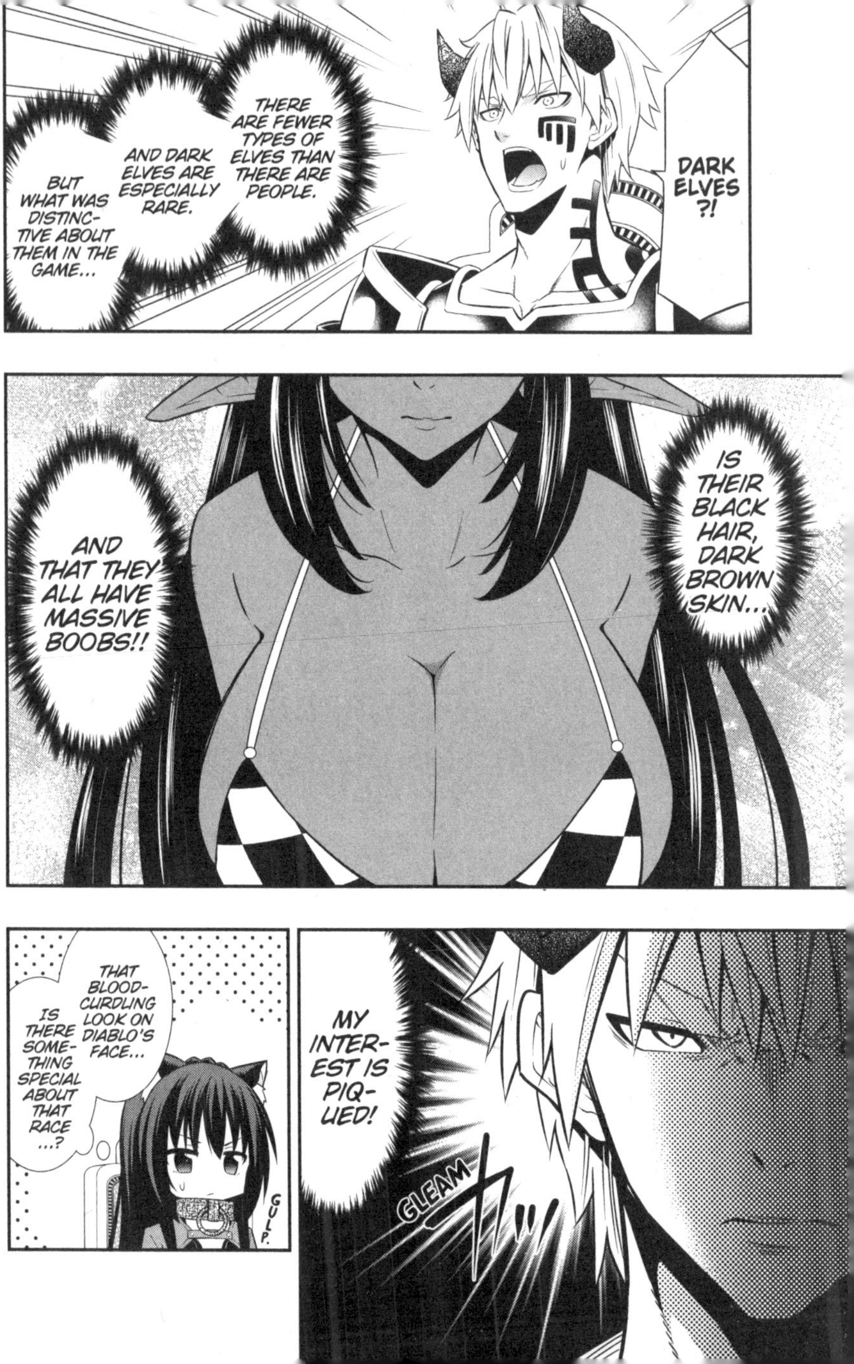
DARK ELVES?!
THERE ARE FEWER TYPES OF ELVES THAN THERE ARE PEOPLE.
AND DARK ELVES ARE ESPECIALLY RARE.
BUT WHAT WAS DISTINCTIVE ABOUT THEM IN THE GAME...
IS THEIR BLACK HAIR, DARK BROWN SKIN...
AND THAT THEY ALL HAVE MASSIVE BOOBS!!
MY INTEREST IS PIQUED!
GLEAM
THAT BLOODCURDLING LOOK ON DIABLO'S FACE...
IS THERE SOMETHING SPECIAL ABOUT THAT RACE...?
GULP.

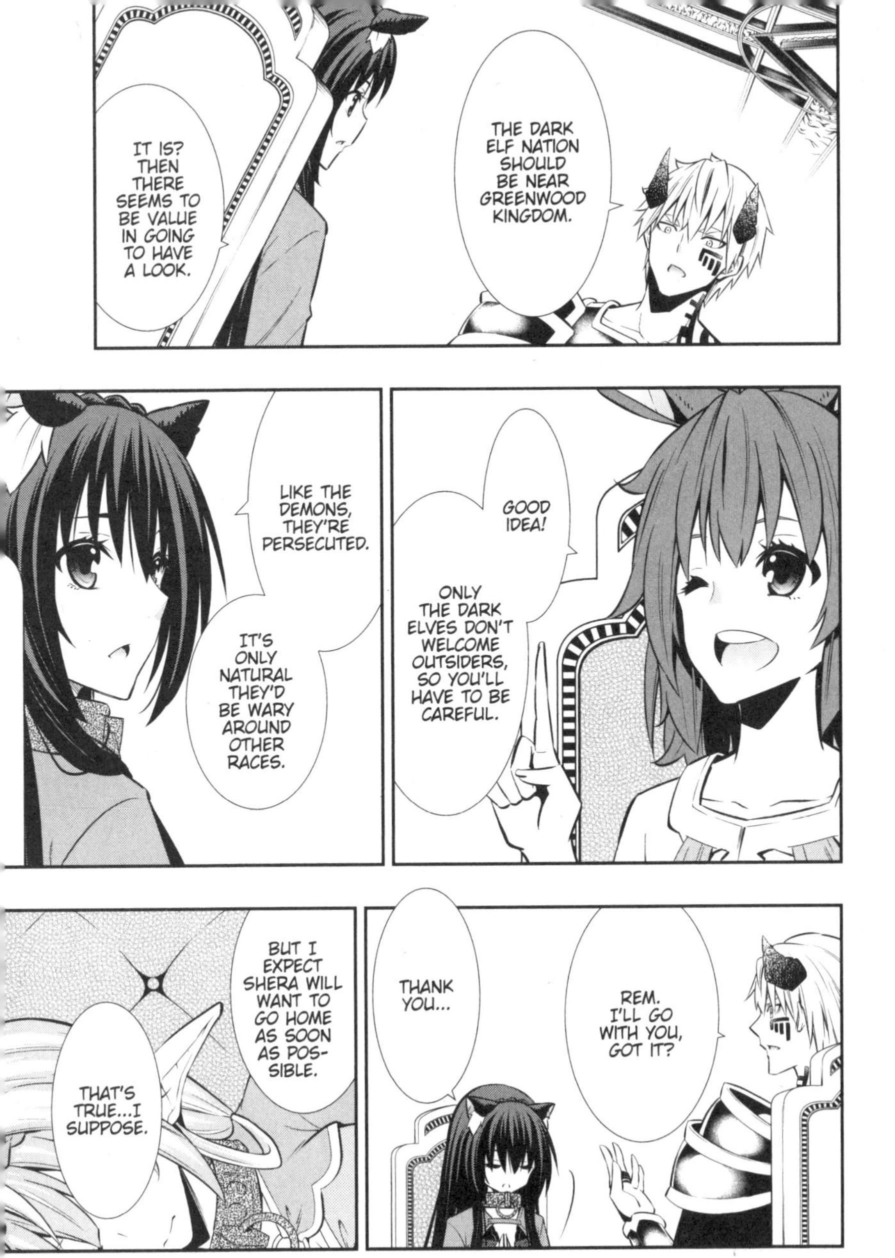
THE DARK ELF NATION SHOULD BE NEAR GREENWOOD KINGDOM.
IT IS? THEN THERE SEEMS TO BE VALUE IN GOING TO HAVE A LOOK.
GOOD IDEA!
ONLY THE DARK ELVES DON'T WELCOME OUTSIDERS, SO YOU'LL HAVE TO BE CAREFUL.
LIKE THE DEMONS, THEY'RE PERSECUTED.
IT'S ONLY NATURAL THEY'D BE WARY AROUND OTHER RACES.
REM. I'LL GO WITH YOU, GOT IT?
THANK YOU...
BUT I EXPECT SHERA WILL WANT TO GO HOME AS SOON AS POS-SIBLE.
THAT'S TRUE...I SUPPOSE.

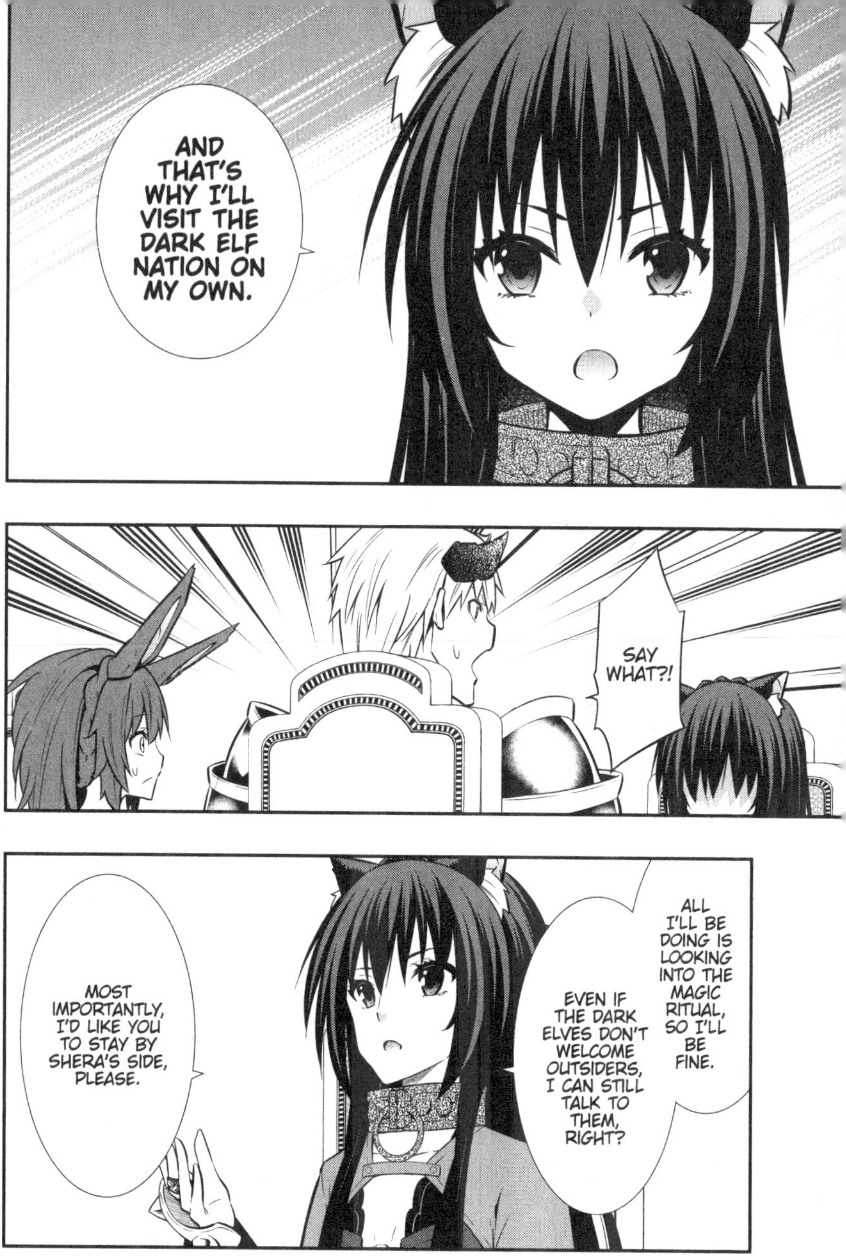
AND THAT'S WHY I'LL VISIT THE DARK ELF NATION ON MY OWN.
SAY WHAT?!
ALL I'LL BE DOING IS LOOKING INTO THE MAGIC RITUAL, SO I'LL BE FINE.
EVEN IF THE DARK ELVES DON'T WELCOME OUTSIDERS, I CAN STILL TALK TO THEM, RIGHT?
MOST IMPORTANTLY, I'D LIKE YOU TO STAY BY SHERA'S SIDE, PLEASE.

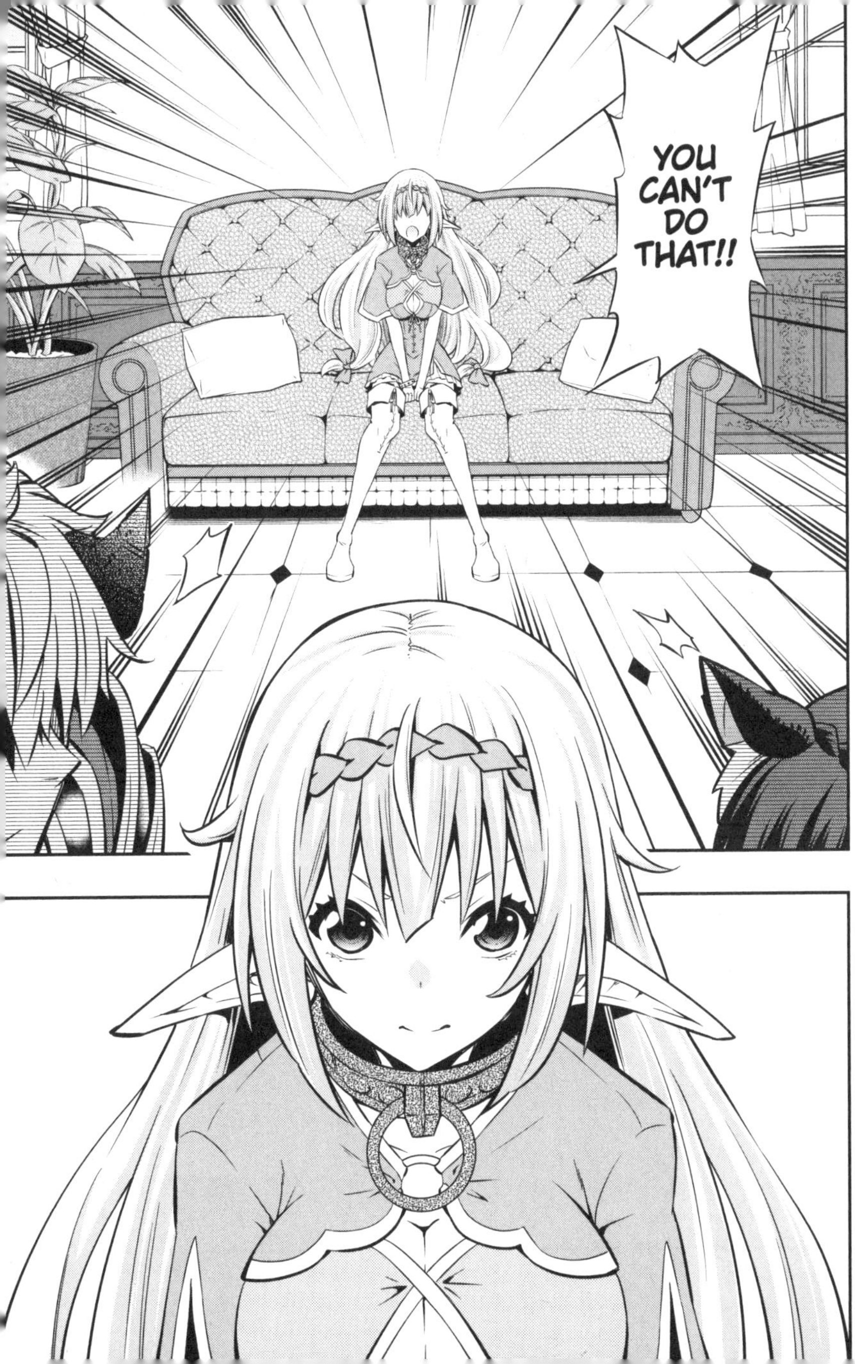
YOU CAN'T DO THAT!!

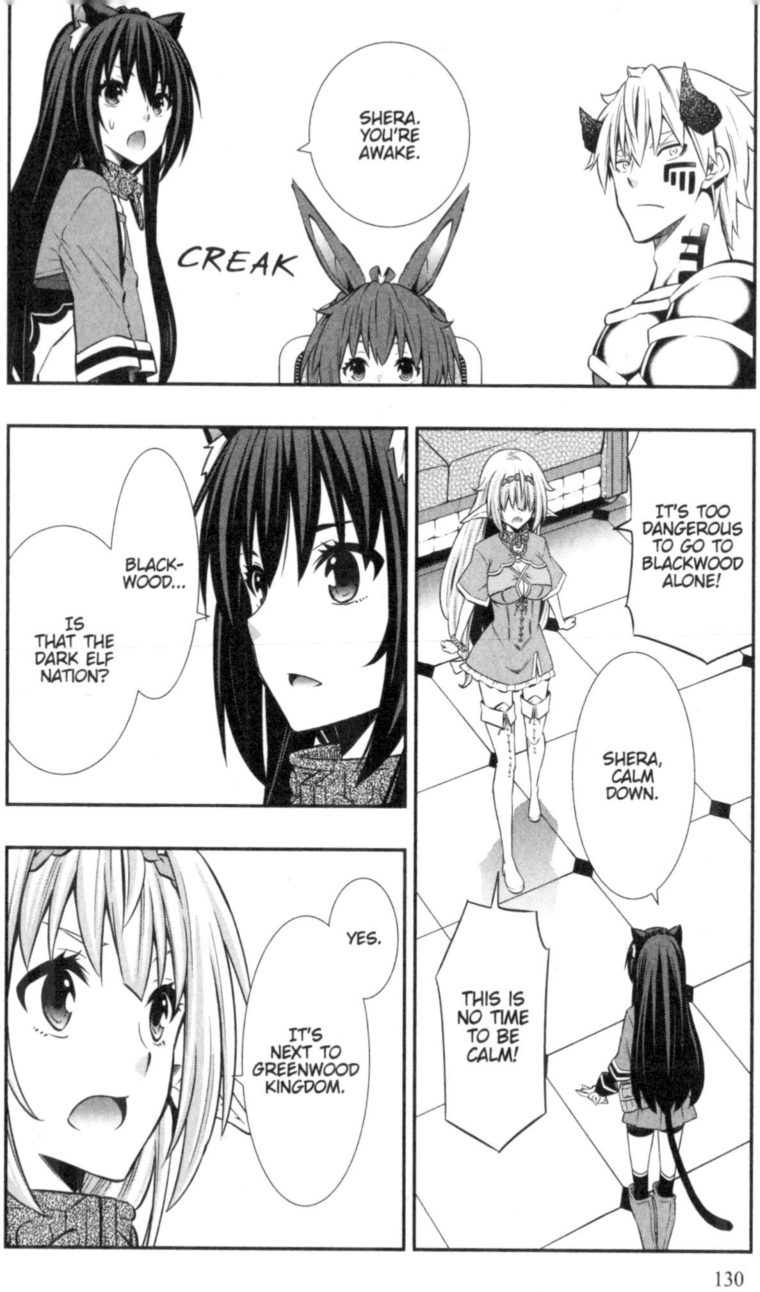
SHERA. YOU'RE AWAKE.
CREAK
IT'S TOO DANGEROUS TO GO TO BLACKWOOD ALONE!
SHERA, CALM DOWN.
THIS IS NO TIME TO BE CALM!
BLACK-WOOD...
IS THAT THE DARK ELF NATION?
YES.
IT'S NEXT TO GREENWOOD KINGDOM.

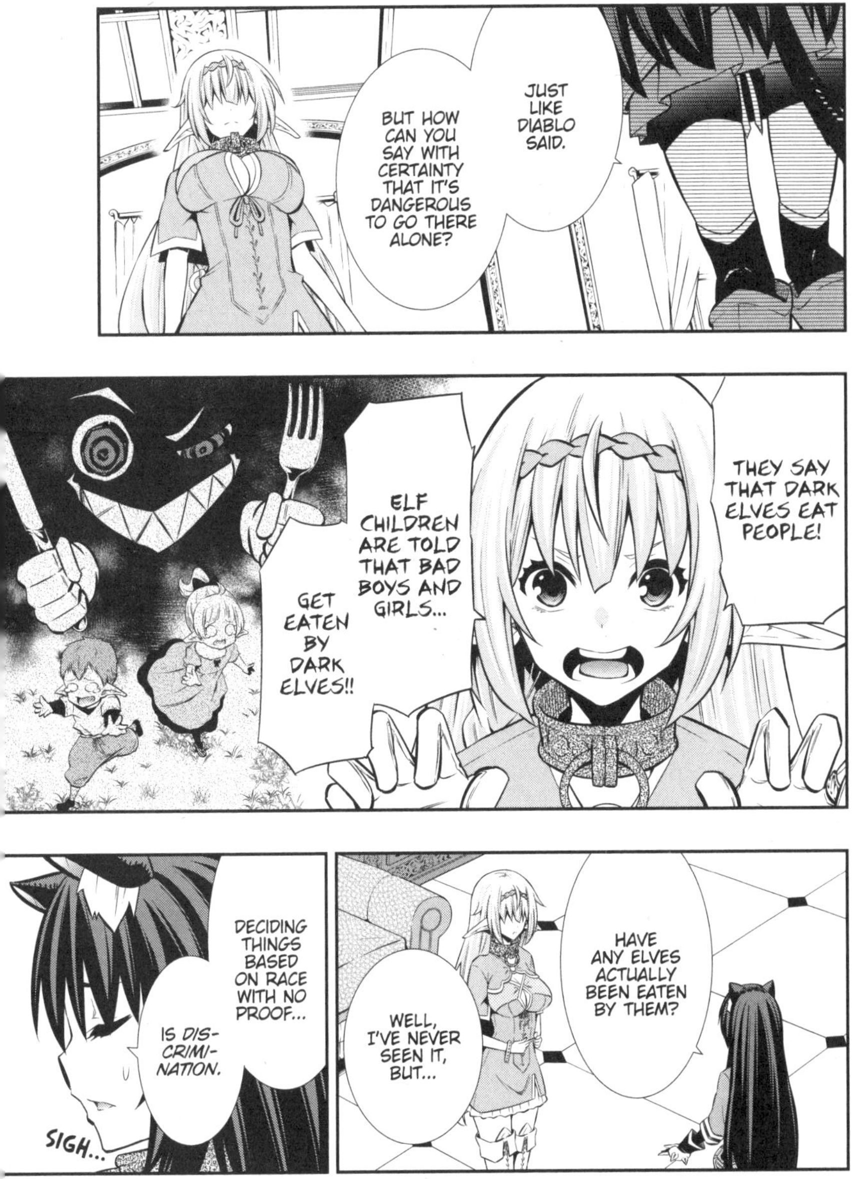
JUST LIKE DIABLO SAID.
BUT HOW CAN YOU SAY WITH CERTAINTY THAT IT'S DANGEROUS TO GO THERE ALONE?
THEY SAY THAT DARK ELVES EAT PEOPLE!
ELF CHILDREN ARE TOLD THAT BAD BOYS AND GIRLS...
GET EATEN BY DARK ELVES!!
HAVE ANY ELVES ACTUALLY BEEN EATEN BY THEM?
WELL, I'VE NEVER SEEN IT, BUT...
DECIDING THINGS BASED ON RACE WITH NO PROOF...
IS DISCRIMINATION.
SIGH...

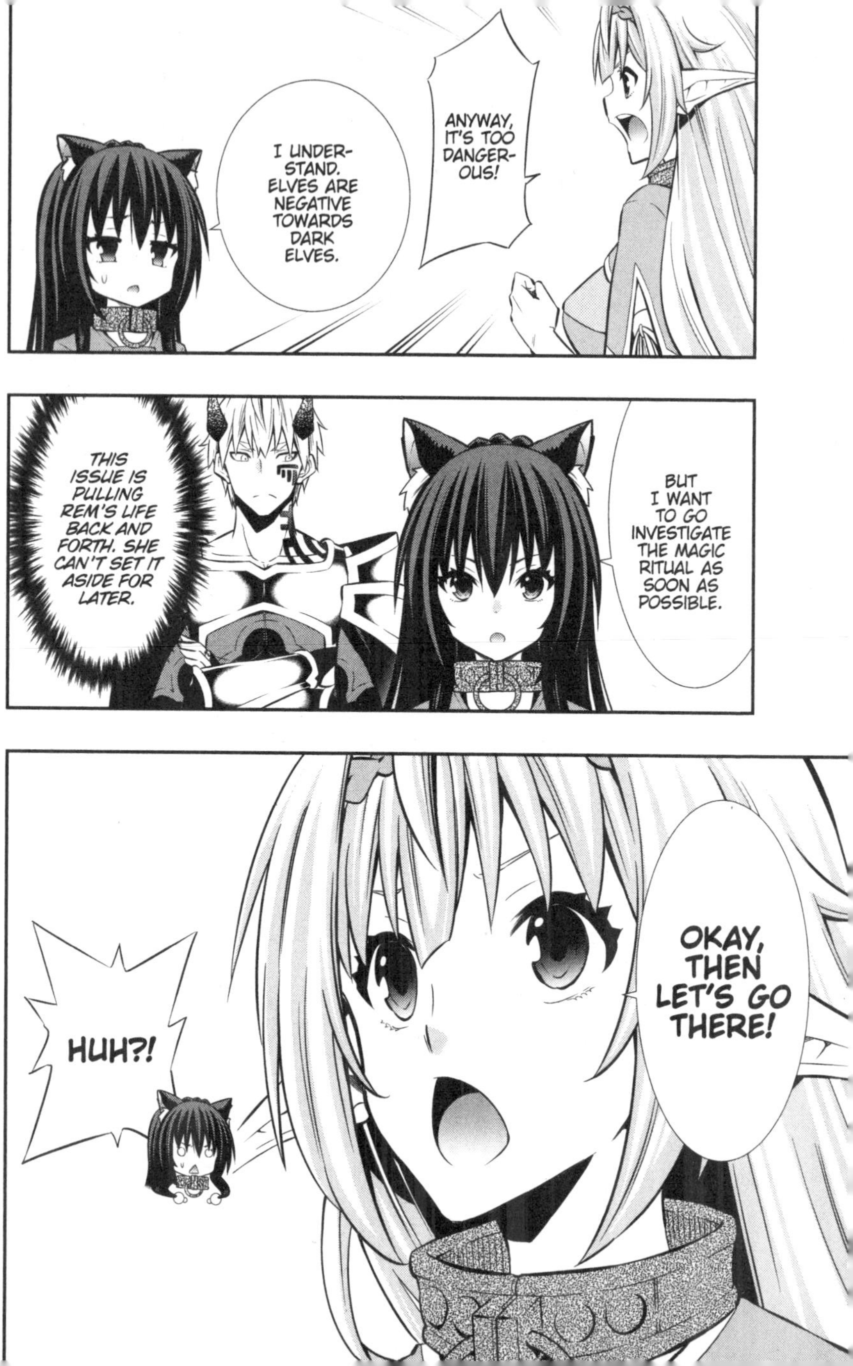
ANYWAY, IT'S TOO DANGER-OUS!
I UNDER-STAND. ELVES ARE NEGATIVE TOWARDS DARK ELVES.
BUT I WANT TO GO INVESTIGATE THE MAGIC RITUAL AS SOON AS POSSIBLE.
THIS ISSUE IS PULLING REM'S LIFE BACK AND FORTH. SHE CAN'T SET IT ASIDE FOR LATER.
OKAY, THEN LET'S GO THERE!
HUH?!

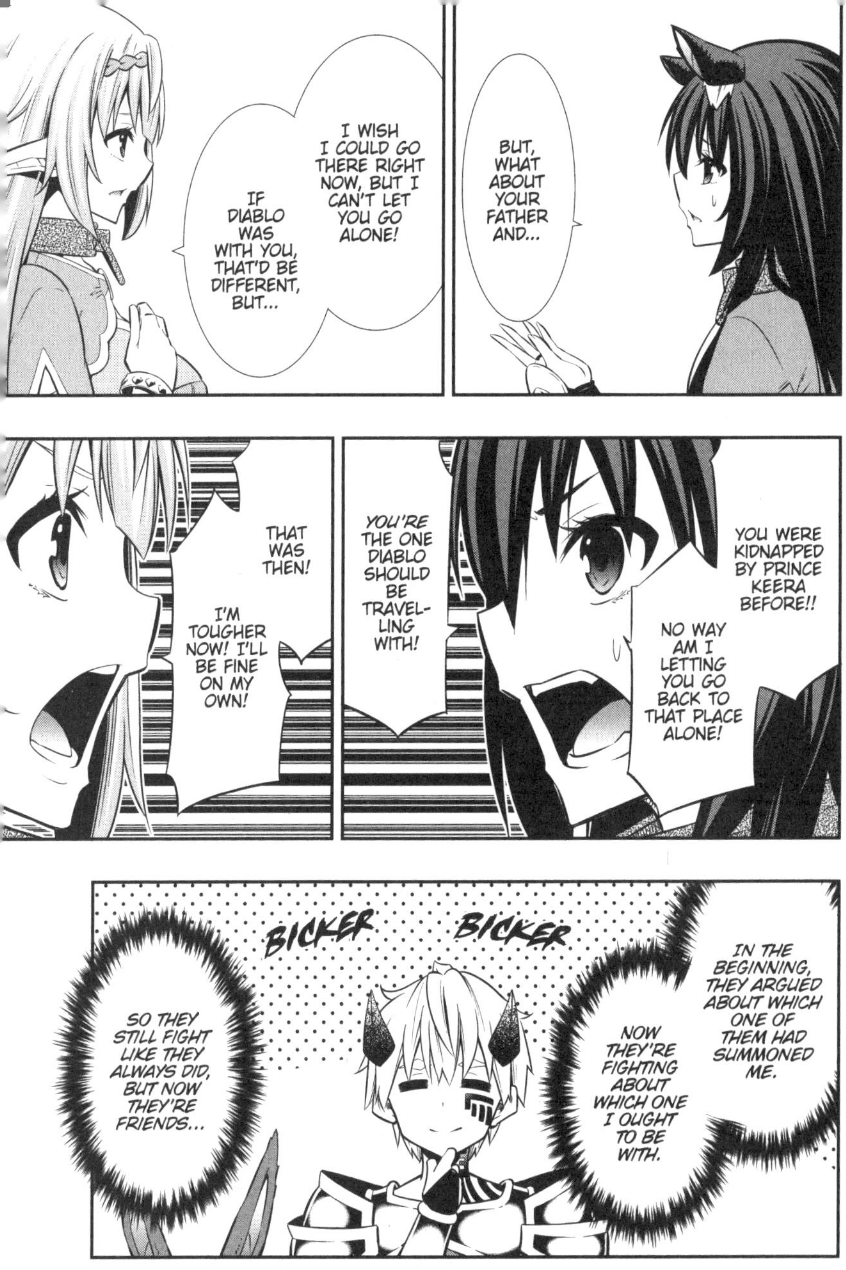
BUT, WHAT ABOUT YOUR FATHER AND...
I WISH I COULD GO THERE RIGHT NOW, BUT I CAN'T LET YOU GO ALONE!
IF DIABLO WAS WITH YOU, THAT'D BE DIFFERENT, BUT...
YOU WERE KIDNAPPED BY PRINCE KEERA BEFORE!!
NO WAY AM I LETTING YOU GO BACK TO THAT PLACE ALONE!
YOU'RE THE ONE DIABLO SHOULD BE TRAVEL-LING WITH!
THAT WAS THEN!
I'M TOUGHER NOW! I'LL BE FINE ON MY OWN!
BICKER BICKER
IN THE BEGINNING, THEY ARGUED ABOUT WHICH ONE OF THEM HAD SUMMONED ME.
NOW THEY'RE FIGHTING ABOUT WHICH ONE I OUGHT TO BE WITH.
SO THEY STILL FIGHT LIKE THEY ALWAYS DID, BUT NOW THEY'RE FRIENDS...

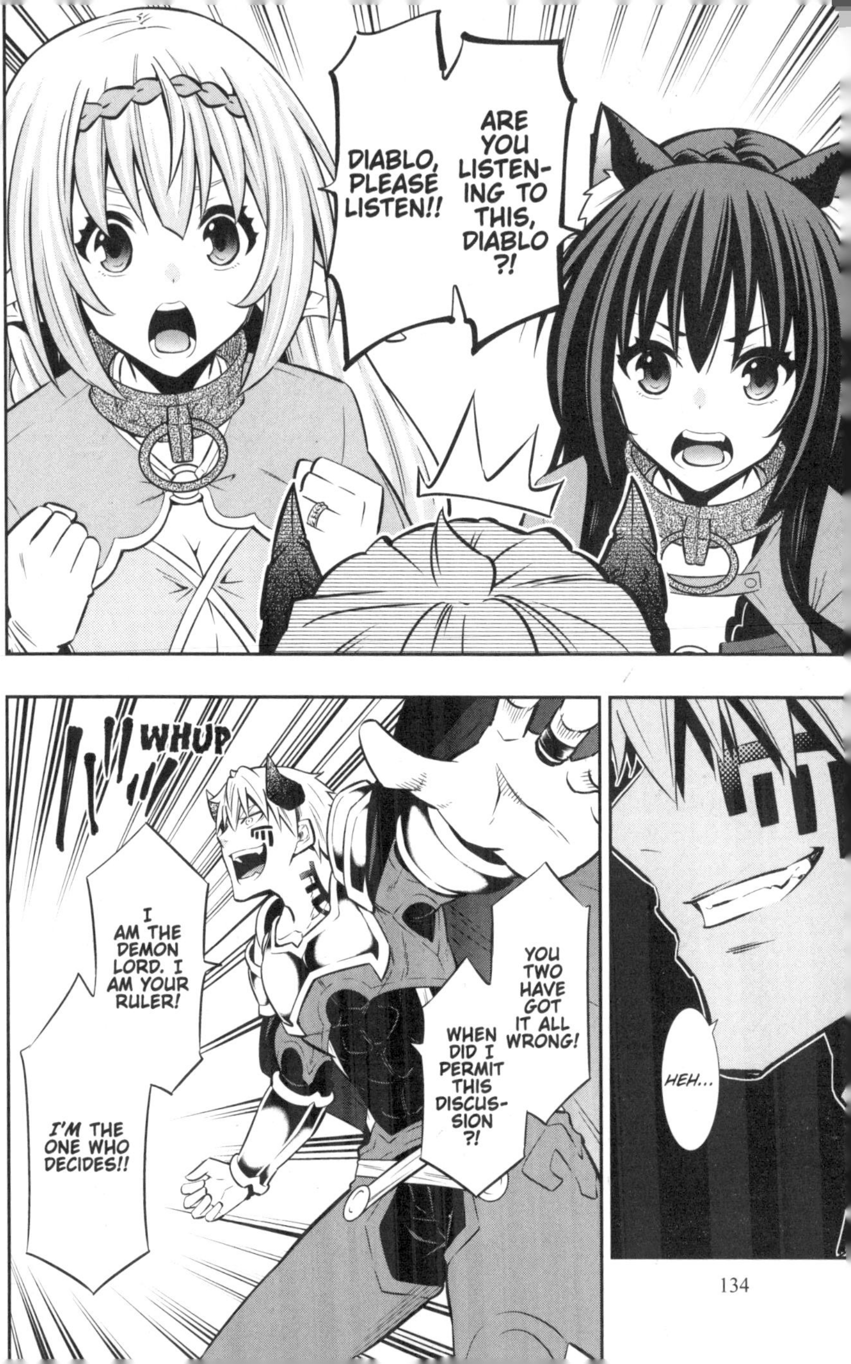

ARE YOU LISTENING TO THIS, DIABLO?!
DIABLO, PLEASE LISTEN!!
HEH...
WHUP
YOU TWO HAVE GOT IT ALL WRONG!
WHEN DID I PERMIT THIS DISCUSSION?!
I AM THE DEMON LORD. I AM YOUR RULER!
I'M THE ONE WHO DECIDES!!

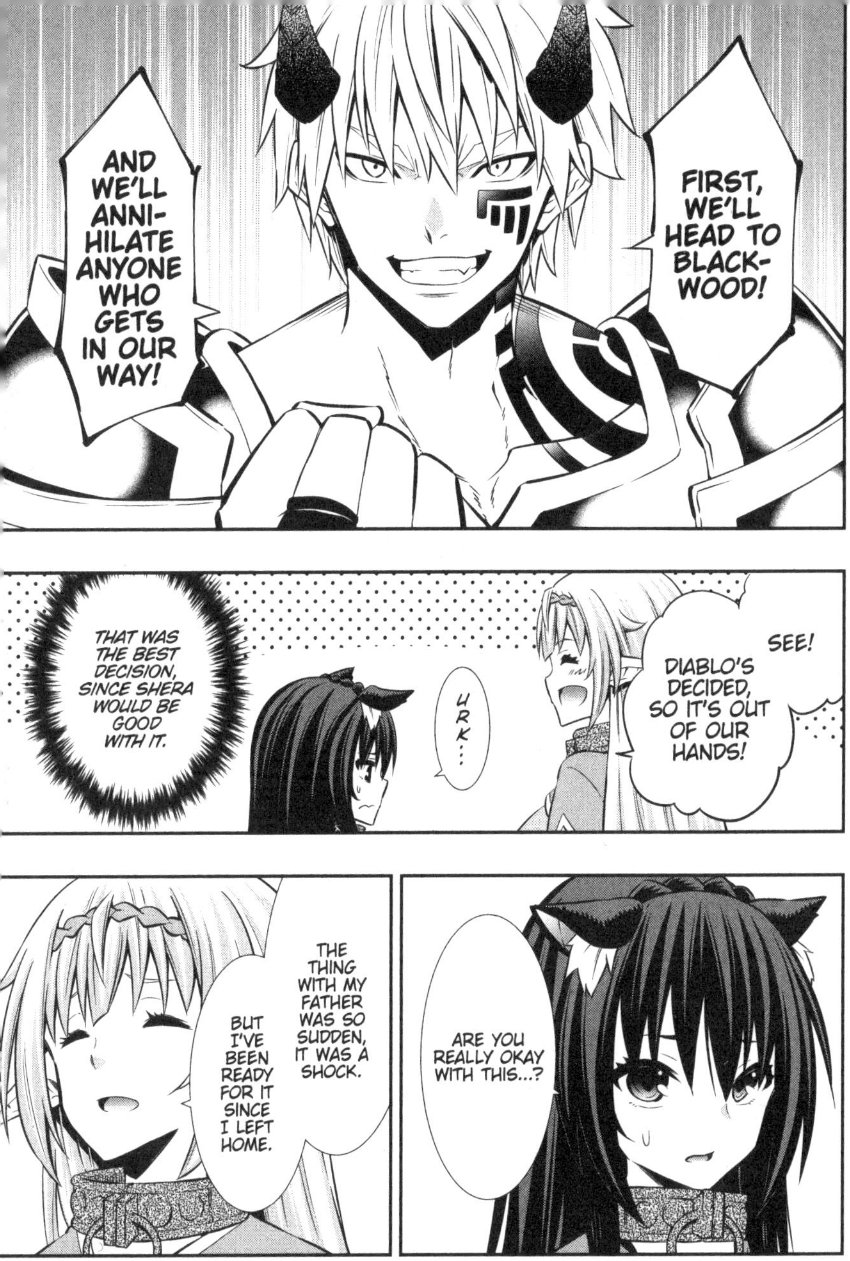
FIRST, WE'LL HEAD TO BLACK-WOOD!
AND WE'LL ANNI-HILATE ANYONE WHO GETS IN OUR WAY!
SEE! DIABLO'S DECIDED, SO IT'S OUT OF OUR HANDS!
URK...
THAT WAS THE BEST DECISION, SINCE SHERA WOULD BE GOOD WITH IT.
ARE YOU REALLY OKAY WITH THIS...?
THE THING WITH MY FATHER WAS SO SUDDEN, IT WAS A SHOCK.
BUT I'VE BEEN READY FOR IT SINCE I LEFT HOME.

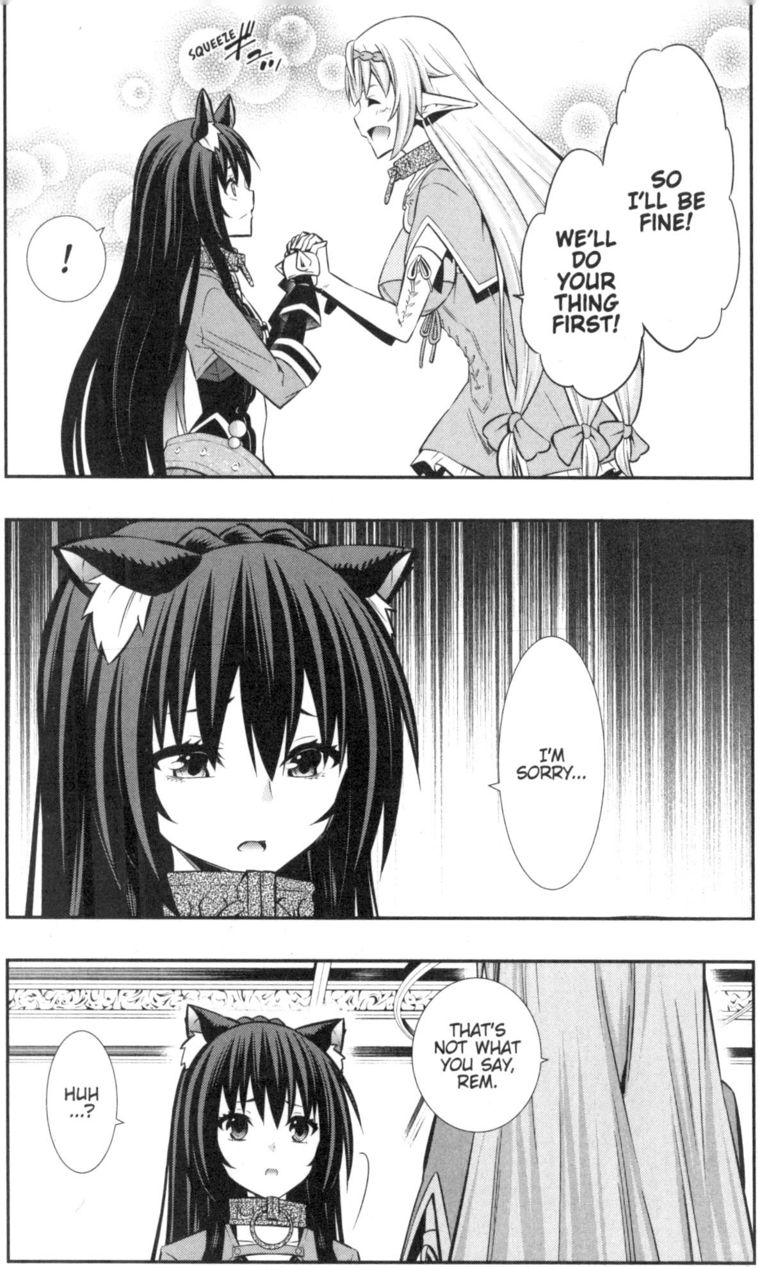
SO I'LL BE FINE!
WE'LL DO YOUR THING FIRST!
SQUEEZE
!
I'M SORRY...
THAT'S NOT WHAT YOU SAY, REM.
HUH ...?

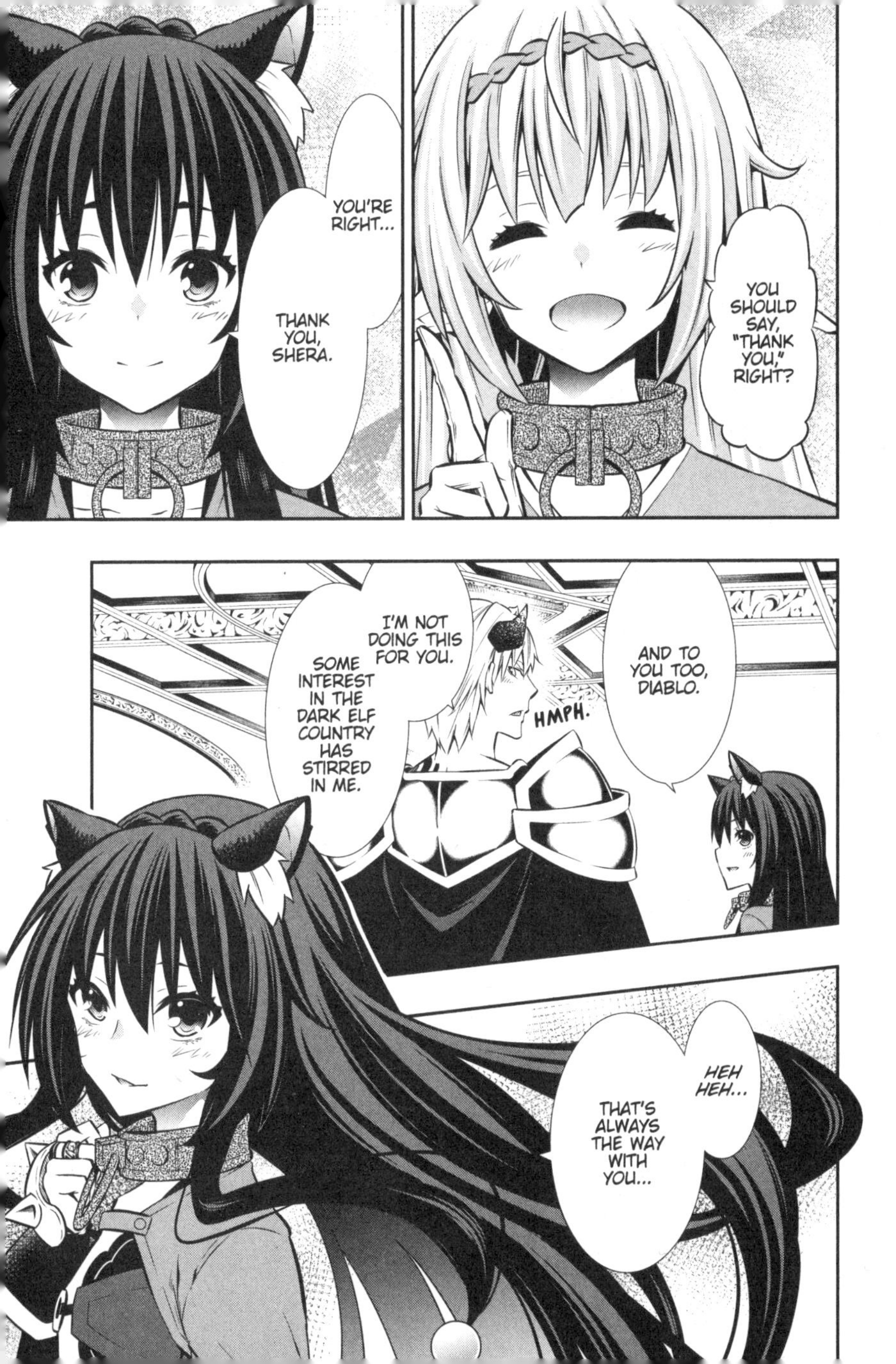
YOU SHOULD SAY, "THANK YOU," RIGHT?
YOU'RE RIGHT...
THANK YOU, SHERA.
AND TO YOU TOO, DIABLO.
HMPH.
I'M NOT DOING THIS FOR YOU.
SOME INTEREST IN THE DARK ELF COUNTRY HAS STIRRED IN ME.
HEH HEH...
THAT'S ALWAYS THE WAY WITH YOU...

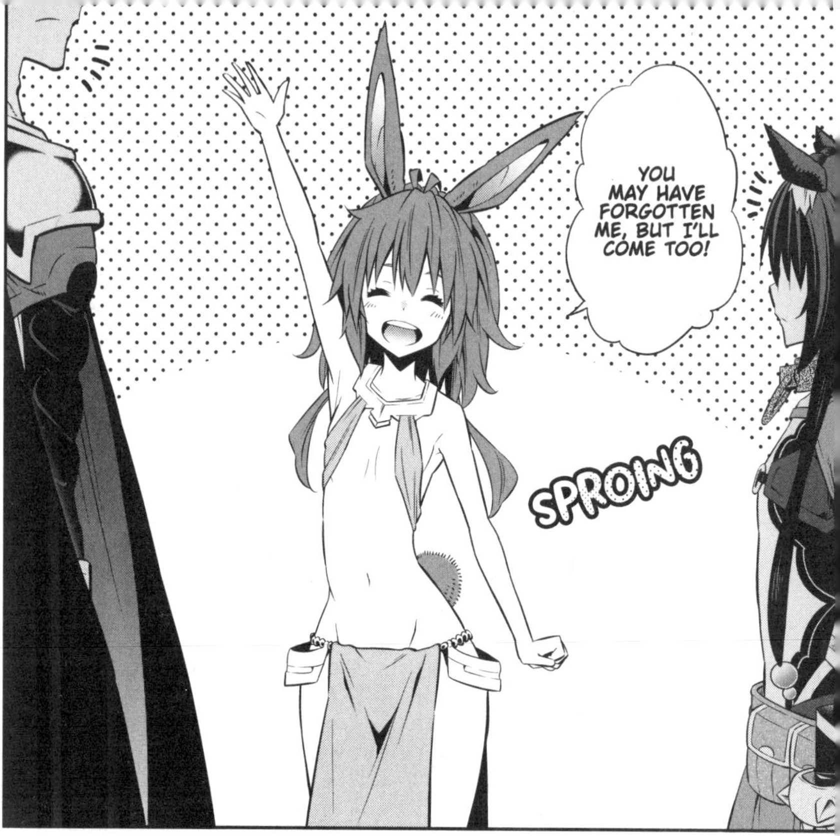
YOU MAY HAVE FORGOTTEN ME, BUT I'LL COME TOO!
SPROING
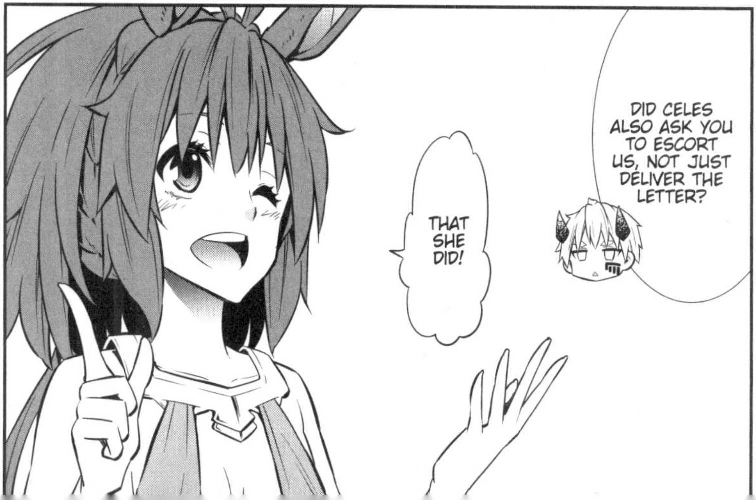
DID CELES ALSO ASK YOU TO ESCORT US, NOT JUST DELIVER THE LETTER?
THAT SHE DID!

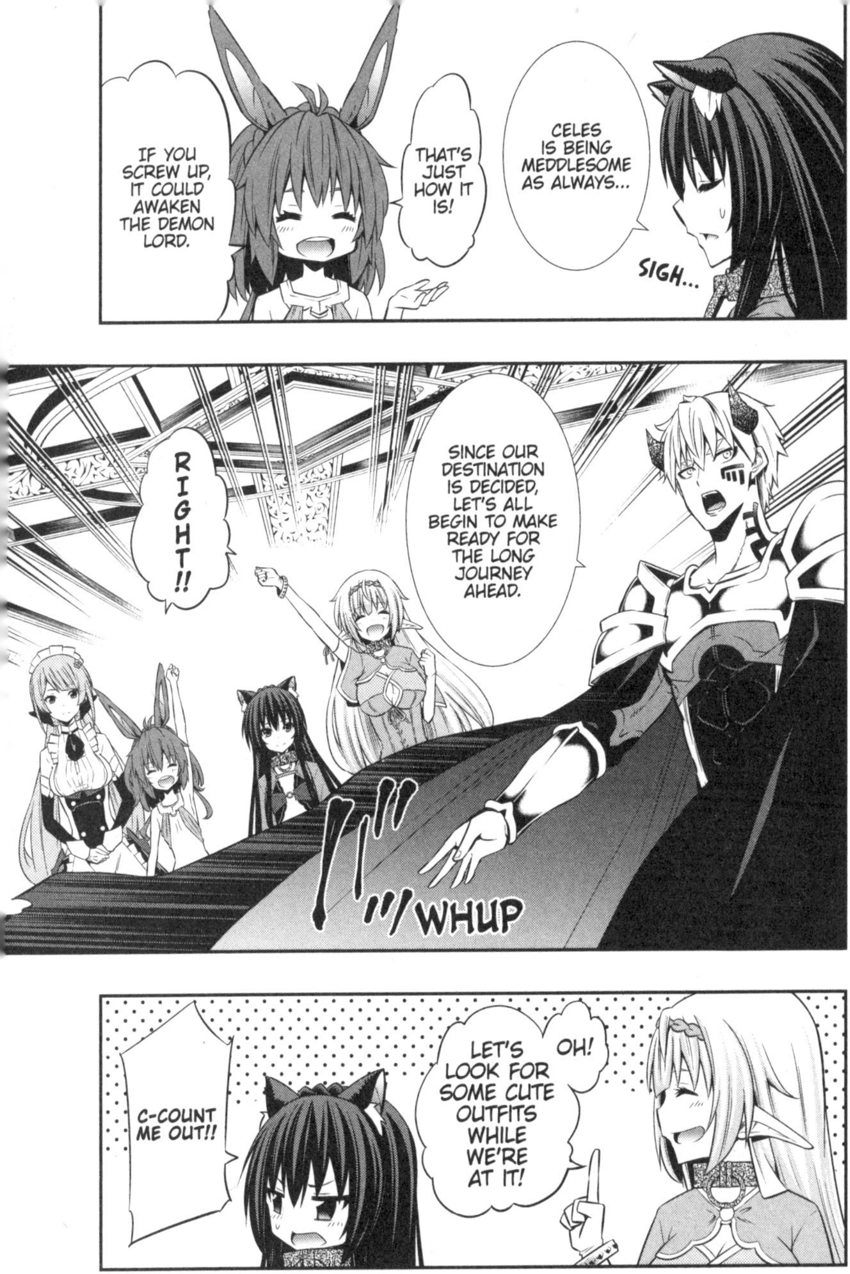
CELES IS BEING MEDDLESOME AS ALWAYS...
SIGH...
THAT'S JUST HOW IT IS!
IF YOU SCREW UP, IT COULD AWAKEN THE DEMON LORD.
SINCE OUR DESTINATION IS DECIDED, LET'S ALL BEGIN TO MAKE READY FOR THE LONG JOURNEY AHEAD.
RIGHT!!
WHUP
OH!
LET'S LOOK FOR SOME CUTE OUTFITS WHILE WE'RE AT IT!
C-COUNT ME OUT!!

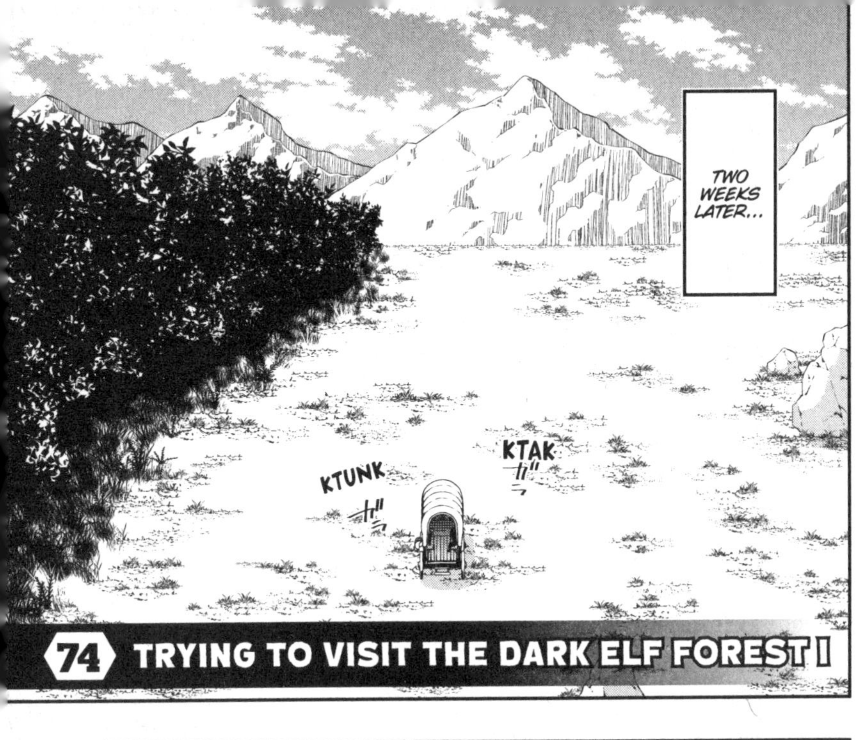
TWO WEEKS LATER...
KTAK
KTUNK

74 TRYING TO VISIT THE DARK ELF FOREST I

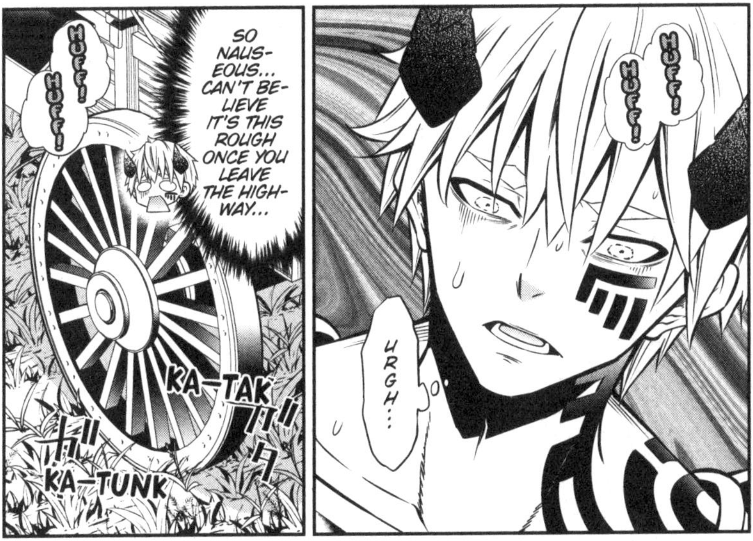
HUFF! HUFF!
URGH...
SO NAUSEOUS... CAN'T BELIEVE IT'S THIS ROUGH ONCE YOU LEAVE THE HIGHWAY...
HUFF! HUFF!
KA-TAK
KA-TUNK

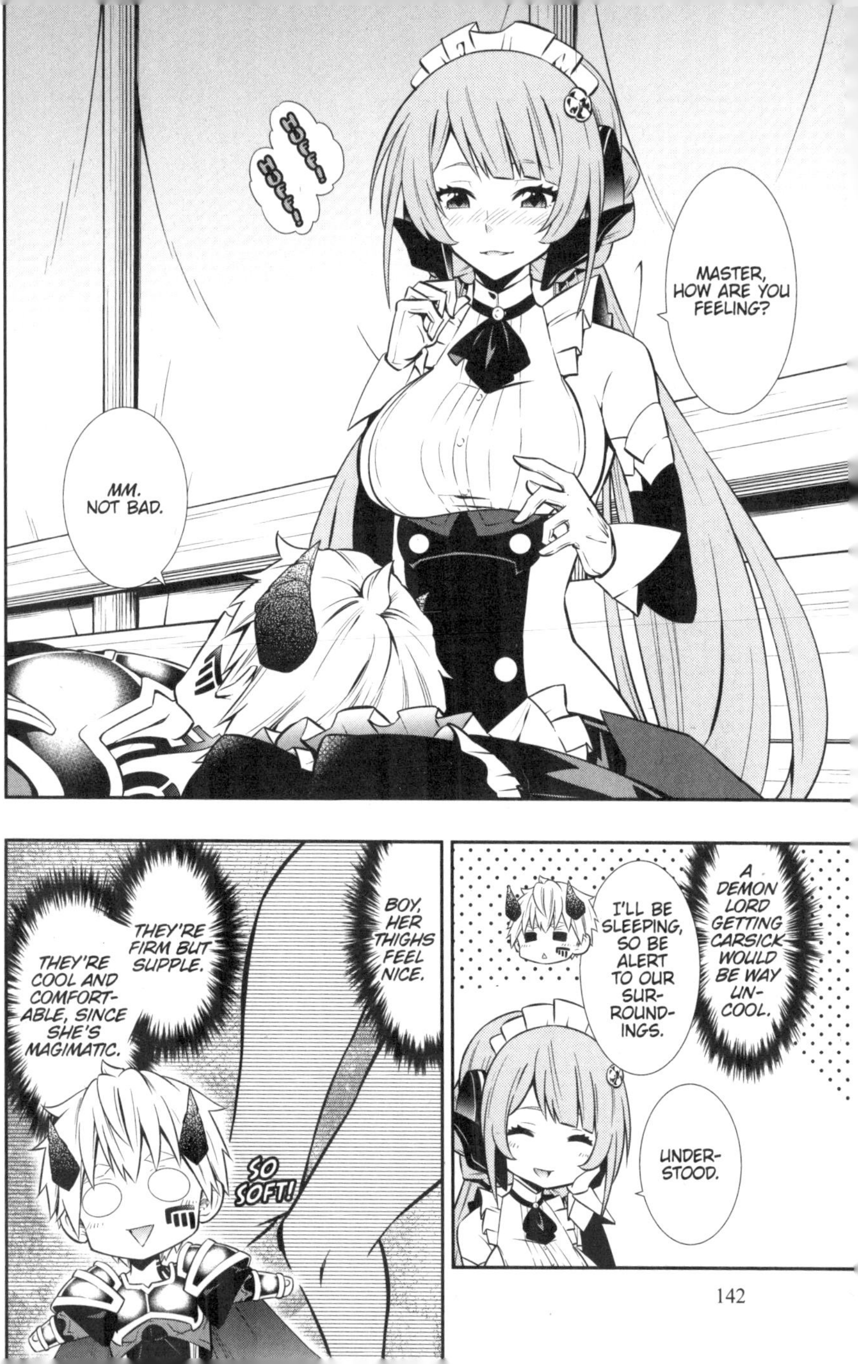
MASTER, HOW ARE YOU FEELING?
MM. NOT BAD.
A DEMON LORD GETTING CARSICK WOULD BE WAY UN-COOL.
I'LL BE SLEEPING, SO BE ALERT TO OUR SUR-ROUNDINGS.
UNDER-STOOD.
BOY, HER THIGHS FEEL NICE.
THEY'RE FIRM BUT SUPPLE.
THEY'RE COOL AND COMFORT-ABLE, SINCE SHE'S MAGIMATIC.
SO SOFT!

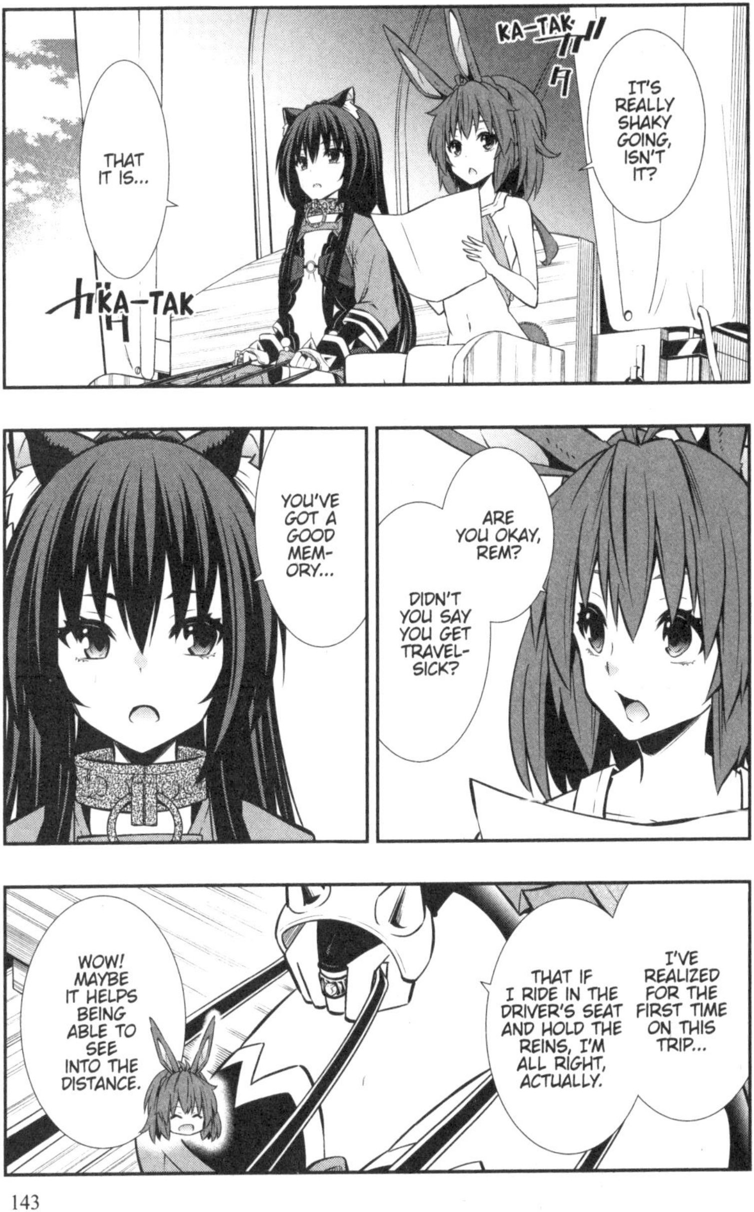
KA-TAK
IT'S REALLY SHAKY GOING, ISN'T IT?
THAT IT IS...
KA-TAK
ARE YOU OKAY, REM?
DIDN'T YOU SAY YOU GET TRAVEL-SICK?
YOU'VE GOT A GOOD MEM-ORY...
I'VE REALIZED FOR THE FIRST TIME ON THIS TRIP...
THAT IF I RIDE IN THE DRIVER'S SEAT AND HOLD THE REINS, I'M ALL RIGHT, ACTUALLY.
WOW! MAYBE IT HELPS BEING ABLE TO SEE INTO THE DISTANCE.

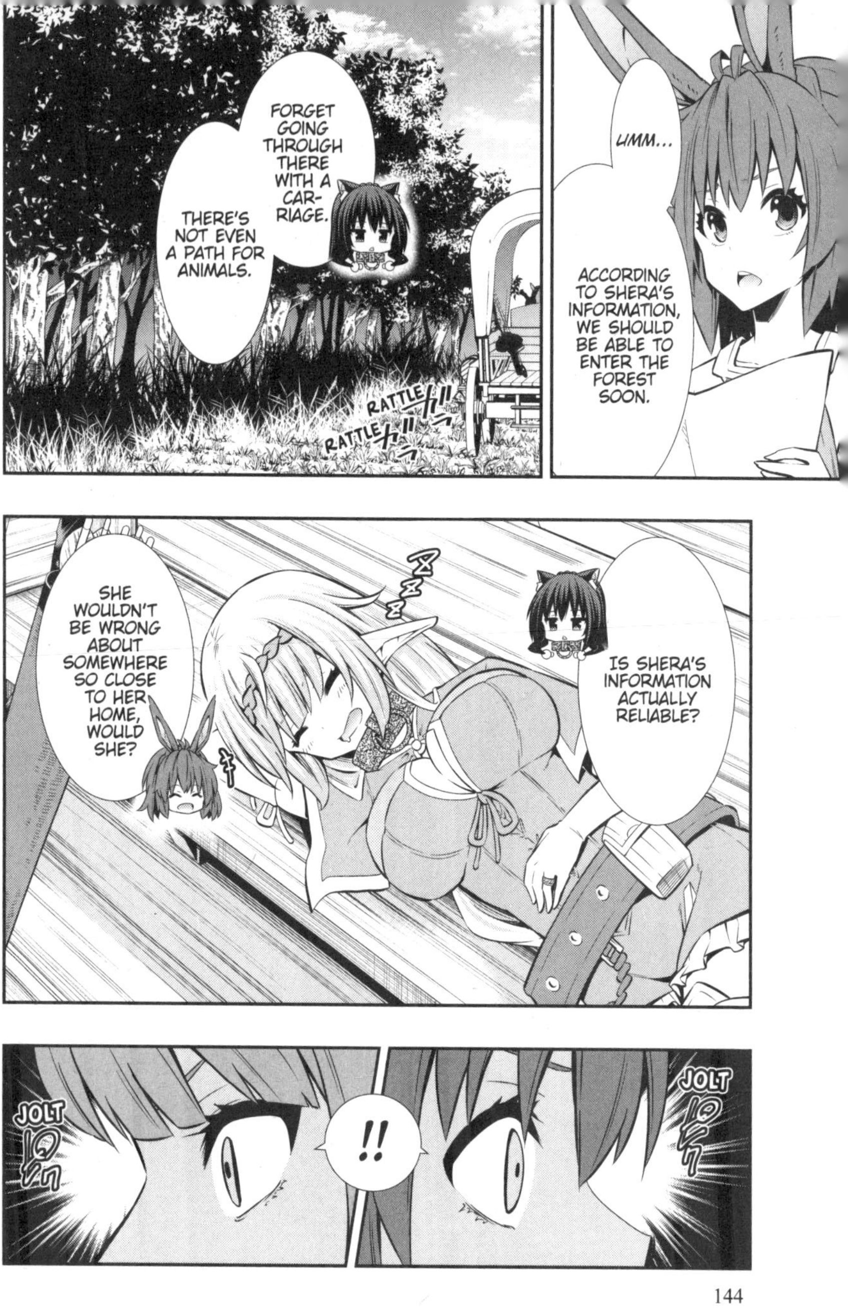
UMM...
ACCORDING TO SHERA'S INFORMATION, WE SHOULD BE ABLE TO ENTER THE FOREST SOON.
FORGET GOING THROUGH THERE WITH A CAR-RIAGE.
THERE'S NOT EVEN A PATH FOR ANIMALS.
RATTLE
RATTLE
IS SHERA'S INFORMATION ACTUALLY RELIABLE?
SHE WOULDN'T BE WRONG ABOUT SOMEWHERE SO CLOSE TO HER HOME, WOULD SHE?
JOLT
!!
JOLT

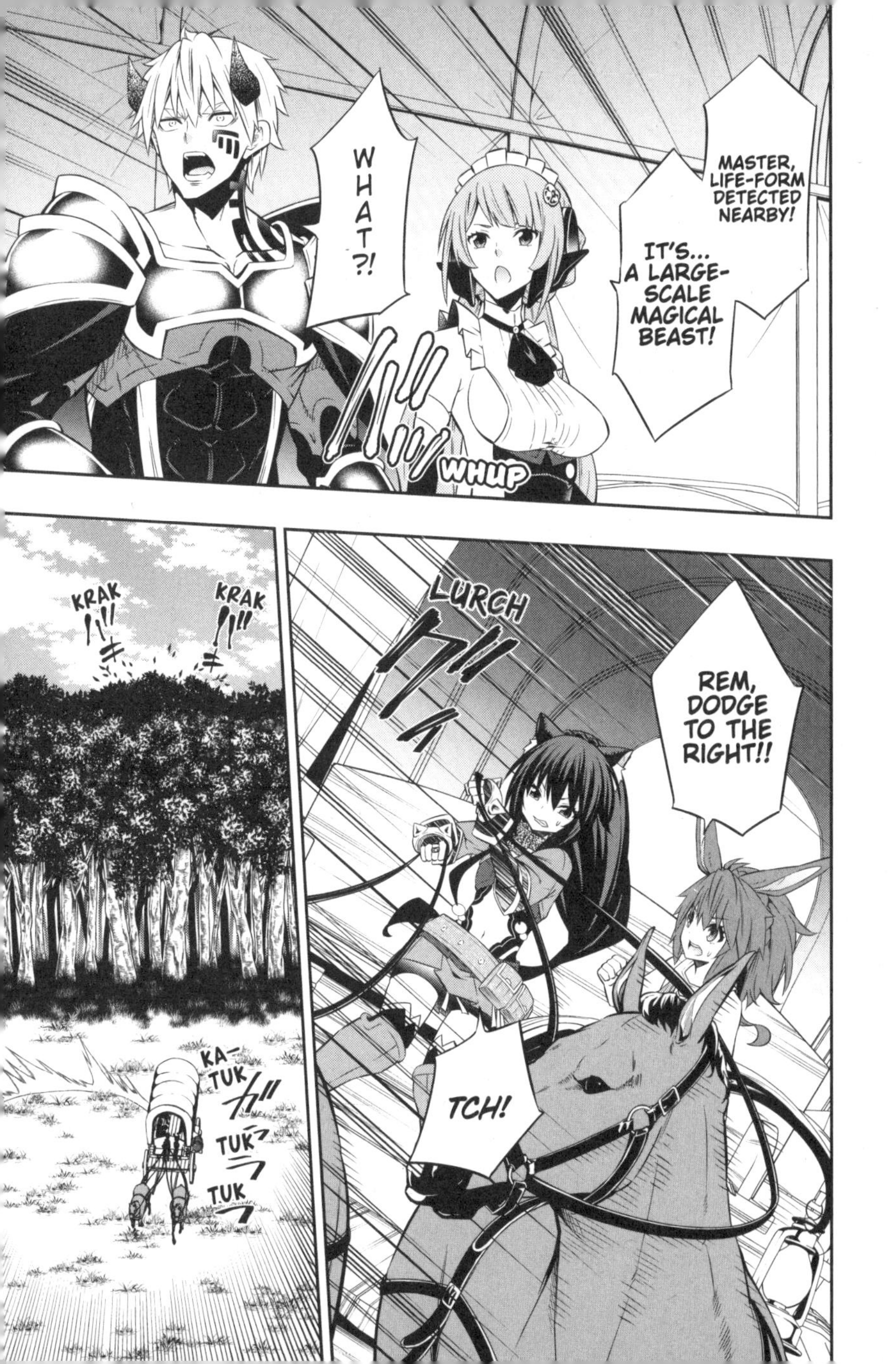
MASTER, LIFE-FORM DETECTED NEARBY!
IT'S... A LARGE-SCALE MAGICAL BEAST!
WHAT?!
WHUP
LURCH
REM, DODGE TO THE RIGHT!!
TCH!
KRAK
KRAK
KA-TUK
TUK
TUK

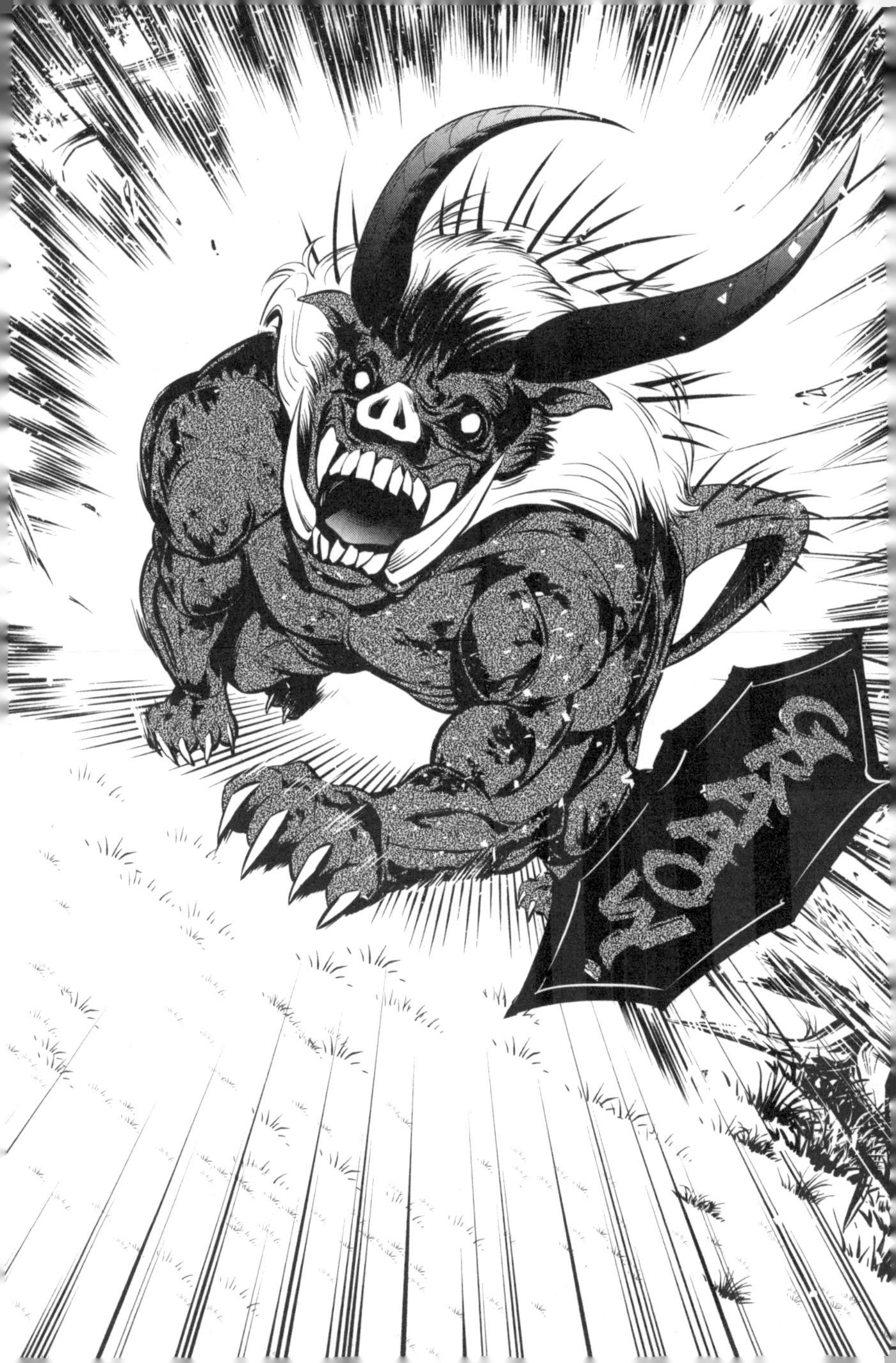
GRAOW!

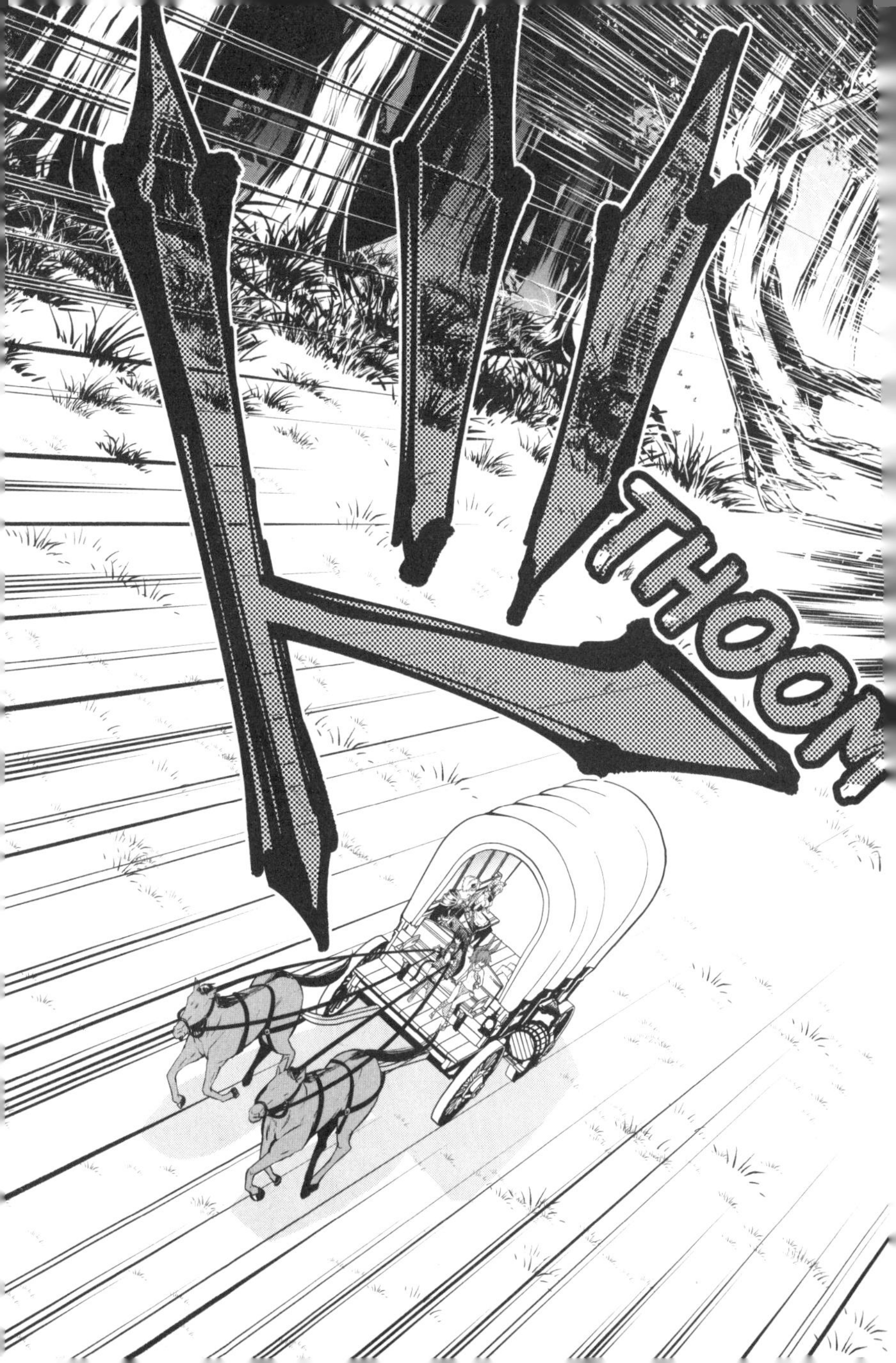
THOOM

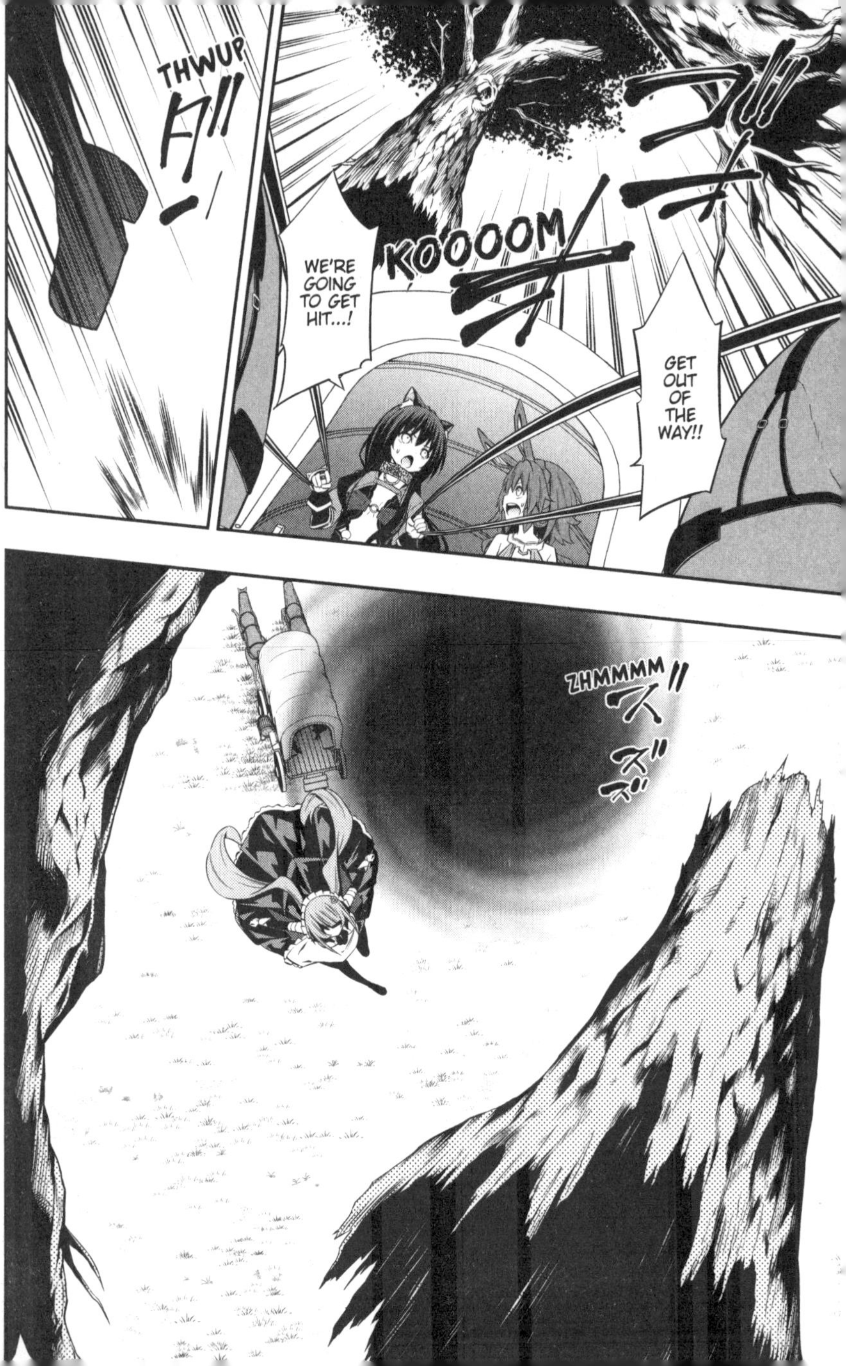
KOOOOM
GET OUT OF THE WAY!!
WE'RE GOING TO GET HIT...!
THWUP
ZHMMMM

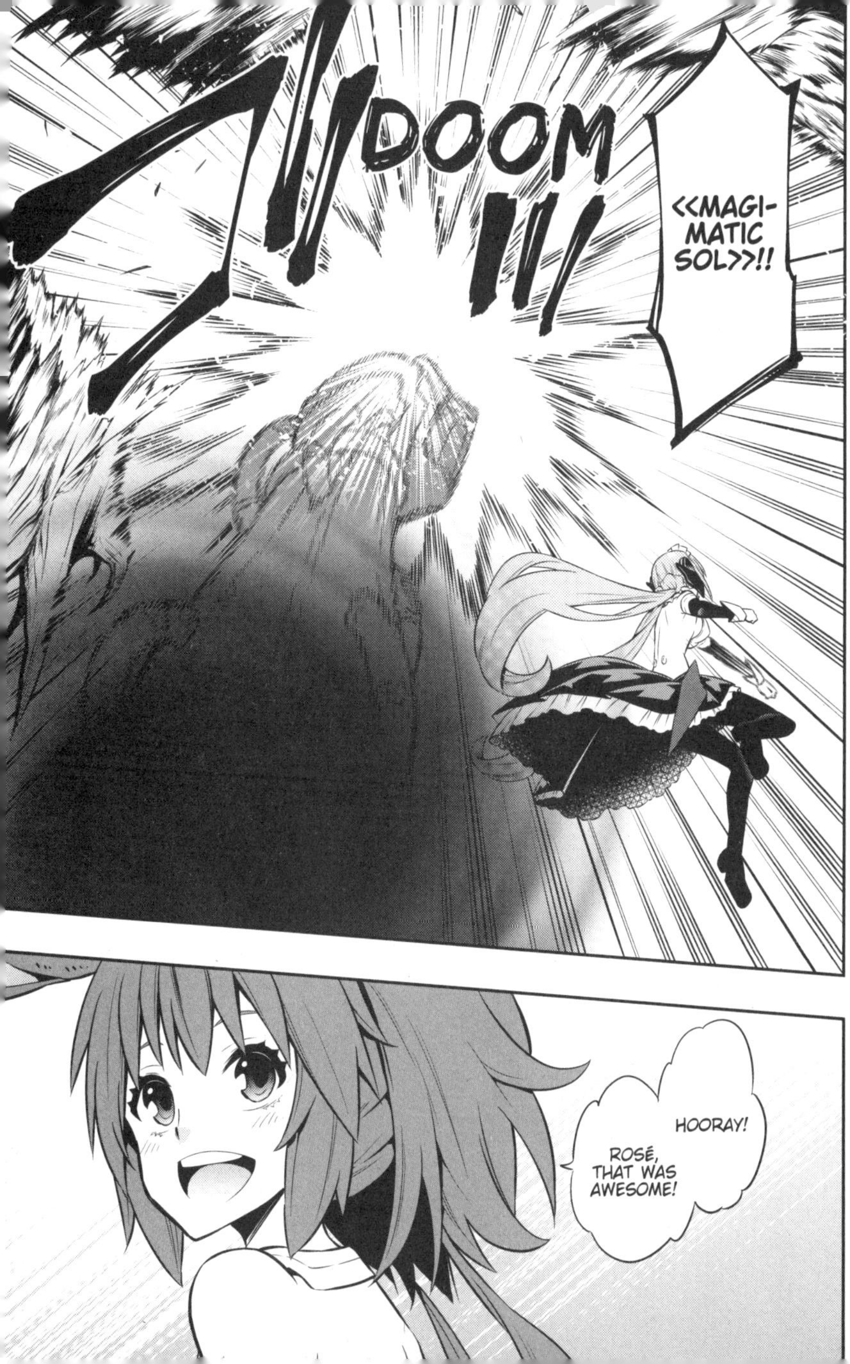
DOOM
<<MAGI-MATIC SOL>>!!
HOORAY!
ROSÉ, THAT WAS AWESOME!

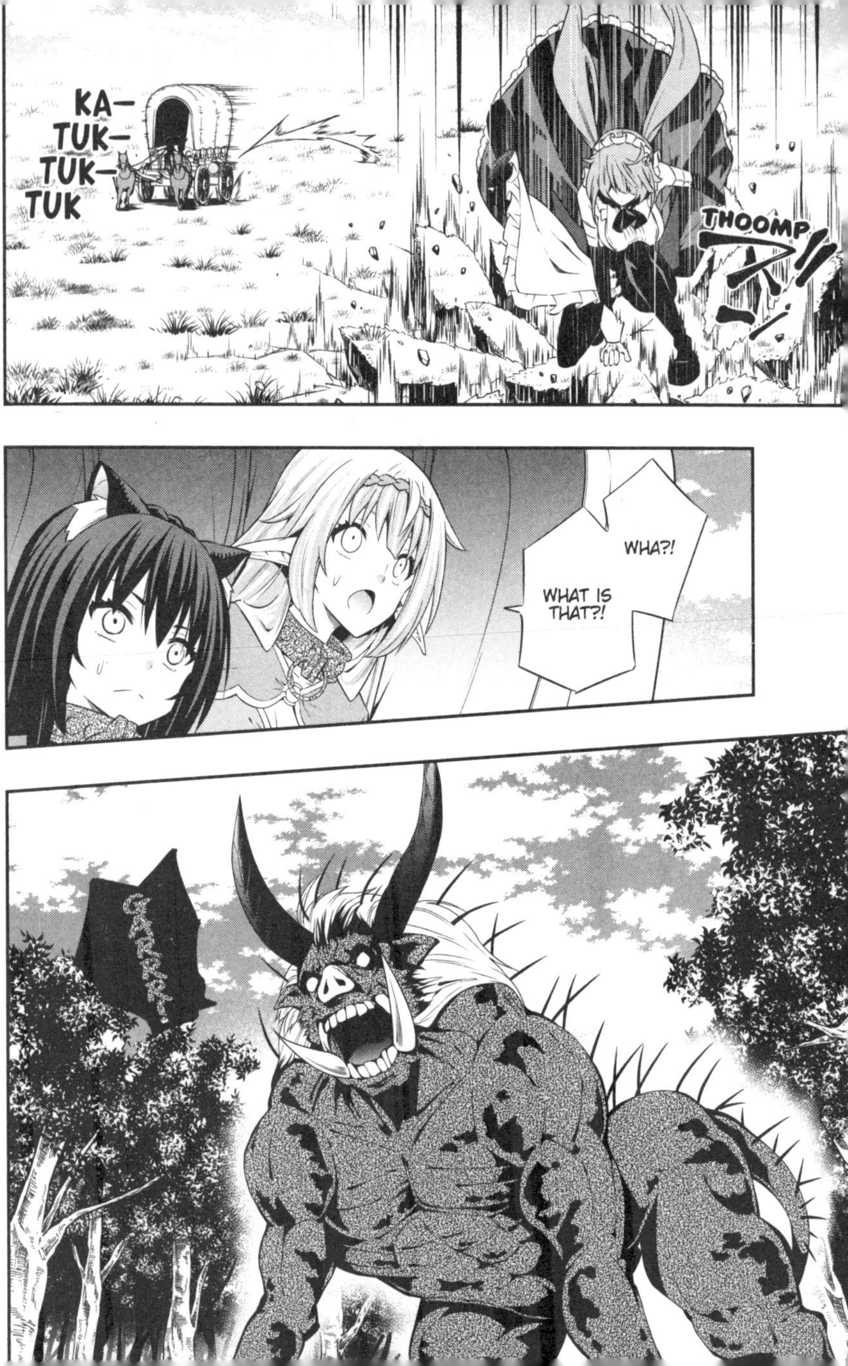
THOOMP
KA-TUK-TUK-TUK
WHA?!
WHAT IS THAT?!
GRRRR!

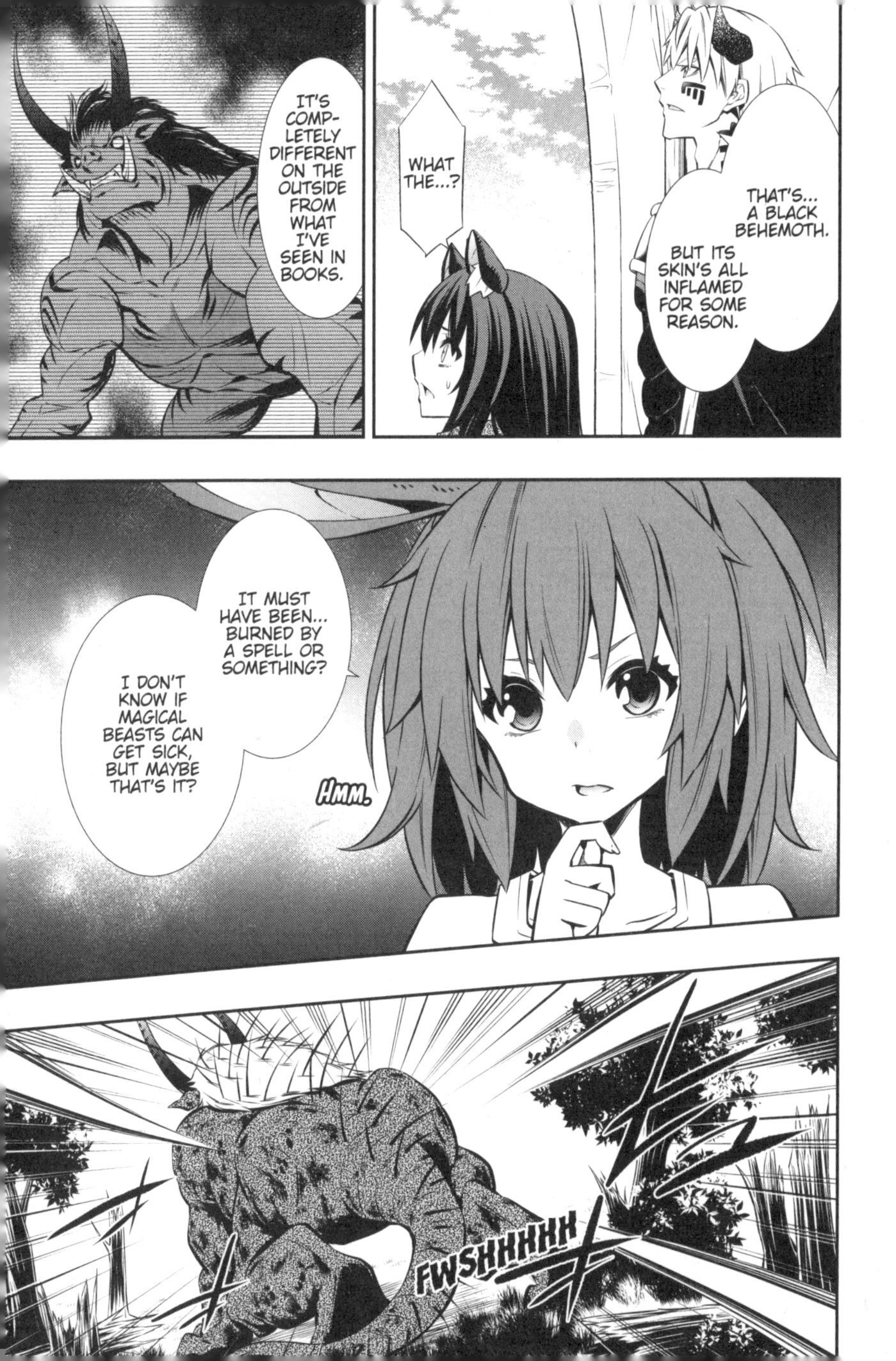
THAT'S... A BLACK BEHEMOTH.
BUT ITS SKIN'S ALL INFLAMED FOR SOME REASON.
WHAT THE...?
IT'S COMPLETELY DIFFERENT ON THE OUTSIDE FROM WHAT I'VE SEEN IN BOOKS.
IT MUST HAVE BEEN... BURNED BY A SPELL OR SOMETHING?
I DON'T KNOW IF MAGICAL BEASTS CAN GET SICK, BUT MAYBE THAT'S IT?
HMM.
FWSHHHHH

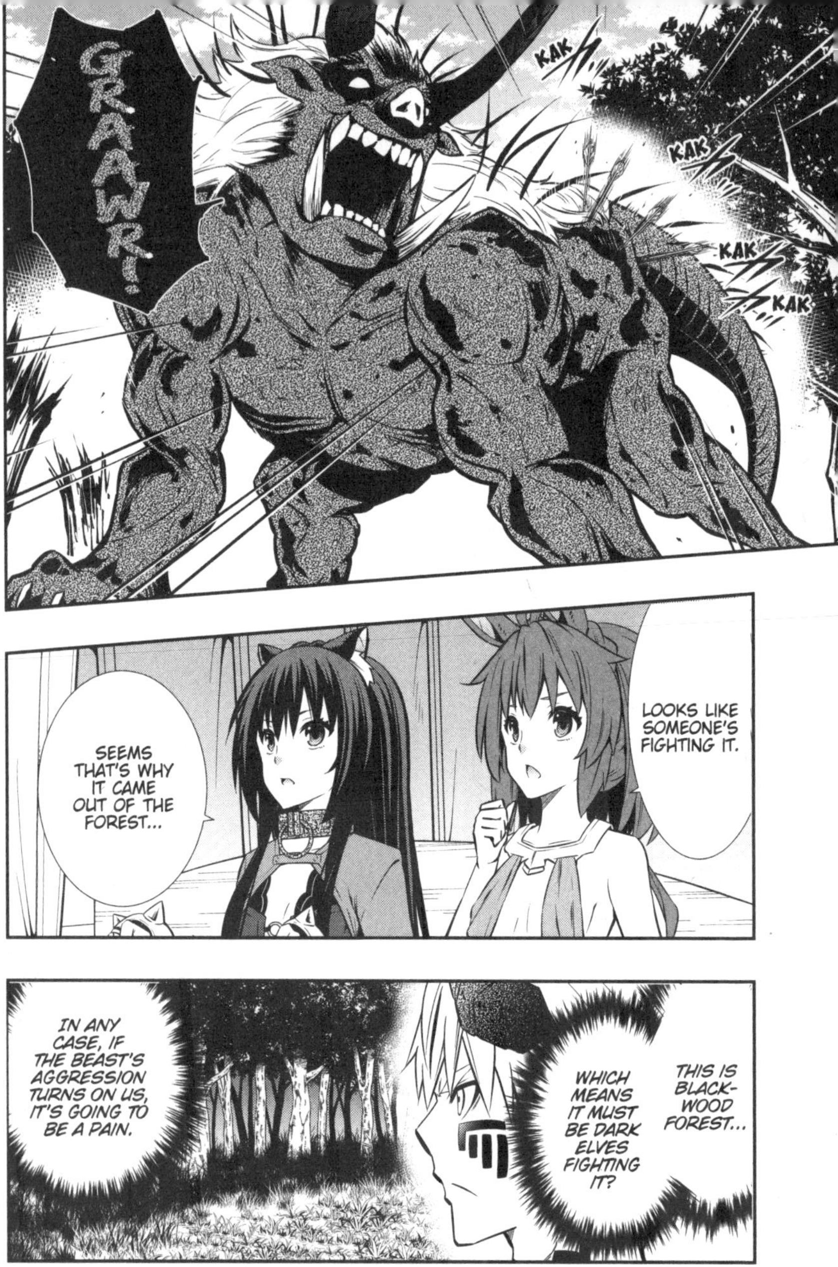
KAK
KAK
KAK
KAK
GRAAWR!
LOOKS LIKE SOMEONE'S FIGHTING IT.
SEEMS THAT'S WHY IT CAME OUT OF THE FOREST...
THIS IS BLACK-WOOD FOREST...
WHICH MEANS IT MUST BE DARK ELVES FIGHTING IT?
IN ANY CASE, IF THE BEAST'S AGGRESSION TURNS ON US, IT'S GOING TO BE A PAIN.

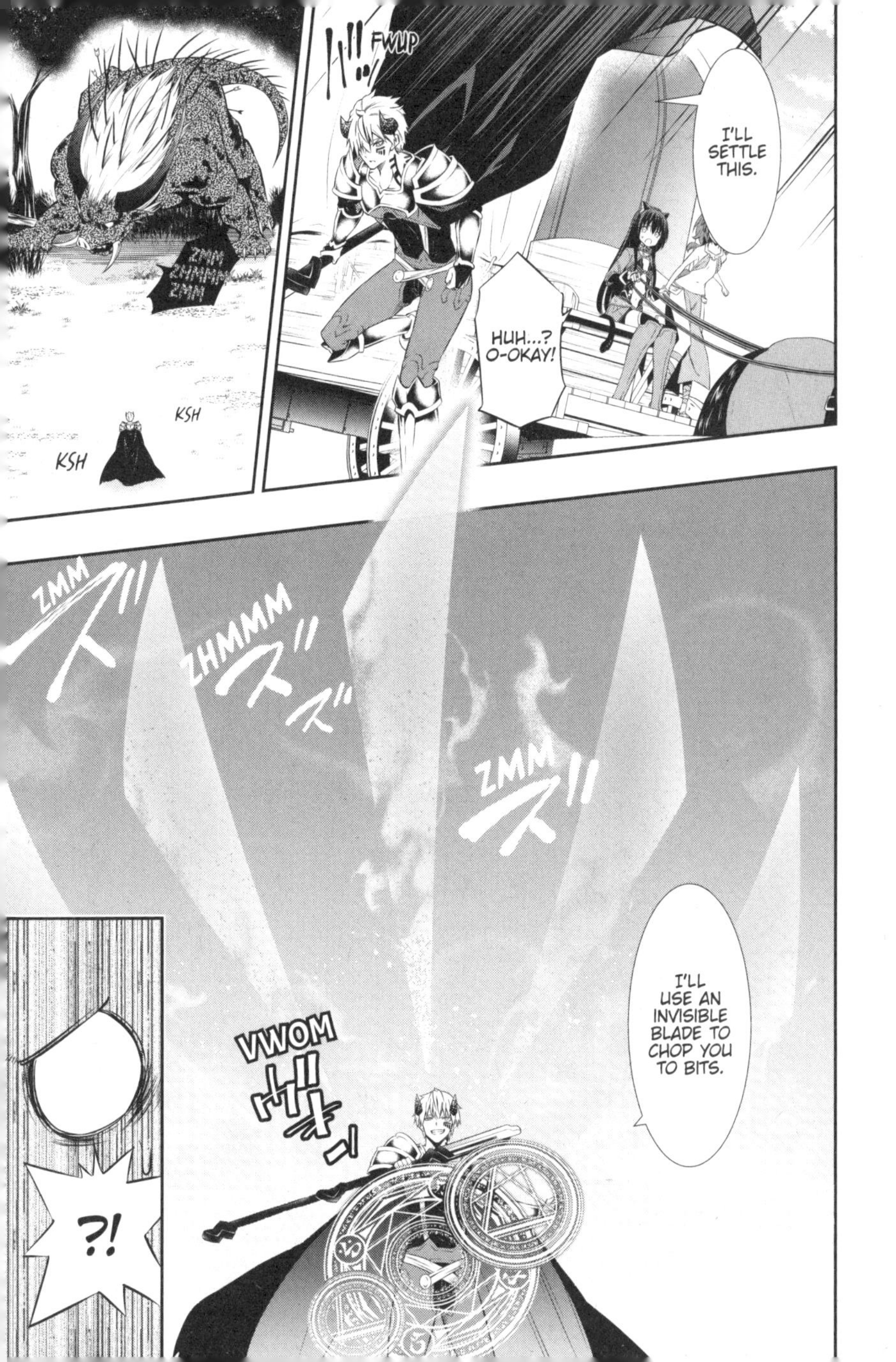
FWUP
I'LL SETTLE THIS.
HUH...? O-OKAY!
ZMM ZMMM ZMM
KSH
KSH
ZMM
ZHMMM
ZMM
I'LL USE AN INVISIBLE BLADE TO CHOP YOU TO BITS.
VWOM
?!

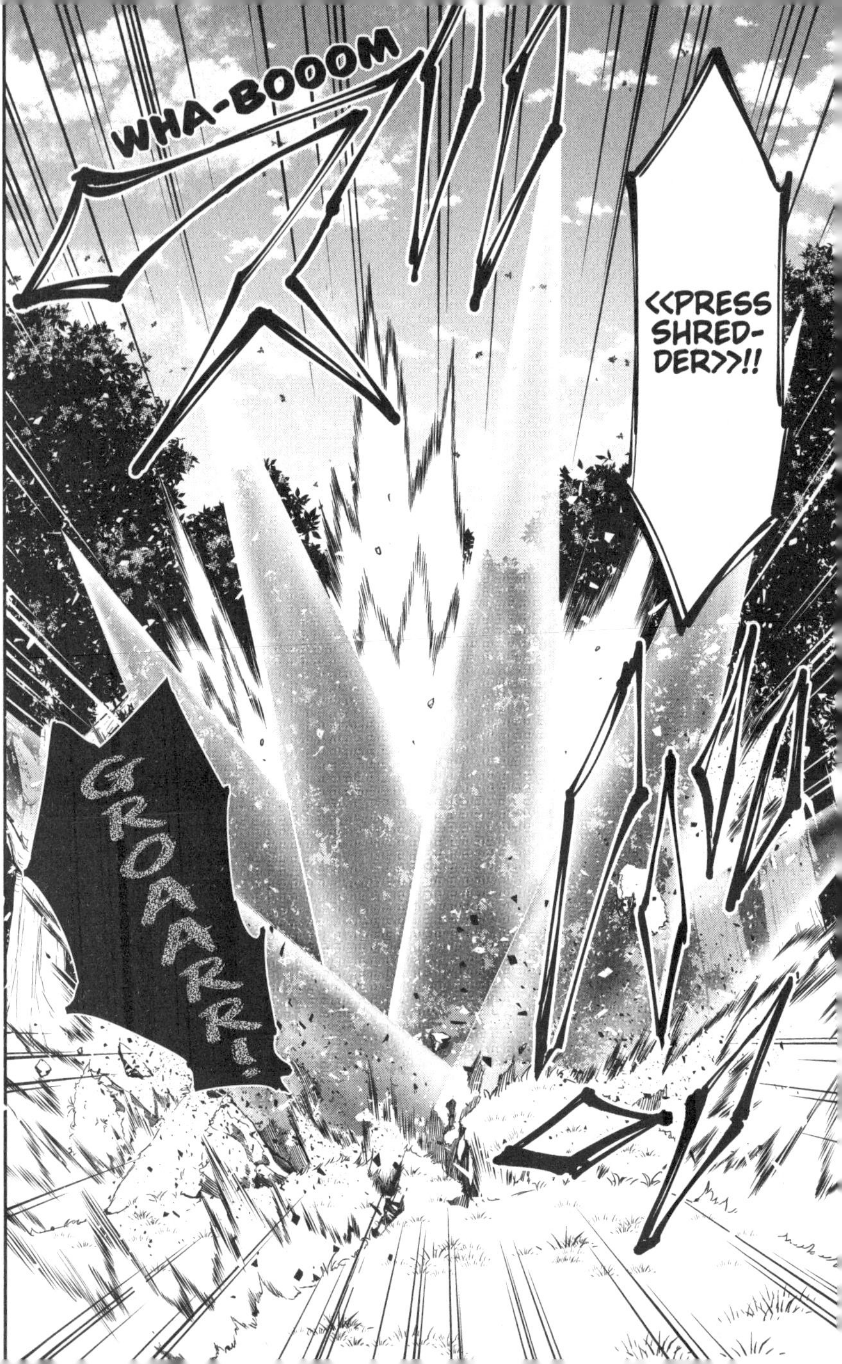
<<PRESS SHRED-DER>>!!
WHA-BOOOM
GROARR!!

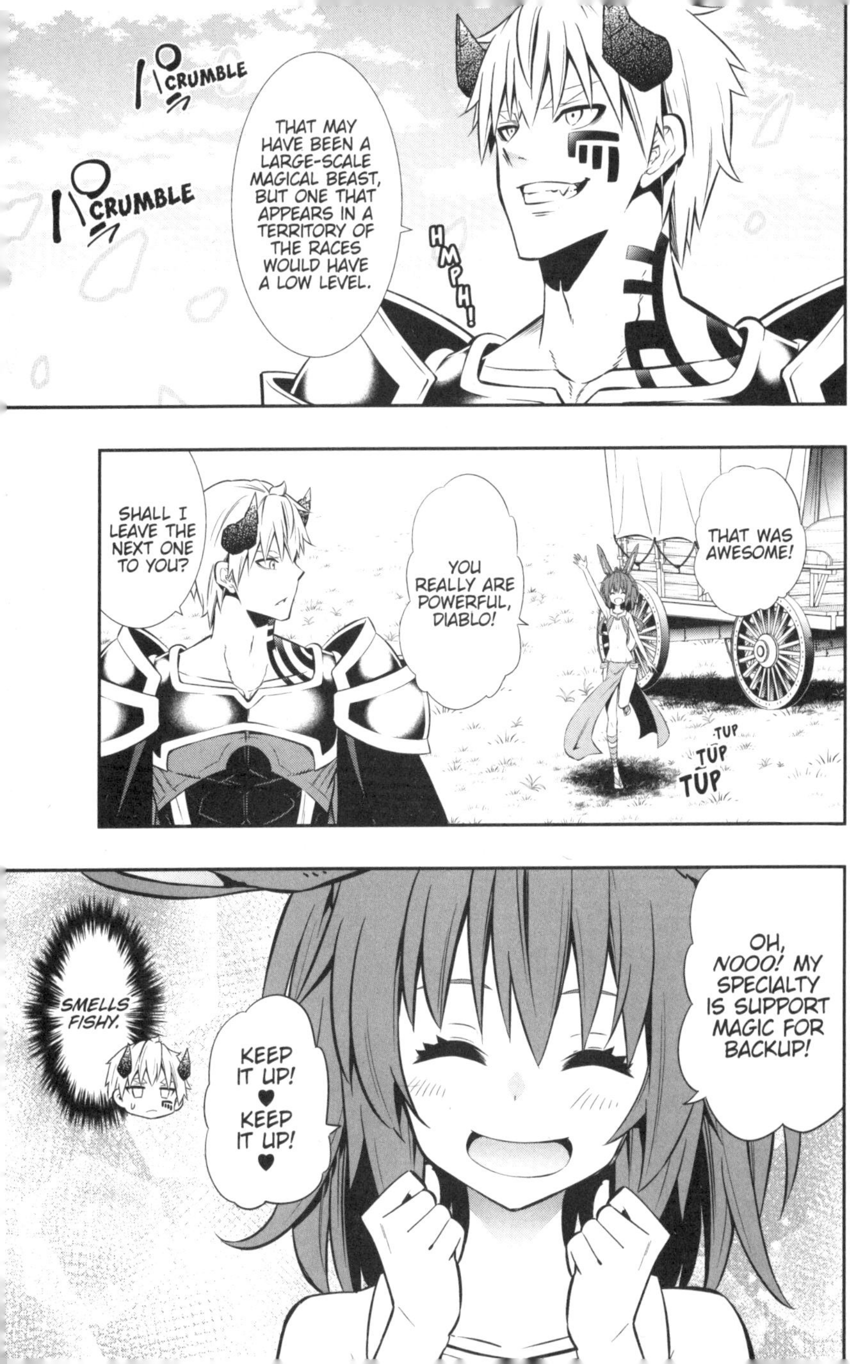
THAT MAY HAVE BEEN A LARGE-SCALE MAGICAL BEAST, BUT ONE THAT APPEARS IN A TERRITORY OF THE RACES WOULD HAVE A LOW LEVEL.
HMPH!
CRUMBLE
CRUMBLE
THAT WAS AWESOME!
YOU REALLY ARE POWERFUL, DIABLO!
TUP
TUP
TUP
SHALL I LEAVE THE NEXT ONE TO YOU?
OH, NOOO! MY SPECIALTY IS SUPPORT MAGIC FOR BACKUP!
KEEP IT UP! ♥ KEEP IT UP! ♥
SMELLS FISHY.

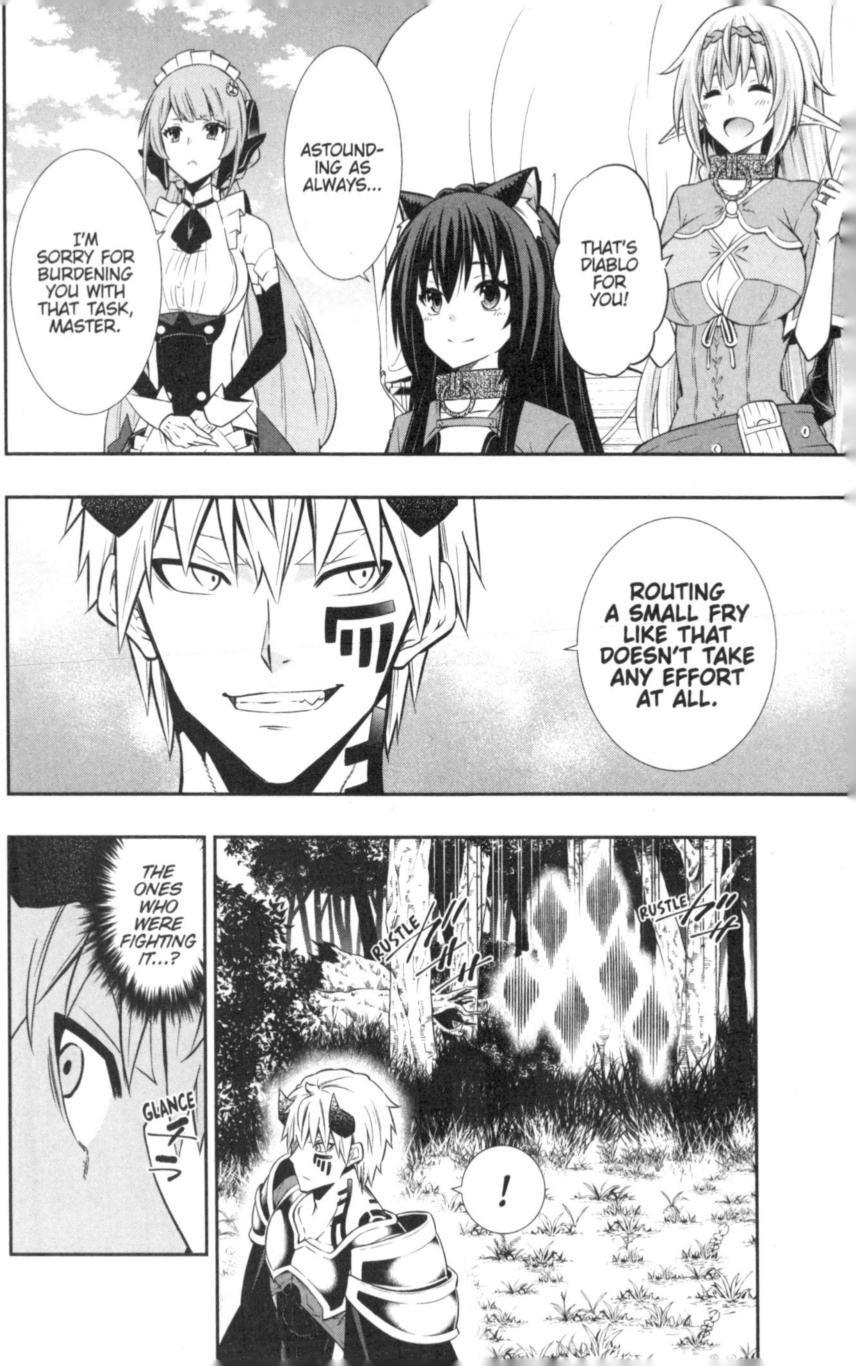
THAT'S DIABLO FOR YOU!
ASTOUNDING AS ALWAYS...
I'M SORRY FOR BURDENING YOU WITH THAT TASK, MASTER.
ROUTING A SMALL FRY LIKE THAT DOESN'T TAKE ANY EFFORT AT ALL.
RUSTLE
RUSTLE
!
THE ONES WHO WERE FIGHTING IT...?
GLANCE

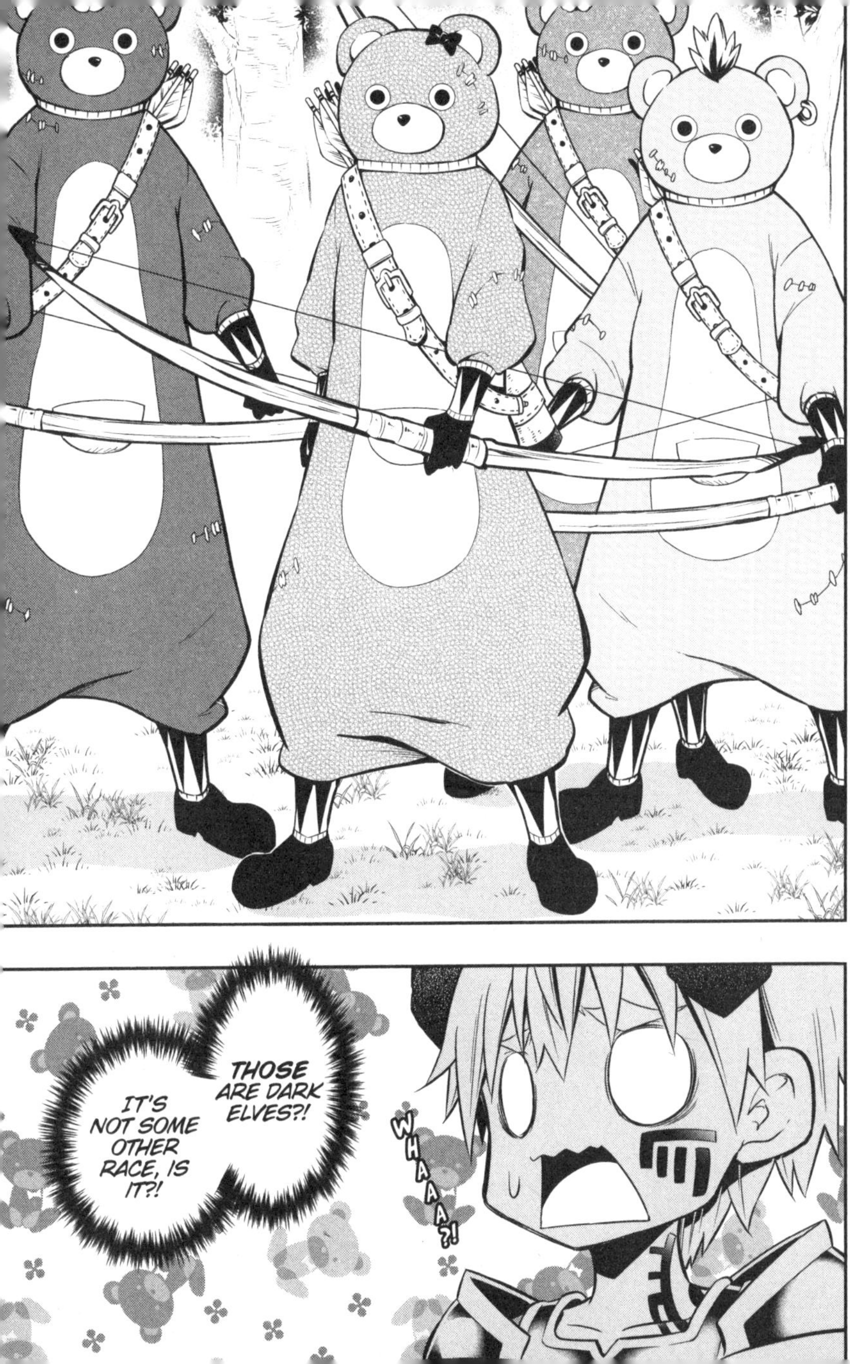
THOSE ARE DARK ELVES?!
IT'S NOT SOME OTHER RACE, IS IT?!
WHAAAA?!

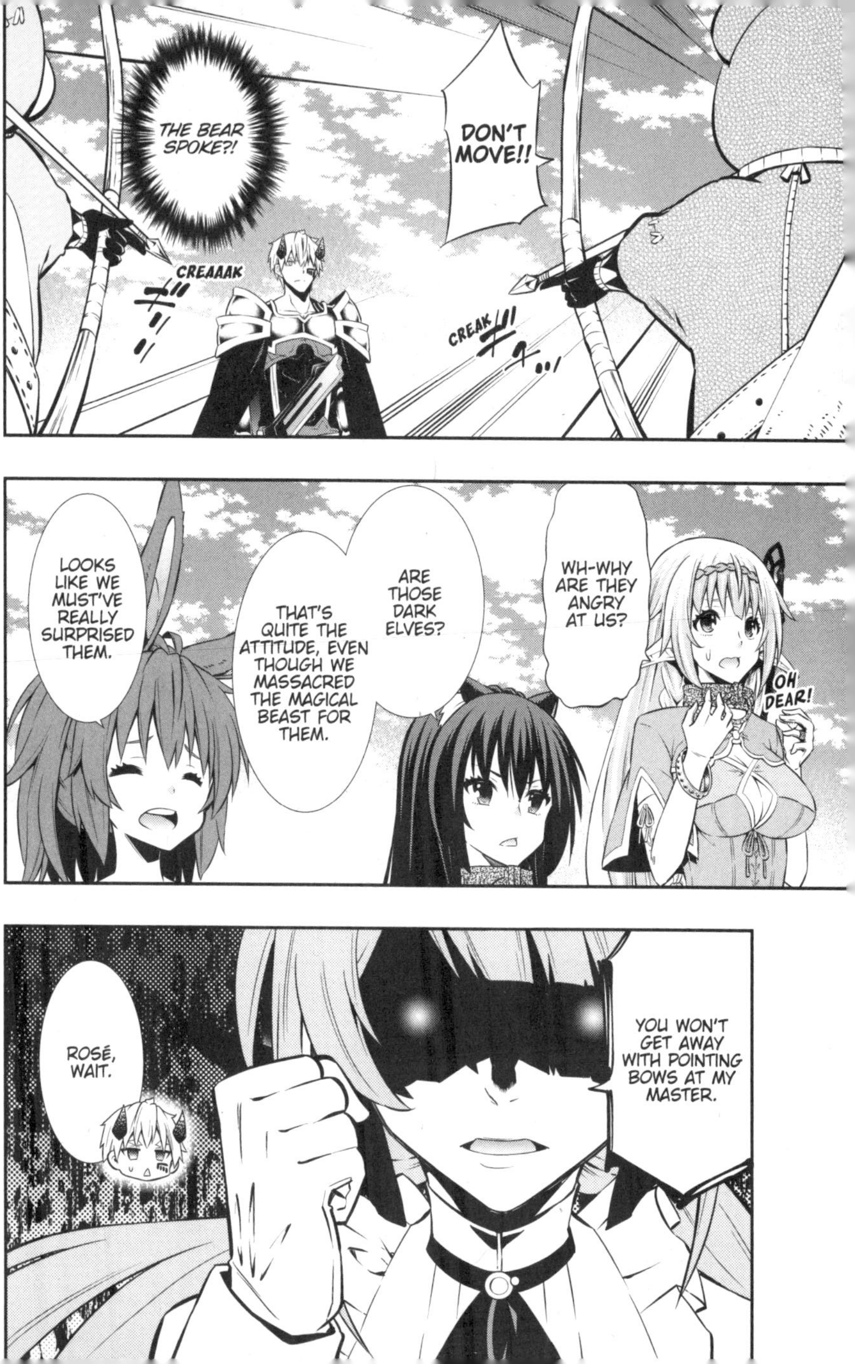
DON'T MOVE!!
THE BEAR SPOKE?!
CREAK
CREAAAK
WH-WHY ARE THEY ANGRY AT US?
OH DEAR!
ARE THOSE DARK ELVES?
THAT'S QUITE THE ATTITUDE, EVEN THOUGH WE MASSACRED THE MAGICAL BEAST FOR THEM.
LOOKS LIKE WE MUST'VE REALLY SURPRISED THEM.
YOU WON'T GET AWAY WITH POINTING BOWS AT MY MASTER.
ROSÉ, WAIT.

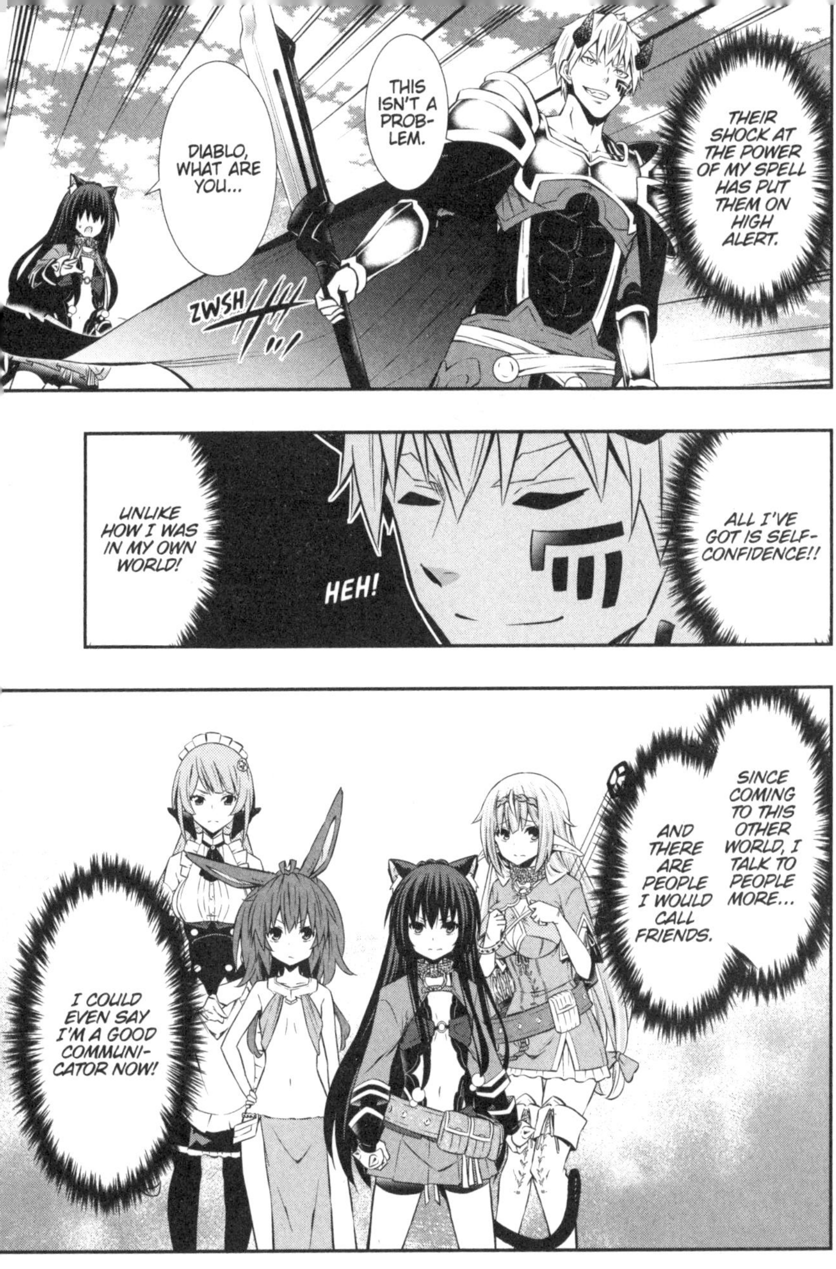
THEIR SHOCK AT THE POWER OF MY SPELL HAS PUT THEM ON HIGH ALERT.
THIS ISN'T A PROB-LEM.
DIABLO, WHAT ARE YOU...
ZWSH
ALL I'VE GOT IS SELF-CONFIDENCE!!
HEH!
UNLIKE HOW I WAS IN MY OWN WORLD!
SINCE COMING TO THIS OTHER WORLD, I TALK TO PEOPLE MORE...
AND THERE ARE PEOPLE I WOULD CALL FRIENDS.
I COULD EVEN SAY I'M A GOOD COMMUNI-CATOR NOW!

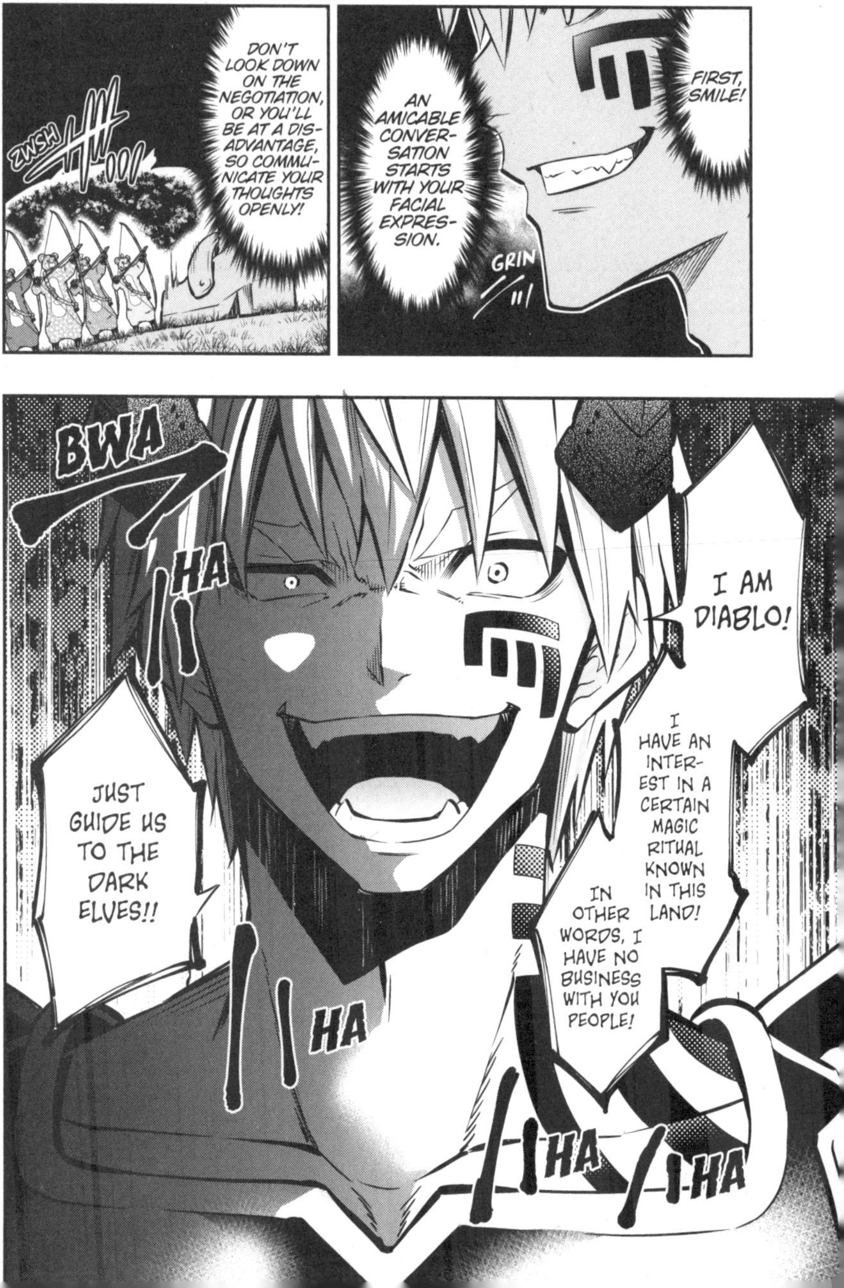
FIRST, SMILE!
AN AMICABLE CONVERSATION STARTS WITH YOUR FACIAL EXPRESSION.
GRIN
DON'T LOOK DOWN ON THE NEGOTIATION, OR YOU'LL BE AT A DISADVANTAGE, SO COMMUNICATE YOUR THOUGHTS OPENLY!
ZWSH
I AM DIABLO!
I HAVE AN INTEREST IN A CERTAIN MAGIC RITUAL KNOWN IN THIS LAND!
BWA
HA
IN OTHER WORDS, I HAVE NO BUSINESS WITH YOU PEOPLE!
JUST GUIDE US TO THE DARK ELVES!!
HA
HA
HA-HA

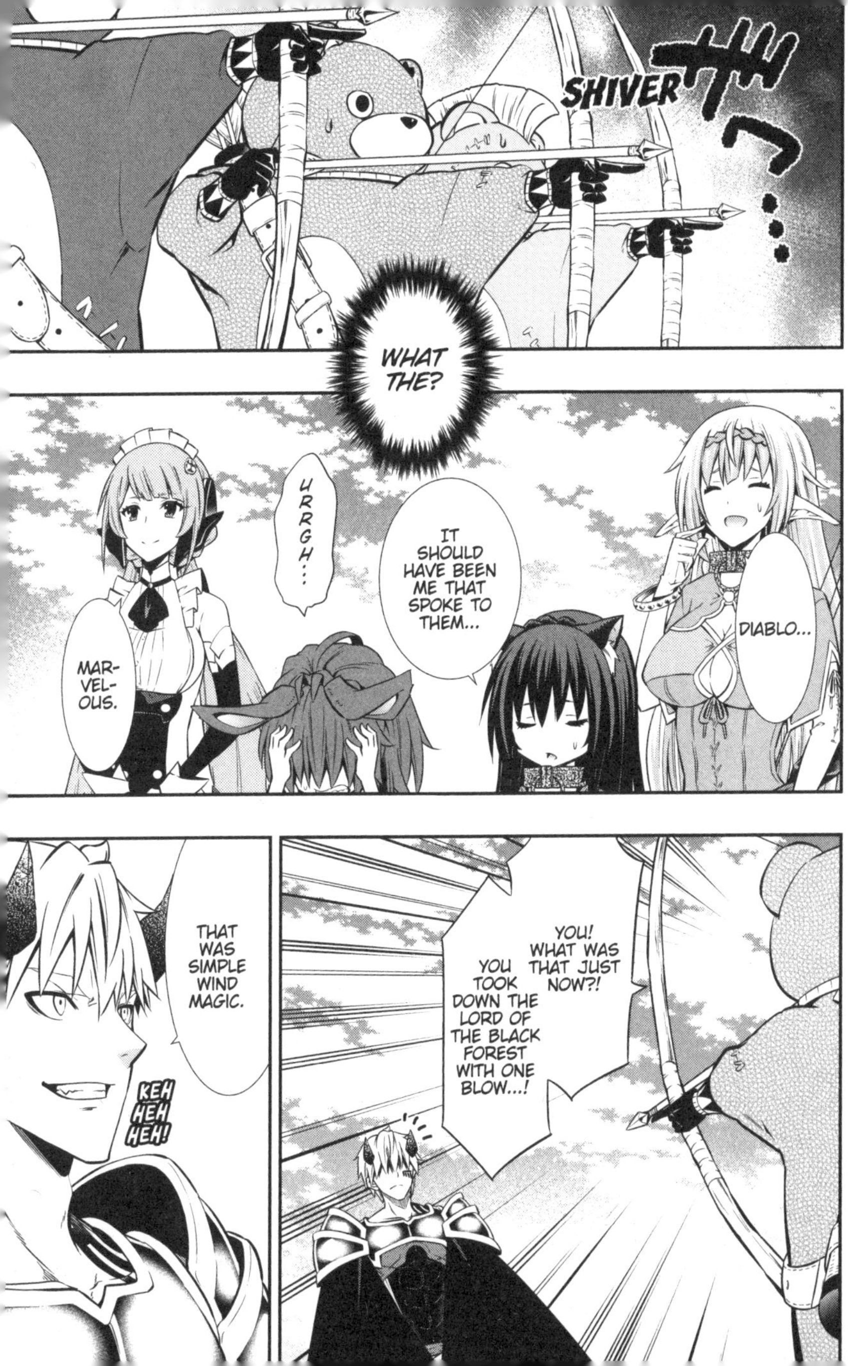
SHIVER
WHAT THE?
DIABLO...
IT SHOULD HAVE BEEN ME THAT SPOKE TO THEM...
URRGH...
MAR-VEL-OUS.
YOU! WHAT WAS THAT JUST NOW?!
YOU TOOK DOWN THE LORD OF THE BLACK FOREST WITH ONE BLOW...!
THAT WAS SIMPLE WIND MAGIC.
KEH HEH HEH!

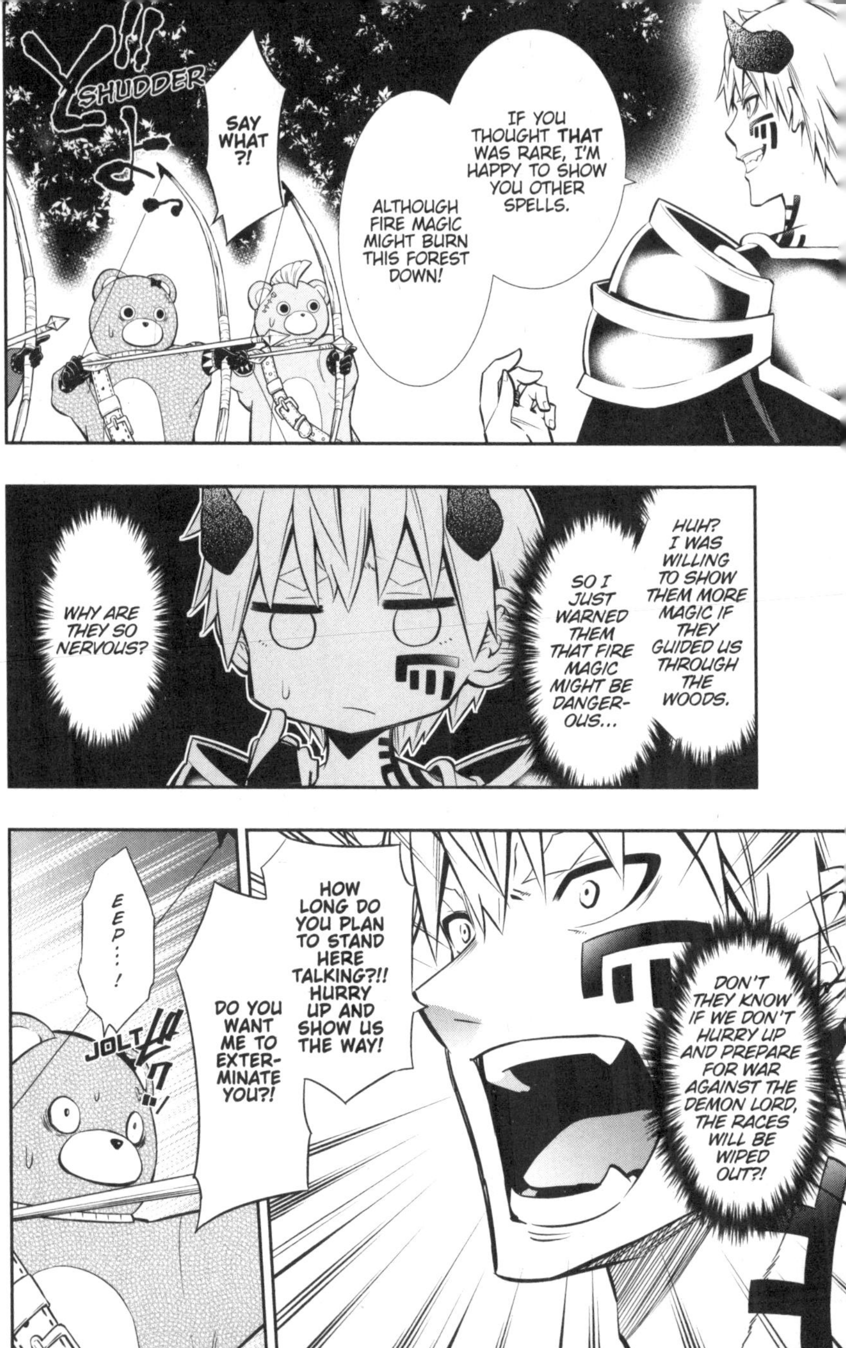

IF YOU THOUGHT THAT WAS RARE, I'M HAPPY TO SHOW YOU OTHER SPELLS.
ALTHOUGH FIRE MAGIC MIGHT BURN THIS FOREST DOWN!
SAY WHAT ?!
SHUDDER
HUH? I WAS WILLING TO SHOW THEM MORE MAGIC IF THEY GUIDED US THROUGH THE WOODS.
SO I JUST WARNED THEM THAT FIRE MAGIC MIGHT BE DANGER-OUS...
WHY ARE THEY SO NERVOUS?
DON'T THEY KNOW IF WE DON'T HURRY UP AND PREPARE FOR WAR AGAINST THE DEMON LORD, THE RACES WILL BE WIPED OUT?!
HOW LONG DO YOU PLAN TO STAND HERE TALKING?!! HURRY UP AND SHOW US THE WAY!
DO YOU WANT ME TO EXTER-MINATE YOU?!
EEP...!
JOLT

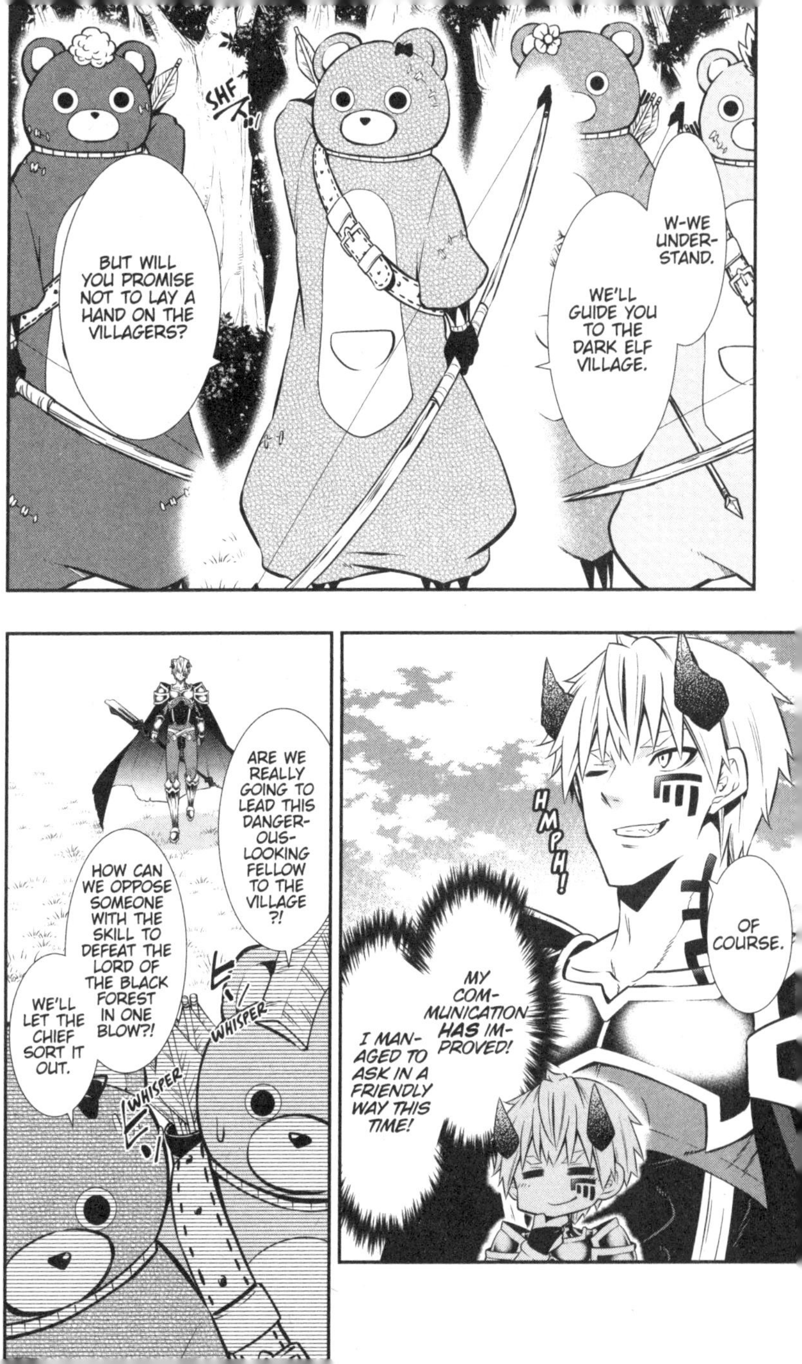
SHF
W-WE UNDER-STAND.
WE'LL GUIDE YOU TO THE DARK ELF VILLAGE.
BUT WILL YOU PROMISE NOT TO LAY A HAND ON THE VILLAGERS?
OF COURSE.
HMPH!
MY COM-MUNICATION HAS IM-PROVED!
I MAN-AGED TO ASK IN A FRIENDLY WAY THIS TIME!
ARE WE REALLY GOING TO LEAD THIS DANGER-OUS-LOOKING FELLOW TO THE VILLAGE ?!
HOW CAN WE OPPOSE SOMEONE WITH THE SKILL TO DEFEAT THE LORD OF THE BLACK FOREST IN ONE BLOW?!
WHISPER
WE'LL LET THE CHIEF SORT IT OUT.
WHISPER

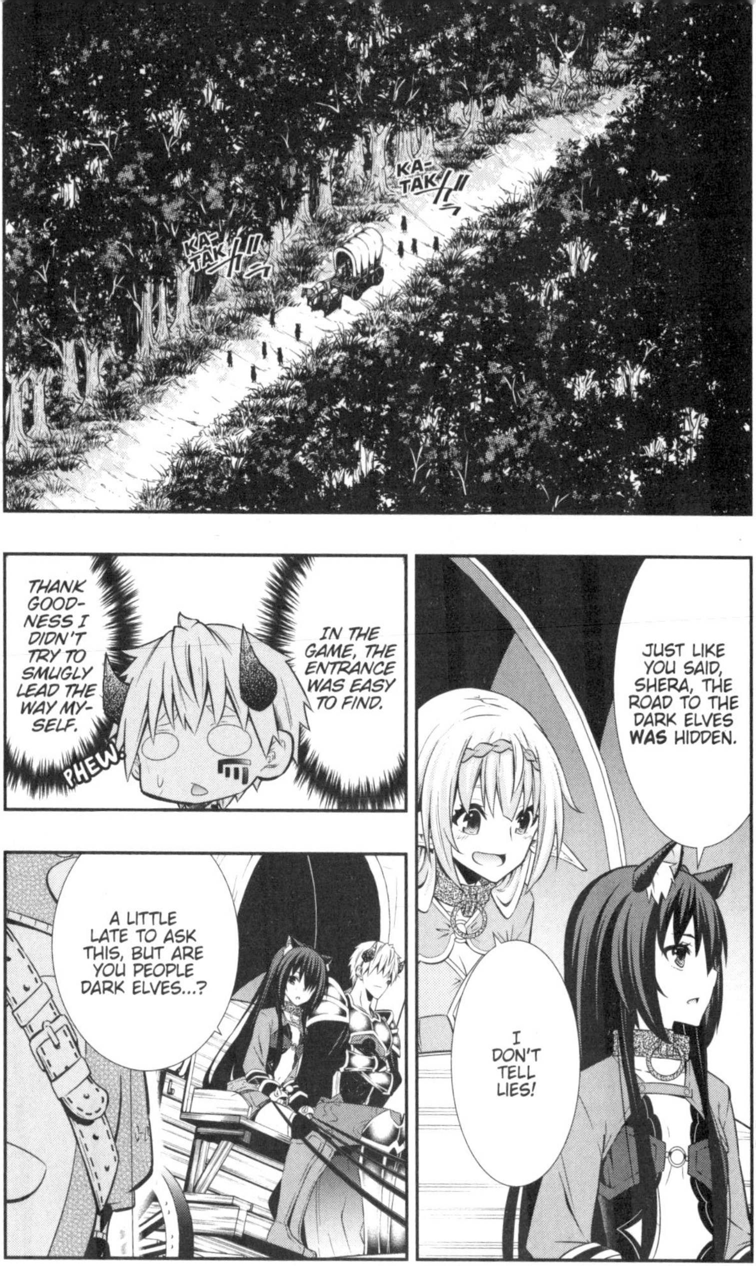
KA-TAK
KA-TAK
JUST LIKE YOU SAID, SHERA, THE ROAD TO THE DARK ELVES WAS HIDDEN.
I DON'T TELL LIES!
IN THE GAME, THE ENTRANCE WAS EASY TO FIND.
THANK GOODNESS I DIDN'T TRY TO SMUGLY LEAD THE WAY MYSELF.
PHEW!
A LITTLE LATE TO ASK THIS, BUT ARE YOU PEOPLE DARK ELVES...?

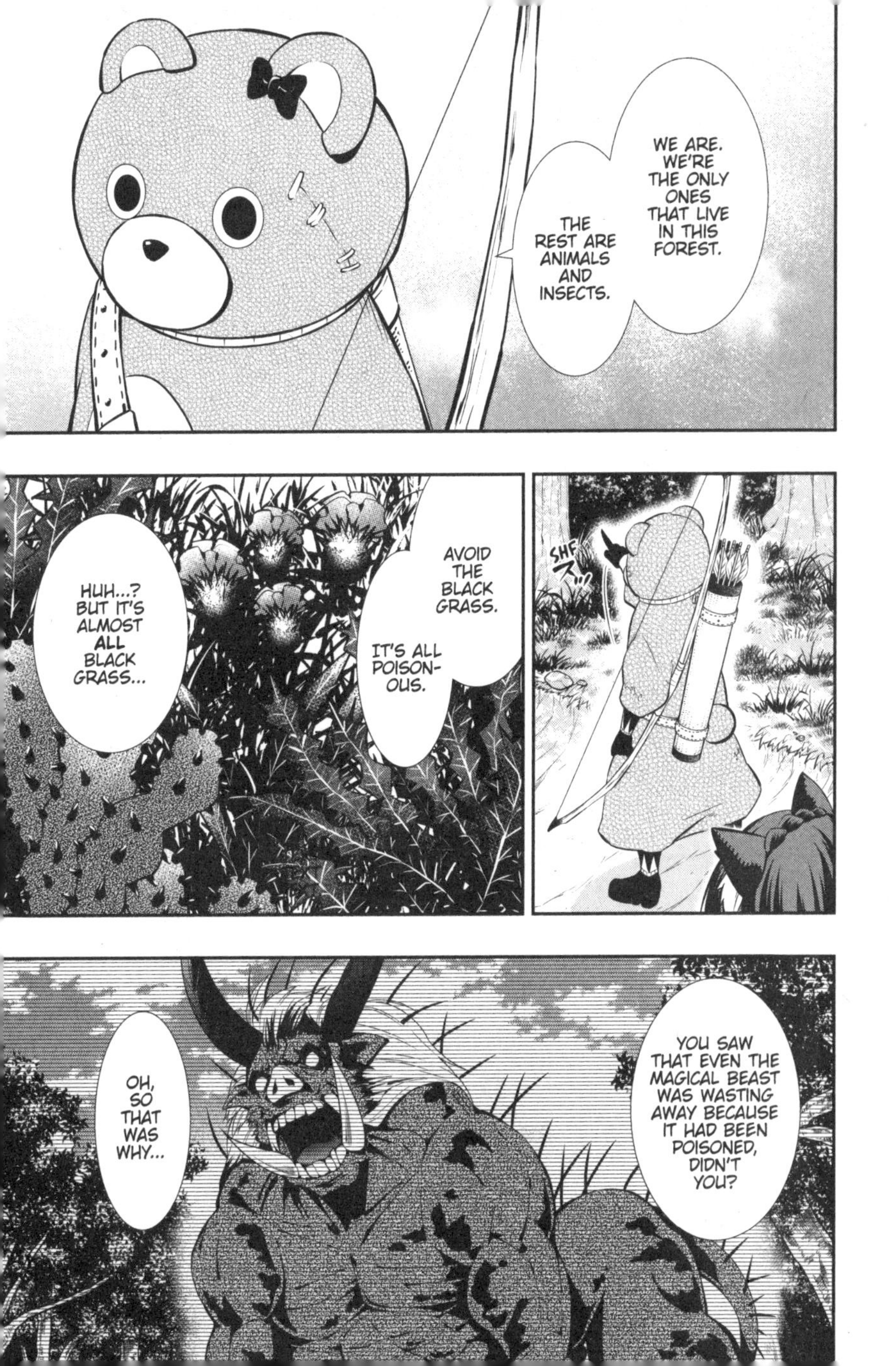
WE ARE. WE'RE THE ONLY ONES THAT LIVE IN THIS FOREST.
THE REST ARE ANIMALS AND INSECTS.
SHF
AVOID THE BLACK GRASS.
IT'S ALL POISONOUS.
HUH...? BUT IT'S ALMOST ALL BLACK GRASS...
YOU SAW THAT EVEN THE MAGICAL BEAST WAS WASTING AWAY BECAUSE IT HAD BEEN POISONED, DIDN'T YOU?
OH, SO THAT WAS WHY...

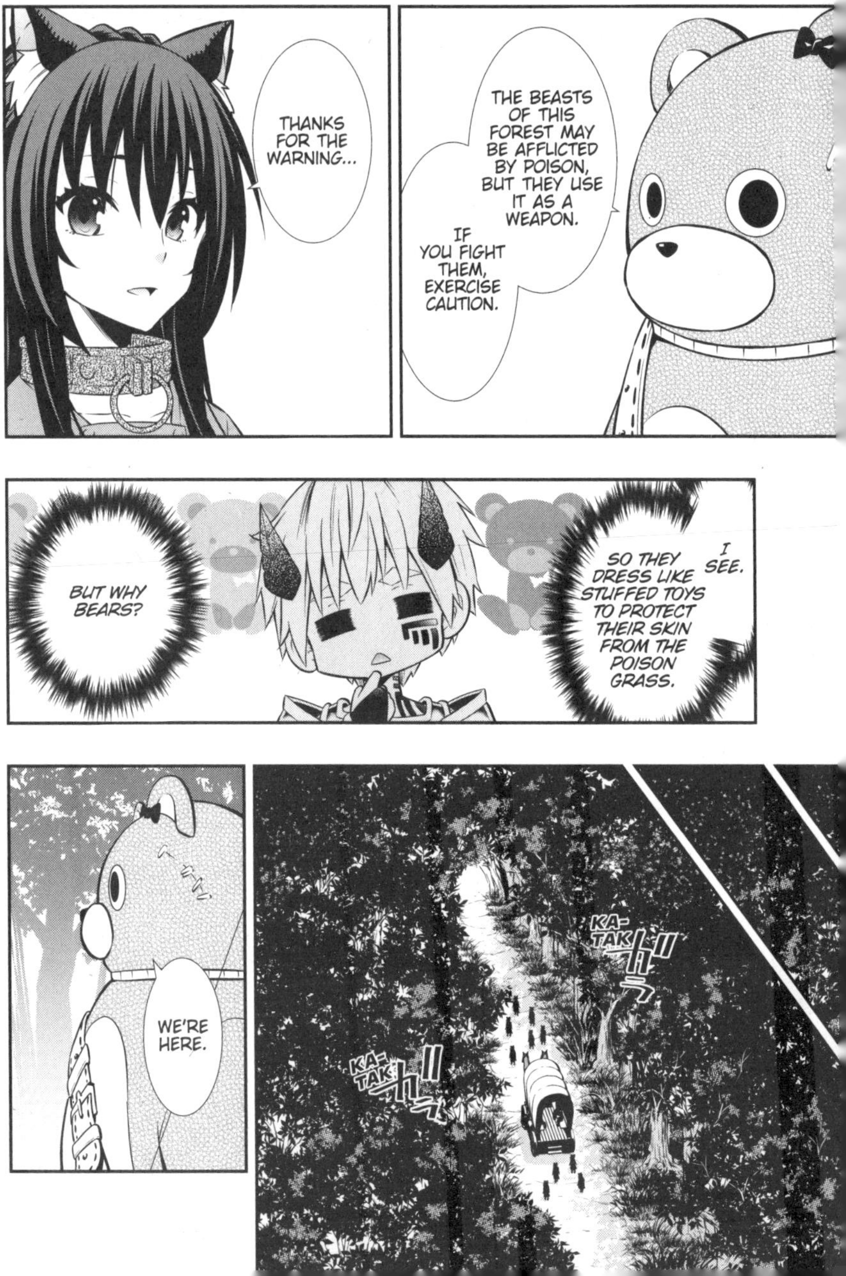
THE BEASTS OF THIS FOREST MAY BE AFFLICTED BY POISON, BUT THEY USE IT AS A WEAPON.
IF YOU FIGHT THEM, EXERCISE CAUTION.
THANKS FOR THE WARNING...
I SEE.
SO THEY DRESS LIKE STUFFED TOYS TO PROTECT THEIR SKIN FROM THE POISON GRASS.
BUT WHY BEARS?
KA-TAK
KA-TAK
WE'RE HERE.

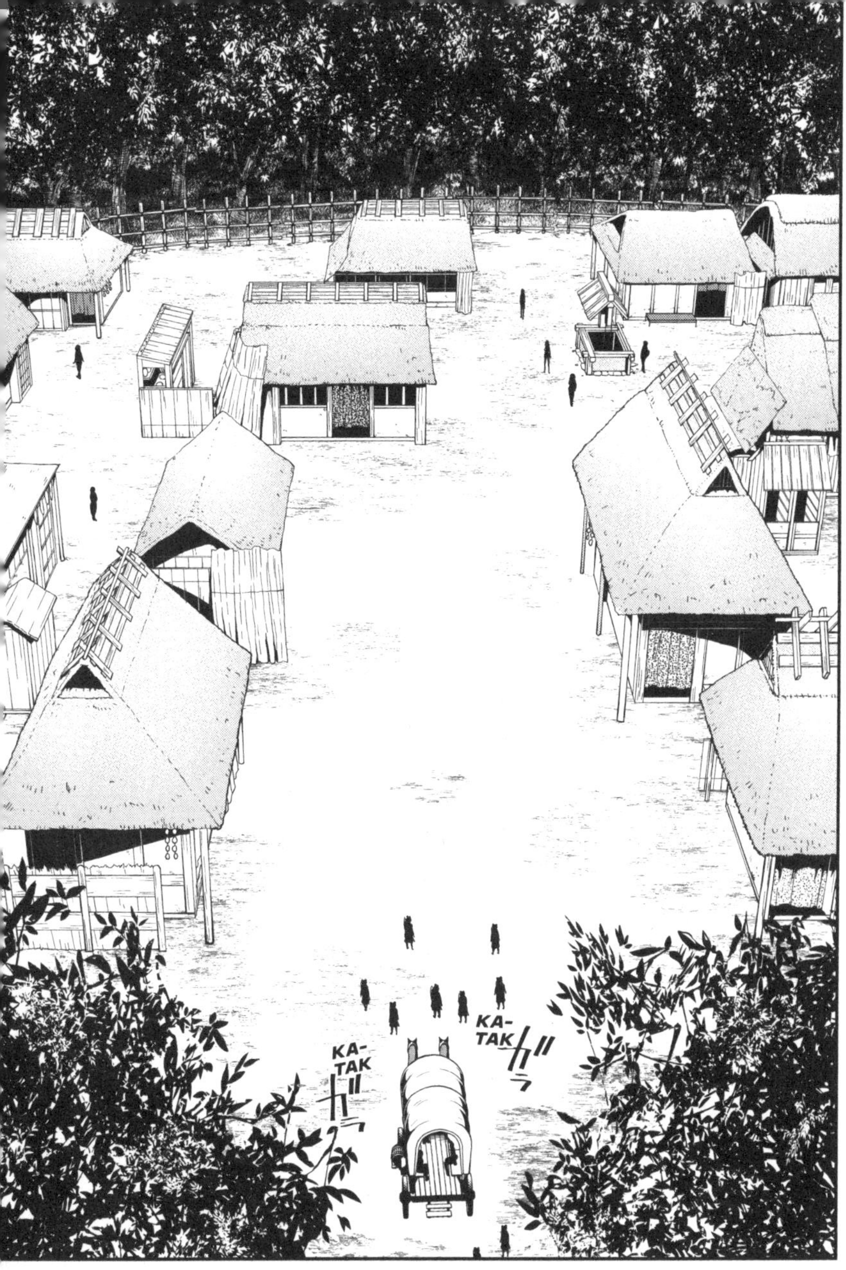
KA-
TAK
KA-
TAK

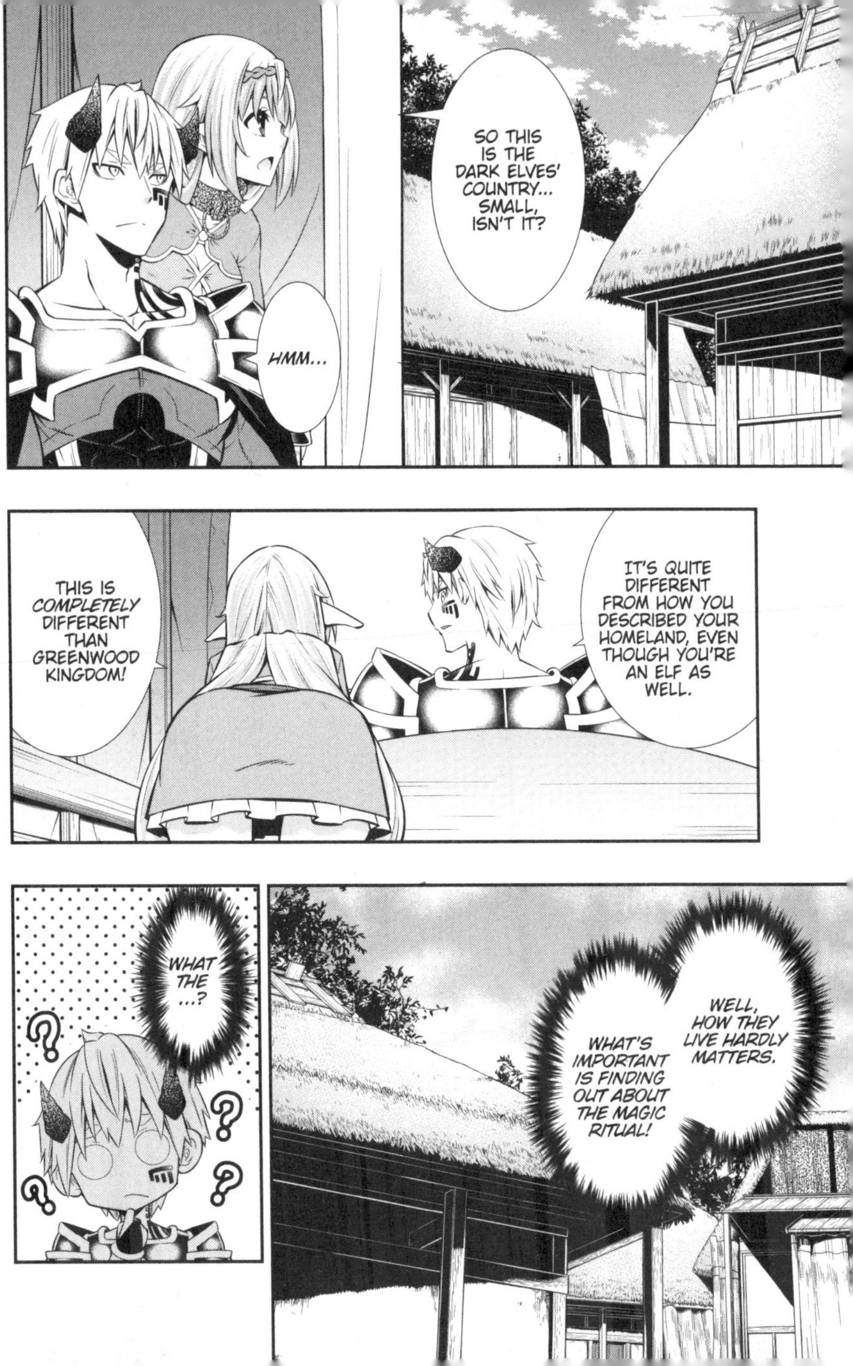
SO THIS IS THE DARK ELVES' COUNTRY... SMALL, ISN'T IT?
HMM...
IT'S QUITE DIFFERENT FROM HOW YOU DESCRIBED YOUR HOMELAND, EVEN THOUGH YOU'RE AN ELF AS WELL.
THIS IS COMPLETELY DIFFERENT THAN GREENWOOD KINGDOM!
WELL, HOW THEY LIVE HARDLY MATTERS.
WHAT'S IMPORTANT IS FINDING OUT ABOUT THE MAGIC RITUAL!
WHAT THE ...?

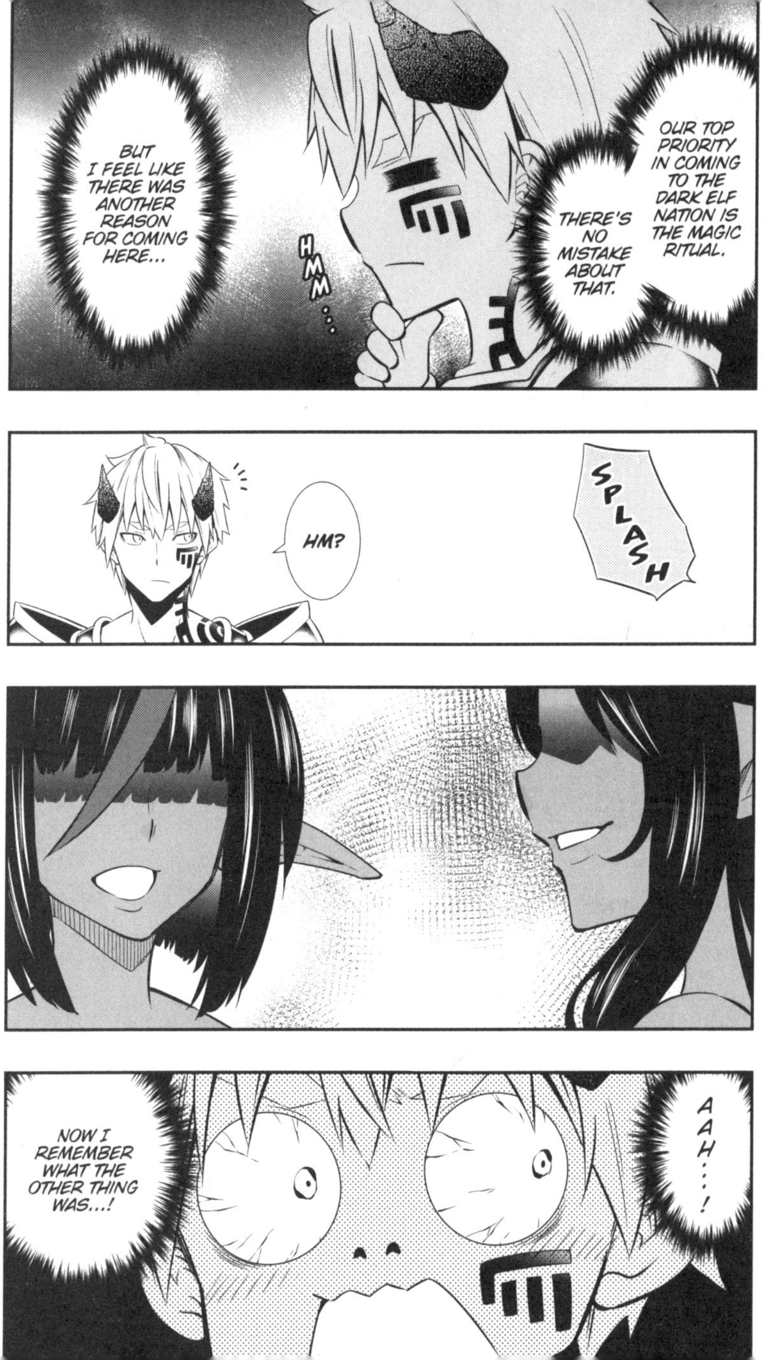
OUR TOP PRIORITY IN COMING TO THE DARK ELF NATION IS THE MAGIC RITUAL.
THERE'S NO MISTAKE ABOUT THAT.
HMM...
BUT I FEEL LIKE THERE WAS ANOTHER REASON FOR COMING HERE...
SPLASH
HM?
AAH...!
NOW I REMEMBER WHAT THE OTHER THING WAS...!

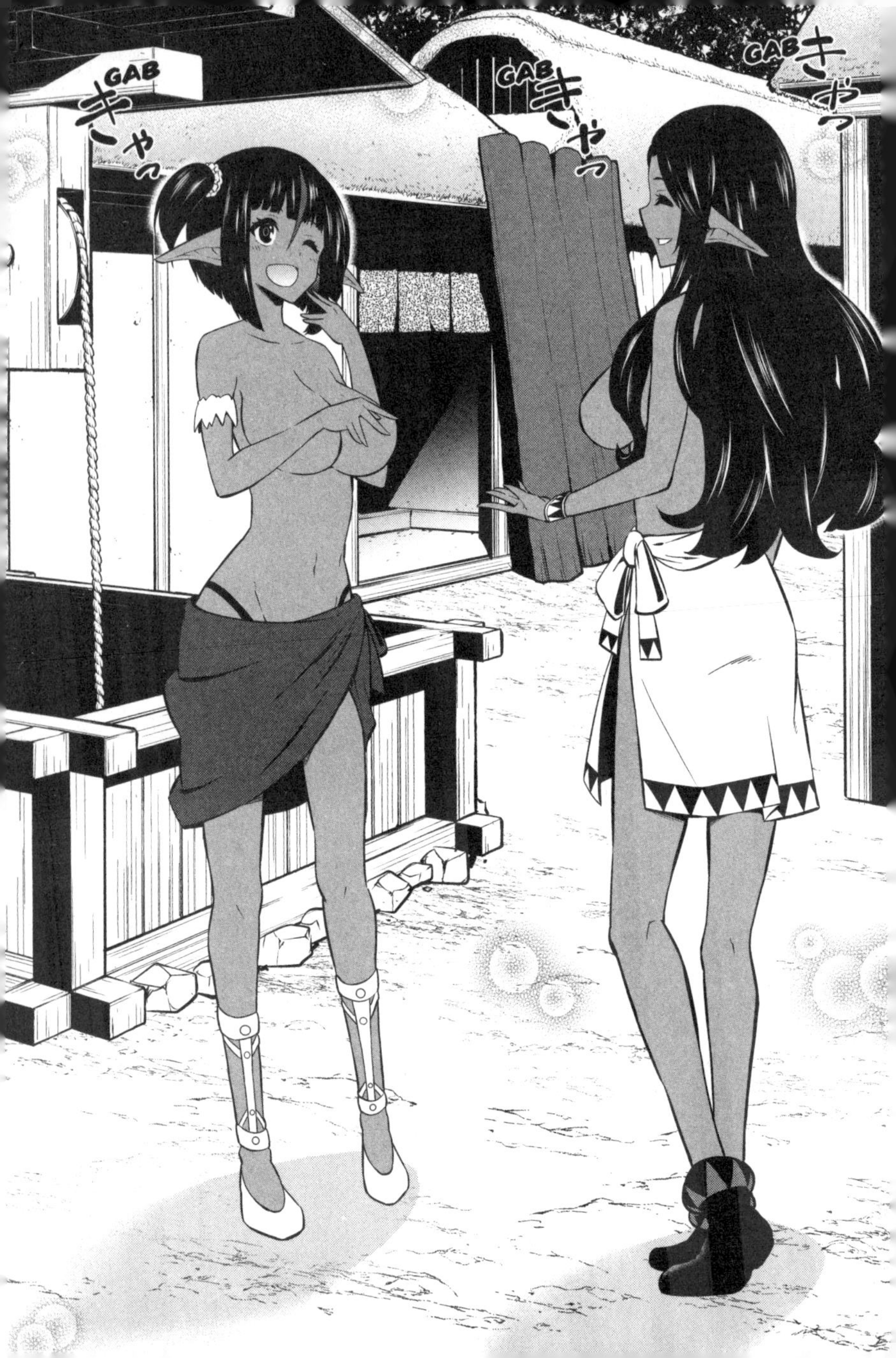
GAB
きゃっ
GAB
きゃっ
GAB
きゃっ

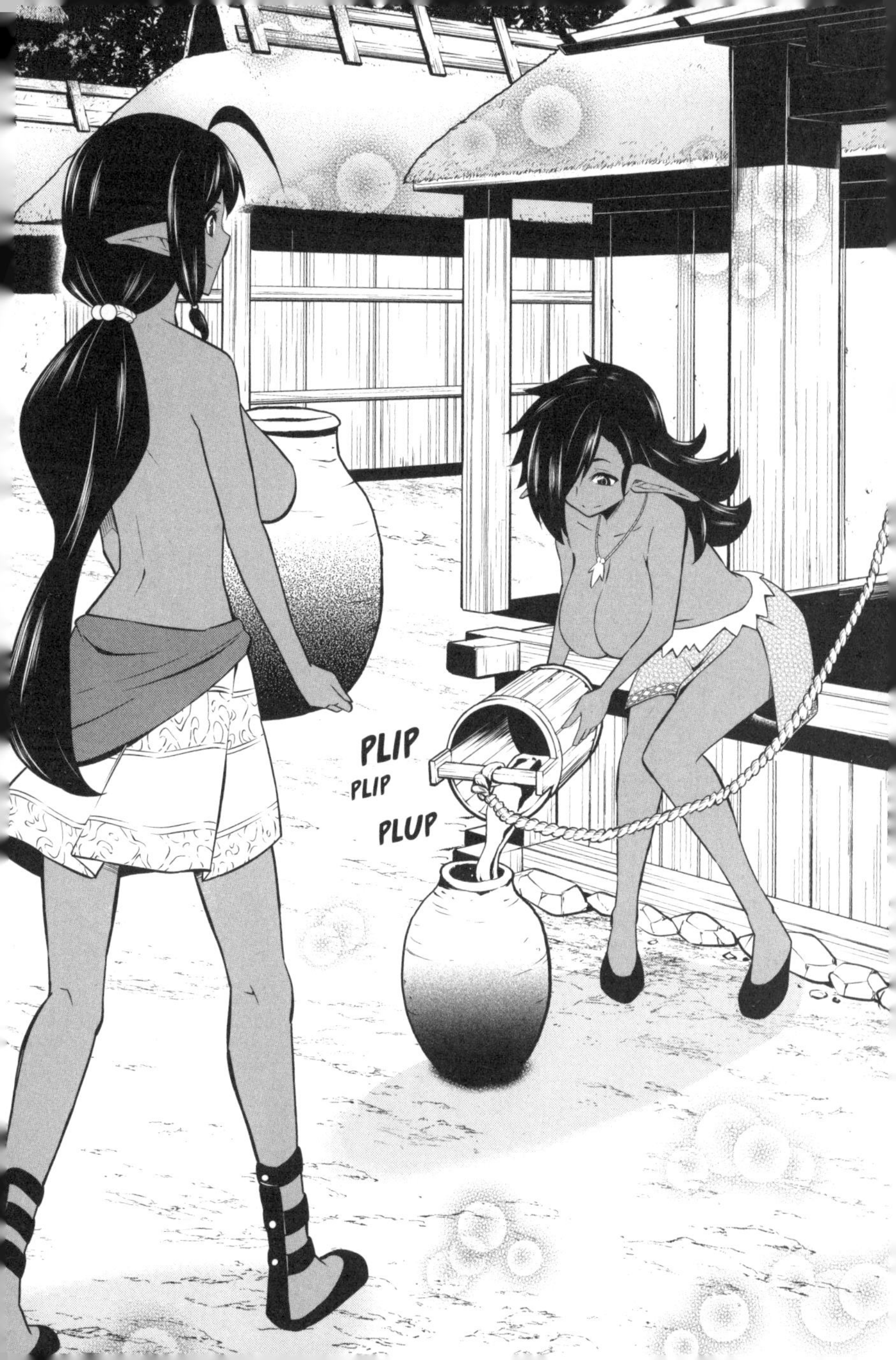
PLIP
PLIP
PLUP

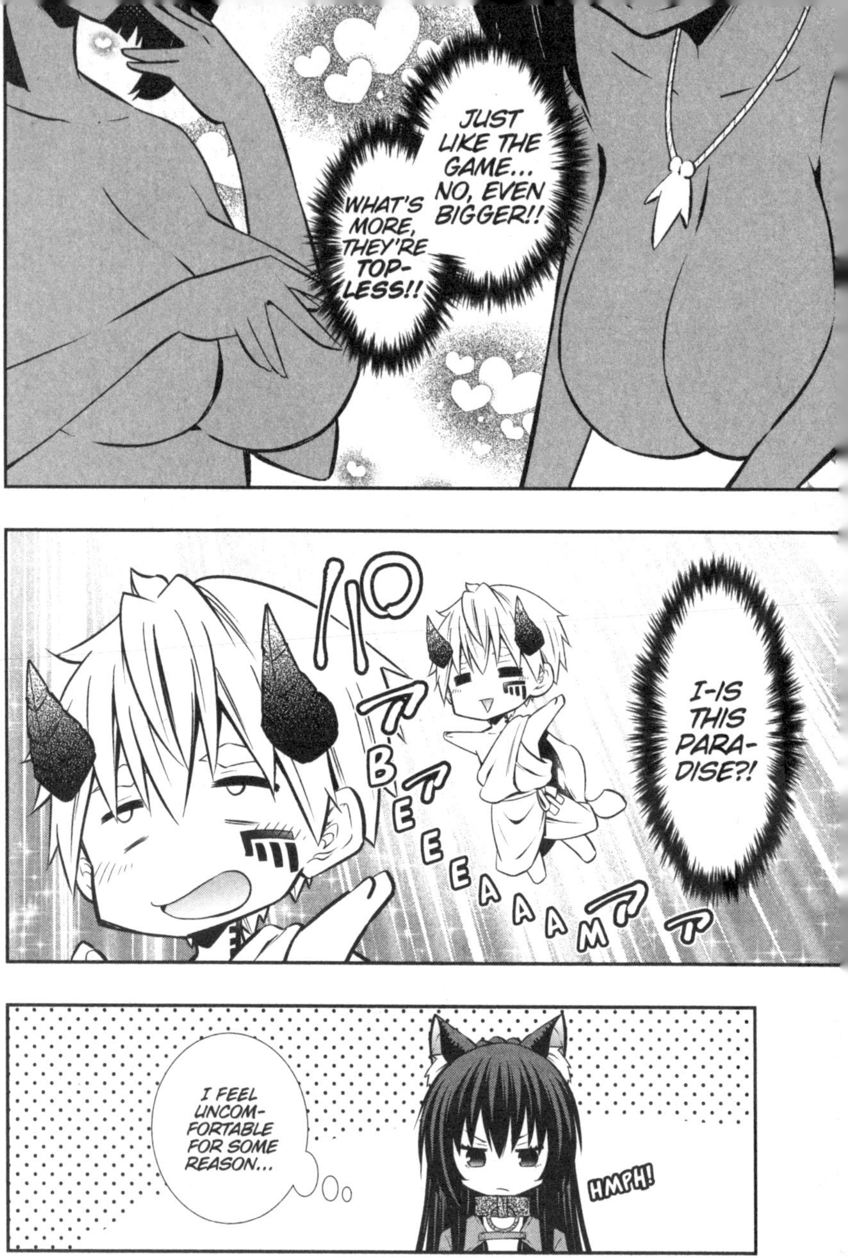
JUST LIKE THE GAME... NO, EVEN BIGGER!!
WHAT'S MORE, THEY'RE TOP-LESS!!
I-IS THIS PARA-DISE?!
BEEEAAAAM
HMPH!
I FEEL UNCOM-FORTABLE FOR SOME REASON...

HOW NOT
TO SUMMON A
DEMON LORD

to be continued...

SPECIAL THANKS FOR VOLUME 15

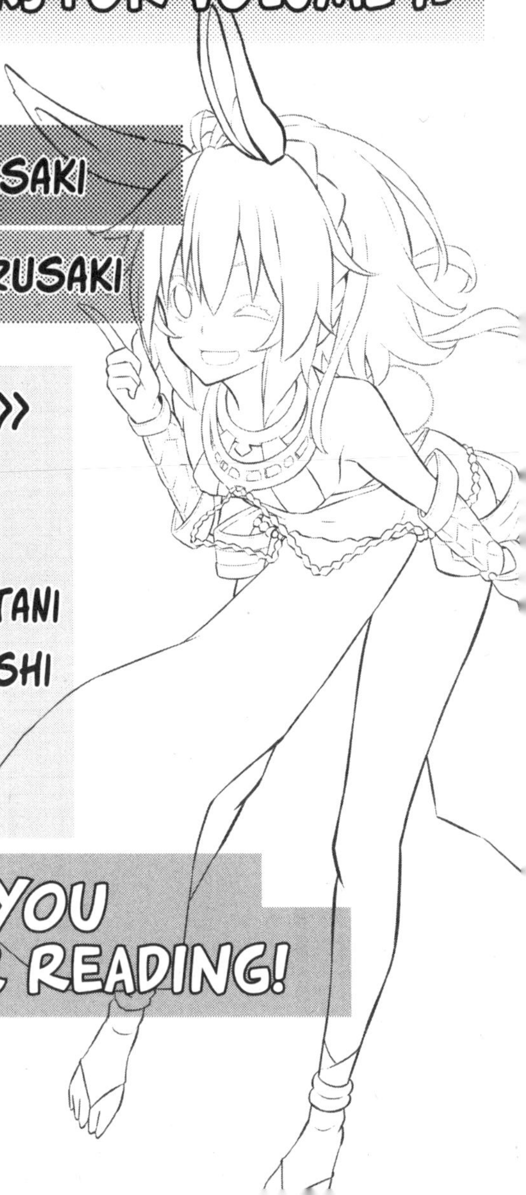

YUKIYA MURASAKI

TAKAHIRO TSURUSAKI

«ASSISTANTS»

DAIKI HARAGUCHI

YUU TAKIKAWA

MASUMI HIGASHITANI

DAISUKE MIYAKOSHI

MINA ITAGAKI

KOMADOGIWA

THANK YOU
FOR READING!

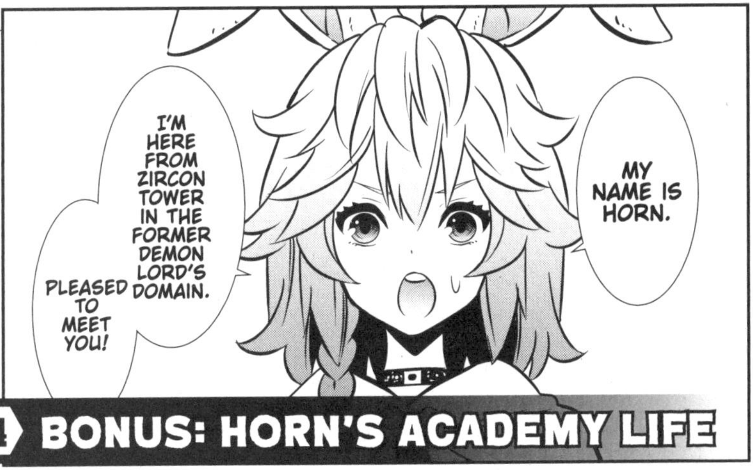
MY NAME IS HORN.
I'M HERE FROM ZIRCON TOWER IN THE FORMER DEMON LORD'S DOMAIN.
PLEASED TO MEET YOU!

74 BONUS: HORN'S ACADEMY LIFE

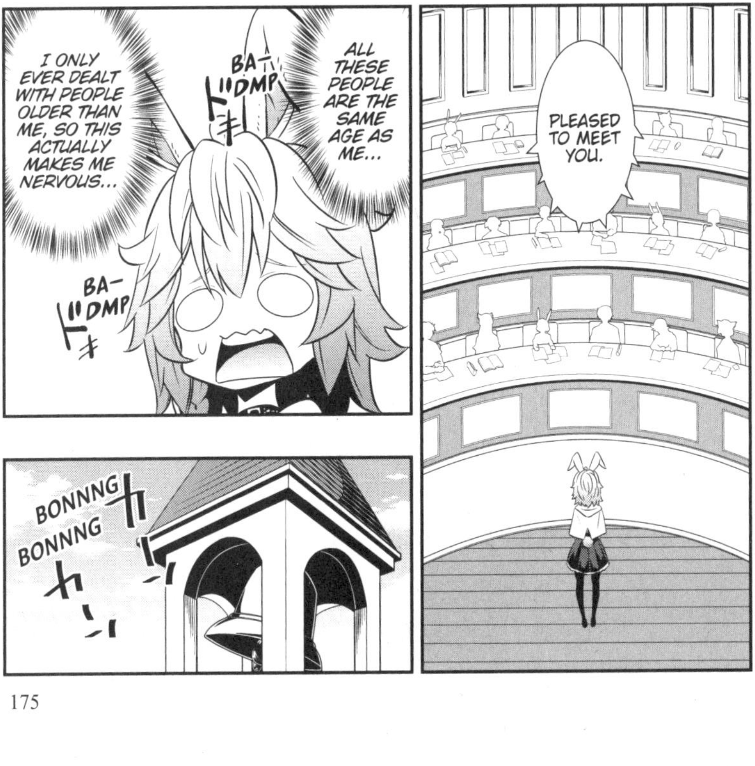
PLEASED TO MEET YOU.
ALL THESE PEOPLE ARE THE SAME AGE AS ME...
BA-DMP
I ONLY EVER DEALT WITH PEOPLE OLDER THAN ME, SO THIS ACTUALLY MAKES ME NERVOUS...
BA-DMP
BONNNG
BONNNG

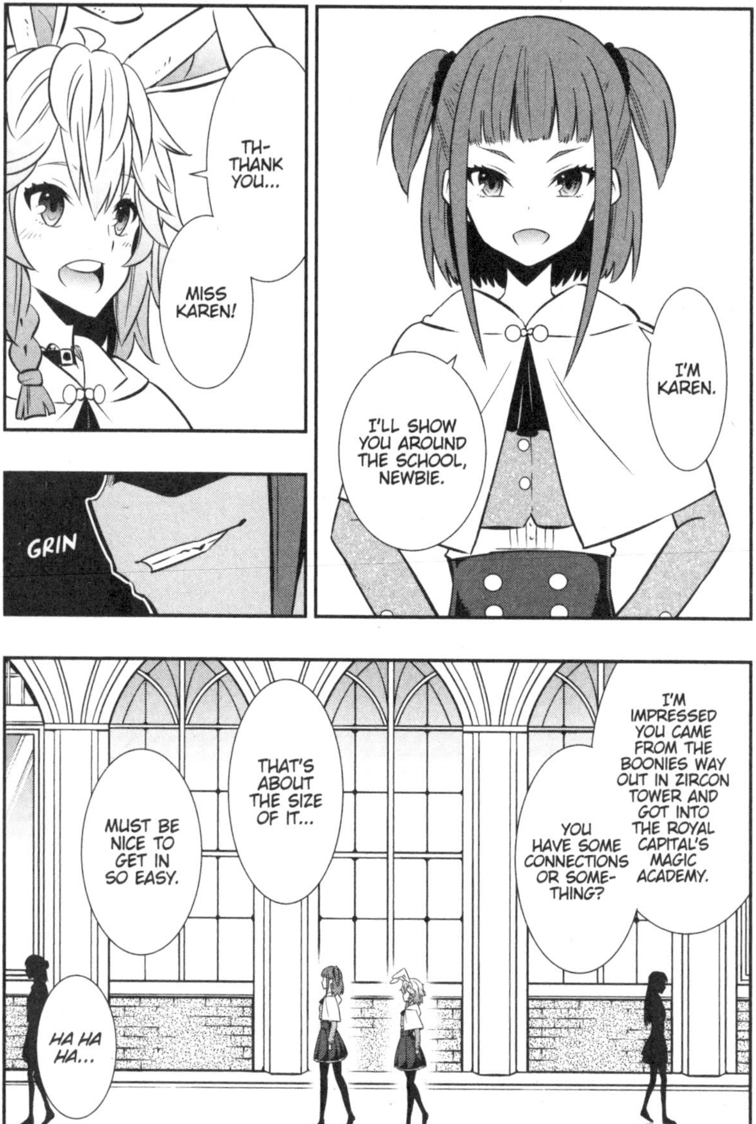
I'M KAREN.
I'LL SHOW YOU AROUND THE SCHOOL, NEWBIE.
TH-THANK YOU...
MISS KAREN!
GRIN
I'M IMPRESSED YOU CAME FROM THE BOONIES WAY OUT IN ZIRCON TOWER AND GOT INTO THE ROYAL CAPITAL'S MAGIC ACADEMY.
YOU HAVE SOME CONNECTIONS OR SOME-THING?
THAT'S ABOUT THE SIZE OF IT...
MUST BE NICE TO GET IN SO EASY.
HA HA HA...

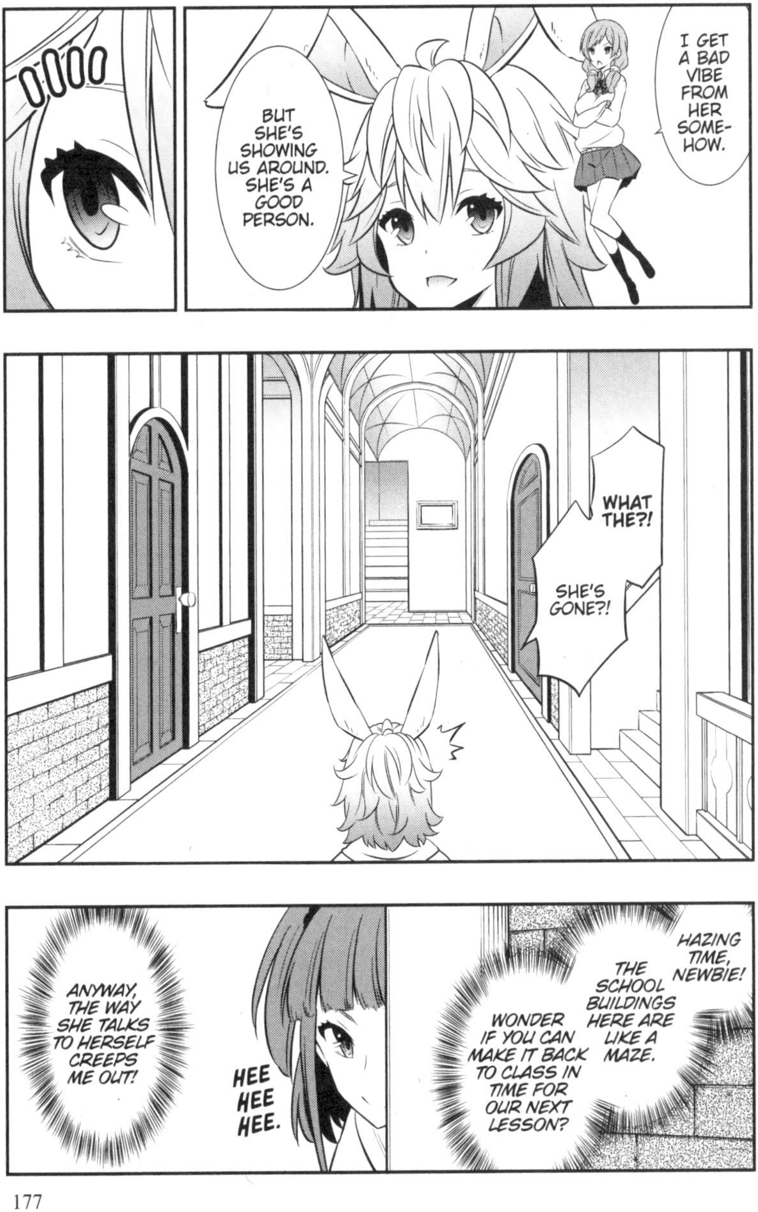

I GET A BAD VIBE FROM HER SOME-HOW.
BUT SHE'S SHOWING US AROUND. SHE'S A GOOD PERSON.
WHAT THE?!
SHE'S GONE?!
HAZING TIME, NEWBIE!
THE SCHOOL BUILDINGS HERE ARE LIKE A MAZE.
WONDER IF YOU CAN MAKE IT BACK TO CLASS IN TIME FOR OUR NEXT LESSON?
HEE HEE HEE.
ANYWAY, THE WAY SHE TALKS TO HERSELF CREEPS ME OUT!

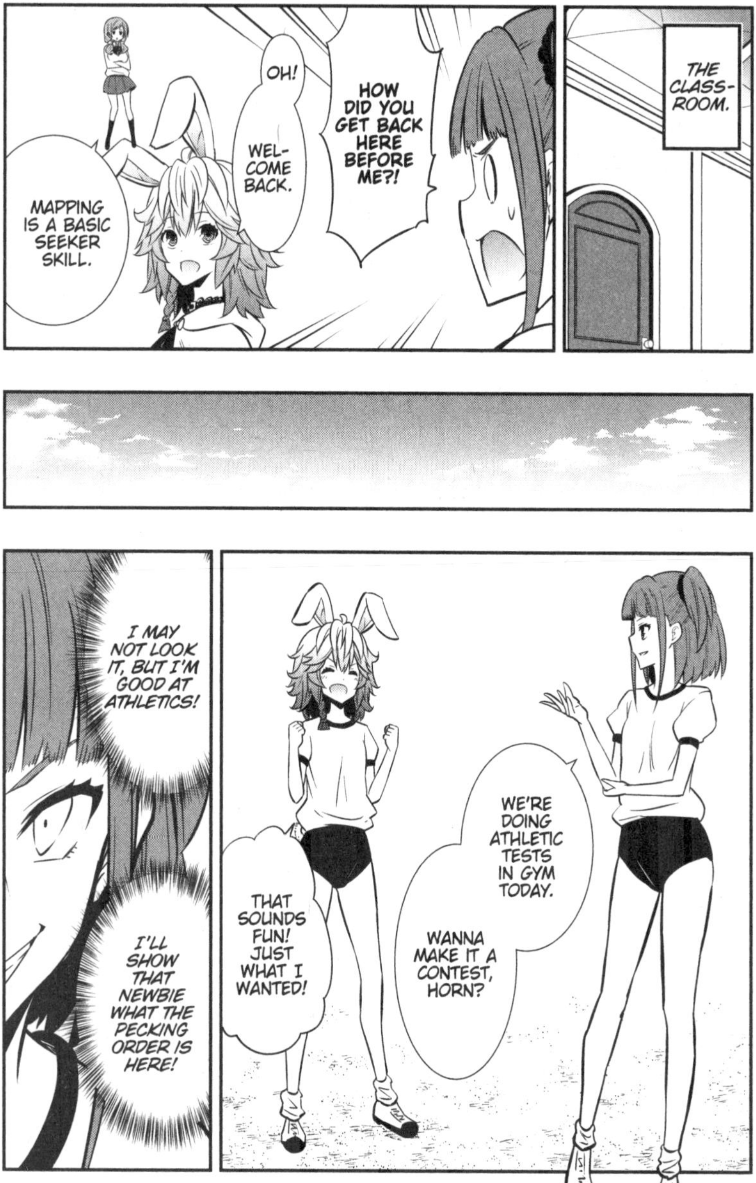
THE CLASS-ROOM.
HOW DID YOU GET BACK HERE BEFORE ME?!
OH!
WEL-COME BACK.
MAPPING IS A BASIC SEEKER SKILL.
WE'RE DOING ATHLETIC TESTS IN GYM TODAY.
WANNA MAKE IT A CONTEST, HORN?
THAT SOUNDS FUN! JUST WHAT I WANTED!
I MAY NOT LOOK IT, BUT I'M GOOD AT ATHLETICS!
I'LL SHOW THAT NEWBIE WHAT THE PECKING ORDER IS HERE!

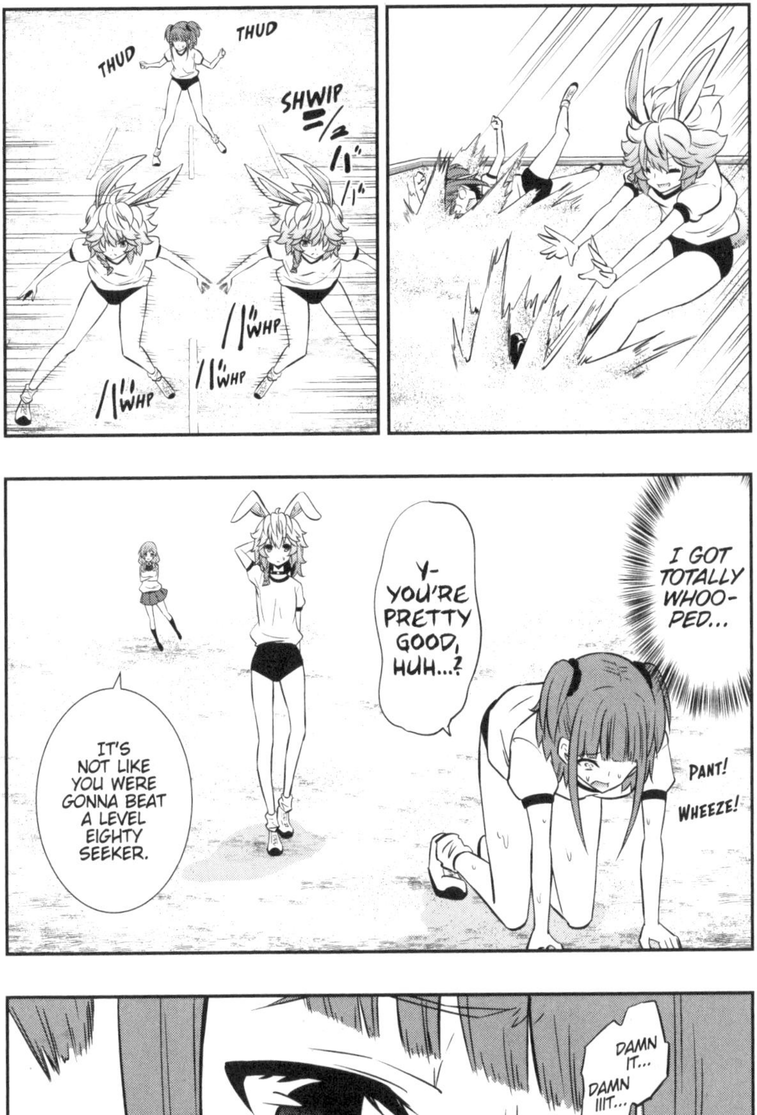
THUD
THUD
SHWIP
WHP
WHP
WHP
I GOT TOTALLY WHOO-PED...
Y-YOU'RE PRETTY GOOD, HUH...?
PANT!
WHEEZE!
IT'S NOT LIKE YOU WERE GONNA BEAT A LEVEL EIGHTY SEEKER.
DAMN IT...
DAMN IIIT...

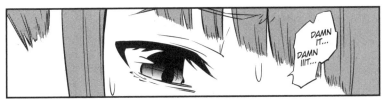

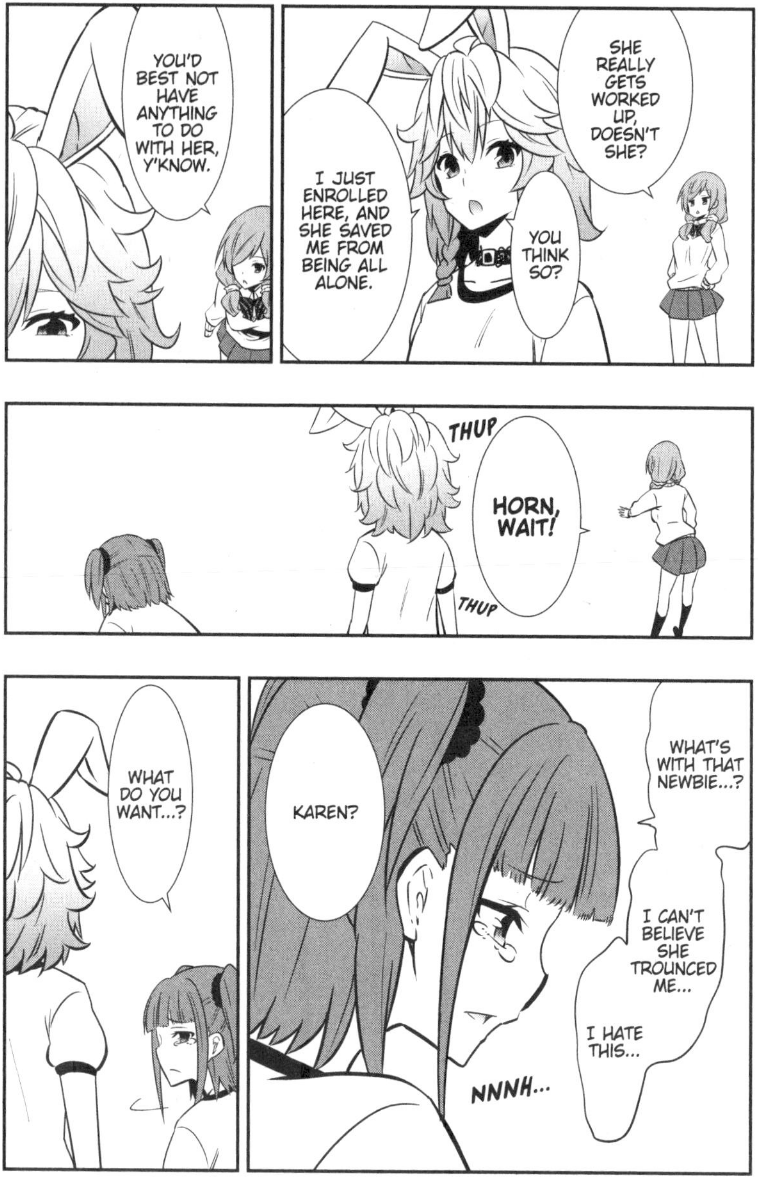
SHE REALLY GETS WORKED UP, DOESN'T SHE?
YOU THINK SO?
I JUST ENROLLED HERE, AND SHE SAVED ME FROM BEING ALL ALONE.
YOU'D BEST NOT HAVE ANYTHING TO DO WITH HER, Y'KNOW.
THUP
HORN, WAIT!
THUP
WHAT'S WITH THAT NEWBIE...?
I CAN'T BELIEVE SHE TROUNCED ME...
I HATE THIS...
NNNH...
KAREN?
WHAT DO YOU WANT...?

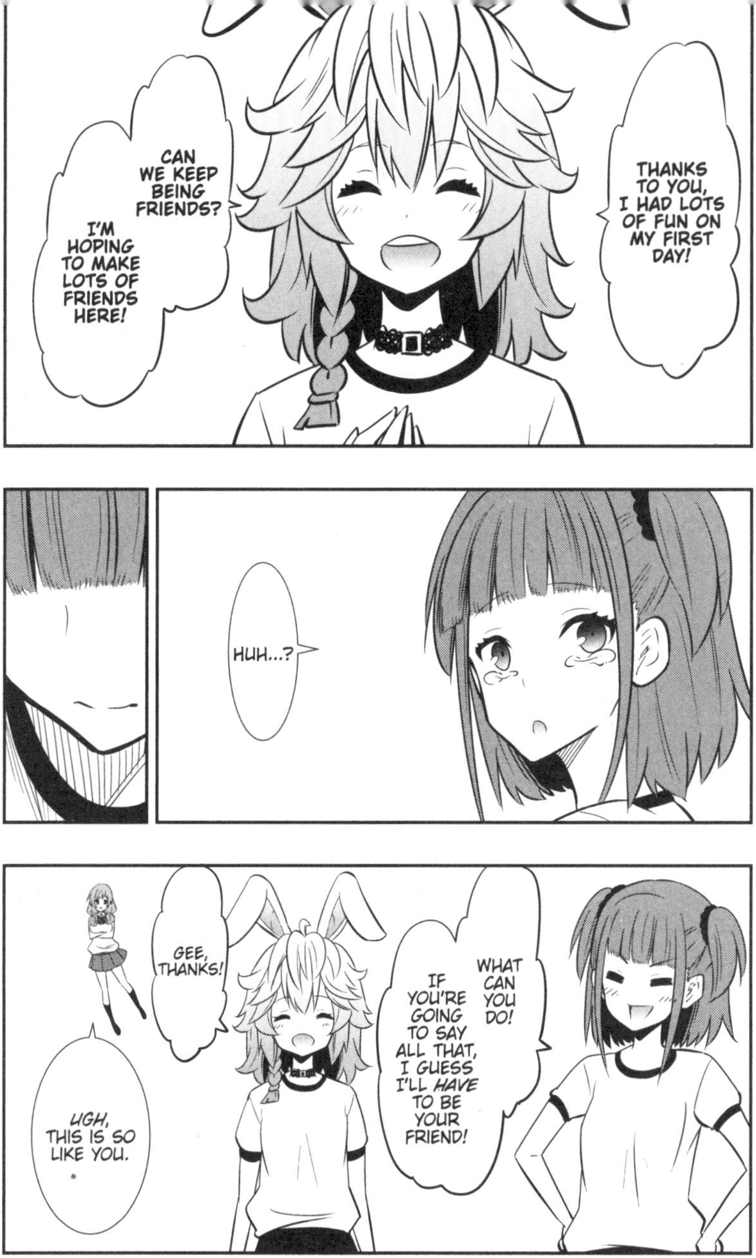
THANKS TO YOU, I HAD LOTS OF FUN ON MY FIRST DAY!
CAN WE KEEP BEING FRIENDS?
I'M HOPING TO MAKE LOTS OF FRIENDS HERE!
HUH...?
WHAT CAN YOU DO!
IF YOU'RE GOING TO SAY ALL THAT, I GUESS I'LL *HAVE* TO BE YOUR FRIEND!
GEE, THANKS!
UGH, THIS IS SO LIKE YOU.

Character Popularity Poll Results

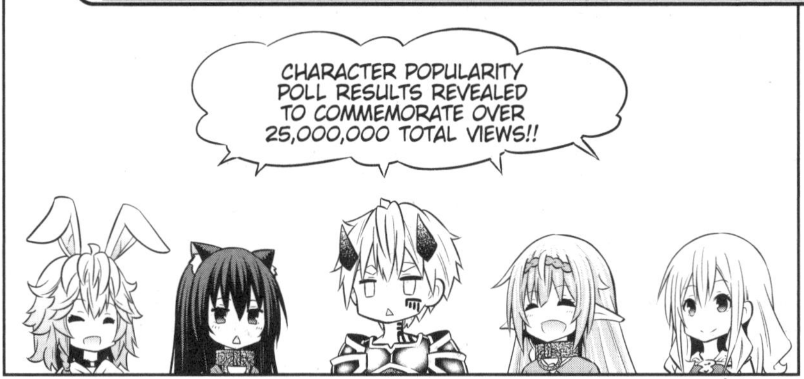
CHARACTER POPULARITY POLL RESULTS REVEALED TO COMMEMORATE OVER 25,000,000 TOTAL VIEWS!!

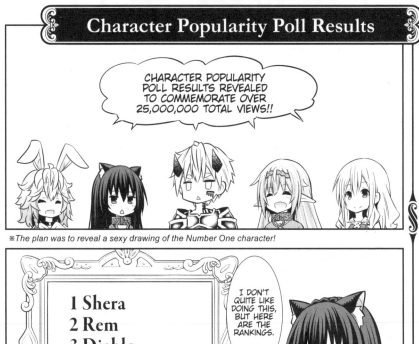

※*The plan was to reveal a sexy drawing of the Number One character!*

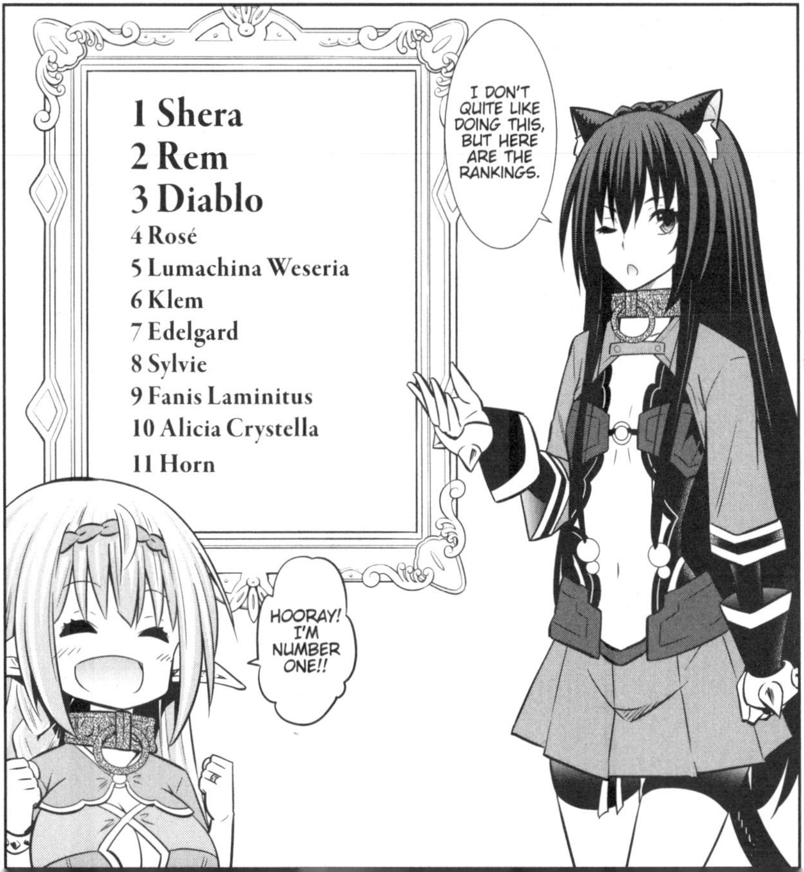
I DON'T QUITE LIKE DOING THIS, BUT HERE ARE THE RANKINGS.
1 Shera
2 Rem
3 Diablo
4 Rosé
5 Lumachina Weseria
6 Klem
7 Edelgard
8 Sylvie
9 Fanis Laminitus
10 Alicia Crystella
11 Horn
HOORAY! I'M NUMBER ONE!!

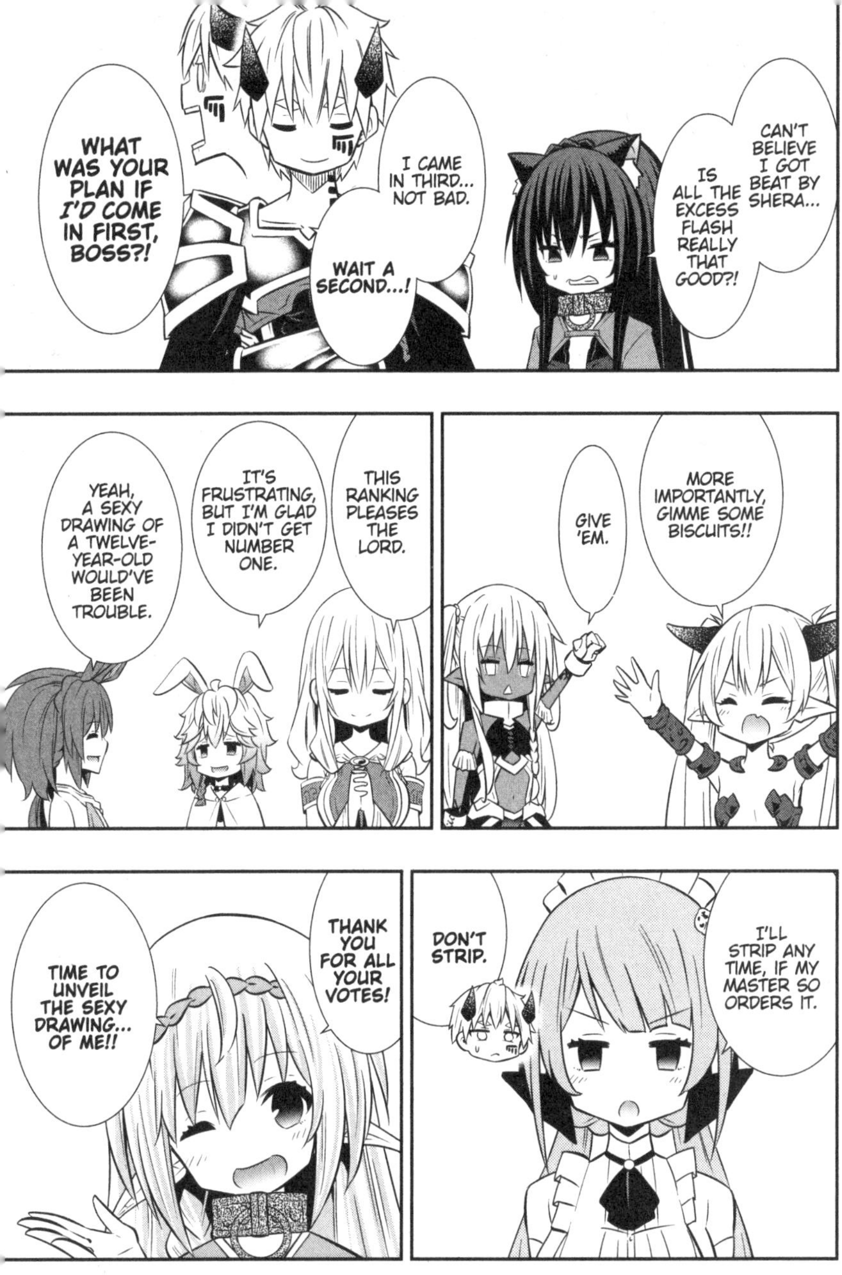
CAN'T BELIEVE I GOT BEAT BY SHERA...
IS ALL THE EXCESS FLASH REALLY THAT GOOD?!
I CAME IN THIRD... NOT BAD.
WAIT A SECOND...!
WHAT WAS YOUR PLAN IF I'D COME IN FIRST, BOSS?!
MORE IMPORTANTLY, GIMME SOME BISCUITS!!
GIVE 'EM.
THIS RANKING PLEASES THE LORD.
IT'S FRUSTRATING, BUT I'M GLAD I DIDN'T GET NUMBER ONE.
YEAH, A SEXY DRAWING OF A TWELVE-YEAR-OLD WOULD'VE BEEN TROUBLE.
I'LL STRIP ANY TIME, IF MY MASTER SO ORDERS IT.
DON'T STRIP.
THANK YOU FOR ALL YOUR VOTES!
TIME TO UNVEIL THE SEXY DRAWING... OF ME!!

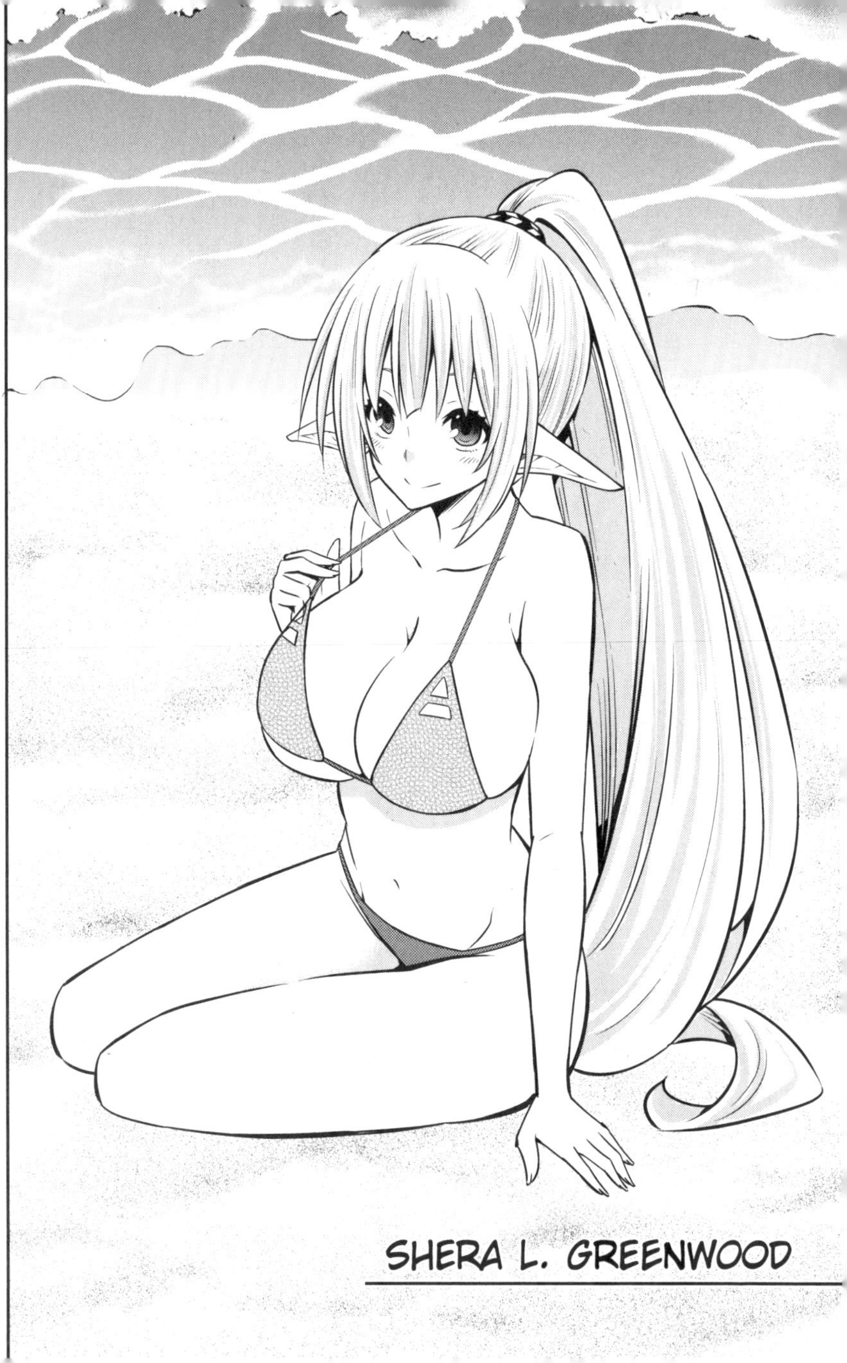
SHERA L. GREENWOOD

HOW NOT
TO SUMMON A
DEMON LORD

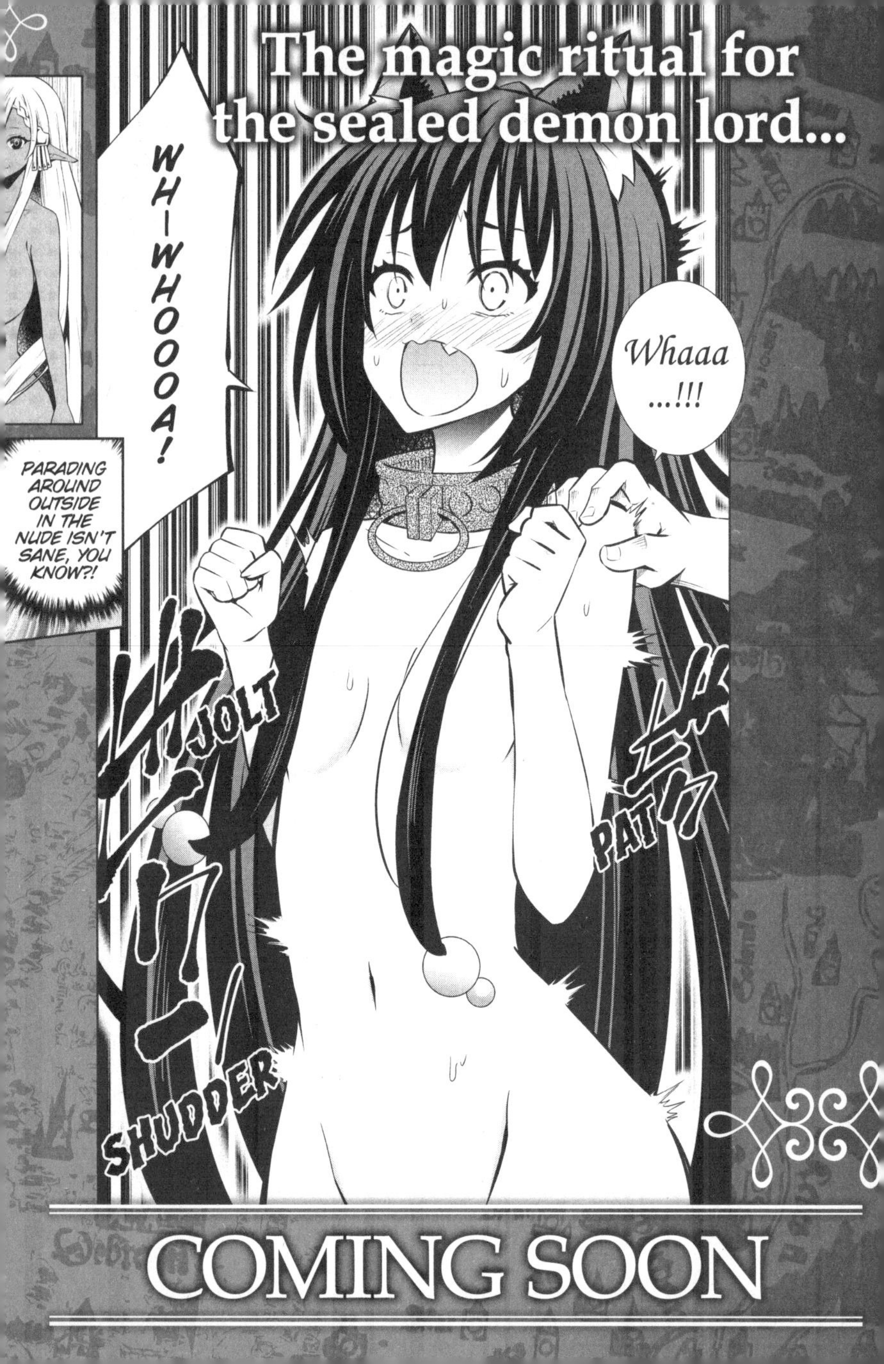
The magic ritual for the sealed demon lord...
Whaaa ...!!!
WHI-WHOOOOA!
PARADING AROUND OUTSIDE IN THE NUDE ISN'T SANE, YOU KNOW?!
PAT!!
JOLT
SHUDDER
COMING SOON

Just what will happen to Rem?!!!

STORY

In search of the ritual to remove the soul sealed within Rem, Diablo and the others visit the Dark Elf village. After some serious negotiating with Rafflesia, the village chief, it's finally decided that the magic ritual will be performed. But on the way to the altar, the unthinkable happens! What is the thing that runs through Rem's body?!

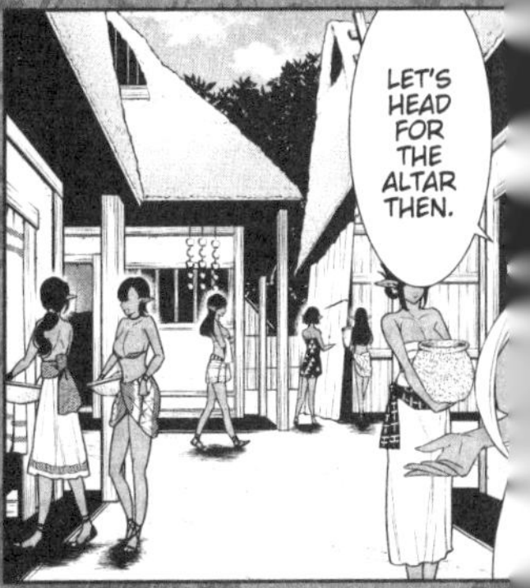
LET'S HEAD FOR THE ALTAR THEN.

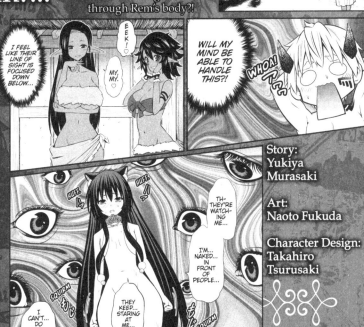

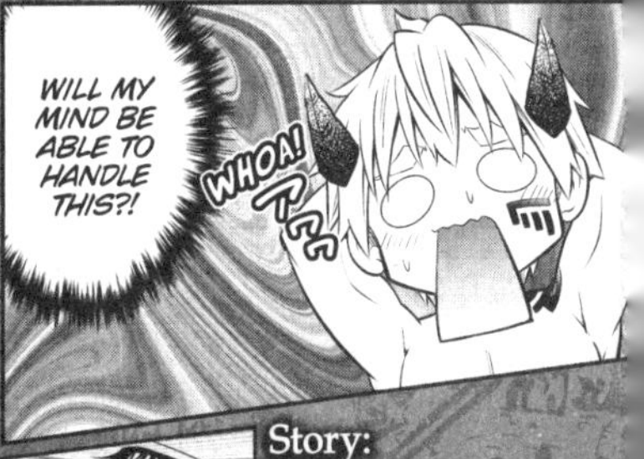
WILL MY MIND BE ABLE TO HANDLE THIS?!
WHOA!

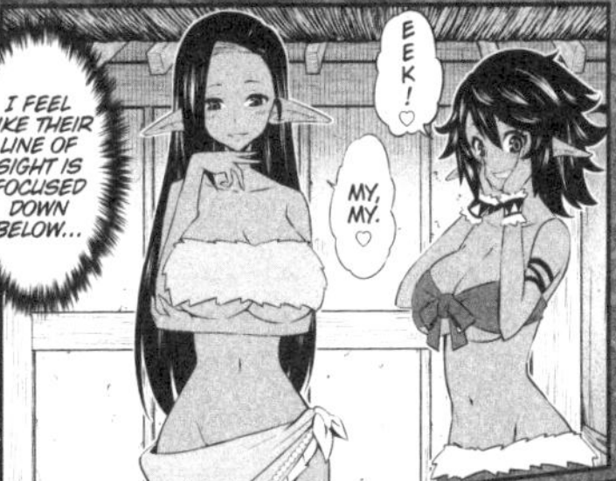
EEK! ♡
I FEEL LIKE THEIR LINE OF SIGHT IS FOCUSED DOWN BELOW...
MY, MY. ♡

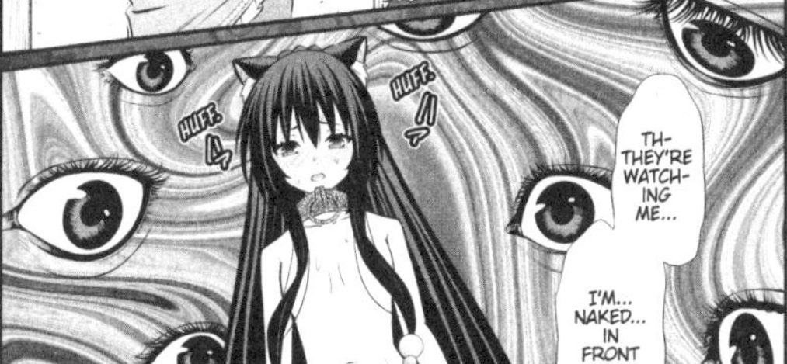
HUFF.
HUFF.
TH-THEY'RE WATCHING ME...
I'M... NAKED... IN FRONT OF PEOPLE...
SQUIRM
THEY KEEP... STARING AT ME...
SQUIRM
I CAN'T... DO THIS...

Story:
Yukiya Murasaki

Art:
Naoto Fukuda

Character Design:
Takahiro Tsurusaki

HOW NOT TO SUMMON A DEMON LORD 16

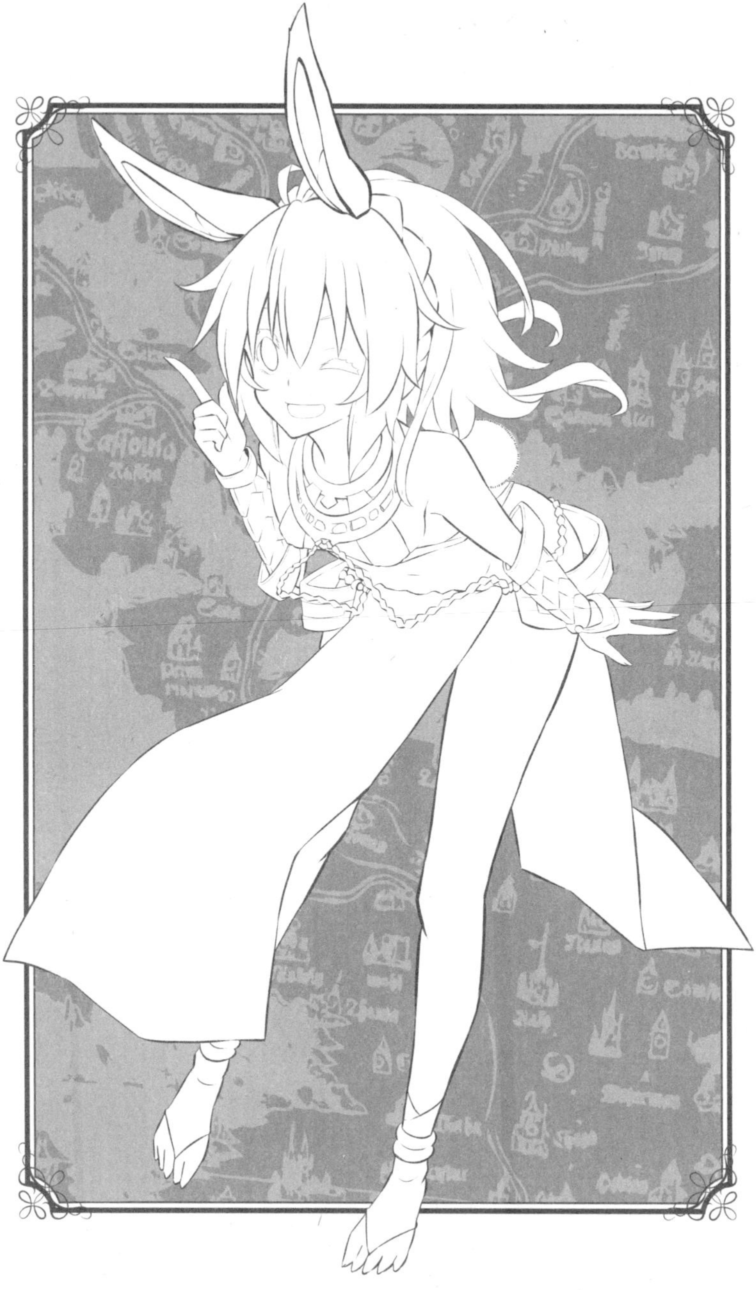

HOW NOT TO SUMMON A DEMON LORD

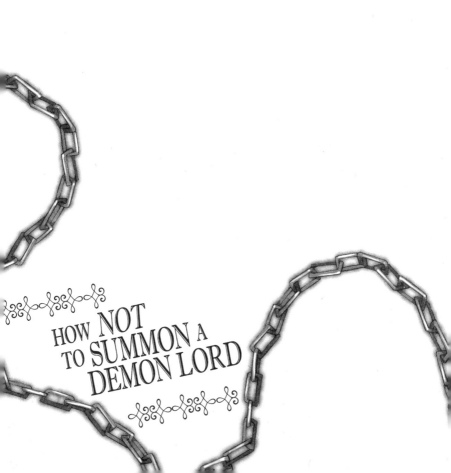